SOCIAL AND ECONOMIC HISTORY OF EARLY DECCAN

SOCIAL
AND
ECONOMIC HISTORY
OF
EARLY DECCAN

SOME INTERPRETATIONS

Edited by
ALOKA PARASHER SEN

MANOHAR
2026

First published 1993
Reprinted 2019, 2023, 2024, 2025, 2026

ISBN 978-81-7304-053-5

Published by
Ajay Kumar Jain *for*
Manohar Publishers & Distributors
4753/23 Ansari Road, Daryaganj,
New Delhi 110 002

Printed at
Replika Press Pvt. Ltd.

CONTENTS

MAP-I AREAS OF STUDY

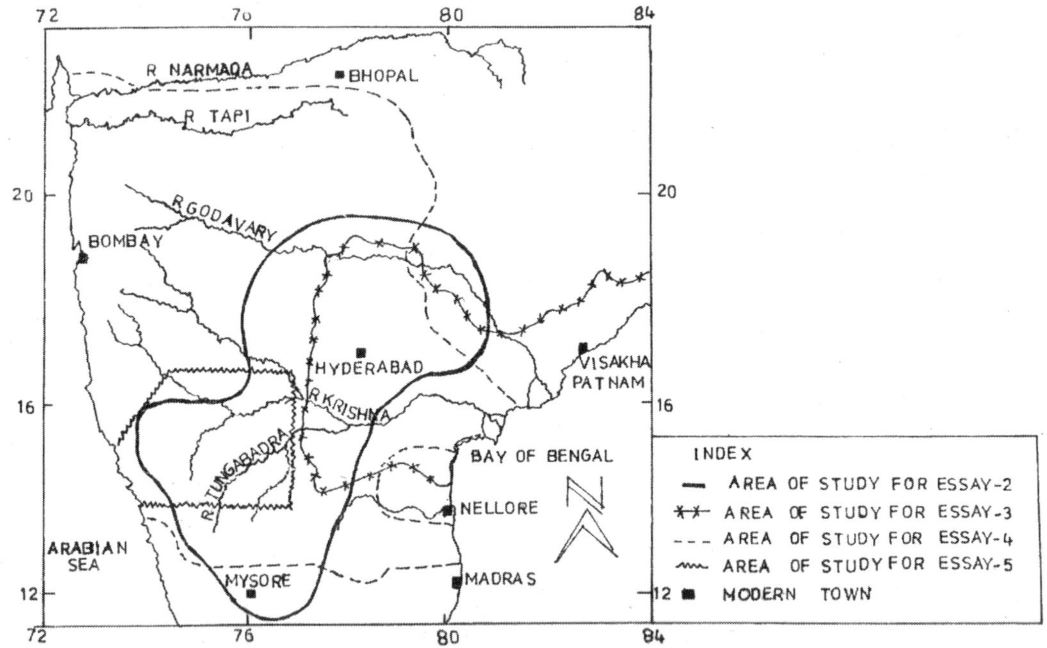

MAP-II
PHYSIOGRAPHY OF THE DECCAN

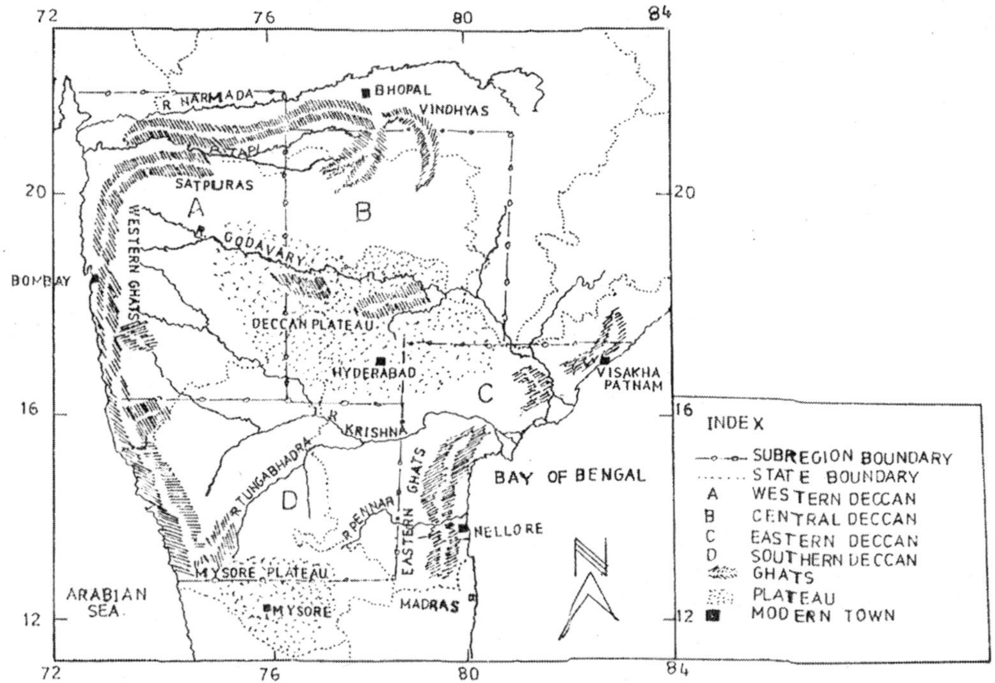

PREFACE

India is a conglomeration of diverse cultural regions wherein each region has its own personality. We have, however, no linear boundaries to define each of these regions and often historians find it difficult to identify a single clear-cut criterion to define historical regions. It is for this reason that Deccan, like other regions of India, has undergone changing historical definitions. Though it is loosely considered a part of South India, it is often ignored that it had its own personality which had undergone transformations during various periods of historical time. This region formed a crucial area for the development of Indian civilization, placed as it was between the north Indian plains and the southern extremity of the Indian Peninsular. Just as there have been changing historical images of the Deccan, its name has also had different forms. It is said to be the anglicized form of *Dakṣiṇa* or *Dakkhiṇa*. In Persian it is called *Dakkan*.

As the Maps included in this volume indicate we have understood the Deccan primarily as the land south of the Vindhyas up to the Krishna-Tungabhadra Basin [roughly between latitude 12° and 20° north and longitude 72° and 80° east]. It is only as a geographical concept that the Deccan has had a stable definition. Defined in a technical way this would be "Deccan a Peninsula of India, south of the Narmada river which would be restricted to the table land between the Narmada and the Krishna, comprising Maharashtra and parts of Madhya Pradesh, Andhra Pradesh, Mysore . . ." [A.M. Webster's *Third New International Dictionary*, USA, 1969, p. 286]. For identifying the heterogeneity of the Deccan in physical terms [Map II] we have sub-divided the whole into four sub-regions of the Western, Central, Eastern and Southern Deccan. [Marked as A, B, C and D in the Maps]. The area of study in each of the accompanying essays form different parts of these sub-regions (Map I) which are not determined by either political or administrative boundaries of any given historical period.

A survey of some of works on the region of study in each of the essays shows that hitherto the historical transformations in the Deccan have been encapsulated in terms of political history. Further that these have been partially treated as a segment of either, the history of India as a whole or, that of South India in particular. Thus, not only are rigid boundaries of historical definitions imposed on the region but its 'centrality' in these histories is understood only in terms of the rise to political significance of dynasties that ruled in these parts with prominence naturally being given to the Sātavāhanas as the first major dynasty followed by such early medieval dynasties as the Chālukyas of Badami, Rashtrakutas, Eastern Chālukyas etc. as they were the ones that were said to be nearest to have reached the 'empire' concept. The other dynasties were treated as part of the 'dark ages'. The historical centrality of the Deccan was thus essentially conceptualized in terms of political monumentality.

Representation of regions only when 'empires' emerged in history has co-existed in existing historiography with another form of representing the Deccan region, namely, that which has been part of the seemingly seamless hegemonizing process of being brought under the cultural influence of either, Brahmanism or Buddhism. Here again a dominant paradigm was at work because the concern of historians was to discover and delineate how these influences penetrated into regions submerging all other small but persistent local cultures and forms of worship. It is not being argued here that these influences should be ignored but what needs to be questioned is the prominence that these factors are given in analyzing the historical forces that went into making the complex personality that was the Deccan.

Having recognized that we do not want to impose a rigid historical definition to the region under study in the present collection of essays we turn to focus on the changing aspects of the social, cultural and economic history of the region from the earliest beginnings to about the 12th century A.D. At the same time, this endeavour does not intend to be an exhaustive account of all these aspects but rather, is an attempt at highlighting some of the salient features involved in the processes of historical change in a society that was spatially and culturally always in contact with external forces. However, there are the internal forces of change in this society that we primarily focus on by way of taking an intrinsic look at both the archaeological and inscriptional sources that are available to us.

The first essay legitimately raises the issue of the rise of Civilization and State in these parts and for this purpose we are almost entirely dependant on archaeological sources, of which, the numismatic sources are particularly valuable. The other three essays relate to subsequent developments in the socio-cultural and economic transition from the ancient to the early medieval period in the Deccan. This has been done by charting out relevant data within the *given parameters* to gain from this a pattern of the broad levels of material and economic change with regard to the social groups being analyzed. Archaeological sources have hitherto been understood variously by historians which gives us a plurality of approaches in its use. We have tried to use this data to improve upon generalizations that a historian can make for understanding the overall dynamics of the cultural processes of change and continuity in a society where literary sources are not available. For acquiring a clarity in this regard and in trying to overcome the problem of a lack of problem-oriented excavations in the Indian context, all data available on the material cultures for some of the important sub-regions of the Deccan has been collated as far as possible.[1] On this basis the subsequent socio-economic and politico-ideological forces of change have been discussed. Thus for instance, one has tried to move away from the overemphasis of the archaeologist's concern with merely describing the monumentality of the Buddhist art and architecture and the historian's undue concern with only the dominance of the Sātavāhanas to ultimately outline the processes of acculturation in a region which even today borders tribal areas of habitation.

For the inscriptional data that do not necessarily mention the caste or class affiliation of any group in a direct way, *the first step* in categorizing the possible nature of social entities has been through such pieces of information as names of individuals, their designations, collective common appellations, functions performed by individuals or functionaries of the State, occupations of individuals or groups particularly in the temple and so on. Subsequently, functions/designations/occupations etc., have been linked to *the context in* which they are mentioned in the inscriptions. Since we are largely concerned with land grants or charters, the underlying phenomena that emerges is the different levels of interaction between social groups and landed property. It must, nonetheless, be mentioned that this type of analysis is suitable for describing primarily the dominant social groups as they are directly mentioned in the inscriptions though it cannot be overlooked that these groups were part of a larger socially stratified society.

For the subject social groups who have no direct visibility in the inscriptions, we have taken cognizance of institutions/ occupations/ practices that imply their existence. In some quarters it has been suggested that social history in fact, "derives its vitality from its oppositional character. It prides itself on being concerned with 'real life' rather than abstractions, with *'ordinary' people* (emphasis added) rather than privileged elites, with everyday things rather that sensational events." [Raphael Samuel, 'What is Social History', *History Today*, March 1985, p. 34]. One has, therefore, not simply stopped with an analysis of the explicitly mentioned social terms/ groups that describe esssentially the elite but have gone beyond this to identify explicitly stated economic/ political/ ideological practices and institutions of exploitation that imply the existence of subject social groups.

The essential aim in these essays has been that the valuable inscriptional data would be of use to ultimately find fundamental explanations of historical change. An essential pre-requisite in our understanding of the given periods of study has been to see how social structure is defined and this has been related to the factor of man's accommodation to his physical conditions at a local level. This has revolved around beginning the analysis with small localities and the rural situation. It must be stated that village society in the past related to, and interacted with, not only social categories but also with defined geographical entities. The individual thus can be placed in the context of family (*kula*), kin group (*gotra*), sub-caste (*jāti*) and caste (*varṇa*). This placement in turn has been related to his situation in a house or extended household located in a village (*grāma*), or small town (*pura*), or military camp (*vāda/vātika*), or city (*nagara*), or province (*viśaya*) and finally, country (*deśa*).

These norms of social and geographical location cannot be sifted and separated from each other in a social analysis and ultimately, these are both related to the primary economic under-pinnings of the nature of land rights and ownership of property in pre-modern India. A small footnote to this categorization would be to recognize explicitly that villages were not a string of hierarchical isolates but had linkages with other contiguous localities. Secondly, though not much work has gone into understanding how village societies in the past reacted to change, it must be accepted as a forewarning that we cannot accept them to have reacted to external change in an uniform way. Therefore, to conclude that there was some kind of typical formulae for social change in the village community must be untenable.

A final third major dimension of recognition in our categorization for social history has been to cautiously approach the data which is primarily garbed in religious and ideological rubric. Though these days it is clearly accepted that we cannot unduly exaggerate the role and impact of religion on early Indian society, at the same time, scholars in handling pre-modern records have once again brought to the forefront the concern as to how one should differentiate the material phenomena from the ideological in the context of Indian society. [Frank Perlin's thought-provoking article 'The Material and the Cultural: An Attempt to Transcend the Present Impasse', *MAS*, 22, 2, 1988, pp. 383-416 raises the theoretical issues at stake]. However, given the constraint that our data comes primarily from the Brahmanical temple one has been cautious in not merely re-speaking the Brahmanical view. Since a major part of the explicit data also states that many grants were made for ostensibly religious purposes we cannot, at the same time, undermine the ideological dimension in the analysis of social groups. It is not difficult to see that the major social groups that benefited from large scale land transactions in early medieval times were religious beneficiaries. The best way to interlink the socio-cultural and economic with the politico-ideological has been by way of mapping out these linkages. In exemplifying ways of mapping and categorizing epigraphical data that has been used to write a social history one has attempted to overcome some of the above stated problems of nomenclature and periodization in the empirical data included in this book for different sub-regions of the Deccan.[2] These are not exclusive studies, that is, one for each of these regions separately. Also, since they have been done over a period of time, they have also registered gradual change and improvements in the presentation and mapping out of the social data from inscriptions.

The study on temple girls [last essay] done between 1982-83 chose a much neglected theme in social history, namely, women. Within this category it was decided to focus on the temple dancing and singing girls as they were consistently mentioned in inscriptions but had hitherto, only been targets of signifying moral degradation in our society. This study focused on a few northern districts of Karnataka between the 8th – the 12th century A.D. and attempted to pertinently relate their social position in the context of their access to the resources from land on which they were solely dependent for the continuance of their profession and religious practices.

The third study done between 1987-89 posed to reflect on the hitherto dubbed 'dark age' in the history of the region. Since political/dynastic details for some periods of history are minimal and not very outstanding, such periods have traditonally been of marginal interest to history. In the present context this also coincided with so-called peripheral regions which were not the seat of 'great empires'. One such period was the Deccan in the post-Sātavāhana times. This study, therefore, took up an indepth analysis of the Vishnukundin inscriptions (copper plates) locatable mainly in the State of Andhra Pradesh to analyze the nature of social and economic changes between the 4th – the 7th century A.D. An important element of this study was to link the socio-economic forces of change to the nature of settlements that the Vishnukundin rule was associated with and the nature of their polity. A further development of these ideas emerged more specifically in the fourth study done between 1988-89. This intended to narrow the thematic focus into only analyzing the social groups and their relationship to the land grant economy. However, what was attempted in this study was to look at this data cutting across three dynasties that ruled over parts of Maharashtra, Karnataka and Andhra between the 7th – the 13th century A.D. Thus, samples of inscriptions issued by the Chalukyas of Badami, the Rashtrakutas of Malked and the Chalukyas of Kalyani and their subordinates have been taken into account. Conclusions based on these studies are in no way absolute but indicate valuable insights into the broad trends in social and economic change. With the help of some Charts we hope to have illustrated at a glance the understanding of this change and the specific problems faced in each case.

The conclusions arrived at in each of these essays are open-ended. On the whole they are tentative indications of broad trends and possible methods that can be pursued to systematically chart out and map the wealth of data available to us in the archaeological and inscriptional sources.[3] This can only be done at the micro level and only when several such studies have been made that we can draw firm conclusions. Nonetheless, we cannot escape from arriving at meaningful definitions of what we have attempted to analyze. In the hope that one has been able to communicate with others and relate ones findings to theirs one will have succeeded in avoiding impositions on them.

As the collection in the Book suggests this has been a collective endeavour. Many of the ideas presented here have been shared and expressed at various classroom lectures, seminars and conferences. Even before such an enterprise was concretely thought of, there was a need felt through my successive interactions with batches of MA and M.Phil. students offering courses in Social and Economic History, that there was a need for a monograph on the early History of the Deccan. In this sense the collective effort has gone beyond the contributors to the volume. Without the enthusiastic response from students and scholars these ideas would have remained fragmented and therefore, I thank all those who helped in putting them together as a cohesive whole.

Krishna Prasad Babu and Tejaswini have been particularly part of this effort since they worked for their research degrees while my Career Award Project was in progress. Their enthusiasm, interest and hard work, not only fueled the earlier nebulous ideas into a meaningful exercise, but well after their research was over they continued to work in the direction of helping to formulate and write for this volume. Without their essays it would have been an incomplete effort in more ways than one. Currently, J. Krishna Prasad Babu is a Lecturer at the Jawhar Bharati College, Kavali, Andhra Pradesh and Tejaswini Yarlagadda is a Senior Research Fellow doing her Phd. at the Department of History, University of Hyderabad.

E. Sivanagi Reddy, Assistant Stapathy in the State Department of Archaeology, Government of Andhra Pradesh, Hyderabad joined our team at a later stage but, nonetheless, has left an indispensable mark on our collecteve endeavour. We owe are sincere thanks to him for having drawn the maps accompanying each of these essays. Though these were done exclusively on the basis of material provided by us, the credit of depicting the data neatly and accurately lies solely with Nagi Reddy. He is also a Ph.D. scholar at the Department of History, University of Hyderabad.

Preparation of this volune would have not been possible without the financial assistance and other facilities made available under the

Career Award bestowed on me for the period 1988-1991 by the University Grants Commission, New Delhi. The formulation and writing of this book was particularly possible because of the time available under the Scheme which provided for the appointment of temporary lecturers so that I was relieved of full-time teaching and could devote my time exclusively for research. I would also like to place on record that the financial assistance under the Scheme enabled me to purchase equipment in the form of a Computer and for travel on field work to various libraries in Madras, Pune and Delhi that expedited the organization and execution of the work. Institutions and Libraries where the work could progress in various stages of its completion need to be thanked for providing the necessary facilities especially the State Department of Archaeology and Museums Library, the Indira Gandhi Library at the Hyderabad University and the Osmania University Libarary in Hyderabad, the National Museum Library and the Libraries of the Indira Gandhi Centre for Arts and Culture and the Indian Council for Historical Research at New Delhi, the Library of the Deccan College in Pune, the Madras University Library in Madras and the Davis Library at the University of North Carolina at Chapel Hill and the Duke University Libraries at Durham in the USA.

It would be meaningless to put in words the support one has got from the family during this enterprise. However, Varun in particular needs to remembered for the long hours of word-processing the manuscript that I shared with him. Kalidas was ever ready to give any help that I asked for and without his constant enthusiasm, spiritedly echoed by Shaunak, it would not have able to enjoy working on the current project. Sushma provided the much needed support and I warmly thank her.

ALOKA PARASHER SEN

Hyderabad
January 1992

NOTES

[1]This work was carried out during 1989-90 and has been part of the data collected for the *Source Book* under U G C Career Award Project.

[2]In particular three M.Phil thesis worked under my supervision and accepted for

the award of degrees by the Hyderabad University. They are : Usha S. Naik, 'Temple Girls in Early Northern Karnataka 700 A.D. - 1200 A.D.', 1983. Some results of this published in Naik and Parasher, 'Temple Girls of Medieval Karnataka' *IESHR*, 23, 1, (1986), pp. 63-91; J.K.P. Babu, 'Socio-Economic Conditions in the Deccan 4th to 7th Centuries A.D. (From Vishnukundin Records)', 1989; P. Tejaswini, 'Social Groups Involved in Production and Administration of the Early Medieval Western Deccan (800 A.D. - 1200 A.D.)', 1989.

[3]For the present literary sources have not been used in these essays mainly because they are limited in scope and content for the period and region of study.

ABBREVIATIONS

ABORI	*Annals of the Bhandarkar Oriental Research Institute*
AI	*Ancient India*
AIIS	American Institute of Indian Studies
APGAS	Andhra Pradesh Government Archaeological Series, Hyderabad.
ARDAM/ARAP	*Annual Report, Department of Archaeology and Museums, Andhra Pradesh*
BACRI	Birla Archaeological and Cultural Research Institute, Hyderabad.
BKI	*Bombay Karnataka Inscriptions* published in *SII* series
BDCRI	*Bulletin of the Deccen College Research Institute*
CSSH	*Comparative Studies in Society and History*
DASSI	*Decade of Archaeological Studies in South India* edited by B.K. Gururaja Rao
DCP	Deccan College Publication
EA	*Epigraphica Andhrica*
EI	*Epigraphica Indica*
EPW	*Economic and Political Weekly*
IA	*Indian Antiquary*
IAR	*Indian Archaeology – A Review*
IESHR	*Indian Economic and Social History Review*
IHR	*Indian Historical Review*
IIAS	Indian Institute of Advanced Studies
JAAP/JA	*Journal of Archaeology, Andhra Pradesh*
JAHRS	*Journal of the Andhra Historical Research Society*
JBBRAS	*Journal of the Bombay Branch of the Royal Asiatic Society*

JESHO	*Journal of the Economic and Social History of the Orient*
JIH	*Journal of Indian History*
JOI	*Journal of the Oriental Institue Baroda*
JPS	*Journal of Peasant Studies*
JTS	*Journal of Telugu Studies*
MAS	*Modern Asian Studies*
OUP	Oxford University Press
PAPHC	*Proceedings of the Andhra Pradesh History Congress*
PIHC	*Proceedings of the Indian History Congress*
SBH	Sacred Books of the Hindus
SII	*South Indian Inscriptions*
'SOCI'	'Sanskrit and Old Canarese Inscriptions' published in the *IA* by J.F. Fleet

LIST OF CHARTS

LIST OF MAPS

1

INTRODUCTION
PROBLEMS OF INTERPRETATION

ALOKA PARASHER SEN

India is a conglomeration of diverse cultural regions wherein each region has its own personality.[1] We have, however, no linear boundaries to mark each of these regions and often historians find it difficult to identify a single clear cut criterion to define *historical regions*. It is for this reason that Deccan, like other regions of India, has undergone changing definitions.

Scholars often tend to go back to 'Original Sources', be they literary or inscripional, to seek for authoritative definitions of regions. The same has been true about explaining the term Deccan which has had different forms and connotations and today, it is considered to be an anglicized form of *Dakṣiṇa or Dakkhiṇa*.[2] This recognition mainly stems from collating scattered references to peoples and lands mentioned in literature and inscriptions which can be today located in what we geographically describe as the Deccan. Literary references to *Dakṣiṇāpatha/Dakkhiṇāpatha* are traced back to Brahmanical texts like the *Ṛg Veda, Aitareya Brāhmaṇa, Arthaśāstra* and the like and to Buddhist texts like the *Vinaya Piṭaka, Sutta Nipāta* etc.[3] to suggest that these generally refered to the southern direction of Peninsular India, lying south of the Narmada.[4] Recent studies prefer to make reference to the more tangible inscriptional material to locate the peoples that inhabited the Deccan region by pointing to the earliest such material in the Aśokan edicts since some of these were also located in the region under study.[5] More frequently, the Gautamiputra Balasri's Nasik inscription[6] is made mention of since it lists the components of the Sātavāhana empire and even names the territorial entities --- Asika, Asaka, Mulaka, Suratha, Kukura, Aparānta, Anupa, Vidarbha, Akara,

Avanti --- all of which are meant to help us identify the historical and political Deccan of the early centuries of the Christian era. However, since pre-modern sources simply describe the tribal/ethnic groups that inhabited the Dakṣiṇa regions or small localities which can be identified by us to have been situated in regions we today broadly delineate as the Deccan, we simply indulge in an exercise of constructing the regions of historical analysis using the perceptions of the ancient authors. In the case of the literary sources the underlying biases of the geographical location of these texts primarily in North India are hardly taken into account. Further, nowhere is a rigid definition of *Dakṣiṇāpatha* given so that it can be equated with more recent perceptions of the same.

Bhandarkar was the first Indian scholar in modern times to write with 'Dekkan' in the title to his book in 1892. His study of the Deccan, however, came to be mainly confined to the Maharashtra region.[7] Within the limitations of the sources of information available at that time this text is largely based on literary sources located in North India to define the early historical phase of the Deccan, *i. e.*, prior to the coming of the Aryans.[8] With this inherent bias Bhandarkar interestingly views the early inhabitants of the Deccan as the *dasyus* of the literary sources[9] later to be dominated by the Nandas and Mauryas who are said to represent the Aryan influence which reached this region through political successes of these rulers.[10] Dubreuil's work was the next impotant study of this region to have 'Deccan' in the title of the work. It defined the Deccan as a larger tract of country which was 'bounded on the north by the Narmada and Mahanadi, on the east by the Bay of Bengal, on the West by the Arabian Sea, on the South by the Nilgiri Hills and the Southern Pennar.'[11] This is largely a work which describes the political history of the region concentrating mainly on the hitherto untapped archaeological and inscriptional sources especially on the post-Sātavāhana dynasties.[12] There is no major shift in the foci of historical analysis and it remains a 'detailed account of the local habitats of the dynasties and their interrelationship.'[13]

More recently, Yazdani's edited work on the Deccan has a relatively specific and political definition of it which is said to coincide with the erstwhile Nizam's dominions[14] and it has been indicated at several places in the *Preface* that the concern was to write a comprehensive History of the erstwhile Hyderabad State. In this definition the Deccan comprises major parts of the present-day

States of Maharashtra, Karnataka and Andhra Pradesh. Being an edited work there are the contributions of several well-known scholars and therefore, the rest of the essays in this Book take into account the political boundaries of the various dynasties that ruled over the Deccan as their individual perceptions of its historical identity. However, the working definition adopted for this edited work takes the Deccan as a historical land in Peninsular India that had stretched from the Sahyadri Parvat and Mahendragiri ranges and the Mahanadi and the Godavari rivers in the north, to the Krishna and Tungabhadra rivers in the South and from Arabian Sea in the west to the Bay of Bengal in the east.[15] Like Bhandarkar, this work too advocated the importance of the settlements of Aryans in the Deccan which in turn had resulted in a cultural change and the example of the Aryan linguistic influence[16] is cited in the Marathi language which had spread over a major part of the western Deccan. In a recent study on *Studies in Historical Geography and Ethnography of the Deccan*, though a broader understanding of the Deccan is indeed given,[17] it is nonetheless, reiterated that in a narrow sense it should only be understood as the present-day Maharashtra State.[18]

Nilakanta Sastri focused on South India as a whole and wrote much after Bhandarkar's seminal work but persisted with the earlier stereotype of emphasizing the role of Aryan influence in colonizing and civilizing the South.[19] In his opinion 'The Deccan is one of the oldest inhabited regions of the world and its pre-historic archaeology and contacts with the neighbouring lands, so far as they are traceable, constitute an important chapter in the history of world civilization'.[20] But he too, like Bhandarkar, has largely used literary sources to explain the process of Aryanization in the opening up of the Deccan to civilization. A large majority of the writings on South India view the history of all regions south of the Vindhyas to be under its purview and therefore, in this type of writing, the Deccan is loosely considered a part of South India. In our opinion, South India may be understood as a comprehensive geographical entity with specific sub-regions in it, but it definitely cannot be viewed as one historical entity. It has recently been pointed out that in the past 175 years the books written on the history of South India have understood their own individual component to be South India as a whole.[21] Undoubtedly these definitions are determined either from the point of view of source material, or, for ideological reasons of providing a vantage point to study the region as a whole. It has been observed by us that in the process, for the northern parts of South India, namely, the Deccan region, it is often ignored that it had its own historical personality which had undergone transformations in various periods of historical time.

Since hitherto, these transformations have been encapsulated only in terms of political history, it is precisely within this context that the historical boundaries of Deccan have been delineated by historians. This can be exemplified from the texts of both Yazdani and Sastri because even though the 'region' in both cases is understood differently, particular sub-regions and localities only emerge to historical visibility when a certain dynasty, well-known for its exploits, can be described or detailed. Indeed, Yazdani as the editor of his volume even admits that major repetitions of descriptions take place in the Volume because 'In describing the ruling dynasties of the Deccan a chronological order has been kept, . . . as some of these dynasties were contemporary and fought against one another for independence, or for the integrity of their territories, the accounts of some political events have been repeated, a proceeding which was inevitable in following the general plan of the work according to which the histories of these dynasties have each been given separately in special chapters, and not in association.'[22] Sastri's work on the other hand, has a conscious vantage point from the extreme South so that the Andhra and Karnataka regions only emerge to prominent light during the early times under the Sātavāhanas and then in a later period under the Vijayanagar rulers.[23] As a result of adopting this format social, cultural and economic history are discussed dynasty-wise in some cases[24] and in others, are treated as a fringe to political history by being relegated to the end of the book in separate chapters of 'Social Conditions', 'Economic Conditions' 'Art and Architecture' 'Literature' and the like.[25] Some writings as is the case with K.S. Subramanian's work, a careful chronological sequence of the religious monuments has been done within the parameters laid down for political history.[26] This compilation is interesting in that it takes up a period of study when political history as traditionally understood was confused with the rule of several dynasties but, Subramanian focuses on the religious monumentality of Buddhism to bring the Andhra region to special attention. This work was written in 1927 and can be contrasted with that of Sastri, in the sense that it understands South India from the vantage point of the coastal districts of present-day Andhra Pradesh.

To him, as was the case with Bhandarkar for Maharashtra, 'the bulk of Āndhradésa or the Telugu-speaking country of today has been a separate linguistic belt from very early times.'[27] Interestingly, since his discussion is of dynasties of the post-Sātavāhana times, the emphasis throughout his book is not merely on political monumentality but the greatness of the Buddhist monuments which glorified ancient Andhra.[28] We must thus accept that the historical perception of the definition of the Deccan as a region of historical inquiry has been very much determined by how political powers began to emerge and change the boundaries of localities. Even when a discussion of cultural aspects are central to the inquiry the political framework was not given up.

In this collection of essays we have chosen to focus on the Deccan partly because of its marginal treatment in texts on South Indian History in particular, but more so, because this formed a crucial region for the development of Indian civilization placed as it was between the north Indian plains and the southern extremity of the Indian Peninsular. It has been fairly well accepted that as one of the 'minor cultural regions' of India it had a personality of its own.[29] Having recognized that we do not want to impose a single rigid historical definition to the region under study, as the Maps[30] included in this volume indicate, we have understood the Deccan primarily in its geographical sense as the land south of the Vindhyas up to the Krishna Tungabhadra Basin. Though there have been changing historical images of the Deccan, it is only as a geographical concept that the Deccan has had a stable definition. Defined in a technical way this would be 'Deccan a Peninsula of India, south of the Narmada river which would be restricted to the table land between the Narmada and the Krishna, comprising Maharashtra and parts of Madhya Pradesh, Andhra Pradesh, Mysore. . . .'[31]

While underlining the fact that the historical Deccan has changed, it has been rightly pointed out that the historical geography of the Deccan is its 'cultural' and human geography at successive stages of civilization'.[32] In general studies of settlement patterns using archaeological data it is also commonly understood that the geographical location of a particular culture influences the development of man's material and other existence.[33] Historical writings of recent decades have significantly brought to focus the question of 'geographical constraints' and man's subjectivity to his surroundings.[34] However, we would like to emphasize that 'though regions are deeply rooted in the geographical context and the cultural specificity of particular entities from the positive angle, they must nonetheless be viewed as part of a larger system. In doing so, we must first address ourselves to the intrinsic description of the material surfaces of change and stability.'[35] For this reason we have delineated several sub-regions within this broad understanding of the Deccan mainly to highlight the variations and not accept any monolithic uniformity. At the same time interregional contact has also to be accepted. Thus B. Subbarao's seminal studies on the delineation of regions on the basis of nuclear areas, areas of relative isolation and areas of isolation [36] have proved valuable indicators for understanding contacts between regions and for moving away from looking at the influence of geography on history merely in terms of how it affected the formation of empires, their successes and failures. Further, his understanding of the regional dimension in terms of cultural contacts, as for instance the earliest contact between the lower basins of Krishna and the Godavari on technological grounds,[37] provided interesting data for the hypotheses about inter-regional cultural contacts in India from very early times.

In contrast, most scholars would like to see these contacts in terms of diffusion as is the case with Allchin's study of the megalith burial complexes.[38] V.V Krishnasastry goes to the extent of identifying the megaliths with the vanquished cults of the Aryas as suggested by the Śatpatha Brāhmaṇa.[39] For the historical periods, though D.D. Kosambi understands the Deccan as approximately South of the Narmada which was subjugated mostly to indigenous rulers,[40] it is suggested by him that agriculture in this region was essentially post-Mauryan. Mauryan penetration into the Deccan is explained as a result of the development of trade and commerce[41] which is thus said to have played an significant role in diffusing dominant material traits. However, Kosambi concedes that large pockets of forest tracts still remained and the Sātavāhana rise should be taken as the first manifestation of the traits of civilization while the pre-Mauryan traits continued and are visible in archaeological terms.[42] Maloney, using the excavations done by Wheeler shows how the Sātavāhana material was super imposed on the already existing iron-age societies.[43] Nonetheless, it remains to be said that particular historical studies on the Deccan that have so far been concerned with delineating political history have paid little attention to understanding the pre-Sātavāhana period. Only recently a small historical account of the tribal kingdoms prior to the rise of the Sātavāhanas has been discussed in Sudhakar Chattopadhaya's work.[44] Interpretations of the Deccan history from the vantage point of the evolution of society with particular reference to the Andhra peoples by K. Satyanarayana also looks at the pre-Sātavāhana stage in general terms.[45] Discussion on the pre-historic stage is present in this work but tribes are understood as an undifferentiated category and the variations in the various archaeological cultures has not been taken into account.[46] Satyanarayana's work goes on to describe the spread of plough agriculture, commodity production and trade [47] and both the State[48] and Buddhism are suggested to have fostered the process in several ways.[49]

It is to de-emphasize the role of external influences, articulated in the early historical writings and based on literary sources or, the more recent authority of the archaeological fact, presented in some works, that in the first essay we have taken up the basic issue of the formation of culture and civilization in the Deccan. In our opinion the Deccan was not a mere transitory zone, nor, was it peripheral from the vantage point of either the North Indian developments or the South Indian ones. The particular nature of the historical transformations here have to be identified in their own terms with a more balanced understanding of its relations with external influences. For the study of polity in South India, the first writings interestingly emerge for the Deccan. This is so because the first integrated study of the available archaeological, inscriptional, numismatic and literary sources for the study of a dynasty, at a regional level, is with reference to the Sātavāhanas. Cultural variations of the various sub-regions of the Deccan are subsumed under the study of the political monumentality of this dynasty.[50] The very nature of these books dwells on giving details of dynastic importance and the political events of the period without any relevant discussion on the social base that made early State formation possible. As discussed in the first essay pre-State society is normally visualized in terms of a 'primitive' tribal one which is not understood to have made any contribution to the formation of civilization.[51] Works by archaeologists on the other hand, have concentrated on a description of the material cultures of the pre and proto historic Deccan[52] without relating it to the changes in the social formation as a whole.

The writings on the rise of the Sātavāhana power in the Deccan has largely revolved around the chronology of the early Sātavāhanas and their original home. I.K. Sarma's work on numismatics, along with the use of the traditional literary sources, has used this recent data also to rewrite on the origin of the Sātavāhanas and their homeland.[53] Ajay Mitra Shastri in a recent collection of essays has sorted out some sensitive problems regarding the original home and issues of the chronology of the Sātavāhanas.[54] The views on chronology fall into two broad categories.[55] The more acceptable is the one that advocates the shorter chronology, with according to Ajay Mitra Shastri, is clearly evident in the light of the available material information. He thus concludes that the Sātavāhanas rose to power in the middle or latter half of the first century B.C.[56] Prior to this period the political history of the Deccan is most commonly understood in terms of the influence of the Mauryan rule. This can be dated, on the basis of the evidence of the Mauryan inscriptions, belonging to the third century B.C.[57] In order to put the present study within a larger perspective we next turn to discuss the broader issues of the study of State in early India to highlight that the hitherto undue emphasis on understanding only dynastic and administrative structure of the Sātavāhana power was not peculiar to studies on the Deccan alone. Therefore, to evolve a better understanding of the early history of the Deccan we need to reject some of the biases and prejudices inherent in the existing historiography on the subject and relate it to recent studies on looking at the larger processes of change in society as a whole, both prior to, and contemporaneous with the rise of the State.

The 'ancient period' cannot be understood as an undifferentiated whole for the present purpose. Indeed, for the period before the twelfth century A.D. we witness two important phases in the growth and nature of State-formation in India, one addressing itself to primary change in the heartland of the Ganges Valley around the mid-first millennium B.C. and the other reflecting the changes in the so-called peripheral zones beginning from roughly around the first century A.D. or so and continuing unevenly in the different ecological zones well into medieval times. Among the problems central to the former is the question of defining the nature of political authority and the attendant social stratification that existed in the transition from a pre-State to a State situation in early India. To the latter there is the added question of the formation of new States at a regional level and the attendant variability in the transition to a State society.

At a theoretical level the nineteenth century was an important period for clarifying notions of the origin of State and empirical studies did help in doing so. Thus, for instance, Engels[58] basing his ideas on the empirical studies of Lewis Morgan[59] concluded that a progressive division of labour and production of surplus were a crucial basis for State-formation. In the twentieth century the evolutionary processes of State-formation have been further clarified and along with these there has emerged the question of discussing the viability of the various historical factors like war, population, irrigation, surplus production etc. in the rise of the State.[60] Many of these views in concentrating on the end result, that is, the State society itself, often led to exaggerated causal explanations of State survival as for instance, Karl Witfogel's 'Hydraulic Deterministic Theory' which propounded that a despotic control of resources like water was essential for State to survive particularly in the Asian societies.[61] Though, at the turn of the twentieth century, it was no doubt agreed upon that State was a social phenomena, it was still left to identify the complexity of the pre-State situation. By the mid-twentieth century, social anthropological researches had addressed themselves to this pertinent issue of the organization of society in the pre-State stage. In doing so Morton Fried [62] divided this into the tribal, ranked and stratified stages before full-fledged State emerged.[63] The importance of these ideas lay in the fact that they emphasized critically the issues of continuity and overlap between the two stages and also clearly suggested that power of the State was centralized in its internal means of regulation and control. Today it is well agreed upon by social scientists that rise of State was not an abrupt transformation or a mechanical process and least of all, it was not divinely ordained as some of the traditional theories on its origin would have us believe. Later rationalizations of the 'divine origins' of the State have to be placed in their historical context to understand their purpose and why they were suggested at all.

With regard to the majority of writings available on understanding the origin of State in early India, we have an undue emphasis on two broad thrust areas of interest :(1) writings describing theories on the idea of the State as found in the *Itihāsa-Purāṇa* tradition,[64] or, the *Dharmaśāstra/Arthaśāstra*[65] views on it, or occasionally, the Buddhist theories of its origin (2) writings describing the various 'empires' in ancient India primarily from the point of view of defining their centralized polities of which the kings get a prominent share of description.[66] Both these pre-occupations have led to a blurring of the lines of distinction between the State and the King in ancient India. Some of the writings mentioned above in the context of early Deccan history reflect this tendency. This view was firmly buttressed by the notion, initiated first by the British administrator historians, that all land in Ancient India was owned by the king[67] thereby leading on to a further misconceived notion that autocratic despotic regimes in ancient times inhibited any change in society. Many of these ideas have now been ably questioned by historians.[68]

The majority of the early works on ancient India which discuss some aspects of State power[69] dwell on its features of polity and focused mainly on the institution of the King who was projected as the sovereign power.[70] However, what is pertinent to note, from the present concern of interest is the fact that, at a given point in historical time, State in Ancient India was indeed defined in clear terms as having *saptāṅga* or seven elements.[71] These components, it must be underlined, are strikingly similar to modern social science definitions of the State.[72] That Historians have chosen to describe and discuss only one of the elements of the State, namely the King, and refused to define its fundamental sources of fiscal and coercive power, may have been due to the fact that many of these early studies were done under the influence of nationalist thinking. It was their concern then to construct an image of a strong, unified, centralized Indian polity which was benevolent in order to effectively counter the critical views on the subject at that time.[73] Many of these views have however, anachronistically become an integral part of our understanding of the State in Ancient India and are hardly questioned because they help us perpetuate certain myths of a glorious, harmonious and just society, ruled benevolently by kings who lived up to the ideals of a bygone era.[74] For existing works on South Indian History that have used the above models of understanding the State a systematic critique is available and we need not divert in trying to repeat these arguments for the present.[75]

Notwithstanding these strongholds of the interpretive dimensions of history, recent researches by historians have, in trying to understand the processes of State-formation in early India, not only questioned the above assumptions, but have also explained more fully how the State in ancient India 'acted both as a 'functional' and 'structural' power entity'.[76] Further, it has also been convincingly brought out that there is an intrinsic value in understanding the perception of the tradition preserved in the ancient literary texts as it reveals the historical consciousness of a society which is best defined 'if viewed in terms of a lineage society and its mutation in time to a State system'.[77] Both R.S. Sharma[78] and Romila Thapar [79] direct their methodological avenues to unveil the processes of State-formation in the Ganges Valley where the seminal beginnings of the State are first found[80] during the first five hundred years of the first millennium B.C.. This period of our history has hitherto been understood as the 'glorious Vedic Age'. One of the *central issues* raised by them is to explain the transition from a tribal/lineage based society to a caste/class based one. In scratching for the roots of this answer is revealed the economic, social and ideological setting of the origin of the State in both the Western and Middle Ganges Valley amidst their ecological and material setting. It is pertinent to note that the earlier emphasis on only the literary sources of the *Vedas* has given way in their works to a close scrutiny of the archaeological sources. Indeed the difference between the *Ṛ-g-Veda* and the Later Vedic Texts not only reflects the focus of habitation in two different zones --- the Sapta Sindhu region and the Ganga Yamuna Doab region --- but, it also clearly suggests two basically different social formations. The former clearly as a pastoral economy and the latter revealing the first stages of the growth of an agrarian economy.[81] It is however only in the Later Vedic times that territory emerged as an important element and together with this the importance of the *rājā* came to be highlighted to have both a higher status and well as more effective control of society through functionaries who were called *ratnins*. Romila Thapar[82] in her analysis finds that 'lineage' would be a better term to define the kin-based relations of the early *Ṛg Vedic* society as this makes it easier to distinguish between the *rājanya* (could be translated as 'senior lineages' or clansmen of the *rāja*) and the *viś* (could be translated as 'junior lineages' or the majority of kin related members of a tribe) as the two major segments of such a society

Sharma and Thapar disagree on the basic issue of what kind of relations of production can be envisaged in the Later Vedic society when the kin-based structures were becoming identified with specific territorial units and when conflicts between them were increasing.[83] According to Thapar there was indeed a stratified society defined more in terms of lineage ties than its relationship to the economic forces of production. The tension of such a society was released by migration and a further expansion of the productive forces that were indeed possible in the Middle Ganges Valley and which is where State ultimately emerged.[84] It would be essentially difficult to pinpoint one single factor as crucial to the evolution of the State in the Middle Ganges Valley but it is clear that the constituents of the *saptāṅga* theory were noticeably absent in the earlier society.[85] The most perfect articulation of the processes that led to the formation of State were witnessed in the kingdom of Magadha. In its victory over the Vrijji Confederacy it symbolically marked the success of a monarchic form of government over the alternate system of the *gaṇa saṅgha* type, loosely translated as a 'republica', where power was shared between many *rājās*.[86] Though concepts of early Buddhism were influenced by this idea of sharing power and this found its way in the organization of the Saṅgha, predominantly both the Buddhist and Brahmanical ideas of the origin of the State justified the monarchic form.[87]

The administrative framework, rudiments of which were found in the *mahājanapadas* of the sixth century B.C. came to be formalized in the *Arthaśāstra*, along with a fuller definition of what constitutes the State as noted above. However, as D.D. Kosambi for the first time vigorously argued, that the significance of this text on statecraft is not merely that it discusses rules of how an ideal state should function, but that it specifies the possible economic means by which this could be done.[88] In this sense the discussions on the State's access, control and use of resources pertaining, both to manpower and material, become the essence of this text. It is an outright spokesman of the advantages to be gained by the State if it pursues the policy of agrarian expansion at the expense of the tribal enclaves. There are detailed explanations on how tribes were to be subdued and converted into a caste peasantry.[89] Though the upholding of the *varṇa* system was integral to its vision of social organization it also suggests the incorporation of new social classes that would carry weight in the governance and maintenance of State power.[90] One aspect that is often neglected in the discussion on the *Arthaśāstra* is that the most powerful State is perhaps having a dialogue[91] with the periphery. This naturally brings us to the question of the processes of State-formation in areas other than the Ganges Valley and the most pertinent issue in this regard has been the extent to which these have been qualitatively influenced by the processes of primary State-formation epitomized in the rise of Magadha as an 'empire' under the Mauryas.

It needs however, to be reiterated that in quantitative terms the study of State in Ancient India, irrespective of the region of study, has hitherto been done almost solely from the point of view of understanding the idea of the State or theories pertaining to it from the largely prescriptive literature on the subject. Therefore, ideas on the State as culled from texts like the *Arthaśāstra* have been used to build images of centralized State structures[92] for almost all periods of Ancient Indian history and for almost all regions. On other hand, this notion of the ideal Indian State has been conveniently used to ignore such issues as the growth of complex property relations and the intricacies of the *varṇa-jāti* in determining the nature of the State structures in different periods and regions in history. Since primary State-formation took place in the Ganges Valley most of the above-mentioned studies have largely concentrated on Northern India. In the present context one shall attempt below a brief look at the recent interpretations of pre-State and early State societies in South India especially those that have been done in understanding the Mauryan period which has hitherto been conventionally understood to be the first centralized and unified empire in India.[93]

The monumentality of the Mauryan State has often drawn the attention of scholars because of the extent of territory that was said to have been under its sway. However, little attention has been paid to the mechanism by which this vast territory, constituted of various societies, States and non-States at different levels of economic development, was controlled.[94] If it is agreed that the Mauryan empire included differentiated political and economic systems, then, as Romila Thapar in her recent writings on the Mauryas[95] has suggested, we need to examine how these diverse regions were integrated and governed. In this context she has appropriately questioned the commonly understood formulation that all parts of the Mauryan Empire were organized on lines suggested in the *Arthaśāstra* or, that it was able to restructure the economies of all areas under its control. A possible alternative suggestion made by her is that within the Mauryan empire we need to distinguish three main components : (1) the metropolitan State which initiated conquest and control (2) the core areas which enhanced the fiscal basis of the empire and (3) the large number of variegated peripheral areas, subservient to the above but continuing much as before.[96] In this understanding only the metropolitan State, namely Magadha, would be organized on a unitary centralized basis whereas the control of the other zones would depend on the local levels of authority particularly in areas where the metropolitan State was interested in exploiting the economic resources, in the form of taxes, tribute, plunder while on war, rather than restructuring the economy of those zones. For the metropolitan State to succeed generation of income from continually new sources was crucial. In exemplifying this Thapar draws our attention to the concentration of the Aśokan inscriptions in parts of Andhra, Karnataka which were rich in precious stones and gold and the Kalinga war to be seen as an attempt to secure a rich agricultural hinterland.[97] Both these areas were effectively used to extend the resource base of the Mauryan State which could no longer be met from the limited zone of the Ganges plains. To sum up this new interpretation of the Mauryan rule in India does not mean 'that there was no empire but rather that control was flexible and that the metropolitan State was seen to be the most important element. . . . Here might also be an explanation of why the *Arthaśāstra* tradition, even though it has known an empire as extensive as that of the Mauryas, visualizes a relatively small State in its discussion on how a State is to be administered. Or why Aśoka takes no grandiloquent titles and on occasion even confines himself to the simple title of *rājā māgadhe* (*rājā* of Magadha). . . . The *itihāsa-purāṇa* tradition also maintains that the Mauryas ruled a kingdom but no distinction is made in terms of its being an empire'.[98]

If the example of Magadha can be seen as where the primary processes of State-formation developed, which ultimately took on a complex form, we are left with an apparent impression that the wider historical change in a highly diverse society like India's was brought about through the interaction of this full-fledged State with other regions. In other words, as a primary State it possibly initiated such changes that unleashed processes of secondary State formation in major parts of the Indian sub-continent. At a theoretical level this distinction between primary and secondary States has been raised and rests on the assumption that the former conquer non-States to bring about the latter. For understanding the empirical reality of State formation in early South India this hypothesis may not wholly hold true. An attempt has indeed been made by Sudarshan Seneviratne[99] wherein he argues that the Mauryan State, primarily through its economic interests, intruded into the relatively simple economies of the Andhra and Kalinga areas and thereby helped in setting the tone for State-formation in these parts which did take place in the subsequent period. At the same time, Seneviratne also argues that certain autochthonous forces in the tribal society of pre-Mauryan times did operate to bring in hierarchies of authority in the form of chiefdoms and these internal changes were equally important in bringing about the transformation to a State society in the Deccan.[100]

It precisely because of these internal changes and the fact that pre-State forms in regions South of the Vindhyas rested on differentiated systems of economic sustenance that we need to look at the Mauryan influence, interacting directly only in some zones, as not being a unilateral imposition. It has been suggested by B.D.Chattopadhyaya[101] that we try and identify the structure of the 'localities' (understood as sort of *janapadas)* which may give us some idea of a sort of proto-State before the rise of the Sātavāhanas. Inscriptional and numismatic evidence that tends to suggest the gradual formation of a stratum of elites at the level of 'localities' prior to the emergence of the Sātavāhanas as a major power has been located in the time span between the second century B.C. to the middle of the first century B.C. What is extremely significant from our point of view in Chattopadhyaya's analysis is the fact that the structure and social bases of the subsequent States in this region had much to do with the visibility of these 'localities'. Thus he writes : 'This process did not by any means come to a stop once the Sātavāhanas rose to power; the penetration of a segment of the Mahāmeghavāhanas of Kalinga in the Andhra region in the Sātavāhana period or the emergence of the Ikṣavākus and the Kadambas in the post-Sātavāhana period may be considered 'local' manifestations of the continuity of the same process.'[102]

In a major part of South India, namely, what is commonly called ancient Tamilakam, a name drawn from the Sangam literary texts, another picture of the complex ways in which the origin of the State must have taken place has been discussed.[103] It is only recently that questions of analyzing this data on more scientific lines has yielded writings that care to define the possible pre-State forms and their gradual transition into a State society.[104] In these works the social formation of early Tamilakam has been delineated on the basis of the ecological concept of the five *tiṇai* or physiographical divisions which have been the basis of various descriptions in the early Tamil anthologies. There was inter-relationship between these various economic zones as depicted in the poems and the areas where plough agriculture existed were obviously more superior in terms of productivity and technology. At the political level the form of power thus represented reflected different types of chiefdoms and their interaction with the *Mūvēntar, i.e.* the 'three crowned kings' that are mentioned in the Sangam texts.[105] These were the Cēra-Cōḷa-Pāṇḍya kingdoms which are generally understood to have been outside the Mauryan empire. It has, however, been argued by Seneviratne that 'The presence of the Metropolitan State in the southern Deccan had some degree of influence on the clan-based petty political entities in south India and consequently triggered-off a series of political confrontations aimed at greater political hegemony over communities and settlements, geophysical areas, resource areas, exchange centres and strategic areas'.[106]

However, in the context of the extreme South understanding the internal dynamics of change in society is even more crucial as these elements continued in later historical times as well. Thus for instance, as Gurukkal has pointed it is very difficult to categorize and label the pre-State form at one given level of political control and function. Similarly, during this early period of Tamil history to visualize 'a centralized political authority of due sanction and legitimation within a defined territory, with regular taxation system, standing army and bureaucracy' is difficult.[107] Thus in his analysis features of State co-exist with those of the non-State even at the level of the Ventar monarchs. It is further suggested that the inhibitions due to which full-fledged State, as is commonly understood, did not emerge even in the *marutam* tracts is because the conditions for the development of plough agriculture were not congenial and continued to be based on communal holdings of resources and kinship based production. These together with the policy of raids by chiefs of the other ecological zones created pressure on the production of the *menpulam* or agrarian areas and in some cases led to their destruction as well. Under these circumstances State-formation was not a simple unilinear exercise in Tamil Nadu between 300 B.C. and A.D. 300.

In reviewing some of the new interpretations which have taken a serious look at the processes of State-formation in early India we hope to have been able to suggest that a need to look afresh at the beginnings of civilization and State in the Deccan also requires attention. Though some of these questions have been raised in the second essay, it has not been possible to discuss the force of the ideological moorings in legitimizing the State.[108] For the Deccan situation in particular the intrusive influence of Buddhism was crucial, emanating as it did from important trading and political centres. Not only through expanding trade links and opening up new areas of economic activity, but also in transforming social symbols of power, it did contribute to forging links with political and institutional power. Brahmanism, on the other hand, played a greater role in transforming the nature of State power and State structure in the period after the fifth century A.D. and was equally relevant in providing ideological justification to it. In the third essay a brief look is taken at this issue with regard to the rule of the Viṣṇukuṇḍin rulers.

One would further like to suggest that it is the social basis of State power and its relationship with caste/class that has to be identified and recognized first and foremost, and a beginning for this kind of study has been made in essays three and four of this book. Many elements of later State-formation were embedded in earlier social formations. Central to this was the question of the ownership of land and cultivation of it. Hitherto, discussion on these aspects has tended to cloud the reality of the early Indian State. Further, the discussion on the 'village community' had been mainly on showing that it was a community of equals and economically self-sufficient and had ignored the questions of tensions within the highly complex *varṇa-jāti* system operating in the villages.[109] Thus for any analysis of the nature of the State particularly in what has been recently labelled as the early medieval period, one has to take into account a study of the system of land grants that proliferated in almost all parts of the Deccan from the early centuries A.D. onwards. This created different patterns of land control which in turn, determine to what extent the State can be defined as *unitary, decentralized or segmented.*[110] Each of these terms suggest ways of looking at the State in early India and rest on categorical methodological assumptions of scholars advocating them. However, none of these ignore that the emergence of landed intermediaries, cutting across traditional divisions of caste, but at the same time, adhering to the principles that maintained it ideologically, economically and politically, had brought in different levels of State power and control. This is what made the instruments of State power increasingly coercive in early India. The geographical horizon of the land grant system in early medieval Deccan has gone on to show that far from evolved States being frozen in form and time, there was a continuous change wherein differentiated systems, particularly the less developed ones, were either, incessantly being incorporated into existing State systems or, were becoming the nuclei of new States. Political history[111] of early India and more so, our so-called regional histories can thus be viewed in a more pervasive manner to understand systems of domination and their interaction with changing social formations which continually found ideological legitimacy for the establishment of new States.

Nearly 100 years ago, in 1896, J.D. Gribble wrote *A History of the Deccan.*[112] This was no doubt a history of the more recent periods in its history and an 'official' one of the Nizam and his family. However, in rationalizing why he took up such a monumental task Gribble wrote in the *Preface* to Volume I : 'Now it seems to me that it is essential for a Deccan boy to know something of the early history of that part of the country in which he lives . . .'[113] Gribble was not alone in his concern about teaching the 'natives' about their past. Indeed, he wrote within a certain perception of local history which most Europeans were familiar with in the nineteenth century and which Hunter, writing his *The Annals of Rural Bengal* in 1868, clearly articulates in the words : 'Every county, almost every parish, in England has its annals; but in India, vast provinces, greater in extent than the British Islands, have no individual history whatever. . . . Nor are the inhabitants themselves very much better acquainted with the history of the country in which they live.'[114] This concern with salvaging the lost past of the different regions of India was pertinently related, at the same time, to discrediting the subject of writing. Thus, as early as 1817, Wilks in writing the Preface to his *Historical Sketches of South Indian History* minces no words in stating that 'the department of ancient history in the East is so deformed by fable and anachronism that it be considered an absolute blank in Indian literature' and this was one of the reasons that led him on to rescue 'from oblivion [its history] before it should be lost forever. . . .'[115] As a result of this utter disgust with an ill-defined Hindu past the very first few pages in Wilk's History of the Deccan, viewed as an integeral part of South India, recreates a picture of lawlessness, chaos, decentralized village communities and the like. It must be stated that this was the necessary preamble which Wilks needed to amplify his statements on the introduction of a new land tenurial structure in Mysore which had been the main purpose of his assignment there.

Irrespective of the fact these administrator-historians wrote for different parts of the country,[116] their ideological assumptions about India and their dominant perception of history was the same. They were burdened by the concern for constrasting the civilized West with the backward and irrational India. The very nature of History as a discipline being absent in the traditional society's vision of its past became a signal for the conscious creation of new images within a scientific paradigm so that it became a justification and provided useful tools for the more contemporary interpretations of Indian society. In the context of the present project we have taken the example of the 'Intellectual Construction' of the 'Village Community' in these writings to exemplify how this has impeded our understanding of the nature of social and economic change in the rural context till today. We continue to talk in terms of a single unified image of an 'Indian village' which has no place for understanding and explaining variability in the premodern records on a regional scale.

Fundamental socio-economic changes in India during the last two centuries have been concomitantly accompanied by the advent of modern scientific ideas rooted in the western intellectual tradition. Though it is common enough for us today to say that village India is identifiable according to its indigenous idioms and beliefs, our intellectual understanding of an everlasting Indian village community is the product of ideas embedded in a western consciousness. A historiographical review of literature on the 'village community' began as a peripheral exercise to our primary concern of defining stages in the economic and social history of the early Deccan up to thirteenth century. However, rather than being peripheral, this enterprise indeed became a central concern as it was found that modern constructions of the ostensibly 'pure village community' of ancient and early medieval India were so misinformed that to do any justice to the subject a detailed account of how these modern images of rural India had emerged in the first place became an essential task. This was pertinent from another point too since the modes of explanation, meaning of terms and definition of villages (*grāma*), located as part of a series of settlements, were so antithetically different in the pre-modern sources that to merely make adjustments with the modern perception seemed untenable. This exercise has also been undertaken at some length to show that knowledge about the Indian village is historical and therefore, its mapping and charting out becomes essential otherwise our knowledge of it would remain essentialized in its under-developed nature, poverty, religiosity and the like. In a sense it can be shown that all attempts to define village life have been a series of historical positions and that we cannot allow these to enunciate principles about its existence without ever attempting to view its pre-modern constructions within the indigenous perceptions of the same. These are found in texts and inscriptions at multiple levels of descriptions and not in terms of one monolithic description. These too, it can be argued, were historical positions embedded in sources largely elaborated by the elites in society. However, it is precisely this unraveling of the changing images of village life and situations that need to be emphasized.

It was western intervention and acclaim that brought to the forefront the definition of the 'village community'.[117] It is important to underline that the notion and the term 'Village Community' had a specific origin in the nineteenth century when administrative reports prepared by officers of the British East India Company had just begun to emerge. These reports Karashima writes, 'In determining from whom they should collect land revenue, . . . 'discovered' the existence of village communities', [118] and goes on to pertinently point out that ever since, 'the term (village community) has come to stay in all intellectual enterprises 'though' its connotation has varied according to the motivation of its users or to the stage of historical studies.'[119] As is well known the latter half of the nineteenth century saw greater imposition of alien concepts of organization and governance. In the present context the definition and transformation of villages, their subjugation and the conscious initiation of the imagery of backwardness of the village communities went hand in hand with a greater systematization, professionalization and regularization of the generation of a new kind of Eurocentric knowledge about India which affected most areas of activity. This is available to us in the form of the linguistic, ethnological, archaeological, Census, land revenue surveys and District Gazetteers. Thus a new set of 'hard core' facts on the peasant, revenue, rent, caste, customs, tribes, popular religious practices *etc.* emerged which owed their authenticity to the fact they were generated by State power. Analyzing this trend in the late nineteenth century Gyan Prakash writes, 'Because the society aggregated from the new units was constituted by an apparently objective and culturally neutral classificatory system of individuals, households, occupations, it became available to more extensive administrative penetration. This', it is significantly pointed out, 'brought the older debates on the nature of Indian village communities, culminating in Baden-Powell's

1892 publication of *The Land System of British India* to an end. The government no longer considered the indirect systems of rule consisting of contractual agreements with village leaders as necessary -- and it reached down to the individuals configured by their caste and tribal status.'[120] Thus a rejection of the old form of knowledge and the creation of a new one on the village in India was complete at the turn of the twentieth century. Dharmapal has summarized the impact of the new socio-economic and political system in the following way : 'When disorganization, impoverishment, subjugation had gone far enough and could not go any further without having adverse effects on the total revenue receipts, the whole of Indian society was placed under a sort of freeze and it then became *the task of scholarship to establish that such disorganization, etc., had been endemic to Indian culture.*'[121] (emphasis added)

The subject matter of most of the early writings on the village was subsumed under such headings as 'land systems', 'property relations', 'revenue assesments'. Thus Maine's [122] and Baden-Powell's studies, which have had a great impact on the later writings, were primarily on land systems and related constituent parts of village organization prevailing at the time and were not in fact, systematic historical accounts of the same drawing upon the medieval and ancient records in any substantial way. Communal ownership of land and the notion of the economic and social independence or self-sufficiency of the Indian Village had been the two main pillars of understanding its negative nature as an unchanging one throughout history and these were forcefully argued in the writings of Maine and Marx.[123] They maintained that the earlier Indian society had been stagnant because it had at its base the self-sustaining village community. They consequently declined to find such historical developments in India as noticed in the West.[124] It must however, be stated that Baden-Powell's study proved an incentive for the subsequent nationalist writings as he put forward the idea and argued that non-communal or individual land ownership had been practiced throughout rural India from ancient times down to the nineteenth century.[125] During the early twentieth century new documents like indigenous inscriptions and Indian textual material like the *Arthaśāstra*[126] came to light and this gradually began to alter the earlier perceptions of village communities in the historical literature. However, the terms of analysis and the subject matter of study continued to revolve around land ownership patterns and revenue systems. It was well into the twentieth century that scholars began to pay serious attention to the questioning of the image of an unchanging and isolate village.

Related to the question of the socio-economic character of the village, a considerable amount of confusion was generated on the political aspects of village control and organization.[127] The most oftquoted stereotypical image that has been perpetuated in this regard is the one drawn from the Minute written by Sir Charles Metcalfe in 1830. It reads : 'The Village Communities are little Republics, having nearly everything that they want within themselves, and almost independent of any foreign relations. They seem to last where nothing else lasts. Dynasty after Dynasty tumbles down; revolution succeeds to revolution; . . . but the Village Communities remain the same'.[128] His praise of the tenacity of the village communities was to become a point of departure for the nationalist historians to, not only cull ancient data to prove that villages were self-governing democratic units but, this also led them to ascribe the distant villages with a glorious, harmonious and ideal past that had been rudely shaken by British intervention. This also generated writings by both Indian and British scholars[129] on the 'real', 'pure' and 'true' India lying in the villages. Unconsciously, the Indian village now came to attain an uniform character, unitary in nature, without conflict and everlasting. This has substantially impeded our understanding of the elements of change in village life and its social structure in pre-modern times. The creation of the ostensibly pure original Indian village of the past is thus a relatively new idea, but it has, with amazing ease, been incorporated into historical texts of both pre and post independent India to define village communities of the past as some kind of isolates unconnected to the larger fabric of society.

The static image of village life in history has permeated to the popular general history texts used at the graduate level. First, on the question of economic self-sufficiency, the conclusion of Nilakanta Sastri's chapter discussing the Cholas reads thus : 'The king, the nobles and the temples drew largely in various ways upon the products of the industry of the common people. But much of this wealth was returned to them in ways that advanced their common good. It was a wonderful social harmony based not on equality of classes or individuals but on a readiness to give and take, a mutual goodwill that had its roots deep down at the foundations of communal life.'[130] Sastri was one of pioneers of South Indian History who had revealed considerable new information from hiterto unpublished epigraphs on village organization, but could not help subscribing to the nationalist ethos of the 'Golden Age' of the past; for the Tamil country this was found in the Chola Empire. This emerges clearly in his writings since, when he goes on to describe the Vijayanagar empire in the subsequent chapter, he writes : 'The autonomy of villages, however, suffered considerable abridgement in this period as their officials came to be linked up more and more closely with the central government and its representatives.'[131] Around this time, that is, the mid-fifties, at a more popular level, the access to a historical picture of an Indian village is made available through Basham's famous *The Wonder That Was India.*[132] This, even more explicitly, configures the unchanging character of the Indian villages in the words : 'The Indian village differed very little from that of the present day, . . . The villagers formed a self-conscious community. . . . This strong sense of the community was one of the chief factors in the survival of Hindu Culture.'[133] The popularity of these notions creeps into texts written purely on Economic History as well. Thus, writing in 1969 Dipakranjan Das in his *Economic History of the Deccan* begins his chapter on 'Associate Life in the Towns and Villages' with the words :'The ideal of communal harmony and co-operation was always a living force in ancient India'.[134]

We need to explain the popularity of these notions about the history of Village India and their persistence in history textbooks particularly since, after the 1950's, most of the earlier assumptions about the unchanging character of Indian villages had indeed been rejected in the anthropological studies and Marxist writings on agrarian history in general. One glaring fact that emerges out of this review is the inadequate nature of research on village history till recent times. Thus, it is startling to note that after the publication of Baden-Powell's work (which had only partially looked at the historical dimension), we have only one full-fledged monograph on the history of the 'village community' published by A.S.Altekar in 1927 called *History of Village Communities in Western India.*[135] After this, apart from an interesting detailed article on 'Origin of Indian Village System' in *Indian Inheritance*,[136] published in 1956, the next full monograph on the history of villages emerges as *Early Medieval Village in North-East India* A.D. *600-1200* by Abhay Kant Choudhary in 1971.[137] In the absence of any serious research on the Indian village after Altekar, it seemed almost natural for historians to incorporate images of the self-sufficient and self-governing villages into text-books without questioning the apparently 'objective', 'authoritative' statements of the earlier Orientalist discourses. The essentialization of rural India as a conglomeration of 'communities' from time immemorial had remained intact, but chapters on 'economic conditions', 'land revenue systems', and other such subjects of inquiry had vehemently argued on the changing concept of the land ownership pattern in ancient and early medieval India.[138] As a result, in the representation of rural history its centrality was subsumed under, what B.D. Chattopadhyaya calls 'such generalities as 'agrarian system', 'agrarian structure', 'ownership of land', 'agricultural production', 'agrarian relations' and so on.'[139]

We take the example of Altekar's writings to exemplify the views embedded in nationalist historiography as this also happens to be the earliest exclusive monograph on the history of village communities in the twentieth century. Altekar ostensibly writes as a Nationalist historian but the simple forcefulness with which Altekar's work reiterates Charles Metcalfe's vision of Indian villages can be be restated in his own words which mark the first paragraph in the Preface to his book : 'The importance of the history of the village communities in India can hardly be overrated; for the *real history of India* (emphasis added) consists of the history of its village communities. Dynasties have come and dynasties have gone, but it is the village communities that have preserved intact the culture and tradition of old Bharatavarsha through several revolutions.'[140] Not recognizing that he has unconsciously borrowed the theoretical and methodological assumptions of the imperialist scholars, Altekar goes on to contrast his own work with that of his predecessors like Maine and Baden-Powell, in pointing out that his work was more acquainted with the ancient Indian sources like the *Smṛtis* and Inscriptions and therefore, by implication, more authoritative than the earlier works which had actually been based on conjectures about the past.

Apart from the command on the so-called 'authentic' sources Altekar uses the scientific method to propound on the glory of the ancient past to show, at the end of each chapter, how the greatness of the respective village institutions and life described by him, gradually declined after the Muslim period. His typical assumption in this regard being, 'The Mohamedan influence was not powerful enough, so the institutions continued to exist but their growth was arrested and efficiency weakened (see *ante,* p.29). The British influence, dominant and all sided, has all but killed most of the village institutions.'[141] It would be wrong to conclude that Altekar accepted the assumptions of the imperialist historians without questioning. However, as Partha Chatterjee explains with regard to the development of the ideology of Nationalism in general, that though the nationalists opposed colonialism through the "cunning of Reason" and their claim that India's ancient history had followed such ideas, they were incapable of ideologically transcending the Orientalists assumptions.[142] The contradictions in nationalist historiography therefore, unconsciously led Altekar to perpetuating the very assumptions that he sought to reject and argue against. This urge cannot be better exemplified than in citing the last part of his text wherein he suggests ways and means by which the revival of the features of the old village institutions could be made with the help of adjustment within the framework of the Reformed Bombay Legislative Council Village Panchayat Act of 1920.[143]

Another feature of nationalist historiography which also emerges in Altekar's endeavours was to contrast the Aryan with the Dravidian. In writing about the Village it would seem that this question was hardly relevant. However, on the other hand, it seems that the major thrust of his attempt was to create a different identity for the Aryan village community. He rejects its association with the Dravidian and goes to great length to explain 'we do not subscribe to the view that the village communities in Western India were Dravidian institutions.'[144] It has been pointed out for ancient history in general that the assertion of the regional identity in historical writing was a natural outcome of nationalist historiography.[145] In that sense there are no major theoretical contradictions between Altekar's writings for Western India -- the Aryan village community -- and what the South Indian historians begin to increasingly describe in the context of the Pallava-Chola-Vijayanagara period for the Tamil country after independence. Unconsciously, however, this becomes the focus on the 'Dravidian' village community which Altekar's work had tried hard to bypass. Indeed, these writings on South India are the next important ones on the history of village communities within the existing methodological framework. The efforts of scholars like K.A.N. Sastri, T.V.Mahalingam, K. Meenakshi, A. Appadoria, Venkkayya and others were largely possible because they draw upon new sources from South Indian epigraphs to create a sort of coherent picture of these communities in

South India. Since they began with the assumption that the village communities were to be understood as a part of the centralized administrative system of the respective empires being discussed by them, they were unable to overcome the basic political contradiction in their explanations of defining a centralized despotic form of government and its co-existence with the local self-governing village assemblies.[146] Apart from the nostalgia of the 'golden age' which was seized upon to be reinforced by describing the local assemblies, these historians also largely perpetuated the Brahmanical vision of society by giving undue importance to descriptions of the *sabhā*, where members of the village assembly were largely *brāhmaṇas*. Though data on the *ur* and the *nādu* was also available, its integration to the larger study was still marginal

We take one example of these writings in the essay written by T.V. Mahalingam specifically on the subject. His 'Village Communities in South India'[147] attempts a vivid portrayal of the village communities of South India beginning with the information gleaned through the Sangam texts up to the inscriptions of the Vijayanagar times . He too begins with Metcalfe's quotation praising the village communities and one does not have to read between the lines to understand Mahalingam's point of view. He clearly states, 'The value of a study of the subject can hardly be exaggerated, for in many cases the foundations of the political and administrative institutions of later times have been traced to the ancient village communities. Even the idea of the corporate personality of a group of people is considered to be a development from them'.[148] We had noted above that the term 'village community' had never been rejected as a convenient point to define the cohesive and uniform nature of the historical village in India, and Mahalingam in accepting this terminology readily defines this as 'a body of persons organized for political, economic, religious and professional purposes. The village community was, therefore, not distinct from village organization which existed in some form from very early times.'[149] He takes the *sabhā,* the *ur* and the *nādu* to describe the three types of village organization. The fundamenttal economic reason that kept the village organization together was the communal ownership of land[150] and it was this that is said to have created 'a feeling of collective recognition of their common interest by residents in the village'.[151] However, in explaining the decline of this sense of collective feeling in later periods Mahalingam resorts to political reasons for the failures. Thus he writes, 'Probably, all was not well with the working of the *sabhā* at the place, its work was hampered by the rise of a factious spirit among its members and hence the government's interference and insistence.'[152] Like Nilakanta Sastri, he too sees the Vijayanagara period as not very conducive to the continuance of the village community in its past glory.[153]

The lack of any interest in describing the conflicts between the political order and the rest of society is the hallmark of this type of writing. Even A. Appadorai's work on economic History sees no relationship between the State and the Economic order [154] and the State erroneously emerges as a static one from the earlier times down to the Vijayanagara period. Nationalist historians separated the historical analysis of the Indian village into village organization/ institutions by which they meant its socio-political features, from the village life, which was meant to indicate the economic features of its existence. Both in Altekar's[155] and C. Meenakshi's [156] divisions of the chapters this emerges very clearly. Further, they visualize no conflict at the level of the village society or, between it and the other levels of power, be it political, economic or religious. The basic unit of analysis is therefore, the united village. Finally, they were comfortable in looking at the Indian village as a uniform category. Apart from identifying an Aryan versus a Dravidian village, they were unable to recognize that there could be major variations in village life in time and space.

As noted above, outside of nationalist historiography, we have no individual works on the history of village communities and this therefore, clearly explains how our vision of the history of rural life in India till recent times has been embroiled in the issues raised about it in the colonial context. Thus, one is forced to move away from particular studies and turn to some of the general issues that have been raised by the anthropological studies and historical studies written within the Marxist framework which try to understand change in Indian society and thereby, naturally draw in the Village. Interestingly, these studies bring into focus the institution of caste as the object of study and therefore, directly move away from the village per se though many of the anthropological studies are in fact, village case studies. The Marxist writings on history focus on the larger issues of agrarian history, labelling the particular social formations and the specific questions of land ownership, peasant subjection and so on, and in this sense, they too move away from the village per se, as a unit of study. Nonetheless, the last thirty years or so have seen a successful questioning of the nineteenth century image of an unchanging self-sufficient village and its placement within the broader context of social and economic change.[157]

But have these approaches really brought about a dramatic change in our perception of the Indian village, or rather, Indian villages in history? Writes David Ludden in his recent analysis of the *Peasant in South India* :[158] 'To scholars of political economy, from Karl Marx to Barrington Moore, Indian Village society seems stolid in the extreme. To cultural sociologists from Max Weber to Louis Dumont, the explanation for Indian peasant intertia lies in village traditions prescribed by the caste system, which persists and resists assaults by capitalist urbanites.'[159] In the present context it would not be possible to review in detail the social anthropological studies on Village India that have come out in large numbers since independence.[160] Implicit in these moves, however, was the search for an authentic India after the end of colonial rule and a moving away from a study of imperial policies and the like. It is questionable whether they were indeed able to ideologically break away from the colonial discourse and it has been argued by Gyan Prakash that they were not able to do so when he writes : 'the concept of a caste-driven and other-worldly India, was reformulated as "traditioinal India" by the modernization theory in the 1960's . . . by providing a social-scientific knowledge of "traditional" social structures and beliefs targeted for modernization.'[161]

The "traditional" and "authentic" India was naturally seen in its villages. In contrast to the image of the nationalist historians these village studies took up a thorough analysis of the meaning and connotation of the term 'village community'. They legitimately raised the issue of stratification in the village and asserted that village had elements of continuity with the past. Dumont's *Homo Hierarchicus* had advocated the essentialization of India in terms of caste.[162] For the village he rejected the use of the word 'community' as it implied equality and argued that villages has always been hierarchical. In the same context he provided a critique on the writings of Maine and Marx which have ever since been justifiably accepted.[163] However, M.N. Srinivas has raised issues against Dumont's attempt to deny that 'the village is a community' and not a mere 'architectural and demographic entity'.[164] In his detailed arguments against the former's position he writes: 'Given such a relationship of acceptance of hierarchy, it ought not to be difficult to conceive of communities which were non-egalitarian, their people playing interdependent roles and all of them having a common interest in survival. The argument that only 'equalitarian' societies can have local communities has to be proved, and cannot be the starting point for evaluating hierarchical societies.'[165] Both Dumont and Srinivas try to draw upon the pre-British empirical situation; they both also place caste as the central feature of analysis, but, arrive at different conclusions about the role of caste in what has now come to be conveniently labelled as "traditional India". Dumont emphasized the ritual content of it while Srinivas saw its true nature in its function and for pre-British India, he concluded that this stemmed from 'strong patron-client relationships, the social framework of production created bonds running counter to caste. . . . The village was no doubt stratified along lines of caste and land, but the productive process made it an interlocking community.'[166]

Well after Dumont, and even within Marxist writings, the super structural importance of caste as an institutional and ritual factor to understand early Indian society has been written about which we cannot go into at the moment.[167] But we would like to draw attention to the fact that an overemphasis on this aspect has hampered studies on both the history of caste and the village. How this is so is best encapsulated in the words of Arjun Appadurai : 'the phantom scheme of "modernity and tradition" though in disrepute, continues to haunt and obfuscate scholarly discussion of change in the caste system. This is partly because, from a strictly enthnographic point of view, Indian villages (which provide the context of most caste studies) often resist historical analysis. *Because there is inadequate documentation, historical information on particular systems of caste (local or regional) is partial, scattered, and cryptic.* (emphasis added) This encourages a reification of "traditional" system, based on a synthesis of textual information, odd bits of pre-British records and scattered information form the early British records. Thus, the attempt to genuinely assess the impact of colonial rule on caste is repeatedly confounded by lack of adequate information on caste as a functioning institution immediately before and during British rule. This encourages arbitrary definitions of the "traditional" system and, therefore, of the nature of contemporary change.'[168]

The above concerns expressed by an anthropologist working within the tradition of using historical data hits at the crux of the issue about the history of rural India, namely, the necessity of first recognizing the vestiage of the village in its pre-modern terms. Historical studies of village society need to be set inside a narrative and interpretive framework that pays due attention to long term trends before British rule and to the village activity affecting those trends. Some work in this direction has begun especially the charting out and mapping of statistical data on the village social structure and economy by a team of scholars led by Noburo Karashima[169] for the South Indian medieval records. Indeed, this has in recent years led to a debate on the appropriate characterization of the early medieval social formation in these parts.[170] Earlier, Stein in his writings on *Peasant State and Society*[171] had spearheaded, with the help of the sociological method, the controversy of the nature of social alliances at the village and *nādu* level which gave undue importance to the role of ritual sovereignty. Stein, however, successfully showed that even in historical terms the self-sufficiency of the Indian village was a myth but replaced it with the notion of self-sufficiency at the *nādu* level.[172] More pragmatically, Karashima's efforts have helped to chalk out the village as entities in the medieval South Indian environment, described their social structure and attempted definitions of their socio-economic and politico ideological existence. This kind of data enables us to positively question the earlier stereotypes perpetuated and garbed in different methodological strategies. Karashima himself refrains from coming to any conclusion on defining the nature of the State in Chola times as being either 'Segmentary' or 'Feudal' and prefers to simply understand the elements of social and historical change.[173]

On the empirical situation on South India the Marxist scholars have not contributed as much but have posed relevant questions in the form of providing a critique to both the above points of views.[174] However, it is well-known that Marxist historians for early India as a whole, have ably questioned the notion of the unchangeableness of the Indian village that was perpetuated in the orthodox Marxist writings of the Asiatic Mode of production. Most pertinently, on a general level they have questioned the notion of India as an undivided subject by their advocacy of understanding the "real" world of class struggles and mode of production. Village India thus was not seen as united and harmonious but divided by caste and class conflict and the forces of change being brought about in society were the result of a change in the relations and mode of production. The writings of Kosambi and R.S. Sharma were the earliest to have raised the question about the viability of the use of the Feudal model to understand transition in early medieval India.[175] For this period, it is interesting to note that they both saw the village as having become increasingly "self-sufficient". Kosambi's theory of Feudalism from above which was largely attributed to State initiative talks of the 'growth of virtually self-contained villages' and a "closed village economy" for the Gupta period.[176] Sharma too sees villages and towns as more self-sufficient between the third and ninth century A.D.[177] The pertinent question here is therefore, to what extent have we in our economic analysis of the village been able to move away from the stereotype of self-sufficient image first advocated in the nineteenth century?

In the above overview of the perceptions of different strands of historical writing on the village we noted that in quantitative terms the maximum had been written by the nationalist scholars. They viewed self-sufficiency primarily in a political sense. For South India this was explained to be so because the people were co-owners of the soils. In the anthropological studies the self-sufficiency was symbolized in traditional society and polity and particularly due to the insularity of caste. The Marxist historians have shifted the analysis in looking at the economic essence of the village which in some periods of history did indicate elements of self-sufficiency. Though they have raised the question of conflict in society at the village level and piled up evidence on the subjection of the peasantry,[178] it still remains to be satisfactorily argued as to how this changed the character of village situations from time to time within specific geographical settings.

Our contention is that in any understanding of the 'village community', of the past, and more aptly, the attempts at writing rural history of the specific regions of India, and their situation today, we need to recognize and take account of the fact that the village society of the past was not a mere string of hierarchical isolates that had no linkage with other contiguous localities. Further, one needs to shift from talking about 'an Indian village' to Indian villages. For alternative ways of writing a rural history we need to address ourselves not to the image of one typical village in history but to the multiple images of it at least, in terms of their location in dry, wet or forest zones. That is, how differentially individual villages existed in the rural landscape. This has been attempted in a brief study by B.D.

Chattopadhyaya entitled *Rural Settlements and Rural Society in Early Medieval India* as this would provide, according to him, a 'geographical profile different' in each case.[179] This in turn, is related to terms used to describe rural settlements in pre-modern sources. A study of these can be used to build upon methods to understand the hierarchies of rural settlements as has been described by Ghosh in his background to the study of the city in early India. Evidence for such an understanding of the terminology of rural settlements in the indigenous sources goes back to as early as the sixth century B.C.[180] For instance, it is clear that *grāma* is one of the most popular terms used to describe these settlements but other terms such as *pallī*; *vāṭaka*, *kheṭaka etc.* would imply that certain villages went through different stages in their formation.[181] Internal changes as well as encroachments into tribal habitats having been a continuous historical process, *pallīs* could, over time change to *grāmas* on the one hand, and *grāmas* to *puras* (or towns) on the other.[182] This would explain legitimately the historical process of *grāma* as a kind of village settlement changing in historical time. As discussed by Choudhary even the textual evidence of text like the *Abidhāna-rājendra* of Vijayarājendra Surīśvara can be drawn upon to show that there was no one definition regarding the boundary of a *grāma.* This text suggests that it could be up to where the cows grazed or, up to where the grass or wood cutters could cover in a day, or else, finally, what was fenced or enclosed.[183] This textual flexibility inherently implies the emergence of new *grāmas* and the possibility of existing *grāmas* expanding in the rural space of both the *janapada* (i.e., habitable territory) and *araṇya* (i.e., forest).

From the historical sources the distinction between a *brahmadeya* and non-*brahmadeya* village is well-known.[184] The important point in this connection, however, is that since such few studies on village history have been done it is somewhat erroneously believed that once a *brahmadeya* was made, it was for eternity. B.D. Chattopadhyaya draws our intention to the fact that this was not always so and that there could be reversion of a *brahmadeya* village back to a non-*brahmadeya.*[185] These changes normally required political authority and will but, necessarily meant that the social structure of the concerned villages and its economic underpinnings were also factors of consideration. Much more research[186] needs to be done to understand the specific nature of economic and social change at the village level, and in understanding these historical changes it has to be kept in mind that village societies all over the country did not react to change in a uniform way, i.e., each probably differed in their response to external stimuli and while some may have adapted, others may have transformed themselves. The historical dimension of when these changes took place has yet to be systematically documented. Further, rigid analytical terms of analysis such as 'political' 'social', and 'economic' tend to inhibit the understanding of change and continuity in the Indian village society and could perhaps more meaningfully be replaced by such terms as socio-political, socio-economic, etc. The debate in the twentieth century is no longer on 'Criticisms of Maine's egalitarian *ur*-community and of single-line evolution. . . . or that communities were 'left to modify themselves separately' but rather, it seems now 'necessary to ask how internal and external worlds (in the village) relate, in general, to encompass continuity as well as change'.[187] Thus a rejection of the idea that the village structure in pre-modern conditions was largely unaffected by outside influences is crucial as, in not accepting this, one tends to impose static images of village life which have become sterotypes through erroneous intellectual understandings of the same.

The essays in this volume have drawn upon two major sources of information, namely archaeology and epigraphy. Hitherto, there have been different approaches to their use and this has raised relevant issues of interpretation. In the following pages some of the more recent studies based on this type of source material have been discussed since it is important to underline the fact that the historian today needs to understand the 'original' sources in the context of trying to explain the broad patterns of change rather than specific events. We begin with a discussion of archaeology as a source of information on which the second essay is primarily based. The other three essays in this volume are based on inscriptions which we turn to elaborate upon subsequently.

Archaeological data has been understood variously by scholars and this is partly what gives us a plurality of approaches in its use by historians. For the purposes of this work we had focused on the southern part of the Indian sub-continent, i.e., on regions or subregions lying south of the Vindhyas. Archaeology based historical works that have emerged in the last two decades or so, i.e., since the 1970's have changed the scope of the discipline to some extent and this is what warrants the review of some of these texts. The fact that today the use of archaeological sources has become challenging for the historian is because of the increasing burdens of specilization that the discipline has undergone in terms of the demands of the scientific approach and techniques emanating from it. Despite these advances in the discipline in general, it is noted by us that in the works under review the theoretical assumptions or hypotheses put forward by both historians and archaeologists [188] do not vary to any great extent and therefore, the ultimate aim of both the disciplines continues to remain only 'finding the facts of the ancient past and putting them in some sort of logical ordering'.

The reason for the above tendency is not difficult to find because the method that has paradigmatically swayed both the archaeologist and the historian in the past has been positivism. The intellectual environment under which the discipline of Archaeology, for instance, was fostered on the Indian soil from the eighteenth century onwards began with : (a) antiquarian interest (b) concern for historical geography and (c) understanding Indian history as part of Universal history.[189] Irrespective of whether it were European biases and prejudices that inhibited their understanding of Indian art and monuments or, the unconditional praise with which some aspects of Indian culture were glorified and described or, still further, the imperial concern with constructing a particular kind of history of British India, we are told that the early scholars were concerned with 'systematic' 'minute' and 'precise' descriptions. These could only be done if artifacts, art objects, inscriptions and sites were identified, deciphered and excavated. All this began to be done with increased tempo in the nineteenth century within the spirit of the methodological framework provided by scientific positivism. Thirty years ago, the great historian of South India, T.V. Mahalingam said at a Seminar 'the art of the Indian historian has been 'factography' rather than 'historiography'. He went on to say :--'This charge has been resented but not disproved; and laborious and very often unconvincing defense against this charge has been put up, but that is not by itself enough to alter the situation.'[190] One would like to add in a similar vein that this partly holds true even today. Not only history, but archaeology too has largely remained 'factographic'. Therefore, though we have amidst us a plurality of approaches to study a historic phenomena, the methodology hardly varies in qualitative terms. In the process of explaining why this was so, Mahalingam writes : 'pre-historical and proto-historical research (and in fact all archaeology) deals with the periphery of history is more technical and mechanical rather than literary and instructive which is the true role of informed history.'[191] In this statement is at once encapsulated the traditional vision of how historians view archaeology. These are assumptions common enough today and such concerns among historians as, for the need of 'systematic explorations and excavations -- both vertical and horizontal -- of a number of still untapped sites, dating of archaeological relics by scientific methods like carbon 14 . . .'[192] are repeated as a matter of routine without ever integrating the existing material collected, into the mainstream of historical research.

Broadly, the works under review are those that purport to be texts only describing the archaeological data under the subject headings defined by their scope of research. These may incidentally refer to other sources like literature when it concerns the historical periods. Their approach is historical but the very nature of work undertaken often means describing pre and proto historic phases only. On the other hand, there are those that are primarily historical texts of a traditional kind using archaeological data selectively to explain mainly aspects of cultural or art history and most often, in these works archaeological data is necessarily understood as corroborative. Very few works would like to integrate the use of archaeological data in understanding basic elements of change in a society's evolution -- be it its art or material culture, its polity or economy, its socio-cultural or ecological environments and so on. The reason for this is that scholars working within the parameters of the traditional approach to history or archaeology shudder to pose, or outrightly avoid, questions of hypothesis and model making. A recent article by Paddayya,[193] with the help of examples from field archaeology, argues how the role of hypotheses is crucial to generate fundamental research. Pertinently, in this article he takes examples from earlier works on archaeology both in India and elsewhere, to show that hypothesis making is not a new phenomena that is said to be only associated with the emergence of New Archaeological studies.[194] Against the above we need to accept that both archaeologists and historians 'construct' the past with either consciously, or, unconsciously delineated hypotheses and theoretical premises. These are visible in the following way : (1) as the region particularly 'chosen' for analysis (ii) as data 'chosen' for analysis which is sometimes new, but often, what is available or given and (iii) as objectives or the possible results of the study. In the brief survey that follows we review a few classical examples of the type of works that have emerged in the last 20 years as indicators of broad trends in archaeological and historical research. This is therefore, by no means an exhaustive review. Before we begin it would be worthwhile to indicate that broad surveys of both archaeological and historical works for the period prior to the one under consideration have been exhaustively done at various thematic levels for India as whole[195]

In using the historical framework of the Sātavāhana-Kṣatrapa times, [196] C. Margadandhu in 1985 published an updated inventory of all kinds of archaeological data pertaining to the Deccan and Western India dividing his work into subject wise chapters such as architecture, metallurgy, tools and so on. This could be taken as a typical example of an archaeology based study which, in using the political terminology of dynastic nomenclature, leaves the erroneous impression that his study is in fact a fresh analysis of the Sātavāhana Kṣatrapa period using archaeological data. In fact, there is no attempt at reconsidering any aspect of the period in the light of new evidence, particularly those pertaining to the material culture of the period. On the other hand, similar case studies on a simple description of the diverse range of archaeological data implicity raise important historical questions. One such is V.V.Krishnasastry's work[197] published by the State Department of Archaeology, Hyderabad in 1983 which focuses our attention on the material cultures of a much neglected area of historical analysis within Andhra Pradesh, namely, Telangana. Therby, he has unconsciously brought to historical visibility a region which has hitherto been consciously neglected in historical texts as one not worthy of representation for the early historical period as it had failed to yield monumental edifices of a certain kind like those found in other parts of Andhra. By implication this means that, in most cases, the choice of where the archaeologist's spade should work was in the past primarily determined by the subjective concerns of what he might expect to find in terms of monumental activity -- be it political, religious or artistic. This work also poses the very crucial question of the interlink between the proto and early historical environments in a given sub-region which has become significant for historians concerned with identifying elements of continuity rather than disruption and insularity. By the mid-70's it is noticed that a tendency to identify, within the linguistic boundaries of present day States, the archaeological remains of the so-called regions of isolation had emerged for South India as a whole. A case in point is A. Sundara's study.[198] Both the above works have brought forth valuable new material on their respective areas of study but, have let facts speak for themselves underlying the commonly held belief that objects of observation need not be subjected to the vagaries of interpretation. On the other hand, the earlier tendency of re-using known data and putting it into different moulds has continued to co-exist with the former, as for instance, K. Krishnamuthy's book.[199] In this context the attempt is at projecting the artistic achievements of a society and not its fundamental links with processes of historical change.

The other type of work which has continued to absorb the archaeologist and the historian reveals a tendency towards systematization of data rather than its analysis for changing existing historical interpretations of the subjects. Some works in this genre like those based on the disciplines of numismatics or architecture, implicitly render a historical posture as compared to those based on describing the cultural superstructure emanating from the use of archaeological sources. Thus studies like S. Nagaraju's[200] concentrates on the architectural features of the early historical period and apart from meticulos descriptions of the rock-cut architecture, á very concerted effort is made to look at the development in the architectural style within a chronological framework which is then used to redefine the chronology of the Sātavāhanas in general. Similar exercises in looking intensively at the coin data from excavations[201] were made in the early seventies so that this material could be integrated into historical analysis. A collection of A.M Shastri's articles in this regard have recently been published together reposing a fresh analysis of knotty problems of Sātavāhana chronology.[202] Efforts in this direction were earlier solidified with the publication of I.K. Sarma's book[203] who also brought to focus the provenance of the new coin data found and thereby, implicitly raised questions fundamental to economic history like quantity and distribution of Sātavāhana coinage, the ratio of different metals used for the coinage and so on. For South India as a whole the work of B.D. Chattopadhyaya[204] remains far-reaching in the questions it has raised about the absence of coinage in certain periods of history and therefore, has given a definitive historical perspective to problems of understanding economic history through a scientific examination of coins. Though the above are significant books as indicators of the new trends that could be exploited for getting a richer historical texture of different historical periods, by and large studies on architecture, coins, sculpture and the like have not gone beyond listing cataloguing and description of individual aspects of the archaeological data. Innumerable studies of the latter kind have emerged in the period under consideration.[205]

At this point one would like to appropriately quote one of the prolific and most active archaeologists of his time. He is the late H. Sarkar of the Archaeological Survey of India who for a long period worked on field excavations and wrote considerably on art history. In an address made just before he died he confesses, 'We focused all our attention on Buddhist Stupas as they yielded fine examples of architecture and sculptural art. The fact that they formed part of a larger social and economic fabric was completely lost sight of.'[206] He has further articulated that 'Unless we (i.e., archaeologists) are aware of what is to be brought to the fore in order to explain or discern a historical process we may not be in a position to even notice its very existence. It is history, it is the developments in the realm of Social Sciences which provide us the needed insight. . . . There is now an increasing awareness amongst archaeologists that they should dig not merely artifacts, structures or works of art but the forgotten life and living of a society in its all possible entirety'.[207] A survey of articles published in the name of outstanding archaeologists as their Commemorative volumes or Festschrifts which have been prolifically brought out in the last two decades would be a good barometer to gauge whether Sarkar's ideas have had any bearing on the archaeologists work in the last twenty years or so.

Archaeology Congress and Seminar Papers edited by S.B. Deo[208] and *A Decade of Archaeological Studies in South India* edited by B.K. Gururaja Rao[209] help to project the state of the art at the beginning of the period under consideration particularly from the point of view of the new data that had emerged from excavations in post-Independent India. A similar Seminar with a narrower focus was held in Hyderabad in 1981 on the Sātavāhanas.[210] In the same year appeared *Madhu, the Shri M.N. Deshpande Festschrift.* It was clear in its focus of purporting to include papers on recent research in Archaeology and Art history only and this is made explicit in its sub-divisional headings of Pre and Proto History, Historical Archaeology, Architecture, Sculpture and Art, Numismatics, Conservation etc. In 1983 was published the *S. R. Rao Felicitation Volume* edited by B.K. Gururaja Rao and A. V. Narasimha Murthi which was slightly broader in its scope and was subtitled *'Recent Research in Indology'*. Though many of the individual articles in both these focused on specialized topics of only description based on archaeological material, the broader dimension of the latter was visible in such articles such as 'Socio-Economic Life in Proto-Historic Karnatak'. From the basic methodological approach the focus remained on an intensive description of the cultural aspects of study. This was also clearly brought out in the essays which appeared in *B.B. Lal's Felicitation Volume* edited by K. N. Dikshit called appropriately *Archaeological Perspective in India since Independence,* New Delhi, 1985. It is true that each of these volumes is often a mixed bag with papers presented for different regions of India and one cannot therefore, generalize about the particular quality of papers thus presented. But, in their very scope, they give an idea of the thrust with which archaeological data has been used by scholars in recent years. It has been noticed by us that in using the term 'Indology' when attached to some of the subtitles, their contents then legitimately include stray papers on some aspects of history, irrespective of whether they emanate from archaeological data or literary data. Thus in *Giridharsri, G.S. Dikshit Felicitation Volume* edited by A. V. Narashima Murthy and K. V. Ramesh subtitled Essays in Indology and brought out in 1987 we have a separtate heading on History, besides the ones on Art, Archaeology, Epigraphy and Numismatics.

As we get closer to the end of the eighties a tendency towards a closer interaction with history becomes evident more explicitly in the two other Felicitation Volumes which have incorporated the scope of history in archaeological studies. These are the Essays in memory of *Shri A. Ghosh* in 2 volumes entitled *Archaeology and History* edited by B. M. Pande and B.D.Chattopadyaya and published in Delhi 1987 and *Ajayasri,* Recent Studies in Indology, the *Ajyamitra Shastri Felicitation Volume* also in 2 volumes, edited by Devendra Handa and published in 1989. Both have separate sections on Archaeology and History but above all, they have essays in particular sections like Numismatics, Archaeology etc. on methodological questions of how archaeological data can fruitfully be understood to explain historical change. Thus for instance, K.M. Shrimali's contribution in *Ajayasri* on 'Early Indian Coins and Economic History : Trends and Prospects', raises questions both for the numismatist specialist and the economic historian and suggests means by which we may go beyond mere classification and description to understand the dynamics and forces of economic change in history. Similarly, in the former the many-faceted dimensions of archaeological data get a perspective from the questions posed in some of the articles. With reference to South India entries such as H. Sarkar's,[211] B.D. Chattopadhyaya's[212], A. Sundara's[213] and others like those of Romila Thapar and B. M. Pande open up a vista of new insights into how situations where archaeological data is the primary avenue of evidence can be made best use of and this concern is expressed both by historians and archaeologists. It however, needs to be reiterated at this point that we do not intend to suggest that since the more recent of the Festschrift Volumes show a greater concern of historical analysis, the contextual approach as seen in New Archaeology is now the order of the day. On the contrary, in quantitative terms, not only in the articles in the above volumes, but even otherwise,[214] the dominant trend is still with issues and methods of traditional archaeology that stems more from the physical description and observation rather than emerging from postulations of the hypothetico-deductive method. The latter to our mind are absolutely necessary for proccessual archaeology and its links with patterns of historical change.

When we turn to have a closer look at studies that are primarily texts on History, the most startling feature that emerges is the limited use of archaeological data and it's integration into understanding mainstream history. For South Indian History in particular we have had the dominant area of historical inquiry revolving around 'eventual' history or what is more simply called history of political change. In this regard the majority of works in the last two decades have shifted to writing the history of sub-regions within the present-day linguistic states of South India. Thus we have examples such as the meticulously collected source material on *A History of South Kanara : From Earliest Times to the Fall of the Vijaynagara*, by K. V Ramesh published in 1970 and based primarily on hitherto untapped inscriptional sources. In the same year a consolidated *History of Karnataka* also apeared edited by P.B. Desai. Various kinds of emphasis on political history of either dynasties or regions emerged as for instance an unusually approached problem in M. Rama Rao's work on *Karnataka Andhra Relations 270* A.D. - *1323* A.D. published in 1974. For the early historical period Sudhakar Chattopadyaya's *Some Early Dynasties of South India* was published in 1974 which consolidated the existing inscriptional and literary sources but had no place for a discussion on the material cultures of the period. This would have been particularly relevant for the chapter introduced by him on the pre-Sātavāhana phase where he postulates the existence of some kind of tribal kingdoms.

One can understand that in the early 1950's the concern of the historians of South India to outline the chief features of the political history of regions south of the Vindhyas within a positivistic framework was needed as the first perceptible data on the subject was just emerging and had to be organized. However, it is difficult to accept text books published in 1979 using an identical framework especially since a lot more information has now been made available from sources like archaeology.[215] Unless this is done for graduate level text books archaeology shall continue to play a peripheral role in history teaching and writing. Collections of essays[216] published in the last two decades have introduced data from archaeology but as it happened these appeared in the form of individual articles of particularistic concern and not those attempting to change our perception of the different levels of historical change in the text-books.

It would however be wrong to conclude that history as a discipline has not taken serious cognizance of the challenges that archaeology poses to enrich our understanding of early history of South India. On a general level two thought provoking essays in a collection called *Essays on South India*[217] initially probed into trends that archaeological data poses for corroborating data from the Sangam texts and the society it depicts. The article by Maloney [218] in this volume is a kind of review of the accomplishment of South India Archaeology and the challenges it offers for future research. On a similar plane, M.G. S. Narayanan[219] in his collection of essays gives a definitive methodological framework to undertake such an exercise. However, the very nature of this work is perfunctory and intends to basically delineate lines for further investigastion. The use of the Marxist method of analysis apart from making use of hypotheses, opens up for historians the possibility of using a multi-disciplinary approach and in this the use of archaeology and social anthropology are particularly relevant. Thus we see that historians using this method at the text-book level like K. Satyanaryana[220] make a conscious use of archaeology and in the process integrate its use to the understanding of historical change. This can be contrasted very startingly with those that use the more traditional approach, i.e., the liberal use of archaeological sources only to define the pre-historic phases. A case in point is the popular text for South India -- K.A.N. Sastri's *A History of South India* which has run into several editions well into recent times as the most acceptable history text-book for South India. A fundamental issue in archaeology that is raised in the West is the crucial role of ecology and environments to understand human adaptation. Today, the threads of "New History" or Annalés school that is pervading the still waters of Indian historiography raises for us the value of archaeology to understand history of climate. *Ecology and Archaeology of Western India* edited by D.P. Agarwal and B. M. Pande[221] opened up this line of investigation and provides us with the methods to use ideas of paleo-climate and paleo-soil etc. to have a continous idea of the history of climate but we have a long way to go before this is available to us at the graduate level textbooks.

To urge that there should be a profound relationship between the two disciplines means that we move away from the common general knowledge understanding of this relationship, namely, that Archaeology is important to Historians only because it provides data or evidence for them. We, in fact, now need to move into the arena of understanding how Archaeological data improves upon the Historian's generalizations or his historical explanantions. To suggest that only some historians make generalizations is erroneous as these are implicity available in all kinds of historical works. Secondly, the barriers that unconsciously emerge between the two disciplines in the name of specialization primarily because of the tools and techniques individually deployed, need not isolate us if we agree to recognize that the wider concern of all socially relevant research is to understand the dynamics of culture change. Indeed, if in particular instances this means deploying the techniques and methods of social anthropology or oral traditions, these should also be unhesitatingly incorporated so that we thereby, gain an interdisciplinary projection of the problem. However, this would naturally entail problem-oriented research and not, as is the practice today, 'item' and 'event' based research.

A review of how old ideas in archaeology persist in historical studies is necessary because it is this which inhibits the growth of the relationship of archaeology and history in India. Historians have over a period of time got used to using decontextualized archaeological evidence in the name of museum pieces, art motifs, inscriptions and coins. This diminishes the value of the material culture found on a larger horizon and within a continuity of cultural change. On the other hand , if contextual archaeological evidence is used fruitfully in the form of a range of data available from scientifically conducted excavations, it would reveal appropriate graphs in a society's history that would in turn give us various shades of the historical processes and bring out either, co-existing cultural patterns or, changing ones in space and time. The essay on 'Culture and Civilization' in the present collection of essays has used arcaheological data to look at overlapping levels of historical transformation which would otherwise not be available from other sources of information. In simple terms this means taking a collective look at the material cultures of a given society in their totality, and not merely its objects of cultural value. We would thus like to submit that enough work has now been done in excavation work in various parts of South India which has to be exploited from a different angle and not from the point of view of cataloguing and furnishing archaeological material to simply decorate the pages of cultural and art history, or, the history of religion.

'The character of inscriptions as source materials'[222] has a lot to do with the context in which the early editing of inscriptions was done. In other words, an examination of the historiography of how epigraphical studies began in India in the eighteenth century was linked to a particular kind of perception of history which is also reflected in our discussion of the relationship between History and Archaeology. Apparently, this would seem a meaningless exercise and could also be misinterpreted as being unnecessarily critical of the yeoman's services done by erstwhile epigraphists. However, this task becomes a necessity. Today, when it has become popular to write on aspects of social and economic history, it is inadvertently forgotten, or, unconsciously ignored, by historians that the structure and purpose of the inscription given to us often falls within a framework of analysis which defines the prime task of a historian to be writing an eventual, political or monumental history. The context in which some of the first editing of inscriptions was done was pertinently consumed with the desire to sketch the barest outlines of the political history of the country or region in particular. Thus, when Fleet wrote that 'for our knowledge of ancient political history of India we are indebted only to inscriptions and not to any historical work bequeathed to us by the Hindus',[223] he was genuinely concerned about highlighting historical information within the dominant nineteenth century parameters of understanding history as primarily political in nature and within the positivistic framework of analysis. Hultzsch had articulated that the decipherment of South Indian inscriptions 'is an undertaking which, besides good linguistic attainments, requires careful training in the methods followed by the European school of Classical philology; and, before all, an earnest and patient desire for truth, --- the object of all science.'[224] The early concerns of scholars like Fleet, Rice, Hultzch, Bühler, Kielhorn, Bhagwanlal Indraji, Bhandarkar and a host of others was therefore, largely with historical issues of chronology, dynastic details, definition and description of administrative divisions. Since the prime task was not writing or analyzing aspects of social history, it meant that any data on social groups was unconsciously interpreted under the rubric of political or cultural history.

It has to be our present concern to specify the problems this early perception and methodology of history had evoked for subsequent writings on South Indian history. The issues of special concern shall be only those pertaining to the writing of socio-economic history and historiogrpahical trends that arise out of the use of epigraphical sources. Notwithstanding the change in the perception of what history can be understood as in the twentieth century, epigraphists continue to define the importance of the study of epigraphy for reconstructing political and cultural history.[225] These advantages which help us define the contemporary events of political and religious importance are said to be the very ones that can, according to Sircar, turn into demerits because after all 'most records . . . give the impression that references to historical events in them are incidental.'[226] In a recent collection of inscriptions for India as a whole[227] [R. Chaudhury, *Inscriptions of Ancient India*, Delhi, 1983] the traditionally accepted areas of epigraphy's importance to history are delineated as those giving information on 'person and events' (p.32), solving 'knotty problems of early Indian chronology' (p. 33), describing 'village administration' (p.35), providing for 'allusions to religion and to donation' (p.35), highlighting 'careers' and 'dynastic chronicles' (p.35), 'commemorating the death of heros in battle' (p.36), 'propagation of religion and morality' (p.37), the 'desire to honour religious saints' (p.37) and 'records of religious endowments are also found in abundance' (p.38). The last few areas listed are significant for writing a social history but these are hardly discussed in depth.[228] While professing in the Preface that inscriptions could be used for socio-economic history, and while also admitting that donative inscriptions are the maximum found, the importance of land grants in this book is nonetheless dismissed in the phrase 'The inscriptions throw light on the land grants, duties , tax, fee, perquisites and privileges.'[229]

Given this estimation of the value of the epigraphic record for historians, it is not surprising that in quantitative terms the majority of books on South Indian history concentrate on dynastic studies or those pertaining to define and describe art and architecture.[230] In recent years there has indeed been an interest in writing about social and economic history but, in most cases, the choice of the period of study is determined by dynastic dates. An example of this type can be cited in A.Vaidehi Krishnamoorthy's *Social and Economic Condition in Eastern Deccan (from A.D. 1000 to A.D. 1250)* wherein in the Preface the author defines the significance of the period chosen for study because it saw the end of the independent rule of the Eastern Chalukyas who now became the feudatories of the Cholas and, 'this Chola ascendancy contributed a great deal to developments in the social and religious life of the people'. This, the author feels was 'responsible for the cultural development of the people at a standard higher than the rest of Andhra.'[231] Whereas, this book does not use a dynastic nomenclature in the title there are innumerable others which do and this explicitly gives the erroneous impression that social conditions were somehow static and special during a particular period of rule.[232] The period of rule of a particular dynasty does not necessarily envisage that it would also afford a suitable periodzation for understanding social change and continuity.

Similarly, in identifying the region of study one has come across many books on social and economic study that use the present day boundaries of linguistic states in a rigid manner to define their subjects of historical concern. Alternatively, the political boundaries of a dynansty's rule in the past are made to, more or less, coincide with these state boundaries thus giving enough rationale for defining the spatial context of writing socio-economic history. G.R. Kuppuswamy's *Economic Conditions in Karnataka A.D. 973-1336 A.D.*[233] takes into account both the period of rule of a dynasty as well as the well-delineated boundaries of the present-day Karnataka into account. A similar study for Andhra is K. Sundaram's *Studies in Economic and Social Conditions of Medieval Andhra A.D.1000 -*

A.D.1600 [234.] A rigid compartmentalization of social history as the scope of study written within this pattern of spatial distribution is Jyotsna Kamat's *Social Life in Medieval Karnataka.* [235] In contrast to these, it is when scholars make socio-economic aspects as central to their conceptual understanding of change in a society, that such rigid dynastic or linguistic delineations disappear. The exceptional example of this is seen in K. Satyanarayana's *A Study of the History and Culture of the Andhras.* [236] The particular note of emphasis here is on the ' Andhra peoples' and not the 'State' or 'political dynasty'.

The most common way in which history text-books describe society in early India is within the mould of the *varṇāśrama* system as defined in the *Dharmaśāstra* literature and 'the social order organized on its basis was held to be the primary duty of the ruler.'[237] In the same text data from inscriptions is presented as a sort of deviation which is noted in the expressions and phrases used to account for it. Thus for instance, Sastri writes 'Some curious instances of mixed castes and their trades occur in the inscriptions.'[238] The terms *varṇa, jāti, kula* and *gotra* to define aspects of social history do occur in inscriptions but there are rarely systematic accounts of how society functioned according the norms laid down. Thus, the question raised is to what extent a bibliocentric view of society is sustainable with the help of inscriptional data. It is clear from our brief surveys that the maximum mention is of the *brāhmaṇa varṇa* and *gotras* of the royal families but no mention of their *varṇa.* The lower orders are, in comparison, mentioned only occasionally. It is important to note here that the professions located in the temple are most frequently mentioned. What emerges from this is that the *varṇa* system in the normative sense cannot be culled from the inscriptional sources and therefore, the methods and approach to writing a socio-economic history has to be reviewed.

Our understanding of Social history, in particular, would have to be defined because the majority of writings on South Indian Social History briefly mentioned above subscribe to a definition of it which we could like to reject at the very outset. This is the kind of social history that John Breuilly[239] calls 'Residual Social History'. This is said to be composed of such 'trivialities' as a study of dress and ornaments, weddings, eating habits, leisure, manners and customs and so on. It goes without saying that this kind of history is only of marginal interest to the historian of any specific kind of History. This type of social history has been contrasted with 'Societal History' by

Breuilly and it has been elucidated as one in which the historian begins with assumptions of some kind of method, most successfully followed in the methods delineated by Marx and Weber. This approach brings together different dimensions of political, economic and ideological history in order to give a history of 'society as a whole' or, a 'social formation'. For South India as a whole, and the Deccan in particular, the maximum work done in the area of Social History is under the rubric of the first type. This is clearly visible in most textbooks that take up a separate chapter on Social Conditions towards the end of their monographs.[240] More specifically, the 1960's and 70's of the present century saw a spurt in the writing of separate researched volumes on social history and economic history,[241] which however, have not done much to change the methodological approach or content of social history by and large. It goes without saying that the inroads of the second type of social history in the writing of South Indian History has been very limited, despite the fact that for India as a whole this approach has generated a serious debate in classifying the nature of the particular social formations for early medieval times.[242]

Given the background of the different types of social history and their application to South Indian History, and in rejecting its maximum application in the first type of social history described above, one has to categorically state that both economic and social history *therefore cannot, or should not be, a blindly accumulated pile of facts.* Connected with this is the fact that social history in particular is not a history of only trivialities and thereby, only of marginal interest to historians. Instead, one needs to begin with a refutation of the existing categories of historical analysis whereby rigid terms of the 'political', the 'economic' and the 'social' that have hiterto been used to underline the elements of continuity and change in early Indian society. For social history this kind of categorization has major pitfalls as its linkage with the other categories gets distorted. Rather, we would like to emphasize in the words of John Breuilly 'it [social history] involves making every kind of history *explicitly confront the social nature of action and institutions.'* (emphasis added) Thus, in our view 'Social history is not a particular kind of history; it is a dimension which should be present in every kind of history.'[243]

One of the important methods advocated in recent years for understanding social and economic history has been the statistical method. For its application to earlier periods of history, however, one has to be wary because *given statistics* are in most cases missing and, if they do survive, they cannot be fully trusted. Extant non-statiatical *insitu* sources can be re-worked within a statistical framework with the help of Computers, as has been done by Karashima for South Indian history to yield hitherto undreamed of results. Though its use by him for social history perse has been limited it has, nonetheless, revealed a way for the study of Chola administrative and social organization.[244] However, a note of caution sounded by Karashima, one of the most ardent advocates of this method himself needs to be re-stated in this context : 'We are also aware of the limitations of the statistical method. One of the problems is *the character of inscriptions as source materials* (emphasis added). In future we plan to examine the credibility of this in relation to the existence of the inscriptions. Our argument in the following section will remain hypothetical in that sense also, besides it being based on preliminary analysis.'[245] The point of warning here is that in advocating scientific methods, historians have to recognize that they are dealing with source material embedded in pre-modern situations which are governed by their own respective rules and definitions.

The alternative perhaps can be charting out this data within the *given parameters* to gain from this a pattern of the broad levels of economic change with regard to the social groups being analyzed. The essential positive steps that have helped us do this in a prelimenary way in the following essays is by establishing the relationship between the social group and its economic underpinnings. Since the inscriptions do not necessarily mention the caste/class/group in a direct way, *the first step* in categorizing the possible nature of social entities has been through such pieces of information as names of individuals, their designations, collective common appellations, functions performed by individuals or functionaries of the State, occupations of individuals or groups particularly in the temple and so on. Once this was achieved, it was not difficult to link up this information, that is, on functions/ designation/occupations etc, to *the context in* which they are mentioned in the inscriptions. Since we are largely concerned with land grants or charters, the underlying phenomena that has emerged is that there were different levels of interaction between social groups and landed property. It must nonetheless, be mentioned that this type of analysis is suitable for describing primarily the dominant social groups as they are directly mentioned in the inscriptions. However, it cannot be overlooked that these groups were part of a larger socially stratified society. For the subject social groups, who do not necessarily have direct visibility in the inscriptions, we have drawn attention to and taken cognizance of institutions/occupations/ practices that imply their existence. In some quarters it has been suggested that social history in fact, 'derives its vitality from its oppositional character. It prides itself on being concerned with 'real life' rather than abstractions, with *'ordinary' people* (emphasis added) rather than privileged elites, with everyday things rather than sensational events.'[246] Therefore, one has not simply stopped with an analysis of the explicitly mentioned social terms/groups that describe essentially the elite but we have gone beyond this to identify the explicitly stated economic/political/ideological practices and institutions of exploitation that imply the existence of subject social groups.

As stated above the essential aim of such an analysis of the valuable inscriptional data was to use it ultimately for finding fundamental explanations of historical change and not mere descriptions of the so-called apparent 'reality' of social life in pre-modern times. An essential pre-requisite of this understanding was to also relate it to the factor of man's accommodation to his physical conditions at a local level. Thus it must be stated that village society in the past related to, and interacted with, not only social categories but also with defined geographical entities. The individual thus can be placed in the context of family (*kula*), kin group (*gotra*), sub-caste (*jāti*) and caste (*varṇa*). This placement in turn has to be related to his situation in a house or extended household located in a village (*grāma*), or small town (*pura*), or military camp (*vāda/vātika*), or city (*nagara*), or province (*viśaya*) and finally, country (*deśa*) which has been briefly attempted in two of the essays. [Charts V - XII] These norms of social and geographical location cannot be sifted and separated from each other in a social analysis and ultimately, both have been related to the primary economic underpinnings of the nature of land rights and ownership of property in three of the essays. [Charts VIII - XV].

A further major dimension of recognition in our categorization for social history has been to approach our data with the recognition that it has been primarily garbed in religious and ideological rubric. Though these days it is clearly accepted that we cannot unduly exaggerate the role and impact of religion on early Indian society, at the same time, scholars handling pre-modern records have once again brought to the forefront the concern as to how one should differentiate the material phenomena from the ideological[247] in the context of Indian society. One cannot at this juncture, for reasons of time available, enter into the pros and cons of this debate. However, given the constraint that our data comes primarily from the Brahmanical temple one has been cautious in not merely re-speaking the Brahmanical view. Since a major part of the explicit data also states that many grants were made for ostensibly religious purposes we cannot, at the same time, undermine the ideological dimension in the analysis of social groups. It is not difficult to see that the major social groups that benefited from large scale land transctions in early medieval times were religious beneficiaries. The best way that the socio-economic could be interlinked with the politico-ideological was to map out the linkages in the charts accompanying each of the essays. Infact, it was 'the contributive potential of temple in the legitimization of a political power, based on social differentiation'[248] that has to be reckoned with.

Given this situation, in discussing the *brāhmaṇa varṇa* in essays three and four, one found that during the 6th to the 8th centuries there is a frequent mention to them by their individual names and as recipients of large, mostly village, grants. This tendency no doubt continues into the next phases but is superseded by their collective mention in groups and ultimately, the temple emerges as the biggest landowner. After the 9th century there is also the frequent mention of the *mahājana*. They emerge as donors, recipients, approvers, witnesses and acknowledgers of grants signifying both their political and economic importance. As powerful rural elites they are sometimes understood as *brāhmaṇas* particularly in the *agrahāra* villages, or, as leading members of the village community. This term is a good example for an analysis of the political, ideological and economic power operating through a powerful social group.

Further, in essay four we have drawn attention to the maximum direct information in the inscriptions to individual names of kings, chiefs, and officials who are sometimes known through their designations. Though it is not difficult from this data to categorize them as indicating different levels of a hierarchy, a a more challenging task is, however, an attempt at locating them within a relative social hierarchy specific to their local milieu. Existing historiography has hitherto analyzed these terms to indicate largely administrative functions. In the brief survey done by us it was found that during the early phases numerous villges were the form of grant made mainly by kings (*mahārāja, mahipatir*) of the main ruling families to *brāhmaṇas* as the chief beneficiaries. At a later stage the tendency of lesser chiefs (*sāmanta, perggade, gāmunda*) to make grants, not necessarily in the form of villages, but also as donors of small measurements of land, goods and tax concessions to the temples. Finally, in the third set of examples one sees that the numbers of donors not only increase from among such categories as officials of the village, lesser chiefs and so on (*mahāpradhān, daṇḍanāyaka, naḷgavunda*) but now, the grants are almost exclusively to the brahmanical temple. Individual recipients of such grants become rare. This broad delineation not only suggests that the power of individual groups varies over a period of time but it also indicates that the quantum of the grant and the its mode of transference also undergoes a change. In other words, the idea of the ownership of land by members of the main ruling family during the early phases seems to have been undermined in the later phases though not completely negated. Though it is not possible to go into the details of the complex pattern of ownership/rights in land that the respective groups had, it clearly emerges that when the lesser chiefs made grants we do not have specific immunities attached to them. Thus with this type of categorization one is able to highlight that rather than being mere administrative functionaries, most rural elites had different levels of access to the productive resources of the community and therefore, were part of a highly stratified society. The function of a certain group can then be best explained in its socio-political and socio-economic context.

Meanings of terms are often difficult to categorically state in the pre-modern context. One such is the term *devadāsi.* In the inscriptions we studied for northern Karnataka in essay five we were not able to find it nor, its equivalent transliterated form. The girls in the temple were known through the words *sule* and *pātra* along with different suffixes and prefixes. The alien context in our understanding of this tradition of temple girls led to it moral condemnation beginning with the writings on it in the nineteenth century largely by administrators and ethnographers. However, it is pertinent to point out that the data in inscriptions gives no information on the morally related issues of their existence in the service of the temples. On the contrary, the maximum information on them is in the context of the land grant economy. We attempted to chart this information out in the following manner. The main purpose of the inscription which mentions temple girls was to record land grants either individually, or, to the temple in which they were prominent beneficiaries. In the process all other information on them their names, designations, numbers, their work etc. was incidental. In the first set of instances we have a few examples of the girls themselves making endowments to the temple implying their access to property which they could dispose of within the traditionally accepted mode of doing so. Here, these girls are mentioned with their names. In the next set are examples of those instances which record independent grants made to temple girls wherein sometimes they are mentioned by their names. In these cases their individuality is emphasized and implicitly, a hierarchy of temple girls serving in the temples emerges. In the third set there are those instances of land gants which were made to the temple but in which it is specified that temple girls are significant beneficiaries. Here, the girls are not mentioned by their individual names but are often part of a larger dancing and singing group serving in the temple who are also recipients of a portion of the same or additional land grant. Finally, there are those instances wherein the existence of temple girls is only implied as the grant is made for a specific function/ritual in the temple which is commonly understood to have been performed by the temple girls. Thus, we would like to emphasize here that the temple girls were integrated in a complex way to the dominant economic and ideological framework of society and in this sense, were automatically also as it happens, the only women in society to have partial access to the productive resources in their own individual capacity, and not through the family structure. Though it may apparently seem that these girls were outside the direct patriarchal authority, in fact, their very existence outside it was the creation of patriarchal values of authority.

All the essays in this collection can thus be seen as initial attempts to overcome the problem of interpretation delineated by us above. To overcome the problem of accepting narrow criteria for defining the region of study we have accepted a broader configuration of the Deccan based on an essential geographical characterization of it. This, it has been suggested, would lend better support for highlighting sub-regional variations rather than the present linguistic boundaries of Maharashtra, Andhra Pradesh, and Karnataka. Since early historic changes cut across these boundaries and also the political boundaries of ancient empires, both of which inhibit our understanding of the overlapping layers of historical transformation, for explaining the social, economic and ideological levels of change, spatial and chronological categories have been reviewed.

The other major problem we have tried to focus on above has been the constraints imposed by the earlier interpretive dimensions. These raised issues of concern at multiple levels. It was imperative to suggest that political dimensions of the past can best be understood against the recent work that has émerged for India as a whole on understanding the processes of State-formation, Similarly, our understanding of village society needs to move away from the nineteenth century constructions of it which, we argued in some form or the other, have continued to persist in scholarship till fairly recent times. Finally, the use of particular kinds of data has to be critically viewed as many of the problems in the existing source oriented works abound with a certain vision of history that inhibits a broader use of the data from both archaeology and inscriptions. Our attempt is a small step in the direction of widening the scope of research on the early History of the Deccan for which this first essay forms a background.

NOTES

1 Sankalia's monumental work has divided India into different zones as culturally diverse regions with a basic emphasis on their technological base. He has clearly taken into account the ecological variants in the study of various cultures. *The Pre History and Proto History of India and Pakistan*, Poona 1974 (First published in 1962-63).

2. Persian sources generally know this broad region by the word *Dakkhan*.

3. H. C. Raychaudhuri, 'Geography of the Deccan' in G. Yazdani, *Early History of the Deccan*, Pt. I-VI, (Indian Reprint edition) 1982, pp. 14-15. First published OUP, 1960. These references are mainly to the geographical landmarks like names of rivers, mountains, forests or regions south of the Narmada or to indigenous/tribal peoples residing in these areas. Some references to the Classical Greek literature has been also made.

4. This is how a 19th century Manual also encapsulates the definition of the Deccan --- Henrich Kiepert, *A Manual of Ancient Geography*, London, 1818, p. 23.

5. As for example I. K. Sarma, *Coinage of the Sātavāhanas*, Delhi, 1980, p. 7.

6. *EI*, Vol. VIII, 1905-6, p. 60.

7. R. G. Bhandarkar, *Early History of the Dekkan . . .*, Delhi (rpt). 1985, pp. 2-4 (First edition was published in 1892 and the second in 1895). Deccan is thus

said to be 'almost identical with the country called Maharashtra or the region in which the Marathi language is spoken.' (p. 2).

8. Ibid., p. 10. This understanding clearly brings forth a north-centric perspective in defining the so-called historical Deccan on the basis of Brahmanical texts.
9. Ibid., pp. 3-5 and pp. 6-13.
10. Ibid., p. 10. The rest of the chapterization concentrates on the major dynasties that ruled over the Western part of the Deccan, namely Maharashtra, beginning with the description of the Cave Temples in Western India (Section IV), followed by a history of the Andhra-bhṛtyas or Sātavāhanas (Sections V-VIII) and the rest of the book is a discussion on various 'empires' of the Dekkan --- those of the Early Chalukyas, Rashtrakutas, Later Chalukyas, the Kalachuris and the Yadavas, (Section X-XIV).
11. J. G. Dubreuil, *Ancient History of the Deccan*, Delhi (rpt.) 1979, p. 1. First published Pondicherry, 1922.
12. Ibid. See particularly chapters II, IV and VIII.
13. Ibid., p. xv.
14. Yazdani, op. cit., 1982, Preface, p. vi.
15. H. C. Raycharudhuri, 'Geography of the Deccan' in Yazdani, op. cit., 1982, p. 3.
16. Yazdani, op. cit., 1982, p. 15. It is however ignored that the development of Marathi cannot be attributed to the early historical times.
17. Sumati Mulay, Poona, 1972. In using the Imperial Gazetteers the divisions of Deccan are given as parts of the modern State of Madhya Pradesh, the former Berar, parts of the former Hyderabad State, and the four districts of the former Bombay-Karnataka. (p. 14).
18. Ibid., p. 4.
19. K. A. N. Sastri, *A History of South India*, OUP, 1966, (4th edition) p. 68; p. 70. First published in 1947, 1955 (Reprint edition 1984).
20. Ibid, p. 2.
21. S. Settar, 'Twentieth Century in Ancient India', Presidential Address, Section I, *PIHC*, Kurukshetra, 1982, pp. 3-4; pp. 33-36. We have an interresting example of a book by K. V. Subramania Aiyer entitled *Historical Sketches of Ancient Deccan*, written as early as 1917 and published from Madras which infact mainly discusses the region of the extreme South and has only one section (Section V) on 'Ancient Polity of the Deccan', Vol. II, pp. 311-377 which largely relates to the Andhra region.
22. Yazdani, op. cit., 1982, p. vii.
23. Sastri, op. cit., pp. 3-9; p. 12.
24. Yazdani follows this format.
25. Sastri, op. cit, 1960 is a case in point --- p. 313ff.
26. K. S. Subramanian, *Buddhist Remains in South India and Early Andhra History 225 A.D. to 610 A.D.*, New Delhi (rpt.), 1981. First published in 1972.
27. Ibid., p. xiv. A futher elaboration of this idea goes on to suggest, according to the author, that 'Telugu language and literature are certainly much older than the earliest Telugu inscription'. (p. 10).
28. Ibid., p. 10 where it is conceded that 'Buddhism gave a great impetus to the

advancement of Āndhra civilization in the earliest period of Andhra history and thus left rich legacies to the succeeding ages.'

29. B. Subbarao, 'The Geographic Factors in Andhra History and Archaeology', *BDCRI,* 1948, p. 168, 171.
30. R.L. Singh, *India - A Regional Geography*, Varanasi, 1971 gives the latitudinal and longitudinal definition of this region as $13^{\circ}59'$ and $20^{\circ}33'$ N and $72^{\circ}54'$ and $80^{\circ}26'$ E.
31. A.M. Webster's *Third New International Dictionary,* USA, 1969, p. 286
32. S.M. Alam, 'The Historic Deccan -- A Geographical Appraisal' in V.K.Bawa (ed.), *Aspects of Deccan History,* Hyderabad, 1975, p. 16. The stability of the geographical definition is also underlined by him. Deccan in his opinion is 'conterminous with the Peninsular tableland and lies south of the Tropic of Cancer. It is defined in the north by the Vindhya and Kaimur watersheds and its out boundary is marked by 300 meters contour line.' (p. 16).
33. S.J. Knudson, *Culture in Retrospect,* Chicago, 1978, p. 61.
34. F. Braudel, *On History,* (Tr. Sarah Matthews), University of Chicago, 1980, p. 31.
35. Aloka Parasher. 'Mechanisms of Trade and Historical Change in the Mid-Godavary Valley: c.200 B.C.- 200 A.D.', *PAPHC*, 10th Session, Guntur, 1986, p. 26. Here the specificity of the material cultures in a given geographical context are discussed.
36. Discussed in essays 3 and 4.
37. B. Subbarao, *The Personality of India,* Baroda 1958, p. 115.
38. B & R Allchin, *Rise of Civilization in India and Pakistan*, Delhi 1983, p. 331; p. 334.
39. *Proto and Early Historical Cultures of Andhra Pradesh,* Hyderabad, 1983, p. 103.
40. D.D. Kosambi, *Introduction to the Study of Indian History*, Bombay, 1956, (reprint) 1975, p. 240.
41. Ibid., p. 241.
42. Ibid., p. 242.
43. C. Maloney 'Archaeology in South India : Prospects and Accomplishments' in Burton Stein, (ed.) *Essays on South Indian History,* Delhi 1976, p. 24.
44. S. Chattopadhyaya, *Some Early Dynasties of South India,* Delhi, 1974.
45. K. Satyanaryana, *A Study of the History and Culture of the Andhras* Vol. I. New Delhi, 1985, p. xiv. It is interesting that even while adopting the Marxist theoretical framework, the history of the Andhras is defined by the traditional category of defining the region namely, the present-day linguistic boundary. The author recognizes this pitfall and admits, 'I have taken the liberty of referring to developments which strictly speaking, fall outside the scope of the present study, but which have relevance to the subject in so far as they took place in close proximity to the present boundaries of Andhra Pradesh'. (p. xiv).
46. Ibid., pp. 24; 28.
47. Ibid., p. 159.
48. Ibid., p. 166.
49. Ibid., p. 142.
50. K. Gopalachari, *Early History of the Andhra Country,* Madras, 1941; Sudhakar

Chattopadhyaya, op. cit., 1974. In the thirty years or so that have elapsed between the writing of these two works there has been hardly any change in approach and method.

51. G. Yazdani op. cit., 1982 discusses this stage as pre-Sātavāhana phase. In K. Satyanarayana's book,op. cit., 1985 a chapter on living pre-history describes the pre-State situation. In a perfunctory manner some text-books also introduce the subject, as for instance, K.A.N. Sastri, op. cit., 1966 pp. 48-59; Hanumantha Rao, *Andhrula Charitra* (Telugu), Guntur, 1983 , pp. 1-10.
52. H.D. Sankalia, op. cit., 1974 ; V.V. Krishnasastry, op. cit., 1983; Bridget and Raymond Allchin, op. cit., 1983. We discuss details of the relation between archaeology and history below.
53. I.K. Sarma. *The Coinage of the Sātavāhanas,* New Delhi, 1980, p. 1.
54. A.M. Shastri, *The Early History of the Deccan Problems and Perspective*, New Delhi, 1987, p. 3.
55. The books that have favoured the shorter chronology are H. P. Ray, *Monastery and Guild*, Commerce Under the Sātavāhanas, Bombay, 1986, p. 2; A. M. Shastri, op. cit., 1987. p. 3; The books that have supported the longer chronology are I.K. Sarma, op. cit., 1980 p. 10; G. Yazdani, (ed.) op. cit., 1982, p. 90; B. S. L. Hanumantha Rao, op. cit., 1983, pp. 61-62.
56. Works done on the basis of the numismatic evidence for the pre-Sātavāhana kings have reinforced the shorter chronology of the Sātavāhanas. This issue has been discussed in detail in essay 2.
57. R.E.M. Wheeler ~ Brahmagiri and Chandravalli, 1947: Megalithic and Other Cultures in Mysore State', in *AI*, no. 4, Delhi (rp), 1984, (First published in 1947-48), p. 201.
58. Eleanor R. Leacock, (ed.), *The Origin of Family, Private Property and State*, New York, 1972.
59. *Ancient Societies*, New York, 1877. (Reprint edition, Arizona, 1985).
60. E. R., Service, *The Origin of the State*, New York, 1975 -- Summarized from pp. 37-46.
61. Karl A. Witfogel is famous for his book *Oriental Despotism*, 1957. His ideas on the subject in the form of a concise statement are available in 'Developmental Aspects of Hydraulic Societies', in *Irrigation Civilizations : A Comparative Study*, Social Science Monographs, Washington, 1955, pp. 43-57.
62. Morton Fried, *The Notion of the Tribe*, Mento Park, 1975, pp. 6-8 on reasons why the pre-State situation has been ignored which is related to the disparaging use of the term tribe.
63. Fried, 'On the Evolution of Social Stratification and the State' in S. Diamond, (ed.), *Culture in History*, Essays in Honour of Paul Kaelin, New York, 1967, pp. 715-730.
64. A trend continuing even today -- See the most recent publication in this regard as Diwakar Tiwary's *Concept of State in the Mahābhārata*, Delhi 1990. This book is written by a Political Scientist and tends to lay greater emphasis on textual analysis rather than on the historical processes that went into making of the State as depicted in the *Mahābhārata.*
65. It is understandable that the *Arthaśāstra* has drawn so much interest as this text discusses ideas which coherently provide the first documented evidence on State in Ancient India. A rationale for this found in G. M. Bongard-Levin,

'Society and State in Ancient India' in *A Complex Study of Ancient India,* A Multi-Disciplinary Approach, New Delhi, 1986, pp. 149-171. This essay particularly discusses the tradition of the *Arthaśāstra* and its relationship to the *Dharmaśāstra* tradition (pp. 152-155).

66. For e.g. studies on the Mauryas and the Guptas prominently discuss the administrative features of these 'empires' focusing on details of kings as 'imperial monarchs'. K.A.N. Sastri, *Age of the Nandas and Mauryas*, Delhi, 1967, pp. 171-201; R.C. Majumdar and A.S. Altekar, *The Vākātaka Gupta Age c. 200-550 A.D.*, Delhi. 1986. (First published 1967), pp. 265-294. It is generally believed that the Gupta king was not as powerful as his Mauryan counterpart R. S. Sharma, *Political Ideas and Institutions in Ancient India*, Delhi, 1968, pp. 261-62.

67. Vincent Smith, *Early History of India,* 4th edition, Oxford, 1924 (First published 1919), p. 1241.

68. For a review of these ideas see Irfan Habib, 'The Social Distribution of Landed Property in Pre-British India' in R. S. Sharma and V. Jha (ed.), *Indian Society : Historical Probings*, New Delhi, 1974, p. 281ff. and R.A.L.H. Gunawardane, 'The Analysis of Pre-Colonial Social Formations in Asia and the Writings of Karl Marx' *IHR*, vol. 2, no.2, 1976, pp. 365-388.

69. U.N. Ghoshal, *A History of Hindu Political Theories*, Calcutta, 1923; K.P. Jayaswal, *Hindu Polity*, 2 vols. Calcutta, 1924; A. S. Altekar, *State and Government in Ancient India*, Benares, 1949.

70. Jayaswal, op. cit., 1924, pp. 90-106, however, goes to pains to show that the republican form of government known in ancient times had significant features of a constitutional Parliamentary system. Such views have been reiterated even in recent studies -- See for e. g. Sudama Misra, *Janapada State in Ancient India*, Varanasi, 1973, pp. 132ff.

71. *Arthaśāstra*, VI.1.1. Kautilya, however, rationalizes as to why the State originated and gives greater importance to the King as one of the elements of the State -- See V.K. Gupta *Kautilyan Jurisprudence*, Delhi, 1987, pp. 18-19. It is also made clear that if any one of these elements is not present the State is destroyed -- Discussed in Tiwary, op. cit., 1990, pp. 70-72; p. 102.

72. Leacock, op. cit., 1972, pp. 228-230.

73. Romila Thapar, 'Interpretations of Ancient Indian History' in *Ancient Indian Social History*, New Delhi, 1978, pp. 11-18.

74. At the popular textbook level this is a common perception of the pre-modern Indian State. For example the case of the depiction of Chola History in K.A.N. Sastri, op. cit., 1966. pp. 204-206.

75. For South Indian History, a historiographical critique of the Nationalist writings has been done by Burton Stein in his essay 'The State and the Agrarian Order in Medieval South India : A Historiographical Critique' in B. Stein (ed)., op. cit., 1976, pp. 64-91.

76. R.S. Sharma, *Origin of the State in India*, University of Bombay, 1989, p. 2.

77. Romila Thapar, *From Lineage to State,* Bombay, 1984, p. 19.

78. R.S. Sharma, op. cit., 1989, p. 4.

79. R. Thapar, op. cit., 1984, pp. 9-12.

80. For the present the Harappan State is not being discussed as written sources for such a study are lacking. A recent attempt to study it have been made by

Jerome Jacobson, 'The Harappan Civilization : An Early State' in J. Jacobson (ed.), *Studies in Archaeology of India and Pakistan*, New Delhi, 1986, pp. 137-172.

81. Summarized from Sharma, op. cit., 1989, pp. 2-30.
82. Summarized from Thapar, op. cit., 1984, pp. 21-69.
83. For an overview of the difference of opinion between these two scholars see R.S. Sharma's review of Romila Thapar's book 'From Kin to Class' *EPW*, June 1, 1985, vol.XX, no. 22, pp. 960-961.
84. Thapar, op. cit., 1984, p. 69; pp. 70-115.
85. Romila Thapar on features of early State in India summarized in 'State Formation in Early India', *International Social Science Journal*, UNESCO, 1981, pp. 655-663.
86. Discussion on *gaṇa saṅgha* in Thapar, op. cit., 1984, pp. 77-83.
87. Thapar, op. cit., 1981.pp. 664-668.
88. D.D. Kosambi, *The Culture and Civilization of Ancient India in Historical Outline,* Delhi, 1970, pp. 133-165.
89. Tribal areas were considered to be permanently those of enemies in the *Arthaśāstra*, VII.10.16. D.D. Kosambi discusses the views of Kautilya in this regard *Introduction to the Study of Indian History*, Bombay 1975 (First published in 1956), p. 25; pp. 230-31; pp. 252-53.
90. *Arthaśāstra*, XIII.4.62.
91. Thapar, op. cit., 1984, pp. 128-129.
92. In a recent article Gerard Fussman even questions the use of this text to build up the image of a centralized polity. He, on the other hand, uses only the inscriptions of Aśoka and the foreign Classical accounts for this study. Details in 'Central and Provincial Administration in Ancient India : The Problem of the Mauryan Empire', *IHR*, vol XIV, nos. 1-2, July 1987 & January 1988, pp. 43-72.
93. This interpretation is the most popular way to depict the Mauryan State and is embedded in all text-book descriptions of the same irrespective of historiographical perspective. For instance, R.K. Mukherjee, *Chandragupta and His Times*, Madras, 1943, pp. 54-55; B.M. Barua, *Asoka and His Inscriptions*, 2 vols., Calcutta 1946, p. 146; p. 153; R. Thapar, *Asoka and the Decline of the Mauryas*, 2nd ed. OUP, 1963, p. 94.
94. Fussmasn, op. cit., 1987-1988, pp. 53-72 details for us the complexity of the Central and Provincial administration of the Mauryan State from a new perspective wherein the centralization of powers at the Centre is questioned.
95. Romila Thapar, *The Mauryas Re-Visited*, S. G. Deuskar Lectures 1984, Calcutta, 1987, pp. 1-31.
96. Details in 'The State as Empire : The Mauryan Case' in Claessen and Skalink, *The Study of the State*, The Hague, 1981, p. 409ff.
97. Thapar. op. cit., 1987,pp. 5-6; pp. 13-15.
98. Thapar, op. cit., 1984, pp. 160-161.
99. 'Andhra and Kalinga : The Processes of Secondary State-Formation in Early India', *IHR*, vol.VII, nos. 1-2, 1981, pp. 54-69.
100. Some of these issues have been elaborated in a recently approved M.Phil Thesis that was worked under my supervision by D. Nagamani, *Material Culture and Social Formations in Early Deccan*, Department of History,

University of Hyderabad, 1990, Chapter III, pp. 128-167.

101. 'Transition to the Early Historical Deccan : A Note' in B.D. Chattopadhyaya and B. M. Pande (ed.), *History and Archaeology*, Essays in Honour of A. Ghosh, New Delhi, 1989, pp. 727-732.

102. Ibid., p. 730.

103. M.G.S. Narayanan questions this approach and has instead provided an alternative way of understanding the early Sangam Polity and Society -- *Re-Interpretations of South Indian History*, Trivandrum, 1977, pp. 1-23.

104. Two recent articles handling this problem in a detailed manner are Rajan Gurukkal, 'Forms of Production and Forces of Change in Ancient Tamil Society', *Studies in History*, vol. 5, no. 2, 1989, pp. 159-175. and Sudarshan Seneviratne, 'Pre-State to State Societies : Transformations in the Political Ecology of South India with special reference to Tamilnadu' paper presented at Seminar on *State in South India*, JNU, New Delhi, 1989 (cyclostyled copy).

105. Rajan Gurukkai, 'Social Formation and Political Processes in Early Tamilakam', paper presented at Seminar on *State in South India*, JNU, New Delhi, 1989, pp. 28-31. (cyclostyled copy).

106. Seneviratne, op. cit., 1989, p. 36.

107. Gurukkal, op. cit., 1989, p. 34.

108. Kesavan Veluthat, 'Monarchical Power in Early Medieval South India : The Image and Reality', paper presented at Seminar *State in South India* , JNU, New Delhi, 1989, pp. 1-36. (cyclostyled copy).

109. The historiographical problems in writing about change at the local level have been inhibited by intellectual constructions of the 'village community' which we shall elaborate upon below.

110. Hermann Kulke 'Fragmentation and Segmentation versus Integration ? Reflections on Concepts of Indian Feudalism and the Segmentary State in Indian History', *Studies in History*, vol. 5, no. 2, 1982, This whole issue is devoted to a study of the State in India in which well-researched contributions have made intensive studies of the historical processes involved in the formation of State in India particularly from early medieval times.

111. In a recent article V. Jha reviews trends on the underlying importance of the study of political history in the context of ancient India in 'Ancient Indian Political History : Possibilities and Pitfalls', *IHR*, vol XIV, nos. 1-2, July 1987 and January 1988, pp. 90-110.

112. London, 1896.

113. pp. ii-iii. Interestingly, the history that he sets out to familiarize the 'natives' with commences only with the 14th century.

114. Vol. I, pp. 3-4.

115. p. xxv; p. xix.

116. There are no such writings for the *early History* of the Deccan per se except for the usual perfunctory references in the first Gazetteers, Archaeological Survey reports and Land revenue surveys. The titles of books writing about South India as a whole tend to cover the early history of parts of the Deccan as is the case with Wilks book cited above.

117. There have been many reviews of how village communities have been understood. Two of the important ones undertaken by sociologists are :

Louis Dumont, 'The "Village Community" from Munro to Maine', in L. Dumont (ed.), *Religion, Politics and History in India*, Paris, 1970, pp. 112-32; M.N. Srinivas, 'The Indian Village : Myth and Reality', in M.N. Srinivas, (ed.), *The Dominant Caste and Other Essays*, OUP, Delhi, 1987, pp. 20-59.

118. N. Karashima, *South Indian History and Society Studies from Inscriptions* A.D. *850-1800*, OUP, 1984, p. 40.

119. Ibid, p. 40. See also Louis Dumont op. cit., 1970. pp. 112-32.

120. Gyan Prakash, 'Writing Post-Orientalist Histories of the Third World : Perspectives from Indian Historiography', *CSSH*, vol. 32. no. 2, April 1990, p. 387.

121. Dharmapal, 'A Note on the Disruption and Disorganisation of Indian Society in the last Two Centuries', *Patriotic and People Oriented Science and Technology Bulletin*, November, 1983, vol. 3. no.2, p. 39.

122. *Village Communities in the East and West*, London 1871. For a full critique of his writings see Dumont op. cit., 1970.

123. Karl Marx, *Capital*, Progress Publishers, Moscow, 1971, III, pp. 333-34.

124. Talal Asad, 'Are there Histories of Peoples Without Europe? A Review Article' *CSSH*, vol, 29, no. 3, July 1987, pp. 594-607 surveys recent views on the subject.

125. *The Origin and Growth of Village Communities in India*, London 1899.

126. The *Arthaśāstra* was discovered and partially published in 1905. It was fully published in 1909 and its English translation in 1915 by R. Shamasastry.

127. This question has been ably discussed by M.N. Srinivas, op. cit., 1970, pp. 28-36 wherein it is argued to show that the relationship between the village and the State in pre-modern times was intricate and complex than had hitherto been recognized by the early writers on the so-called autonomy of the villages.

128. Minute in *Report of the Select Committee of the House of Commons*, 1832, Vol. iii, Appendix 84, p. 331. Metcalfe, it is well-known revived this characterization of villages first made by Thomas Munro in his celebrated *Fifth Report from the Select Committee on the Affairs of the East India Company*, 1812. For details see Dumont, op. cit., 1970, p. 70 ff.

129. For example S. J. Thomson, *The Real Indian People*, London, 1914; C. F. Andrew, *The True India*, London, 1939.

130. Op. cit., 1966, pp. 205-206.

131. Ibid. p. 308. Under the Cholas the villagers are said to have asserted their local autonomy only when local oppression became unrestrained as a result of the weakening of central control. Thus local-self government is said to have flourished under the benign rule of benevolent despots. *Cf.* pp. 204-205.

132. London, 1954.

133. Ibid., pp. 190-191.

134. From the First to the Sixth Century A.D., Delhi. 1969, p. 150.

135. Till recently this is the only work that takes a chronological look the development of village settlements at a regional level cutting across periods. In the light of new sources, however, some of his fundamental assumptions need critical questioning.

136. II, Bharatiya Vidya Bhavan, Bombay, 1956.

137. [Mainly a socio-economic study], Calcutta, 1971.

138. The writings of such nationalist historians as K.P. Jayaswal op. cit., 2 Vols., 1919-1924 and U.N.Ghoshal *Agrarian System in Ancient India,* Calcutta, argued to show that there had existed in ancient India private ownership of land. Simultaneously, other nationalists scholars continued to emphasize on the corporate nature of rural and urban activities as in R.C, Majumdar's *Corporate Life in Ancient India*, Calcutta, 1920.
139. *Aspects of Rural Settlements and Rural Society in Early Medieval India*, S. G, Deuskar Lectures on Indian History and Culture, 1985, Calcutta, 1990, p. 2.
140. Op. cit., 1927. p. iii. Apart from a minor change in the wording, the total import of the views expressed are identical to Metcalfe's.
141. Ibid., p. 125.
142. *Nationalist Thought and the Colonial World - A Derivative Discourse,* London, 1986, p. 30; pp. 168-9.
143. Op. cit., 1927, pp. 128-133.
144. Ibid. p. vii. The book ends with an Appendix on the subject entitled 'Dravidian Civilization and Village Communities'.
145. Romila Thapar, op. cit., 1978, Chp. I.
146. Burton Stein has provided a suitable critique of these writings in his 'The State and the Agrarian Order : A Historiographical Critique' in Stein, op. cit., 1976. pp. 64-91.
147. In S.P. Gupta and K.S. Ramachandran (eds.). *Readings in South Indian History*, Delhi, 1977, Chapter 14.
148. Ibid., pp. 94-95.
149. Ibid., p. 95.
150. Ibid., pp. 96-97.
151. Ibid.
152. Ibid., p. 100.
153. Ibid., p. 103-104.
154. Stein, op. cit., 1976, p. 66.
155. In fact he has divided his whole work into two distinct parts -- 'Village Institutions' and 'Village Life'.
156. *Administration and Social Life Under the Pallavas*, Madras, 1938.
157. R. S. Sharma, (ed.), *Survey of Research in Economic and Social History of India*, ICSSR Publication, New Delhi, 1986 presents essays that give a wide historiographical review of the subject.
158. Princeton, 1985.
159. Ibid., p. 5.
160. Some of these published in the *EPW* have been collected and edited by M.N. Srinivas, op. cit., 1955.
161. Op. cit., 1990, p. 392; 393.
162. Paris, 1970.
163. Op. cit., 1957.
164. Op. cit., 1977, p. 56; p. 57.
165. Ibid., p. 57.
166. Ibid. pp. 56-57.
167. For a review of the sociological and historical works on caste see Suvira Jaiswal, 'Studies in Early Indian Social History : Trends and Possibilities', *IHR*, vol.VI, nos.1-2, July 1979 - January 1980, pp. 1-24.

168. *Worship and Conflict under Colonial Rule,* A South Indian Case, Orient Longman reprint 1983, pp. 7-8. This problem makes him move away to take up the Hindu Temple, as opposed to caste, as a locus of study which can more easily relate to the economic and political domain on the one hand, and the religious and cultural on the other.
169. Some results published in Karashima, op. cit., 1984.
170. For a Marxist review of Karashima's work see M.G.S. Narayanan, 'Review Article', *Tamil Civilization*, vol.3, no.1, March 1985, pp. 57-71 and *IESHR*, vol. XXII, no. 1. January-March, 1985, pp. 95-101.
171. OUP, 1981.
172. The varied issues this has raised for studies in social stratification and economy of villages is discussed in R. Champakalakshmi, 'Peasant State and Society in Medieval South India : A Review Article', *IESHR*, vol.XVII. nos. 3 & 4, 1981, pp. 411-426; D.N. Jha. 'Validity of the 'Brāhmaṇa-Peasant Alliance' and the 'Segmentary State' in Early Medieval South India', *Social Science Probings,* vol. 1, no. 2. June 1984, pp. 270-296.
173. Karashima, op. cit., 1984. Preface.
174. As mentioned above several review articles on both Stein's and Karashima's book have been written by scholars. For an overview of the Marxist point of view on this period for India as a whole see D.N. Jha's Introduction in *Feudal Social Formations in Early India*, Delhi, 1986. It must be pointed out that Karashima's data on village records from original inscriptions which has been statistically organized may become the source of debate -- Aloka Parasher, 'Feudal Formations', *Social Scientist*, no. 171-172, August-September 1987, pp. 122-125.
175. The evolution of Kosambi's views on the subject have now been put together in A. J. Syed (ed.), *D.D. Kosambi on History and Society, Problems of Interpretation*, Bombay, 1985, See particularly Parts I and II. R. S. Sharma, 'Problem of Transition from Ancient to Medieval in Indian History', *IHR,* vol I, no.1, March 1974, pp. 1-9; pp. 81-84; 'Indian Feudalism Retouched', *IHR*, vol.I, no.2, September, 1974, pp. 320-327.
176. Op. cit., 1956, p. 226; 281.
177. *Indian Feudalism*, New Delhi, 1965, Chapter, 3, p. 127 ff.
178. B.N.S. Yadava, 'Immobility and Subjection of Indian Peasantry in Early Medieval Complex', *IHR*, vol.I. no.1, March 1974, pp. 18-27. See also G.K. Rai, *Involuntary Labour in Ancient India*, Allahabad, 1981.
179. Op. cit., 1990, p. 12 ---- the three regions chosen to exemplify this point are Bengal, western Rajasthan and South Karnataka.
180. A. Ghosh, *The City in Early Historical India*, IIAS, Simla, 1973, Chapter 3, p. 32; pp. 35-37; pp. 38-39. Also discussed in B. D, Chattopadhyasya, 'Urban Centres in Early Medieval India : An Overview' in R. Thapar, and S. Bhattacharya (ed.), *Situating Indian History*, OUP, 1986, pp. 8-33.
181. The term *pallī* is generally understood as a pastoral or cowhered settlement, *vāṭaka* is said to be one with some kind of enclosure, *kheṭaka* is regarded as one surrounded by hills and rivers and so on. Details discussed in R. N. Mishra, 'Village Life and Settlements in the Light of Vākataka Inscriptions' in B.N.Pande & B.D. Chattopadhyaya, *Archaeology and History,* Essays in memory of Shri A Ghosh, vol. II. Delhi, pp. 643-644. All possible village

settlements from the Vākataka inscriptions have been charted out and mapped by K. M. Shrimali, *Agrarian Structure in Northern Deccan and Central India, A Study of Vakataka Inscriptions,* Delhi. 1987.

182. B. D. Chattotpadhyaya, op. cit., 1990, pp. 2-3.
183. A.K. Choudhary, op. cit., 1971, pp. 70-71.
184. A seminal article by Karashima contrasting these two types of villages is a case in point, op. cit., 1984, pp. 3-15. Examples of political authority suppressing resistence when non-*brahmadeyas* were made *brahmadeyas* in D. N. Jha,'Presidential Address', Section I, *PIHC,* Waltair, 1979 and R. N. Nandi, 'Presidential Address', Section I, *PIHC,* Annamalainagar, 1984.
185. Op. cit., 1990, pp. 7-8. Example cited from M. S. Randhawa, *A History of Agriculture in India*, Vol. I. Delhi, 1980, p. 462.
186. Essay four in this volume looks at some details of the social groups at the local level and the grants made to them.
187. Peter Robb, *Rural South Asia, Linkages, Change and Development,* New Delhi, 1986, pp 7-8.
188. As far as scientific Archaeology in its theoretical aspects is concerned, very few efforts have been made in India to use it. For details see K. Paddayya & S.B. Deo, (ed.) *Recent Advances in Archaeology,* Poona, 1983, Introduction. Therefore, we cannot conclude as Chang has done for American Archaeology : 'In contemporary American Archaeology, there is much justified emphasis on the use of archaeology for social science ends.' K. C. Chang, 'Some Theoretical Issues in the Archaeological Study of Historical Reality in R.C. Dundell & E.S.Hall. *Archaeological Essays in Honour of Irving Rouse*, The Hague, 1978, p. 13.
189. Summarized from Dilip K. Chakrabarti, 'Ideas and Discoveries in Indian Archaeology,' *IHR,* vol. V, nos. 1-2, 1978-79. pp. 91-108.
190. (Ed) Romila Thapar and S. Gopal, *Problems of Historical Writing in India*, New Delhi, 1963, p. 31.
191. Ibid.
192. Ibid.
193. 'The Role of Hypothesis and Traditional Archaeology', *BDCRI,* vol. 47-48, 1988-89, pp. 239-247.
194. Louis Gottschlak, *Generalization in the Writing of History,* Chicago, 1980 argues that all kinds of historical works harbour generalizations, some do it explicitly while others, do it implicitly.
195. For different aspects of Archaeology by archaeoligists of the Deccan College, Pune see *BDCRI,* 2 vols, 1974-75. For a survey of Social and Economic History see R. S. Sharma (ed.), *A Survey of Social and Economic History,* ICSSR, Delhi, 1986 and for various aspects of History in general the Presidential Addresses of the Ancient Section *PIHC,* between 1969-1988.
196. *Archaeology of Sātavāhana Kṣatrapa Times*, New Delhi.
197. *Proto and Early Historical Cultures of Andhra Pradesh.* Some aspects of this work have been reviewed and highlighted in *IHR*, vol. XIII, nos. 1-2, July 1986 & January 1987, pp. 183-185.
198. *The Early Chamber Tombs of South India : A Study of the Iron Age Megalith Monuments of North Karnataka,* Dharwar, 1975.
199. *A Cultural Study,* Delhi. 1977.

200. *Buddhist Architecture of Western India,* Delhi. 1981.
201. A. M. Shastri, *Coinage of the Sātavāhanas and Coins from Excavations,* Nagpur, 1972.
202. *Early History of Deccan --- Problems and Perspectives,* Delhi, 1987.
203. *Coinage of the Sātavāhanas,* Delhi. 1980.
204. *Coins and Currency Systems of South India 275-1300 A.D.* New Delhi, 1977.
205. For Andhra, for instance, we have Krishnamurthi's *Andhra Dance Sculpture,* Hyderabad, 1975, also published in 1975, N. S. Ramaswamy's *Amaravati : The Art and History of the Stupa and Temple,* Radhakrishna Sarma's *Temples of Telingana,* Hyderabad, 1972, *Temple Sculpture of Andhra Pradesh* by Rajendra Prasad published in 1978, *Forts in Ancient and Medieval Andhra* by Ramachandra Murthy in 1979 and others.
206. *PAPHC,* vol. X, 1986, p. 2.
207. Ibid, p. 1.
208. Nagpur, 1972.
209. Dharwar, 1978.
210. (Ed.) P. Sitapati. *Sātavāhana Souvenir,* State Department of Archaeology and Museums, Government of Andhra Pradesh, Hyderabad, 1981.
211. 'Emergence of Urban Centres in Early Historical Andhradeśa', Vol. I, p. 621 ff.
212. 'Transition to Early Historical Phase of Deccan: A Note', Vol. II, p. 727 ff.
213. 'Studies in Ash Mounds', Vol. I, p. 313 ff.
214. The recent publication of K.P. Rao, *Deccan Megaliths,* New Delhi, 1988 is a case in point.
215. We have in mind the text edited by Chopra, Ravindran and Subramainiam called *A History of South India,* Delhi, 1979.
216. *Aspects of Deccan History* (ed.) V. K. Bawa in 1975, *Readings in South Indian History* (ed.) S. P. Gupta. K. S Ramachandran in 1979 and *South Indian Studies* (ed.)R. Nagaswamy in 1978.
217. (Ed.), Burton Stein, New Delhi, 1976.
218. Ibid., pp. 1-40.
219. *Re-Interpretations of South Indian History,* Trivandrum, 1977.
220. *A Study of the History and Culture of the Andhra People,* Delhi, 1975.
221. Delhi, 1977.
222. N. Karashima, op. cit. 1984, p. 189.
223. M. S., Ramaswami Iyengar, *Eminent Orientalists,* Madras, 1922, p. 205.
224. Preface to *South Indian Inscriptions,* Vol. I. ASI, Madras, 1890, p. v.
225. D.C. Sircar, *Indian Epigraphy,* Delhi, 1965, pp. 17-22.
226. Ibid., p. 23.
227. Radhakrishna Chaudhury, *Inscriptions of Ancient India,* Meenakshi Prakashan, Delhi, 1983.
228. Ibid., pp. 38-39. It is interesting to note that the information on social history that is highlighted refers to the mention of 1000 *Brāhmaṇas* in the Champaka record of the Vakataka king of which 49 are mentioned by name.
229. Ibid. Preface; p. 40.
230. S. Settar, op. cit., 1982. References to such works for the first half of the twentieth century.
231. Secundrabad, 1970, both the quotations from p. ix. Both Statements convey

elements of a satisfaction with cultural imperialism.

232. Examples in A.S. Altekar's *The Rashtrakutas and their Times*, Poona, 1934; and S. Sankaranarayan's *The Vishunukundis and their Times*, Delhi, 1977.

233. Research Publication Series No.22, Karnatak University, Dharwar, 1975.

234. Treveni Publications, Machilipatnam, 1968.

235. Abhinav Publications, New Delhi, 1980.

236. People's Publishing House, New Delhi, 1982.

237. K.A.N. Sastri, op. cit, 1966, p. 319.

238. Ibid., p. 319.

239. 'What is Social History', *History Today,* March, 1985, pp. 34-42.

240. K.A.N. Sastri, op. cit., 1966, Chp. on 'Social and Economic Conditions' is typical of this type.

241. Some of these have been listed above. For South India the writings of Burton Stein and Noburo Karashima during this period stirred the still waters of South Indian Historiography. Both of them, however, did not advocate the Marxist method as had been done by D.D. Kosambi and R. S. Sharma for Northern and Central India during this period.

242. See Introduction, D.N. Jha, *Feudal Formations in Early India,* Delhi, 1987.

243. Op. cit, 1985, p. 40.

244. N. Karashima, op. cit., 1984, Chp. 2, 'Integeration of Society in Chola Times', pp. 56-68.

245. Ibid., Notes to Chp 2, fn. 47, p. 189.

246. Raphael Samuel, 'What is Social History', *History Today*, March 1985. p. 34.

247. Frank Perlin's thought provoking article 'The Material and the Cultural : An Attempt to Transcend the Present Impasse', *MAS.,* 22, 2, (1988), pp. 383-416 raises the theoretical issues at stake.

248. Ashok Shettar, 'Aspects of Agricultural Expansion in Early Medieval Southern Karnataka', in K. Veerathappan (ed.), *Studies in Karnataka History and Culture*, (Vol II Proceedings of the Karnataka History Congress), Mysore, 1987.

2

CULTURE AND CIVILIZATION
THE BEGINNINGS

ALOKA PARASHER SEN

The nature of cultural expansion in regions immediately south of the Vindhyas has never been fully discussed. Often the Deccan regions have been considered to have acted only as a bridge in carrying the highly evolved norms of civilized life from the north Indian plains to the extreme South; the latter two being considered the prime progenitors of 'civilization' in India though their origins may have initially varied. To this understanding is also added the element that, if the Ganges valley Vedic civilization and the Tamil civilization of the Sangam age were not the only stimuli for the development of Indian civilization, then the common feature and true ethos of Indian life developed from ideas initially visible in the Indus valley civilization.[1] This essay is an attempt at suggesting ways of understanding the origins of civilization in early Deccan by emphasizing on the internal processes of change rather than looking at it only in terms of external influences. It further focuses its inquiry on those regions of the Deccan which have hitherto been considered 'regions of isolation'. Through this analysis we go on to suggest that the transition to civilization cannot be looked at without highlighting the variations in the pre-civilization stage . We thus argue that the process of the development of civilization in early Deccan may have interacted with similar processes in other parts of the country but, it had its own individual character which, once identified, would enable us to look at the totality of early Indian civilization in a positive and holistic fashion.

The underlying premise that has been hitherto implicitly accepted by most historians of India is that civilization as a progressive development diffused from the above - mentioned three select areas of the Indian subcontinent into the so-called secondary centres, which initially being non-civilized barbarian societies, *were forced to undergo the civilizing change at a later stage*. In other words, it is believed that the local traditions of technological material and other equipment in areas of the Deccan were not strong enough to bring about a breakthrough. The use of the concept of 'civilization' as a progressively desirable goal and that of the diffusion of a 'high' culture to a 'low' one, has led historians to unconsciously ignore the nature of internal historical change in the so-called "marginal" areas of isolation. The popularity of this generalization of the diffusion of civilization from certain core regions of the Indian subcontinent to the rest of the country, stems from the inherent value judgments in favour of the connotation of 'progress' attached to the term 'civilization'.[2] This has unfortunately had its negative effects in that it has unconsciously led to an exaggeration in the use of the concept of diffusion to understand almost every instance of culture change.[3] At another level in quantitative terms, many of the areas such as the Deccan have received little or no attention, or, only recent interest, simply because the origin and foundation of 'civilization' as the mainstream of development was not found here.

Our present concern is to take an intensive look at the foundations of the historical structures of the Deccan by identifying periods of overall change which do not necessarily coincide with political change. Indeed, our particular interest would also like to indicate that even before the origin of the State in these parts we find differential systems of political and economic organization which ultimately help us characterize the specific socio-political evolution of some of the earliest societies in these parts. The Deccan defined most commonly as the land south of the Vindhyas up to the confluence of the Krishna-Tungabhadra is constituted of various sub-regions, [MAP II] each rooted in a geographical specificity. Thus, in defining the roots of the distribution of the earliest material cultures, (Charts I A & B and Charts III A & B) one cannot but rule out the question of an unilinear transition from one productive system to another. The reference here is to the overlap situations at many of the sites , between the Neolithic-Chalcolithic and Megalithic phases and between the Megalithic and Early Historical ones. On the other hand, in the central Deccan it may be noted that there is a near total absence of the Neolithic-Chalcolithic phase but a substantial emergence of the Megalithic one.

In specific terms this raises the question of the transition from the proto-historic situation known to us from the innumerable megalith remains strewn all over the Deccan, and the elements of their interaction with the beginnings of the historical cultures again, known rather uniformly in the Deccan from the Ṣātavāhana layers of habitation. It is here, i.e., between the late centuries B.C. to the early centuries A.D. that the major problems about the diffusion of civilization, and the transition from tribe to civilization and State are addressed. Some scholars view the Sātavāhanas as the harbingers of the golden period and the duration of their rule as 'the vehicle of social transformation from a lower to a high state of society.'[4] However, in particular, it is the question of Mauryan presence in many parts of the Deccan which brought with it the first documented evidence, that has often been taken as the beginning point for the rise of civilization in these parts.[5] Those scholars who advocate a longer chronology for the Sātavāhanas (i.e., their rule beginning at the close of the third century B.C. or, early second century B.C.) do not have difficulty in explaining that the decline of the Mauryas in some parts of the Deccan was followed by the rise of the Sātavāhana power. However, in recent years it has become common to accept the shorter chronology which places the rise of the Sātavāhana in the middle of the first century B.C. In this case the period after the Mauryas in some parts of the Deccan is followed by a gap which historians have tacitly left unexplained as a grey area. Below, we focus a bit more closely on this gap which we prefer to call the pre-Sātavāhana phase because though it may coincide with the later Megalith levels of habitation in some sub-regions, it is not identical with it. Further, each sub-region of the Deccan throws up different elements of political and economic orgainzation during this period, known mainly from numismatic data, which suggests the emergence of small 'janapada-like' "localities"[6] presaging the rise of the Sātavāhana state.

In the present context 'civilization' for us does not simply denote the superstructure of a society expressed only through its intellectual endeavour. Rather, keeping in line with more recent definitions, 'civilization' in fact, must be considered as a kind of culture with a very complex set of behavioural patterns known to us from a range of activities of a particular society.[7] Evolutionary ideas having pervaded the disciplines of sociology, anthropology and archaeology, it came to be understood that civilization as the most progressive end of the spectrum was to be contrasted with pre-civilization. The latter necessarily denoted a stage inhabited by primitive peoples–savages and barbarians– implying their wildness, animality and generally as people constrained only by nature. Needless to add, these must be considered pre-requisite stages towards formation of state and civilization. Further, these pre-requisite stages we feel cannot be simply explained away by the use of a rigid, and very often an ambiguous term like 'tribe'.[8]

Following Lewis Morgan, Gordon Childe ultimately formalized the conception of the first civilizations as urbanized with the following linked features such as social surplus, full time specialists living in cities, a ruling class, writing, monumental buildings, long distance trade and finally, an institutionalized form of political organization based on force and termed as the State.[9] There are many scholars who have questioned Childe's ten criteria of civilization particularly with regard to its applicability to temperate Europe.[10] More fundamentally, E.R. Service even questions the notion that the rise of civilization was founded on the origin of the State.[11] Within the broad evolutionary framework of the nineteenth century anthropologists showed that in the pre-civilization stage primitive societies, denoted by the general term tribal, were segmented kin groups that were egalitarian in their relations to each other. However, significantly both the terms primitive and tribe acquired a pejorative meaning indicating a barbarous condition.[12] This unconsciously led to establish the concept of a dichotomous relationship between civilized/non-civilized.[13] Modern anthropological theory of the last few decades has now almost totally done away with the singular use of the term 'tribe' to describe the pre-civilization stage. As far as the term primitive is concerned, it is best understood as simple, early, original or primary lacking highly developed governmental institutions.[14] It is essential to accept this before we even attempt an understanding of the difference between primitive and civilized. And further, it is the continuum between these two stages which needs to be established rather than its dichotomous distinction.

Two of the scholars who have tremendously helped us in explaining the origin of civilization, particularly of State, with their studies in ethno-history, are Service and Fried.[15] Briefly, they delineate the following stages in socio-political evolution of societies : (i) 'egalitarian' societies {terms used by Service were 'band' and 'tribal' for this stage and later substituted by 'segmental'} (ii) 'ranked' societies {called 'chiefdoms' by Service} (iii) 'stratified' societies and (iv) States.[16] Fried's departure from the Marxist analysis is that *differential economic control and power was likely among hereditary kin groups rather than simply groups of owners and non-owners*. In agreeing with this view one would nonetheless, like to emphasize that this did not happen universally in all regions at the same time. The variations in the process of this transformation and the complexity with which it took place needs to be emphasized. Further, it are the stages that lead up to this transformation which determine the pace of this change.

In contrast to north India and the extreme South where there is a substantial amount of literary evidence available for the early historic period,[17] for a major part of early Deccan history we do not have such material. Hitherto, Puranic accounts of the Kali Age kings have been extensively used, along with epigraphical data, to reconstruct a chronological framework of the political suzerainty of the Sātavāhanas in these parts as the first 'empire-builders' in the Deccan.[18] For this early period, historical accounts have generally concentrated on the Greek Classical writings to dwell upon aspects of economic history as trade, towns and the like.[19] Inscriptions and coin finds too have been used in identifying and labelling the relative importance of certain regions of the Deccan.[20] Whereas extensive reliance has been given to these sources, no corresponding effort has been made in organizing the archaeological data that has expanded manifold in recent years. For understanding not only the expansion of civilization, but also its peculiar nature, embedded as it was in the distinct evolutionary process of the pre-civilization stage, we need to look more closely at archaeological data and give primacy to it. Here we need to be forewarned of the limitations of the traditional approaches to archaeological data.[21] This kind of source material can give insights not only into the details of the cultural segments in different sub-regions but, at the same time, enables us to highlight the transitional aspects of these cultures into the historical period.

To add to the problem of the limited nature of source material for the study of early Deccan history, an unconsciously neglected historiogrphical issue has been the different ways in which the Deccan has been understood by historians and archaeologists.[22] This has been mainly done on the basis of the availability of data that has enabled the description of the pre-historic and early historic environments.[23] It needs to be stated here that all research has explicit or implicit hypotheses, which Hill writes : 'guide the selection of research problems and the nature of the data to be collected'.[24] Several examples of this can be given and though it would be wrong to suggest that such definitions or demarcations of the Deccan were consciously delineated, they have nonetheless come to be accepted as rigid historical constructs. This has most obviously meant that those sub-regions of the Deccan which had failed to yield monumental Buddhist edifices (like those found in the 'Western Deccan' or the Krishna-Godavari Delta region of the 'Eastern Deccan') or, those lacking concrete evidences of Mauryan contact such as the inscriptions of Aśoka (with their concentration in the 'Southern Deccan'), were inadvertently not taken up for historical inquiry, or, taken up only when the Mauryan contact first began.[25] Further, the apparently startling 'historical' edifices of these select sub-regions pre-occupied most archaeologists and historians who mainly dwelt on an intrinsic descriptions of these.[26] It has been pertinently pointed out recently by B.D. Chattopadhyaya that, 'the stages leading up to the period of the Sātavāhanas are, however, . . . far from clear.'[27] This is relevant for all sub-regions of the Deccan.

In the context of the present paper it is difficult to take a close look at all the sub-regions in terms of their cultural evolution which went into the making of early historical society in the Deccan as a whole. In spatial terms we confine ourselves to sub-regions conventionally termed as the Southern Deccan or the Mysore Plateau region and the Central Deccan or the Hyderabad Telangana Plateau region. [Indicated in MAP II and III as B and D] Both these have one thing in common in being dubbed areas of relative isolation as they had neither large tracts of alluvial soil, as was the case in the Eastern Deccan, nor, did they have strategically located port towns facilitating as outlets of trade as in the Western Deccan. More pertinently, these two sub-regions provide significant data on the stages leading up to the cultural processes identified as the stage of civilization. Below, we intend to highlight some of these crucial aspects pertaining to the antecedent stages leading to civilization and briefly, to the civilizational stage in order to thereby identify the specific nature of society in early Deccan that has been hitherto neglected.

MAP-III

MAJOR CENTRAL AND SOUTHERN DECCAN SITES

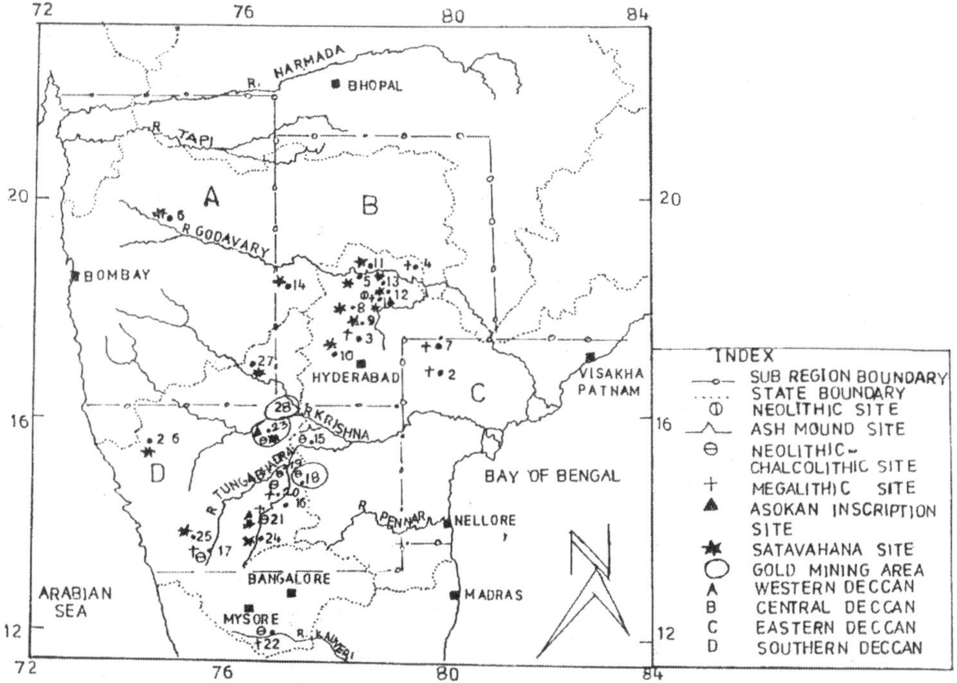

LIST OF SITES IN MAP III [CENTRAL AND SOUTHERN DECCAN]

S 1 PEDDABANKUR

S 2 POLAKONDA I

S 3 KADAMBAPUR

S 4 POCHAMPADU

S 5 KOTILINGALA I & II

S 6 PAITHAN

S 7 WARANGAL

S 8 KARIMNAGAR

S 9 DHULIKATTA

S 10 KONDAPUR

S 11 KARNAMAMIDI

S 12 CHINNABANKUR

S 13 VEMUNURU

S 14 TER

S 15 UTNUR

S 16 KUPGAL

S 17 HALLUR

S 18 PIKLIHAL

S 19 TEKKALAKOTA I & II

S 20 SANGANAKALLU I

S 21 BRAHMAGIRI

S 22 T NARSIPUR

S 23 MASKI

S 24 CHANDRAVALLI

S 25 BANAVASI

S 26 VADGAON MADHAVPUR

S 27 SANNATI

S 28 KOEDEKAL

KEY:

S = SITE NUMBER ON MAP III

It has been now recognized that in pre and proto-historic Deccan a great diversity of culture is visible. Further, archaeological evidence reflects how there was the co-existence of a hunting and gathering economy with a pastoral and agricultural one.[28] This is evident beginning with the Late Stone age and Mesolithic settlements through into the Chalcolithic and Iron age settlements.[29] Allchin further states that during the earliest stages of settled life, *i.e.*, among the Neolithic-Chalcolithic communities of the Deccan, some sort of craft specialization and even trade can be postulated. In this light he would qualify Childe's definition of the pre-urban economy being only 'relatively' self-sufficing.[30] The origin and growth of the internal distribution and communication system, particularly with regard to the exchange of objects commonly used in daily activities, is crucial to our understanding of 'pre-urban' and 'urban' situation in these parts. For instance, as pointed by Allchin, the technical uniformity of the fine blade industries of the Late Stone age, Neolithic and Chalcolithic cultures of Karnataka, Andhra, Maharashtra, Western India and the Indus plains shows culture contact 'both in space and time'.[31] It would have atleast required a rudimentary organization of labour, craft and trade for inter-regional contact to be viable. Indeed, Sundara has aptly suggested, 'The Krishna-Tungabhadra Doab region proved to be a contact zone of the developed Neolithic of the lower Krishna and the Chalcolithic culture of the upper Krishna'.[32]

At least, three broad phases of food producing cultures for the Southern Deccan, beginning around *c*.2300 B.C., have been postulated[33] (Chart I A). Some are contemporary to the Indus Valley civilization. The earliest (*c*.2300 B.C. - *c*.1800 B.C.) Neolithic cattle keeping economy was limited geographically to 'the nuclear area that today represents the Andhra Pradesh Karnataka State boundary'.[34] It is represented graphically and evident to us from the numerous Ashmounds (dung heaps) that have been excavated at sites like Utnur, Kupgal *etc.*[35] Here, there is little sign of cultivation and cattle played an important role in the economy. The construction of these cattle pens has been rarely found on the banks of rivers and their locale indicates seasonal movements. It is significant that the introduction of copper in Southern Deccan resulted in a more settled way of life and this emerged roughly around *c*.1500 B.C. This is characterized by a peasant economy based on dry farming of millets, grams and domestication of pigs, sheep fowls *etc.*[36] Enough evidence for this type of habitational settlement is found at sites like Utnur,

Hallur, Piklihal, Tekkalakota, Sanganakallu, Brahmagiri, T. Narsipur, Maski *etc.* (Chart I A & B). Their settlement pattern in all the micro-regions is said to have been uniform in that 'Settlements along the low hilly ranges are close to streams and away from major watersheds'.[37] As noted above a network of exchange was prevalent in the different regions of the Deccan and also with other regions of India which meant that these were far from isolated units of production. Further, the continuity of occupation and evolution and adaption to different economic systems of production from the first through to the third phase is a marked feature in these parts.

When we come to the period of iron age settlements, though there is a striking uniformity of the Megalith or iron using cultures in South India as a whole, we recognize that at some sites, they are superimposed on different levels of development of the preceding phase of Neolithic-Chalcolithic settlement. The case of Hallur is significant in that besides the fact that there is a Chalcolithic-Megalithic overlap, to-date it presents the earliest C^{14} dates for the use of Iron in the Deccan, *c.*1000 B.C.[38] Though this early evidence is limited, it raises a wider probability and as argued by Maloney the spread of iron technology in general can be understood to have great implications for the diffusion of an agricultural economy based on rice cultivation.[39] Among the other sites, which show the overlap of Megalithic culture with the preceding Neolithic-Chalcolithic one, are Brahmagiri and Maski. T. Narsipur and Sanganakallu both have evidence of earlier habitation and are important Megalithic sites as well. The upper limit of Megalith levels almost every where merges into the historical period identified in Andhra Pradesh and Karnataka by Sātavāhana remains (Chart I B).

It has been pointed out that iron was more profusely used in the Deccan than in the north[40] though its technological variations reveal a lack of prosperity.[41] The diffusion of this technology was associated with the distinctive Black and Red Ware almost uniformly all over South India.[42] The development of a more complex social and economic pattern of existence was thus set and there emerged a way of life that was different from the earlier agricultural life based on dry farming.[43] However, we know far greater details about their burials than about their habitation area and generally, the former was situated away from the latter or any area of tilled land.[44] Dilip K. Chakrabarti in writing about 'Issues of the Indian Iron Age' points out that in the context of the iron age in Southern Deccan in particular and the South Indian Peninsula as a whole, 'the early historic period . . . did not begin till the third century B.C. The period between *c.* 1,100-1,200 B.C. and *c.* 3rd century B.C. is a long one and suggests a substantial iron age occupation of the region', and further questions, 'but have we really got beyond the enumeration of megalithic burial types and related assemblages?'[45] Indeed, the iron age base of its early historic period has been only partially and imperfectly understood. It is precisely because of this neglect that the importance of the Megalith cultural phase to define the relationship and link between the proto-historic and early historic phases at certain excavated sites and the question of the rise of urbanization and the processes leading to civilization have been taken up for this study.

Hitherto, an overemphasis on the diffusionist theory had left little room for understanding indigenous development of cultural processes. Today, even in writings on the north Indian Ganges Valley early historic urbanization there has developed a critical view of the apparently 'revolutionary' role that iron may have played in the formation of urban centres.[46] In this context an alternative is found in the work of Erdosy who would like to see the crucial indicator for the rise of urban centres 'in the development of a hierarchy of settlement types on a regional scale' and therefore, regard the 'sociocultural transformations accompanying the rise of cities as the central issue'.[47] Thus, rather than bemoaning the lack of the role iron played in the transformation of the Deccan society into a fully urban one during the centuries B.C., we need to first and foremost identify the gradual aggregation of social groups in different settlements and place them in an essential continuum leading towards Civilization. In this transition the Deccan reflects a heterogeneous picture and we, therefore, need to emphasize upon the importance of the existence, or co-existence of particular sub-regions as independent, or semi-independent entities contributing to the whole region's historical development. We cannot also suggest a unilinear stage of development from pastoralism to agriculture wherein one mode of production gives way to another. Thus, the details of not only the economic structures but also of the political and social systems that controlled and manoeuvred these diverged conspicuously in each of the sub-regions.

In the sub-region of the Southern Deccan the transition to the early historical stage is significantly marked by the presence of the

Mauryas through the location of the Aśokan inscriptions.[48] [MAP III] These are particularly situated around the two sites of Maski and Brahmagiri which have also been excavated and show a continuous habitation from very early times. (Chart IA&B) However, it is not simply Mauryan presence which should be marked out for mention for, this is also the locale for a sizeable cluster of Neolithic-Chalcolithic settlements and between them is sandwiched the enigmatic megalith culture. All the other sites under discussion are located in the near vicinity of Brahmagiri and Maski, on both sides of the river Tungabhadra. They are Piklihal, Tekkalakota, Sanganakallu and Hallur. [MAP III] We feel that although all these present very valuable data on the antecedent stages to civilization and are rich Neolithic-Chalcolithic sites, they become less important in terms of the material remains found during the early historical period. (Chart II). Since the questions of the origins of iron age technology[49] are interconnected with the cultural and economic milieu in which it emerged we turn to describe it next.

Tekkalakota for instance, is basically a Neolithic-Chalcolithic site with no evidence of iron but, as has been pointed out in a survey of the Black and Red ware pottery, it is one of the few sites which gives significant associations of this pottery in the Chalcolithic context dated to around 1400 B.C.[50] It is further significant that in the midst of the gold mining region only this site has yielded gold ornaments at level I which is identified as the early Neolithic period.[51] In emphasizing upon the concentration of Neolithic sites in this area like Maski, Piklihal, Anandgal, Kotekal, Watgal, Lingsugar and other small settlements, [MAP III] Allchin states that almost all these are 'within 5 miles of the auriferous zones.'[52] He further goes on to suggest that, 'small scale and local extraction of gold was already taking place during the Neolithic period.'[53] With the limited technology available at the time one must agree with Allchin's suggestion that gold mining at this stage was mainly on the surface. It nonetheless, continued here in a remarkably permanent way.

Hallur can perhaps be taken as a typical example of a site which best reveals the permanent nature of habitation from the early Neolithic pastoral phase up to the iron age (Chart I A & B). It has been pertinently pointed out by R.C. Gaur that 'At Hallur it has been claimed that there is a transitional phase between the Neolithic and the Iron age, but there is no definite evidence to prove this transition'[54] since the blade industry of the Neolithic does not continue into Period II in the middle levels of which the iron is said to appear. However, what is most significant at this site is the occurrence of iron notably during its early phase. The early iron age is also represented at Piklihal and has been identified at Brahmagiri in the burial pits with stone slabs excavated by Wheeler, antedating the later cist graves.[55] With respect to the earliest phase of iron a matter of considerable importance is the 'overlap' situation obtained at Hallur for the Chalcolithic and Iron age levels and as mentioned above, here the C^{14} dates suggest an opening of the period as early as 1100 B.C. However, it is interesting to note that the early historical phase at this site does not yield any substantial remains except for a fair amount of pottery–Black and Red Ware, Russet-Coated Painted Ware–indicating merely an occupation of the period.[56] (Chart II) Thus, though C^{14} dates for iron age levels in the Deccan now confirm that this metal was known here almost as early as it was known in the North, if not earlier, it does not seem to have unleashed a socio-economic transformation at Hallur in the historical period as an 'Urban' centre. Nonetheless, we cannot discard Hallur because of its seemingly 'non-urban' character, because, as we intend to dwell upon below, it is the nature of the well-settled Chalcolithic communities of these parts that needs re-definition.

At Piklihal and Brahmagiri (Chart II) is also represented a succeeding phase of iron age which is said to coincide with the Sanganakallu evidence of iron and Maski period II. This is the phase of a relatively greater use of iron and whereas, in the earlier phase the settlements yielded a substantial stone-axe and blade industry, it is now found on a diminished scale. At all these sites the depth of iron age occupation is less than four feet.[57] Sanganakallu, like Hallur, fades away during the early historical period. When compared with Maski, Piklihal, situated not very far from it, does not have a well-represented habitation area during the historic phase. Its material prosperity gradually diminishes and just before the early iron age there seems to be an intrusion (Chart II).

Not ignoring the variations in the relative prosperity of this cluster of sites both during the iron age and the early historical period, it remains significant that these settlements continued to persist, in the near proximity of each other, for a fairly long period of time before the intrusion of Mauryan presence in these parts. It is now generally understood that it is precisely because these must have been traditionally centres of some economic/social/political power that it motivated Aśoka to choose this as an area to inscribe his message of *dharma*.[58] As early as 1962 Allchin candidly put it : 'the Aśokan edicts of the south reflect a very material interest in the area, and though they may also proclaim to the sincere Buddhism of their author they tempt us to ask whether this was not rather a case of the banner of the Dharma following the prospectors than vice-versa?'[59]

Of all the sites mentioned above, Brahmagiri remains to-date the most extensively excavated and, therefore, has been the most discussed. Material remains found here in a specific context have often been used as indicators to measure the importance of iron age in the south in general[60] and the relationship of iron age and early historical phases with the Mauryas.[61] Here,[62] as well as to some extent at Maski, the iron age ensemble is followed by that which yields what has been conventionally called 'Russet coated' or 'Andhra Ware'. These remains have often been compared with those found at Arikamedu and thereby, the date for fixing this phase is not earlier than the opening of the Christian era.[63] To put it in another way, the Mauryan contact in the archaeological record must be visualized to have taken place in the iron age, defined generally as the Megalithic period. Further, it is clear that the last phase of the megalithic culture at Brahmagiri seems to be co-existent with the first phase of the Sātavāhana levels of habitation. The overlap situations at Brahmagiri both during the Neolithic-Megalithic period and the Megalithic and Early Historical ones, together with the convincing evidence of cultural similarity of data from burials and habitation areas, makes this the site par excellence for a study of the transition to the early historic period in these parts.[64] It can supposedly also be considered the only site, among those discussed above, to have had a full mature development and to be thus characterized as 'urban' during the early centuries A.D. The early historical remains at Brahmagiri, particularly those identified with the Sātavāhana layers of habitation[65] are significantly found at other sites in the region like Chandravalli, Banavasi, Vadagaon-Madhavpur and Sannati (Chart I B & II). These sites indicate rich material remains in the historical period with no substantial antecedent stages of either the Neolithic-Chalcolithic or early iron age settlements. In other words, there is a shift from the traditionally habited sites of the previous cultural phases.

Thus, during the early centuries A.D. , it is suggested by scholars that Brahmagiri, Chandravalli, Sannati, Vadagaon-Madhavpur and Banavasi graduated into being called urban centres.[66] Adhering clinically to the criteria set forth for defining urban in the existing historiography, N.R. Banerjee comes to suggest that there was a lack of prosperity and no 'urban bias of the megalithic builders' of South India.[67] More specifically, Ghosh adds that iron age megalithic habitation levels at Brahmagiri and Maski do not show signs of prosperous towns.[68] And further, Dilip K. Chakravarti in characterizing the urban phenomena in the whole of India during the early centuries A.D. which was marked by an uniform prosperity, points out that *only now* (emphasis added) there is 'the undisputable evidence of urban settlements in areas like Mysore, Kerala, Madras and Andhra where the earlier evidence seems to lie vague and doubtful.'[69] The concern in all these views is primarily to come to some sort of consensual definition about the end result of the urban configuration available from the material remains at these centres notwithstanding that, so far, no problem-oriented excavations have been conducted in these parts and what has been done, is of a limited kind. Thus, taking this sub-region as a whole we cannot simply contend ourselves with the conclusion that at least some of the above-mentioned centres developed into urban ones and thereby suggest that the civilizational stage was partially achieved in these parts though at a later stage when compared to north India. By accepting an apologetic explanation historians tend to unconsciously look for uniform patterns of urban growth when in fact, none exist and consequently, overlook the complex cultural traits that went into the making of these settlements in the pre-urban phase. One has only to turn to the 'overlap' situations at many of the sites to realize that the urban phenomena was not sudden and further, that the form it took was at variance with what emerged in other parts of India during the same period.

This variance was ultimately linked to two interrelated aspects of the socio-economic formation in these parts : (1) the nature of social stability and (2) the nature of economic activity that drew the communities here in the first place. The nature of community settlement of particularly the Megalithic times has raised more questions than answered them. There are as many opinions about the authorship of the megaliths in South India and the Deccan as there have been books and articles written on them right from the nineteenth century when they were first discovered. Mcintosh details these to conclude that 'the major elements of the South India megalithic culture are in the main indicative of *strong continuity from the preceding Neolithic cultures,* from which it derives most of its material culture and a considerable number of its funerary rites.'[70](emphasis added). He, however, does add that certain features of the megalith graves like horse finds, horse trappings do indicate contacts with the Eastern Mediterranean and West Asia. Nonetheless, in highlighting the former conclusion he has drawn heavily on the syncretic views of Allchins who have listed about half a dozen possible influences on the development of the Megalithic culture in India.[71] Significantly, a point often missed by scholars in the analysis of the Allchins' in their emphasis on the indigenous nature of the Megaliths is that, it is pertinently based on the artifactual assemblage associated with these burial monuments and not on the hypothesis of their supposed racial affinities. Thus, they take pains to point out : 'There can be little doubt that many of the traits already established in the Neolithic persisted right through the Iron Age.'[72] To this, may also be added the views of Kennedy on the possible composition of the population of South India during the Iron age, wherein he concludes, 'the skeletal record of the megalith-builders does not provide the slightest reason to accept the hypothesis of a sudden displacement of populations in connection with the beginnings of the megalithic cultural complex.'[73] Though scholars like Leshnik[74] and Parpola[75] in their analysis tilt towards a Indo-Iranian or Aryan origin for the Megaliths and thereby heavily support the diffusionist theory, we would like to re-consider this issue by agreeing with the former explicated views and suggest that though the complexity of the inter-mingling of the Neolithic and Megalithic cultures in the Deccan cannot be directly proved, it is strongly indicated in material terms by the 'overlap' situations at some of the sites discussed above and further, the considerable evidence now heaped upon the indigenous development of iron working in Peninsular India[76] are strongly indicative of traditions of continuity rather than dysjunction and total external imposition.

That there was a continuous habitation at these sites is generally accepted by scholars but what is unconsciously ignored in the historical analysis is that these existing complex cultural traits were not obliterated during the succeeding historical stages of habitation despite the multiplicity of habitation areas or the non-uniform nature of the 'overlap' situations at the particular excavated sites.[77] The element of continuity further tends to be underplayed as often the use of the term 'tribal' or 'tribe'[78] to indiscriminately describe and club together all pre-State groups creates not only a discontinuity between the pre-civilization and civilization stages but also pejoratively dismisses the importance that these well-entrenched communities played in the formation of the civilized society. On the contrary, when new elements were subsequently added due to inter-regional trade and contact as a consequence of the Mauryan intrusion or, later, with the Indo-Roman contact, it was done on a solid foundation of economically differentiated communities.[79] These continued to nonetheless be organized on the basis of kinship ties. In *The Mauryas Re-visited*[80] Romila Thapar rightly postulates that since the political nucleus of the Mauryan empire was so far away from this region their mechanisms for appropriating the wealth available in these parts must have been dependant to a large extent on the pre-State groups and their network of lineage and kin.

Given the lack of literary sources for the Deccan as a whole it is very difficult to go into details of the exact nature of society in describing the dominant elements of kin-based relations during this period of transition from the megalith to the early historic. However, recent numismatic researches have brought to light certain evidence of pre-Sātavāhana chiefs who issued their own coins. A significant point to be recognized here is that the dates of these vary from sub-region to sub-region. In this cotext it has been pertinenetly pointed out by B.D. Chattopadhyaya that punch-marked coins of the Deccan, which began with the Mauryan period and continued to be manufactured in the early centuries of the Christian era, can in fact, be associated with specific 'localities'. These were followed by uninscribed cast coins and uninscribed die-struck coins, and they all provide a necessary background to the emergence of 'local' inscribed coins series of the Deccan.[81] P. L. Gupta[82] has made a recent attempt at analyzing these coins series from the numismatic and archaeological point of view to conclude on some of the major issues of their dates and distribution. First and foremost, he has rightly classified the big lead coins with inscriptions issued by local dynasties in the Deccan, sub-region-wise. They are listed as 'Kuras in the Panchganga basin (Kolhapur); Sadakanas in and around Chitaldurg district; Hastin in the Krishna valley; an unknown dynasty in the Tungabhadra basin and Sadas in the Mahishaka country'[83] which, he says, 'existed continuously till they were uprooted by the later Sātavāhanas in the time of Sri Yajña Sātakarni or a little earlier in circa second-third centuries A. D.'[84] The Kura, Sadakana and Hastin coins are impotant from the perspective of the Southern Deccan as they reveal the political profile of this sub-region after the Mauryan period and before the rise of the Sātavāhanas.

In exemplifying the importance of this period for a study of the pre-requisite stages leading to civilization we turn to elaborate upon some details of settlements in the Central Deccan which also provides valuable numismatic data [MAP II and III]. Regarding the sequence of the proto-historic cultures in the Central Deccan there is a notable absence of their contact with the Mauryan influence and this is significantly different from the other major sub-region taken up for detailed inquiry and described above. Also, here there are no major Chalcolithic sites.[85] Moreover, the subsequent picture that emerges here is slightly different since most of the Megalith sites do not have antecedent layers of habitation (Chart III A and B). Though it is often pointed out that there is a striking uniformity of the Megalith or iron using cultures in the South, it is important to underline that they are imposed on different levels of the preceding phase of settlement. Some of them like Polakonda, Kadambapur and Peddabankur have a little evidence of Neolithic remains but this is substantially less than what has been found in the context of the Southern Deccan. However, to put the mid-Godavari Valley in archaeological perspective it must be stated that this area reveals sites that range from the lower Paleolithic and Mesolithic ones on the one hand, and Neolithic and Megalith ones on the other.[86] Further, microliths are associated not only with hunting and gathering cultures but have also been found in abundance continuously right from the Neolithic times up to the historical layers of habitation.[87] These are of course commonly found in other parts of the Deccan and South India, associated with Chalcolithic levels and Allchin finds an explanation for a great demand for microliths by these communities in that there was probably a short supply of copper and bronze.[88] The complexity of the co-existence of archaeological cultures and their interaction with each other, as also their sequencing in the particular local situations, reflects upon the overlapping time scales of the historical transformation. This is intrinsic to the character of the early social formation in the Deccan which leads us to summarize that the transition from Neolithic to Chalcolithic and their interaction with the Megalithic occurred independently and variably in select parts of the Deccan and evolved gradually under different local environment.

The concern with identifying important archaeological sites in the Central Deccan has been of recent interest.[89] Sir Mortimer Wheeler's Maps [90] published in 1948 of the different sites from the pre to the early historic phase show a total blank for the Central Deccan. During the early years of independence the concern with identifying the Buddhist sites particularly in coastal Andhra[91] was predominant and the question of undertaking problem oriented excavation in so-called 'regions of isolation' was considered of little importance. This has unconsciously undermined our understanding of this region as, therefore, it has emerged in negative light and one where the history of the monumental is absent. The importance of the Central Deccan got prominence in the context of excavations conducted by the State Department of Archaeology and Museums, Government of Andhra Pradesh since the 1960s[92] which has also brought to the forefront the major issue of the Sātavāhana origin and early rule being located here[93] raising legitimate questions about the region's crucial role in the transition from pre-State to State society.[94]

Habitation in this region is indicated by a systematic finding of sites ranging from as early as the Lower Paleolithic and the Mesolithic stages.[95] In this context it has been noted : 'Most of the lower and middle Paleolithic sites are found on the red sandy or clayey soils. Mesolithic sites occur both on the red and black soils. Neolithic, Megalithic and Sātavāhana sites are generally found on black sticky or brown soils.'[96] The rich crop of early historical sites in almost every alternate village in the taluks of Warangal and Karimnagar has been noted[97] but explanations for the reason why this was so in relation to the antecedent cultures has not been discussed. Of all these, Kondapur is the one where evidence can be traced back to the Middle Stone Age and it has been postulated that it was a factory site for stone blades and flakes.[98] Kondapur situated in Medak district, about 70 kms from Hyderabad, is one of the earliest excavated sites in this region.[99] [Map III] Microliths of the Late Stone Age are also evidenced here and in archaeological terms this site becomes important again with the introduction of iron.[100] Though Paleolithic and Mesolithic materials are not available from any of the other early historical sites from the Central Deccan, it is well recognized that the Karimnagar region in general is rich in evidence available for these cultures, particularly spread around the river Godavari and its tributaries.[101] This is indicative of a very substantial food gathering economy that persisted in these parts from very early times.

The other major early historical sites [MAP III] in the Central Deccan are Peddabankur and Kotalingala, both in the Peddapalli taluk of Karimnagar district and Dhulikatta, situated about 10 Kms from Peddabankur (Chart III A and B). Of these, at Dhulikatta below a sterile layer which underlies a Sātavāhana deposit a few microliths like cores, blades, and flakes have been found.[102] Significantly, it is at Peddabankur that the antecedent cultures are interesting. It was a Neolithic site of considerable scale indicated by the scores of ground stone tools found here.[103] Some Neolithic axes and microlith implements were found at the early historical levels of habitation as well.[104] Peddabankur has Megalith burials along with a habitation area and has yielded considerable amount of Megalith related artifacts like horse remains, tools and implements of iron, cattle remains and so on.[105] According to K.P. Rao at Megalith levels here brick structures were also encountered and he has identified two distinct phases as Period I (c. third century B.C.) as Megalithic and Period II (second century B.C. to second century A.D.) which yields cultural remains of the Sātavāhana times.[106] The continuity of cultures at this site is therefore striking and very clearly there is an indication of the overlap of cultures. In a region which even today borders the tribal areas, it is not unusual to postulate that there was an inter-dependence between different kinds of subsistence patterns. This may perhaps be one of the reasons that lead the excavator to style Peddabankur as a 'Sātavāhana village'.[107]

The Neolithic stage in these parts is best exemplified with the excavated material from Polakonda in Warangal district and Kadambapur in Karimnagar district (Chart III A and B). At Polakonda two phases of stage I of the Neolithic and the Late Neolithic have been found. The latter has been radio-carbon dated to 1300 B.C.[108] During the Megalith phase the burials are situated at a distance of one Km from the habitation and in the proximity of large irrigation tanks.[109] Interestingly, the historical site here is to the North of the village and has three levels of occupation—Pre-Sātavāhana, Sātavāhana and medieval.[110] Unlike Peddabankur which stands out for its historical remains, Polakonda has rich Neolithic material but at both the continuity of settlement, whether of the local indigenous people or, along with outside immigrants, is an important feature. However, in contrast to both these, the site of Kadambapur, with its location in the midst of important historical sites of Dhulikatta, Kotalingala and Peddabankur, gains added significance first as a Neolithic settlement and then as a Megalithic burial site.[111] Though there are no historical remains available from here, the megalith material is rich in the usual iron objects and Black and Red Ware vessels and like Polakonda it also lies in the proximity of irrigation tanks.[112] It is worth pointing out that in and around the Kadambapur area several small sites with early historical material remains have been found. Karnamamidi situated on the north bank of the river Godavari in Adilabad district and Chinnabankur 4 Km north of Peddabankur in Karimnagar district are only known to us as early historical sites[113] [MAP III].

Pochampadu, and perhaps Kadambapur, are most representative of megalithic sites in the region. Krishnasastry has noted that both of them have burial furniture in conformity with that of Vidarbha.[114] At Kadambapur five Megaliths (4 pit burials and 1 cist burial) with some habitational deposit were noted. All, except one of them, were secondary burials and three out of the five were multiple burials. A remarkable find was an iron dagger with a copper hilt[115] indicative of importance of the person buried. In contrast Pochampadu had very few skeletal remains though pottery and iron objects were found in good number. A rectangular platform used for exposing the dead bodies was also located.[116] The repertoire of iron objects pertaining to war, agriculture and household activity at these and other megalith sites tells us of the extent and diversity of its imposition on the Neolithic sites as well as the general implications of the use of iron technology for agriculture and craft production. Weapons include daggers, knives, wedge-shaped blades, lances, spearheads with barbs, arrow-heads, swords of single and double edge and amidst all this, significant pieces of horse bits and stirrups need to be mentioned. While skeletal remains of horse were found at Pochampadu, bits of saddlery in the form of curb-chains have been found at the megalith levels of Peddabankur.[117] Again while agricultural implements such as flat-axes, sickles, spades, hoe-blades, knives have been found at many sites, at Pochampadu and Peddabankur in particular, we also find the bone remains of such domesticated animals as cattle, sheep, goat, swine which probably indicate that these formed part of their diet.[118] However, by far the most striking aspect of the megalith economy in this sub-region was its ability to generate iron objects on a large scale. This is undoubtedly related to the availability of iron in this region.[119] It has been pointed out that a 'number of ancient iron working spots were located in Karimnagar region at Regonda, Tellakunta etc.' At the latter site enormous deposits of iron slags and nodules of calcium carbonate indicate this. Indeed here, 'the entire hill range is scattered with iron ore'.[120]

Two aspects of the pre-Sātavāhana situation need to be emphasized in the development of the early historical sites in the Central Deccan. One of these was related to the particular nature of the economy which rested on the small-scale production of iron related artifacts and the other, to the substantial existence of pre-Sātavāhana levels of habitation, not necessarily related with the Megalithic material remains. We suggest this primarily on the basis of archaeological and numismatic data found at Kotalingala which is discussed below. Indeed, the stratigraphy of the excavation independently suggests a clear pre-Sātavāhana level.[121] At Peddabankur, Dhulikatta and Kondapur considerable amount of iron objects were present and at the former two Megaliths and All Black Ware pottery was also found.[122] At Kotalingala, apart from iron slags and ore found here in plenty, as the largest mound excavated in this region, coins of King Chimukha (equated with king Simuka of the *Purāṇas*) as 'founder of the Sātavāhana dynasty' were also collected.[123] The mound here was about 50 hectares in extent and 6 metres above the plains and during the course of excavations revealed significant pre-Sātavāhana levels of habitation. Further, it is strongly suggested that this was a Fort which on the north side, along the course of the river, showed the presence of a wharf.[124] On both the right and left banks of the Godavari, Kotalingala is surrounded by small early historical sites, and at Vemnuru, a site of 3-4 hectares, 'the presence of iron slag and iron ore may indicate the existence of an indigenous iron industry'.[125] The defence structures at Kotalingala as well as its location hint at its political and commercial importance right from pre-Sātavāhana times.

Dhulikatta, a corrupt of Dhulikota, literally means a mud fort. The settlement here was about 18 hectares in extent with two huge brick-built gateways and a deep moat outside the fort. The mud brick fortification has been traced to the pre-Sātavāhana times, though the main fort has been dated to Sātvahāna times, i.e., between 100 B.C. -- 200 A.D.[126] The most outstanding structural monument discovered and excavated here, dated to the last quarter of the third century B.C., is a Buddhist Stūpa.[127] It has been pointed out that the beginnings of Buddhism at Dhulikatta was possibly pre-Sātavāhana because no anthropomorphic representation of the Buddha is found here.[128] The Stupa is located outside the Dhulikatta city, surrounded by fertile black soil, and situated on a well connected trade route to places like Nagarjunakonda and Dhanakataka.[129] It's role in trade cannot be denied because of the silver Roman coins found here.[130] With all these features, Krishnasastry has conceded that Dhulikatta developed into a full-fledged 'walled town of the Andhras'.[131]

On the other hand, it has been graphically portrayed that Peddabankur represents 'a curious amalgam, indicating occurrence of continuous habitation from the Neolithic-Chalcolithic period onwards'[132] leading to its designation as a village. On the basis of the early reports on Peddabankur, Margabandhu has noted that there are two phases of structural development at this site : the early period dated to c. 250-100 B.C. and that which continues into[133] the Sātavāhana period c. 50 B.C.–200 A.D. However, apart from the suggested pre-Sātavāhana structural remains at Peddabankur, there are two significant finds that determine its character. On the one hand, 'a series of square and rectangular cisterns and brick platform with pieces of iron slag and two ovens indicate it to be a blacksmith's forge'.[134] On the other, the site and its surrounding areas are covered by alluvial black soil exposing at places a microlith industry.[135] This in no way undermines Peddabankur's importance as a production centre of particularly iron goods[136] and the fact that scores of punch-marked silver, Roman denari and Sātavāhana coins have been found here leads to the conclusion that it was also probably a mint centre.[137] In fact, in some senses the appellation 'market town' to it seems apt.[138]

It has been pointed out that Kondapur does not yield imposing architectural remains,[139] though both religious and secular buildings have been excavated here. However, as at Peddabankur large earthen water basins with two furnaces and innumerable iron objects like sickles, chisels, nails, knives, spearheads, hoes, forks and also possibly a plough-share, have been found.[140] Like Peddabankur, here too, no striking fortification walls have been found. On the other hand, considerable evidence of plain houses built of either brick or rubble has been excavated. The plan of these houses is not clearly discernible but in all probability these were the residences of the ordinary inhabitants of Kondapur. Here, there are some indications to show that they housed people from different social strata.[141] The overall pattern of the style of architecture at Kondapur, it has been pointed out, was rather plain and simple but 'quite efficient and skilful'.[142] This is true of even the religious, mainly Buddhist buildings found here which are the maximum number of all excavated structures at this site. They are ascribable to the Hinayana sect.[143] In the Karimnagar region, to the north of Kondapur, the Dhulikatta Stupa was easily linked with such others located at Phanigiri, Gujulabanda and Thirmalagiri and these of course are all part of the larger network of Buddhism in Andhra Pradesh.[144] There are a few label inscriptions indicating the donations of *gahapatis* at Dhulikatta[145] but on the whole, the simplicity of these early Buddhist sites in the Central Deccan is striking.

Despite considerable excavation work neither Peddabankur nor Kotalingala have distinctly yielded any evidence of religious structures. No evidence at all of any Brahmanical temple or sculptures has been found, though several terracotta figurines of Mother Goddess and Yakshas have been discovered in large numbers.[146] Other evidence such as the worship of serpent (Naga cult)[147] hardly proves that elements of Brahmanical cults were prevalent here, as Krishnasastry tends to suggest. The evidence in question is a figure of a snake made of iron found at Peddabankur. Krishnasastry traces back the antiquity of Naga worship to Vedic times,[148] though one would rather like to agree with Shrimali's assessment that there was the incorporation of the pre-Aryan Nagas and their forms of worship into the Brahmanical system from very early times in the Ganges Valley. According to him this particularly took place in the land of the Kuru Pañcālas even though they were traditionally considered to be the best of the *āryas*.[149] Indeed, it was not only Brahmanism that assimilated the folk elements of Naga worship but both Buddhism and Jainism showed an anxiety to do so.[150] In the context of the Central Deccan the incorporation of the five-hooded Naga Muchilinda protecting the feet of Lord Buddha is found on a slab of the northern *ayaka* platform of the Stūpa at Dhulikatta.[151] This, as well as Yaksha forms at the same Stūpa,[152] have to be seen as part of the larger Buddhist ideology of even making the Nagas share in the relics of the Buddha.[153] Thus, Nagas as protectors and worshipers of the Buddha are seen prolifically illustrated at Amaravati as well which is considered to be the best representative of Buddhist art in the Deccan.[154] In a general sense, however, all over India the term Naga continued to be understood primarily in the sense of a classificatory term for forest people. Given the lack of any other evidence for the existence of Buddhism or Brahmanism from the site of Peddabankur, one would like to suggest that the above-mentioned Naga 'figure' of iron probably represents a part of the belief system of tribal peoples. Their co-existence with the more settled communities is postulated on the basis of evidence from Peddabankur itself where scores of Neolithic ground tools and microliths were found at early historical levels of habitation and this therefore, clearly suggests the existence of such populations.

Against the above background one has noted that all the above sites had significant pre-Sātavāhana elements. In the Central Deccan Kondapur and Dhulikatta have the common feature of Buddhist edifices, Peddabankur and Kondapur share features of being important 'mint centres', Kotalingala and Dhulikatta both have evidence of fort-like structures. Importantly, Kondapur and Dhulikatta have clear evidence of the early form of Buddhist art and all three, Kotalingala, Dhulikatta and Peddabankur, have important pre-Sātavāhana features in their structural and material remains. The fundamental question is that if in the early historical period these centres had developed urban features, the forces represented in the proto-historic cultures that made this possible and, the mechanism through which local groups participated in the spheres of economic, social and political activity, during this period have to be focused upon.[155] The most significant point in this regard is the discovery of several pre-Sātavāhana coins along with early Sātavāhana coins, some of them in a stratified context, at Kotalingala.[156] Unlike the numismatic evidence from Dhulikatta and other places, the Kotalingla finds are outstanding because a number of coins of a certain Chimukha (25), 'founder of the Sātavāhana dynasty' have been collected.[157] Several others of the early rulers of this dynasty like Sātavāhana (234) and Satakarni (47) have also been found.[158] Apart from these, those of Samagopa (68), Mahātalavara (13), Gobadha (17) and Narana (9), open up a new vista of the pre-Sātavāhana history of this region. Parabrahma Sastry identifies the Gobhadra and Samagopa coins with the Sunga dynasty of Vidisha that ruled over these parts.[159] Thakur Raja Ram Singh in a recent analysis identifies them with the descendants of the Andhakarattas referred to by Budhagosha who ruled, according to him, from Kotalingala as pre-Sātavāhana Andhra Kings.[160] One cannot agree with Singh's view that there existed here a 'confederation of Petty and Tribal rulers and other kingdoms controlled by Andhra Kings' and the latter he sees as ruling from Kotalingala.[161] From our point of view these clearly highlight the fact that some form of specific political authority had become a force continuously from pre-Sātavāhana times in the Central Deccan where the Mauryan presence cannot be archaeologically located.[162]

There is no doubt, however that power relations were rooted in old kin ties in post-Mauryan Deccan as a whole. A series of coins reflecting the rise of local rulers in the context of post-Mauryan Southern Deccan discussed above firmly suggested the rise of a politico-economic power base still rooted in local kinship ties. Epigraphic sources from the Andhra region of the Eastern Deccan also gives us similar evidence as for instance, the mention of Kubiraka *rāja* of the relic casket incscription found at Bhattiprolu of the third century B.C., Somaka *rāja* of an inscription of the second century B.C. found on an the outskirts of Vaddamanu, Aira Māna Sada of the Velpuru epigraph and so on.[163] The prefix '*go*' in the names of chiefs like Gobadhra and Sama gopa, who are said to have ruled from Kotalingala, may indicate their origin in pastoral communities. A stone pillar, now lying in a paddy field one kilometre away from the Kotalingala fortress, bears a label inscription *Nāga Gopi Nikāya*,[164] meaning 'assemblage' or 'group' of Nāga Gopi which may have also referred to a kin group living in a settlement outside the fortified township. The location of Dhulikatta amidst fertile black soil and the considerable number of granaries in the fort area may indicate that the ruling clans here were probably from powerful landowning agricultural communities. It is impossible to establish a connection, political or otherwise, between the various ruling families who were in control of these fortified towns and the surrounding populations and more particularly, how the nature of authority from pre-Sātavāhana times was transformed in Sātavāhana times, but that there was a concerted need felt by them to defend themselves is evident in their attempts at fortifying their settlements.

Peddabankur too probably had an independent political and economic existence. Both here, as well as at Kondapur, a large number of coins, punch-marked ones and also early Sātavāhana types, have been found. I.K. Sarma suggests that Peddabankur was a mint centre.[165] Krishnasastry locates this mint in Enclosure II where scores of coins were found during excavation.[166] Sarma deduces this particularly on the basis of a large number of terracotta moulds found in stratified deposits and the existence of hundreds of small die-struck pieces in pots. Two hoards of punch-marked coins have also been found here.[167] A variety of coins of different types were reported also from Kondapur and this had led Yazadani to designate it as 'an important Andhra town where coins were minted'.[168] Here too, thousands of punch-marked and early type of Sātavāhana coins were found along with a discovery of coin moulds to which the punch-marked coins fitted.[169] The co-existence of a variety of coin types at these centres converges on an obvious conclusion, namely, that the regional economy was dependent on trade and commercial transactions of a certain magnitude.

That a surplus had been generated by the well-settled communities of the Central Deccan during the early centuries A.D. is evident enough from the structures they built to store it, as also the other manifestations of urban life. However, as delineated above the early history of habitation and cultural evolution in this region had helped in gradually transforming pockets of the food-gathering economy particularly from the Megalithic phases of habitation. These have been generally found in close proximity of the early historical sites [MAP III]. The expansion of the agrarian base was therefore linked with the proliferation of early historical sites in the region. It is in this phase that it can be postulated that there was an increase in population. In the sites under discussion the maximum number of iron implements have been recovered from Peddabankur and Kondapur. The impact and use of the iron technology must, nonetheless, be understood in the context of a limited ecological base, where because of the non-availability of fertile tracts, other than along the river, large scale agricultural operations were not possible. Village settlements thus continued to be dependent on other modes of production such as pastoralism, gathering and fishing. But, what is particularly striking is that even small settlements in the mid-Godavari valley give evidence for the production of iron objects. In this way it would be possible to suggest that the existence of social groups, organized most probably on kinship lines, were involved in the craft production of smelting and forging iron.[170] Thus, we submit that trade in these parts was stimulated not so much by the export of an agricultural surplus, but rather, by the supply of iron objects and other related commodities,[171] a process which began in proto-historic times. This explains the existence of such large number of coins of various types at many of these places. It would not be an exaggeration to state that it was the capacity of the dominant social groups in the region to maintain the networks of trade and production that resulted in the growing strength of certain local elites. Even in pre-Sātavāhana times, their practice of striking the coins with their names inscribed on it is evidence of this. Political power in pre-Sātavāhana times was necessarily segmented, but under the new forces of social change these groups interacted with each other to ultimately establish the larger network of the Sātavāhana empire which covered other sub-regions of the Deccan as well.

Taking into consideration the archaeological data described above for the two sub-regions of the Southern and Central Deccan, it has been our main aim to highlight the salient features of the formation of the early society which due to the geocultural and techno-economic, as well as institutional constraints and possibilities, developed an individual character, different in content and style from other sub-regions of the Deccan, and also from other parts of India. Rather than dismissing the so-called 'tribal' nature of this society we have tried to emphasize that civilizations of the classical type, i.e., those that develop in a primary form, need not be the sole criteria to be located in an uniform way in all regions of the country. Even in its classical form, its characteristic features are foreshadowed in earlier stages of society. The term civilization is thus a relative concept and should not be defined in terms of the appearance of some single attribute like writing or arts. Hitherto, scholars have used this criteria to conclude that 'a grade of cultural evolution we call civilization was achieved between 200 B.C. and A.D. 300, even though particular features such as literature, monumental brick construction or coin hoards did not appear evenly in all the nuclear centers of the south'.[172] Maloney writes this for South India as a whole, focusing on Tamil country.[173] In this context he also informs us 'But there is no evidence of early civilization between the gold-bearing zones of Karnataka and Madurai. Likewise the tract between the Godāvarī and the Kāvēri has little to offer as regards early civilization.'[174] However, in our analysis, the continuum of directional change from the pre-civilization to the civilizational stage has been given a marked emphasis to look at civilization only in terms of a type of culture that was not achieved at an arbitrarily demarked point. In this sense simple cultures in so-called peripheral regions contribute to the development of civilization through a two-way interactional integration and thus, defining the internal processes of change are fundamental to characterizing any given society.

NOTES

1. M.G.S. Narayanan, 'Trends and Prospects in Historiography', Presidential Address, Section I, *PIHC*, 39th Session, Hyderabad, 1978, pp. 15-16, raises the plea to look afresh at the 'roots' of Indian Civilization. In recent years scholars working on the hitherto select areas of Indian civilization have also recognized that 'contributions made by the inhabitants of other regions' to this process have been neglected. See Gregory Erdosy, *Urbanization in Early Historic India*, BAR International Series, 430, 1988, p.1.
2. Ruth Tringham, 'The Concept of "Civilization" in European Archaeology' in J.A. Sabloff and C.C. Lamberg-Karlovsky (ed.), *The Rise and Fall of Civilizations*, California, 1980, pp. 470-484 has discussed this at length in the context of the unfair comparison that has been made in identifying stages of civilization in temperate Europe with those in the Mediterranean.
3. An example of this is in the use of the term 'Aryan' by scholars even though they adopt different methods of historical analysis. *Cf.* K.A.N. Sastri, *A History of South India*, OUP, (4th ed. rp.), 1984, p. 69 and K. Satyanarayana, *A Study of the History and Culture of the Andhras*, vol. I, New Delhi, 1973, p. 100. For an elaboration of a questioning of this idea — Aloka Parasher, 'Early History of Andhra — Some Interpretations', *PAPHC*, 9th Session, Kurnool, 1985, pp. 184-191.
4. Yetukuri Balarama Moorty, 'Sātavāhana Era A Transition from Tribal Culture to National Culture' in *The Andhra Pradesh Journal of Archaeology*, Sātavāhana Special, Dr. N. Ramesan Commemoration Volume, vol III, no. 1, 1990, p. 64. The existing commonplace interpretations of transition from 'tribal culture' to an 'agricultural society' in the context of Andhra history has been expressed in this brief paper, pp. 57-64.
5. Clarence Maloney, 'Archaeology in South India : Accomplishments and Prospects' in Burton Stein, *Essays on South India*, New Delhi, 1976, pp. 25-27; Vimla Begley, 'From Iron Age to Early Historical in South Indian Archaeology' in J. Jacobson, (ed.), *Studies in the Archaeology of India and Pakistan,* AIIS, New Delhi, 1986, p. 299; Romila Thapar, *The Mauryas Revisited* (S.G. Deuskar Lectures on Indian History, 1984), Calcutta, 1987, p. 4ff.
6. A term borrowed from B.D. Chattopadhyaya's suggestions on the formation of "some form of proto-State formation at a local level" before the rise of the pan-Deccan emprie of the Sātavāhanas — 'Transition to the Early Historical Phase in the Deccan : A Note', in B. M. Pande & B. D. Chattopadhyaya, *History and Archaeology*, New Delhi, 1987, vol. II, p. 728.
7. *Encyclopaedia Britannica*, vol. 5, p. 831.
8. K.Satyanarayana, op. cit., 1975, on the use of the term 'tribal stage' and particularly his chapter 'Living Prehistory'; A. Ghosh, *The City in Early Historical India*, IIAS, Simla, 1973, p. 13 on his doubts whether people in the South had "shed their tribal character" even during the Mauryan period.
9. V.G. Childe, 'Civilization, Cities and Towns', *Antiquity*, vol. 31, March 1957, p. 36 and which is elaborated by him in *What Happened in History* (1st published 1942), Penguin Books, (rp.), 1964, pp. 31-32; p. 97 ff.
10. Sally Green, 'Introduction' in V.G. Childe, *Man Makes Himself*, First

Illustrated edition, Wiltshire, England, 1981, pp. 8-23. Also by R. Tringham, op. cit., 1980, pp. 472-474.

11. Elman R. Service, *Origins of the State and Civilization, The Process of Cultural Evolution*, New York, 1975, p.178.
12. Morton H. Fried, *The Notion of Tribe*, California, 1975, pp. 3-10.
13. R. Tringham, op. cit., 1980, pp. 473-478.
14. E.R. Service, op. cit.,1975, pp. 47-50.
15. Ibid., pp. 44-46; M.H. Fried, 'On the Evolution of Social Stratification and the State' in Stanely Diamond (ed.), *Culture in History : Essays in Honour of Paul Kaelin*, New York, 1960, pp. 713-731.
16. A variety of perspectives on early State-formation is now available in the exhaustively accumulated and theoretically coherent studies on the subject in two volumes edited by H.J.M. Claessen and Peter Skalnik (ed.), *The Early State*, The Hague, 1978 and *The Study of the State*, The Hague, 1981.
17. For north India it has been pointed out that availability of textual data has not necessarily led to 'a better understanding of archaeological and cultural materials' (p.110). It has been thus noted that in dealing with Vedic literature the limitations of the 'Aryan' model have emerged and in describing urban centres from Buddhist and Jaina sources 'material remains and their chronologies have been often adapted to fit these descriptions' (p.110). Details of how this has happened in Anna King, 'Some Archaeological Problems Regarding Gangetic Cultures in Early Historical India', in Kenneth A.R. Kennedy and Gregory L. Possehl (ed.), *Studies in Archaeology and Palaeoanthropology of South India*, AIIS, 1984, pp. 109-119.
18. Sudhakar Chattopadhyaya, *Some Early Dynasties of South India*, Delhi, 1974, pp. 25-31; p.33 ff. Unlike most other books of this type on dynastic history he introduces a brief account of pre-Sātavāhana times.
19. D.R. Das, *Economic History of the Deccan*, Delhi, 1969, p. 216 ff; K. Satyanarayana, op. cit., 1975, pp. 136-154.
20. H.P. Ray, *Monastery and Guild*, Commerce under the Sātavāhanas, Delhi, 1986, p. 33 ff. for details on the Western Deccan; H. Sarkar, 'Emergence of Urban Centres in Early Historical Andhradeśa', in B.M. Pande & B.D. Chattopadhyaya, op. cit., 1987, vol. II, pp. 631-641 takes examples from the Eastern Deccan.
21. Two important books for the Deccan in terms of the detailing of significant new archaeological data are V.V. Krishnasastry, *The Proto and Early Historical Cultures of Andhra Pradesh*, State Department of Archaeology and Museums, Archaeological Series 58, Hyderabad 1983 and A. Sundara, *Rock Cut Chamber Tombs of South India*, 1972. Both these are studies based on a regional scale but have payed no attention to explain the cultural processes they observe on the basis of this new data.
22. Namely, the generalized way in which the terms Western Deccan, Eastern Deccan and Southern Deccan have been introduced in the titles of Books. Textbooks on the historical Deccan use it from their own vantage point of view as in the case of R.G. Bhandarkar, *Early History of the Dekkan*, 1894, New Delhi (rp.), 1975 (mainly Maharashtra part); K.V.S. Aiyar, *The Historical Sketches of Ancient Deccan*, Madras, 1917 (mainly coastal Andhra); G. Jouveu Dubreuil, *Ancient History of the Deccan*, Pondicherry, 1920

(includes some parts of Tamil country); D.C. Sircar, *Successors of the Sātavāhanas in the Lower Deccan*, Calcutta, 1939 (mainly coastal Andhra) and so on.

23. Thus we have only particular parts of the Deccan being described largely in terms of their cultural and artistic heritage, for example, K.R. Subramanyan, *Buddhist Remains in Andhra and History of Andhra between 225 and 610 A.D.*, Madras, 1932; F.R. Allchin, *Neolithic Cattle-Keepers of South India*, Cambridge, 1963; Vidya Dehejia, *Early Buddhist Rock Temples*, London, 1972; S. Nagaraju, *Buddhist Architecture in Western India*, New Delhi, 1982; Amita Ray, *Life and Art of Early Andhradeśa*, New Delhi, 1983.
24. J.N. Hill, 'The Methodological Debate in Contemporary Archaeology : A Model', in David L. Clarke (ed.), *Models in Archaeology*, 1972, pp. 61-107.
25. Similar historiographical situations obtained in the context of an analysis of European proto-history and early history. A discussion in Maurizio Gualtieri, 'Fortifications and Settlement Organization : An Example from Pre-Roman Italy', and R.F.J. Jones, 'A False Start? The Roman Urbanization of Western Europe', in *World Archaeology*, vol. 19, no. 1, June 1987, pp. 30-57.
26. H. Sarkar, op. cit., 1987, vol. II, pp. 631-632 has significantly raised questions about this pre-occupation of archaeologists and historians and suggested a new direction for forthcoming studies on this region.
27. B.D. Chattopadhyaya, op. cit., 1987, vol. II, p.727.
28. F.R. Allchin, 'The Relationship of Neolithic Later Settled Communities with those of Late Stone Age Hunters and Gatherers in Peninsular India', in R.S. Sharma & V. Jha (ed.), *Indian Society : Historical Probings, Essays in Honour of D.D. Kosambi*, New Delhi, 1974, pp. 45-66.
29. For the mid-Godavari Valley there is interesting evidence wherein Neolithic tools were found at historical levels of habitation, V.V. Krishnasastry, op. cit., 1983, pp. 22; 24; 35. Implications of this discussed in Aloka Parasher, 'Social Structure of Settlements in the Central Deccan' in Indu Banga (ed.), *The City in Indian History*, Delhi, 1991, pp. 40-44.
30. B. & R. Allchin, *The Birth of Indian Civilization*, Penguin, 1968, pp. 266-267; Clarence Maloney, op. cit., 1976, p. 3 points to the fact that at Brahmagiri, for instance, the introduction of microliths just below the level containing evidence of food-production and cattle keeping (c. 2300 B.C.) 'heralds a rather abrupt cultural change and may represent intrusive influence.'
31. Allchin, op. cit., 1968, p. 277. Evidence of this for the Neolithic phase at one of the most systematically excavated sites Nagarjunakonda discussed in B. Subbarao, *Personality of India*, Baroda, 1958, p.115.
32. A. Sundara, 'Cultural Ecology of the Neolithic in India', in S.B. Deo and K. Paddayya, ed., *Recent Advances in Indian Archaeology*, Deccan College, Poona, 1985, p. 41.
33. B. & R. Allichin, *The Rise of Civilization in India and Pakistan*, New Delhi, 1983, General distribution pattern and chronology of the early phase — pp. 286-287. For a review of the most recent work done on the Neolithic stage of food production in the Southern Deccan see A. Sundara, op. cit., 1985, pp. 39-43.
34. Maloney, op. cit., 1976, p. 9.

35. F.R. Allchin, *Utnur Excavations*, Andhra Pradesh Archaeological Series, No. 5, Hyderabad, 1961; *Neolithic Cattle Keepers of South India*, 1968 discusses in detail the full implications of these mounds in determining the economy and culture of these pastoral communities. He clearly ascribes them to the Neolithic period. However, work by archaeologists after him tend to place them in the post-Neolithic period but there is still no unanimity on the subject. Iron age connections suggested by V.R. Rami Reddy, 'An Outline of the Pre and Protohistoric Cultures of South Western Andhra Pradesh', *Journal of Karnatak University*, vol. VIII, Dharwar, pp. 125-136. Though not identical with this view, A. Sundara too dates these mounds in some parts of Karnataka to between 1200-700 or 600 B.C. (p. 323). Details of various views on this subject have been discussed by him in 'Studies in Ash Mounds', in B.M. Pande and B.D. Chattopadhyaya, *Archaeology and History*, New Delhi 1987, vol. I, pp. 313-324.
36. Allchin, op. cit., 1983, General distribution pattern and chronology of the third phase — pp. 287-288. It has become increasingly difficult to differentiate the Neolithic horizon from the Chalcolithic in the Southern Deccan. For a recent survey of a list of all the sites that have been excavated and reported in all the three phases of the Neolithic-Chalcolithic cultures in South India see M.L.K. Murty, 'Pre-Iron Age Agricultural Settlements in South India : An Ecological Perspective', *Man and Environment*, XIV, 1, 1989, pp. 65-67.
37. M.L.K. Murty, op. cit., 1989, p. 69.
38. M.S. Nagaraja Rao, *Protohistoric Cultures of the Tungabhadra Valley*, Poona, 1971, p. 15. See also M.S. Nagaraja Rao, 'Earliest Iron-Using People in India and the Megaliths', in *Madhu Recent Researches in Indian Archaeology and Art History*, 1981, pp. 25-32. In the latter article he discusses evidence from Tadakanahall, a site 8 kms from Hallur which shows that the Megalith burials here are related to the overlap phase of Neolithic-Chalcolithic and Early Iron age at Hallur. Pottery and iron tool types are similar at both places. This evidence is therefore suggested to be the earliest evidence for Megalith burials datable to *c.* 1000 B.C. It nonetheless needs to be pointed out that D.P. Agarwal feels that further confirmation about the antiquity of iron in South India is necessary — *The Archaeology of India*, London, 1982, p. 257.
39. Maloney, op. cit., 1976, pp. 8-9 suggests a diffusion of rice cultivation and the Dravidian languages with the Megaliths. B.K. Thapar, 'Maski — 1954 : Chalcolithic Site of the Southern Deccan', *AI*, vol. XIII, pp. 14-15. Deo, on the other hand, argues on the basis of the evidence mainly from the Vidarbha sites and also from Brahmagiri and Maski that the Megalithic people were mainly pastrolists, op. cit., 1985, pp. 90-91; p. 94. N.R. Banerjee, *The Iron Age in India*, New Delhi, 1965, p. 210 gives emphasis to the role played by irrigation in agriculture in the megalith society.
40. In the early 1950s D.H. Gordon suggested this but later changed his mind. However, he maintained the view that iron was bought to India by 'a people who buried their dead in cairns'. Discussed in B.R. Subrahmanyam, 'Appearance and Spread of Iron in India — An Appraisal of Archaeological Data', *JOI*, vol. XIII, no. 1, Sept. 1963, pp. 351-353.
41. N.R. Banerjee, op. cit., 1965, p. 214. Earlier views that the earliest evidences of iron working can be observed only in the Ganga-Yamuna doab and then

'the knowledge diffused to other parts of the sub-continent' is no longer accepted. For earlier views Cf. Subramanyan, op. cit., 1963, p. 357.

42. Allchin, op. cit., 1983, p. 334.
43. M.S. Nagaraja Rao, op. cit., 1971, pp. 123; 136.
44. Ibid., p. 49. M.S. Nagaraja Rao is of the opinion that megalith people settled on riverine beds in the Southern Deccan. For details on different aspects of the socio-economic life of the megalith period on South India and the Deccan see B.K. Gururaja Rao, *Megalithic Culture in South India*, Mysore 1972, Chapter 10 and 12; K.P. Rao, *Deccan Megaliths*, Delhi, 1988.
45. Dilip K. Chakravarti, 'The Issues of the Indian Iron Age', in S.B. Deo and K. Paddayya, (ed.), op. cit., 1985, p. 76.
46. Anna King, op. cit., 1984, pp. 110-111.
47. G. Erdosy, op. cit, 1988, pp. 2 & 4. A small attempt to looking at the relationship between different types of settlements at a subregional level of the mid-Godavari Valley and defining the possible nature of their urban characteristics has been made in Aloka Parasher, op. cit., 1991, pp.19-46.
48. Location of Aśokan inscriptions, recently mapped out by Gerrad Fussman, 'Central and Provincial Administration in Ancient India : The Problem of the Mauryan Empire' *IHR*, vol. XIV, nos. 1-2, 1987-1988, p. 47; p. 4; pp. 64-67; Vimla Begely, op. cit., 1986, p. 301.
49. N.R. Banerjee's comments on Dilip K. Chakravarti's paper, op. cit., 1985, pp. 77-78 rightly points out that a clear picture of the chronology of iron age sites is far from clear though of all the iron using cultural groups the Megalithic culture is the best documented.
50. H.N. Singh, 'Black and Red Ware — A Cultural Study' in D.P. Agarwal and Dilip K. Chakravarti ed., *Essays in Indian Proto-History*, Delhi, 1979, p. 272; pp. 280-281.
51. Allchin, op. cit., 1983, p. 287.
52. F.R. Allchin, 'Upon the Antiquity and Methods of Gold Mining', *JESHO*, vol 5, 1962, p. 209.
53. Ibid., pp. 209-210.
54. R.C. Gaur's comments on Dilip K. Chakravarti's paper, op. cit., 1985, p. 80.
55. Allchin, op. cit., 1983, p. 329.
56. M.S. Nagaraja Rao, op. cit. 1971, p. 68.
57. Allchin, op. cit, 1983, pp. 329-330.
58. This view has been systematically argued by several scholars and was first suggested by Maloney, op. cit., 1976, p. 25. Discussed in Sudarshan Seneviratne, 'Kalinga and Andhra: The Process of Secondary State-Formation', *IHR*, vol. 7, no. i-ii, 1981; R. Thapar, *The Mauryas Revisited*, Calcutta, 1987, pp. 13-14; p. 25.
59. Allchin, op. cit, 1962, pp. 208-209.
60. S. Nagaraju and B.K. Gururaja Rao, 'Chronology of Iron Age in South India' in D.P. Agarwal and Dilip K. Chakravarti (ed.), *Essays in Indian Proto-History*, vol. 5, ISPQS' History and Archaeology Series, Delhi, 1979, pp. 321-329.
61. Maloney, op. cit., 1976, pp. 25-26; Vimala Begely, op. cit., 1986, p. 304; p. 306.
62. M. Wheeler, 'Brahmagiri and Chandravalli, 1947 : Megalithic and Other Cultures in the Chitaldurg District, Mysore State', *AI*, no. 4, 1947-48, pp.

180-310.

63. Allchin, op. cit., 1983, p. 330.

64. Nagaraju & Gururaja Rao, op. cit., 1979, pp. 323-324; pp. 327-28; Amita Ray, op. cit., 1983, p. 26.

65. Wheeler, op. cit., 1947-48, p. 208; p. 232.

66. This is how they have been listed by scholars who have reviewed the recent archaeological discoveries in Andhra Pradesh and Karnataka in P. Sitapati (ed.), *Sātavāhana Seminar Souvenir*, 1981, *e.g.*, Banavasi, it is noted was famous in literature as the oldest capital city in Karnataka.

67. N.R. Banerjee, op. cit., 1965, p. 214.

68. A. Ghosh, *City in Early Historical India*, IIAS, 1973, pp. 12-13.

69. Dilip K. Chakravarti, *Purātattva*, no. 7, 1974, p. 89.

70. J.R. Mcintosh, 'The Megalith Builders of South India: A Historical Survey' in H. Härtel (ed.), *South Asian Archaeology*, Berlin, 1981, pp. 467-468.

71. Details in B. & R. Allchin, op. cit., 1968, pp. 229-230.

72. Ibid., p. 232.

73. K.A.R. Kennedy, *The Physical Anthropology of the Megalith Builders of South India and Sri Lanka*, Canberra, 1975, p. 75.

74. L.S. Leshnik, *South Indian Megalithic Burials : The Pandukal Complex*, Wiesbaden, 1974.

75. A. Parpola, *Arguments for an Aryan Origin of South Indian Megaliths*, Madras, 1973.

76. Dilip K. Chakravarti, 'The Beginning of Iron in India', *Antiquity*, vol. L, June 1976, pp. 114-124.

77. Begely, op. cit., pp. 300-301 takes pain to point out that both at Brahmagiri and Maski the continuous area of habitation is limited.

78. Maloney, op. cit., 1976, pp. 11-12 compares the iron age situation in South with the "primary civilizations" and poses a question as to 'when was a grade of cultural evolution that can be called civilization achieved?' emerge in South India. H. Sarkar, op. cit., 1987 goes to the extent of suggesting 'we are here not concerned about their antecedent stages' when discussing the growth of the city in Andhradeśa.

79. This can be suggested on the basis of the special construction of certain types of burials and value oriented grave goods Wheeler, op.cit., 1947-48, p. 197 and B.K. Gururaja Rao, op. cit., 1972, p. 184. That there were economically differentiated communities in the pre-State society has been theoretically formulated and discussed in Sudarshan Seneviratne, op. cit., 1981, p. 54; pp. 57-58; Rajan Gurukkal, 'Forms of Production and Forces of Change in Ancient Tamil Country', *Studies in History* (new series), vol. 5, no. 2, 1989, pp.159-160.

80. Op. cit., 1987, pp. 13-16.

81. B. D. Chattopadhyaya, op. cit., 1987, p. 729.

82. 'Coins from Archaeological Excavations in Deccan' paper presented and circulated at the *Colloquium on South Indian Archaeology*, Birla Archaeological and Cultural Research Institute, Hyderabad, January 10-21, 1990, pp. 237-310.

83. Ibid., pp. 305.

84. Ibid., 306.

85. V.V. Krishnasastry, op. cit., 1983, Part II of the book is notably divided into two chapters : Chapter III The Neolithic Period and Chapter IV The Megalithic Period.
86. Thakur Raja Ram Singh, 'Prehistoric Sites in Karimnagar Region, Andhra Pradesh', *JAAP*, vol. I, no. 2, 1979, pp. 4-9; V.V. Krishnasastry, 'Archaeology in Andhra Pradesh', *DASSI*, Dharwar, 1978, pp. 45-58.
87. V.V. Krishnasastry, op. cit, 1983, p. 22, 24; Aloka Parasher, op. cit., 1991, p. 28; p. 40ff.
88. B. & R. Allchin, op. cit., 1968, p. 267, p. 277.
89. For the present purpose Vidarbha is excluded for discussion. Excavations in this region too were taken up only in the last two decades or so — *IAR*, 1961 — 62, pp. 32-34; S.B. Deo, *Excavations at Takalghat and Khapa 1968-69*, Nagpur, 1970; *Mahurjhari Excavations, 1970-72*, Nagpur, 1973.
90. Op. cit., 1947-48, Maps on Microlith, Megalith and Indo-Roman sites.
91. Clearly visible in the reporting of the *IAR* from 1954-55 to 1959-60; 1973-74; 1974-75.
92. No systematic report of these have so far been published though material remains found here have been discussed in V.V. Krishnasastry, op. cit., 1983 which has been reviewed in *IHR*, vol. XIII, no. i-ii, 1986-87, pp. 183-185.
93. V.V. Krishnasastry, op. cit., 1983, p. 203.
94. Aloka Parasher, op. cit., 1991, pp. 45-46.
95. *IAR*, 1974-75, p. 1. There is no uniform terminology to describe these Stone age cultures and sometimes they are referred to as the Early, Middle and Late Stone Ages.
96. T.R.R. Singh, op. cit., 1979, p. 3.
97. V.V. Krishnasastry, op. cit., 1983, p.123.
98. B. & R. Allchin, op. cit., 1968, p.76.
99. It was first excavated by the Archaeology Department of His Highness the Nizam's Dominion and reported in the *Annual Report*, 1940-41; G. Yazadani, 'Excavations at Kondapur—An Andhra Town (c. 200 B.C. - 200 A.D.)', *ABORI*, vol. XII, pts. iii-iv, 1941, p. 177ff.
100. Allchin, op. cit., 1968, p. 76; Amita Ray, op. cit., 1983, p. 86.
101. V.V. Krishnasastry, op. cit., 1978, pp. 47-50; Thakur Raja Ram Singh, op. cit., 1979, pp. 1-10 and 'Living Conditions of Paleolithic Man in Godavari Valley from Basar to Bhadrachalam, A.P., India', *JAAP*, vol. II, no. 1, 1984, p.10; See also — K.N. Prasad and T.R.R. Singh, 'Observations on the Vertebrate Fossils from Karimnagar and Adilabad Districts, A.P.' *JAAP*, vol. II, no. 1, 1984, pp. 59-61 and T.R.R. Singh, 'Some Unique Discoveries in Stone Age Archaeology in Telangana Region, A.P.', *JAAP*, vol. II, no.1, 1984, p. 35. Thakur Raja Ram Singh has personally toured this area and links up the material finds with the geological and ecological factors obtainable in these parts.
102. *IAR*, 1974-75, p.25.
103. V.V. Krishnasastry, op. cit., 1983, p. 22.
104. Ibid., p. 24; p. 35.
105. Ibid., pp. 95-97.
106. K.P. Rao, op. cit., 1988, p. 65.
107. Krishnasastry, op. cit., 1983, p. 124.

108. Ibid., p. 22; p. 50.
109. Ibid., pp. 78-79; p. 103; p. 239.
110. Ibid., p. 27; pp. 129-30.
111. Ibid., pp. 25-26.
112. Ibid., pp. 92-95; pp. 105-106; p. 239.
113. Ibid., p. 125; pp. 127-128; p. 240.
114. Ibid., p.115.
115. *IAR*, 1974-75, pp. 3-4.
116. *IAR*, 1963-64, p. 1; K.P Rao, op. cit., 1988, p. 23.
117. Krishnasastry, op. cit., 1983, pp. 94-97.
118. Ibid., p. 106.
119. Currently serious efforts at understanding the iron ores and technology of "Deccani 'wootz' production" are being made by Thelma Lowe. For details see the following papers by her : (1) 'Refractories in High-Carbon processing : A Preliminary Study of the Deccan Wootz-Making Crucibles' in P. E. McGovern, M. D. Notis (ed.), *Cross-Craft and Cross-Cultural Interaction in Ceramics,* American Ceramic Society, Westerville OH, 1989, pp. 237-251; (2) 'Solidification and the Crucible Processing of Deccan Ancient Steel' in R. Trivedi, J. A. Sekhar, J. Mazumdar (ed.), *Principles of Solidification and Materials Processing*, vol. 2, Oxford and IBH, New Delhi, 1989, pp. 729-739; (3) 'Indian Iron Ores and the Technology of Deccani 'wootz' Production' presented at the Iron Paleometallurgy and Cultures International Symposium. Universite de Technologies de Compiegne a Sevenans, Belfort, November 1-9, 1990, pp. 1-12.
120. Ibid., p. 107.
121. V. V. Krishnasastry, 'Archaeological Discoveries in AP', in B.K. Gururaja Rao (ed.), A *Decade of Archaeological Discoveries in South* India, Dharwar, 1978, p. 74; P. L. Gupta, op. cit., 1990, p. 306 hopes that the publication of the Kotalingala report would reveal much of the knowledge we need of this period and may add to the existing limited information known from the Nevasa excavations. He is of the firm opinion that the origin of the Sātavāhanas lay in the Northern part of the Deccan and not to its Southern or Eastern parts. Pre-Sātavāhana levels from excavation have also been reported in this region from Vadluru in Nizamabad District and Polakonda from Warangal Distirct — Krishnasastry, op. cit., 1983, pp. 129-130.
122. Ibid., p. 94; p.126; p. 244; pp. 218-19; Amita Ray, op. cit., 1983, p. 86. At Peddabankur Black and Red Ware and Red and Coarse Red is also found.
123. Krishnasastry, op. cit., 1983, p. 126; p. 132. Hitherto though the coins collected from here were analysed by Parabrahma Sastry in *JAAP*, Vol. I, 1979, the excavated material has been discussed here for the first time.
124. Krishnasastry, op. cit., 1983, p.126.
125. Ibid., p.125.
126. *IAR*, 1974-75, p. 3; 1975-76, pp. 2-3; 1976-77, pp. 4-5.
127. Krishnasastry, op. cit., 1983, p. 125; pp. 144-145; pp. 225-226.
128. Amita Ray, op. cit., 1983, p. 82.
129. Krishnasastry, op. cit., 1983, p. 125; p.135.
130. Amita Ray, op. cit., 1983, p. 83.
131. Krishnasastry, op. cit., 1983, p. 124.

132. Amita Ray, op. cit., 1983, p. 82.
133. C. Margabandhu, *Archaeology of Sātavāhana Kshatrapa Times*, Delhi, 1985, p. 25.
134. Ibid.
135. Krishnasastry, op. cit., 1983, p. 124.
136. It is significant to note that to its south are located four important megalith sites of Kadambapur, Budigapally, Singapur and Hanumakonda. [MAP III].
137. I.K. Sarma, *Coinage of the Sātavāhana Empire*, New Delhi, 1980, p. 35 — The Sātavāhana coins found here are of the early types.
138. Krishnasastry, *Sātavāhana Seminar Souvenir*, Hyderabad, 1981, p. 4.
139. Krishnasastry op. cit., 1983, pp. 123-124; Yazadani, op. cit., 1941, p. 177; Amita Ray, op. cit., 1983, p. 86; C. Margabandhu, op. cit., 1985, p. 27.
140. Amita Ray, op, cit., 1983, p. 86.
141. Aloka Parasher, op. cit., 1991, pp. 34-35.
142. Sreenivaschar's Introduction in M.G. Dikshit, *Beads from Kondapur*, Hyderabad Archaeological Series, no.16, Hyderabad, 1952, p. 1.
143. G. Yazadani, op. cit., 1941, p. 182.
144. Details discussed in H. Sarkar, op. cit., 1987, p. 5. See also, Aloka Parasher, op. cit., 1991, p. 36; pp. 40-41.
145. Krishnasastry, op. cit., 1983, p. 226.
146. Ibid., pp. 186-88. — seals and sealings with Brahmi characters; pp. 224-225 — mother goddess and evidence for other forms of primitive religion.
147. Ibid., p. 224. The iron figure of the serpent described here has two perforations at the head and one below which are said to represent the two eyes and its mouth.
148. Ibid., pp. 224-225.
149. K. M. Shrimali, *History of Pañcāla, Vol-1 — A Study,* New Delhi, 1983, pp. 27-29; p. 121.
150. Ibid., pp. 119-120; p. 133.
151. Krishnasastry, op. cit., 1983, p. 178; Plate 61. The earliest representation of this in Buddhist art is from Sanchi. It is also potrayed at Amaravati — J. Ph. Vogel, *Indian Serpent - Lore or The Nagas in Hindu Legend and Art*. Varanasi (Rp.), 1972, p. 130.
152. Krishnasastry, op. cit., 1983, Plates 89, 90 — figures of Yakshas.
153. Vogal, op. cit., 1972, p. 43, Plate X opines that these depictions are comparatively late in the development of the cycle of legends surrounding the great decease.
154. Ibid, p. 43; p. 73; p. 95; p. 99; p. 103; p. 109; p. 126; p. 129.
155. Aloka Parasher, op. cit., 1991, pp. 40-44.
156. Thakur Raja Ram Singh, 'The Pre-Sātavāhana Andhra Kings of Central Godavari Valley. The Andhra Kings of Asmaka, Mulaka', *Recent Archaeological Studies in Andhra Pradesh*, Kakatiya University, Warangal, March 1987 (cyclostyled), p. 8.
157. Krishnasastry, op. cit., 1983, p. 126 and p. 132. P. L. Gupta, 'Kotalingala Find of Post-Mauryan Coins', *Numismatic Digest*, vol. II. pt. ii, December 1978, pp. 31-32 does not agree with the view that Chhimuka was the same as Simuka and who should be considered the progenitor of the Sātavāhana family.

158. T.R.R. Singh, op. cit., 1987, p. 8.
159. Parabrahma Sastry, 'Coins of Simuka Sātavāhana Discovered', *JAAP*, vol. I, no. 1, 1979, pp. 136-137.
160. T.R.R. Singh, op. cit., 1983, p. 14.
161. Ibid., p. 3.
162. P. L. Gupta, op. cit., 1978 p. 33 clearly postulates that these rulers should be simply considered local rulers of the Karimnagar region, who like the Kura and Sadakana rulers of other regions of the Deccan, became powerful after the decline of the Mauryas.
163. P. V. Parabrahma Sastry, 'Political System in Early Coastal Andhra', in Devendra Handa (ed.), *Ajaya Śrī, Recent Studies in Indology*, Delhi 1989, pp. 71-72. Parabrahma Sastry writes that "regarding the political activity in Andhra Pradesh during the pre-Sātavāhana period. . . . The information is too meagre to reconstruct any dynastic history." Though this may be true from the point of view of writing traditional dynastic history, for our present concern the above evidence from all the sub-regions of the Deccan throws valuable light on transition from the prelitetate to the literate early historical stage emphasizing on the internal dynamics of the assertion of politico-economic power.
164. Krishnasastry, op. cit., 1983, p. 148.
165. I.K. Sarma, op. cit., 1980, p. 35.
166. Krishnasastry, op. cit., 1983, p. 139.
167. Ibid., p. 200.
168. G. Yazadani, op. cit., 1941, p. 180.
169. 'Kondapur Excavations', *Annual Report*, 1940-41, p. 20.
170. This idea was first elaborated in Aloka Parasher, op. cit., 1991, p. 39ff.
171. Krishnasastry, op. cit., 1978, pp. 1-4; op. cit., 1983, pp. 151-52; pp. 154-65. At the site of Bommareddy Palli an iron slag mound of considerable extent and height was noticed — T.R.R. Singh, op. cit., 1987, p. 4. Dhulikatta Krishnasastry, op. cit., 1983, and Kondapur were famous for terracottas while Kondapur was 'unequalled by any other single site in India' where the largest amount of bead materials have been found in excavation — Dikshit, op. cit., 1952.
172. Maloney, op. cit., 1976, p. 33.
173. Ibid., pp. 21-22; p. 24; p. 33.
174 Ibid., p. 22.

CHART - IA
EARLY HABITATIONAL EVIDENCE — SOUTHERN DECCAN

		Phase I
c. 2300 - *c.* 1800 B.C. STONE Neolithic	Primary Neolithic Phase. Dated by c 14 results from *Utnur	Present at Lower Neolithic of *Piklihal Maski* I, parts of *Brahmagiri* IA
		Phase II
c. 1800 - *c.* 1500 B.C. COPPER Chalcolithic	First metal objects. Dated by c14 results from **Tekkalakota I, Sangankallu I.I and Hallur I (layers 12-14)	Present at upper Neolithic *Piklihal, Brahmagiri* IA and IB *Sangankallu*I.1, *Tekkalakota I* and Hallur IIA (layers 10-11)
		Phase III
c. 1400 - *c.* 1050 B.C. COPPER/BRONZE Chalcolithic	Probably derived its traits from Jorwe phase in Maharashtra	Present at Tekkalakota II and Hallur (layers 8-9). It is very prominent here. Intrusion at *Piklihal, Sangankallu,* I.1, *Brahmagiri* ?
		Phase IV
c. 1020 - *c.* 950 B.C. IRON Megalith	The early opening c14 dates of this phase from Hallur*** Introduction of iron takes place at the close of the Neolithic-Chalcolithic phase.	Earliest phase at *Hallur*(4-7 layers) and *Piklihal* (site VI layer 3).*Brahmagiri, Maski, Sangankallu*

CHART - IB
SEQUENCE OF MATERIAL EVIDENCE — SOUTHERN DECCAN

Site Name		*Cultures*
Piklihal	:	Lower Neolithic and Upper Neolithic — very rich. Intrusion, early iron age, historic period — area of habitation diminishes.
Tekkalakota	:	Microliths, Neolithic with copper objects — regular finds. Chalcolithic. No iron.
Sangankallu	:	Microliths, Neolithic with copper objects — regular finds. Chalcolithic. Early iron age.
Hallur	:	Neolithic with copper objects — well excavated area. Chalcolthic. Early iron age. Historic period — No stratified area of habitation but pottery of the period.
Maski	:	Early Neolithic, Copper objects — Hiatus. Early Iron Age. Historic period — Mauryan inscription, coins, Roman affinities.
Brahmagiri	:	Microliths, early Neolithic, Neolithic with copper objects. Chalcolithic complex — intrusion. Early Iron age. Historic period — Mauryan inscriptions, Roman contact, Fine pottery, few coins.
Chandravalli	:	Transitional phase between early iron age and historical period — Brick structures, Roman influences, Pottery.
Banavasi	:	Historical period — Mauryan? Brick structures, coins.
Vadagaon Madhavpur	:	Historical period — Brick structures coins. Pottery — Red Ware, russet coated painted ware.

* F.R. Allchin, *Neolithic Cattle Keepers of South India,* 1963.

** M.S. Nagaraja Rao, *Stone Age Hill Dwellers of Tekkalakota,* 1965.

*** *Ibid., Protohistoric Cultures of the Tungabhadra Valley,* 1971.

B. Subbarao, *Stone Age Cultures of Bellary,* 1948.

CHART - II

EVIDENCE OF CIVILIZATION — HISTORICAL PERIOD *c.* A.D. 400 — SOUTHERN DECCAN

NAME	LOCALE	EARLY SEQUENCE CENTURIES B.C.	SĀTAVĀHANA CENTURIES A.D.
Brahmagiri[1]	Chitaldurga District 30 miles south of Bellary Town	Microliths, Neolithic-Chalcolithic Iron and Megaliths. Southernmost location of Aśokan Edicts. 3 copies of minor R.E.I. Town Isila is mentioned where a Mahamatra was stationed --*Brick structure* perhaps a Chaitya	Wheeler defines early historic culture 1st century A.D.-3rd century A.D. as 'Andhra' (p. 202) —Fine *pottery* turned on fast wheel rouletted designed ware — Roman contact Russet-coated ware. —*Coins* are rare — very few ascribable to Sātavāhanas. —*Iron* objects, beads of *terracotta,* agate carnelian.
Chandravalli[2]	Chitaldurga District In a valley adjacent to Chitaldurga hill	Probably only occupied from the beginning of the Christian era. The second last layer has pottery of the *transitional phase* between iron age and early historical period.	Krishna is the first to describe the early historic culture here as Sātavāhana (p.17). --On the basis of *pottery* — yellow painted ochre coloured ware — Wheeler has defined 3 phases i.e Early, Middle and Late. i)First yellow painted ware exists along with megaliths ii)soon becomes abundant and iii)diminishes. Rouletted designs - penetration of Roman influences. —*Coins* half a dozen Roman ones. Sātavāhana coins and their feudatories. Coin chronology late centuries B.C. - early centuries A.D. Coin of Tiberius-Roman Emperor. A silver punch-marked coin. —*Brick structure* - Residential. Size of bricks agreeing to those from other Sātavāhana sites. —Glass bangles, use of potters - wheel, Mediterranean amphora.

Maski[3]	Raichur District on the banks of the Maski stream flowing into R. Tungabhadra	Similar with Brahmagiri, Neolithic economy, copper objects Iron. The famous minor R.E. that mentions Aśoka's name. 54 miles S.W. two more Aśokan edicts Amidst a number of ancient gold working sites scattered all over the region	Thapar considers 1st to 3rd century A.D. as the early historical period here. The russet-coated painted ware cannot be called 'Andhra'. —Fast wheel *pottery* in red slipped ware and black and red ware. Varied designs on pottery which is generally sophisticated. Russet coated ware. Rouletted ware of Roman affinity (all dated later) —*Coins,* Iron implements —Rich variety of *beads* in diverse materials *Bangle* industry with those of period III being more developed. Shell and glass bangles with decoration. *Terracottas* — female figurative moulded in round wearing jewellery, hand-moulded parrot.
Piklihal[4]	Raichur District. A village three miles south of Mugal town	Sequence is similar to Maski. Lowest level is a *very rich* Neolithic phase (important). Is within short distance from Maski	The early historical phase here witnesses characteristics of the culture similar to Maski and Brahmagiri. But the area of habitation in small *Not a rich site* and seems to have been abandoned during this period. —Pottery — red, black and black and red wares, russet coated painted ware. —Dated to 1st century A.D.—300 A.D.
Banavasi[5]	North Kanara Dist. On the banks of R. Varada.	Reputed oldest capital town of Karnataka. Flourished in Mauryan times. *Mahāvaṁsa* 4th century A.D. mentioned Vanavasi as an important centre to which Aśoka sent a Buddhist mission.	Early historic phase here is characterized by huge brick structures. The foundation of fort wall equated stratigraphically with Sātvāhana occupation level —Pottery — the red ware, black and red ware, the russet coated painted ware, few sherds of imitated rouletted ware. —Below *Coins* of Sātavāhana kings, a punch-marked coin was found. Soap stone coin mould of the Roman type. No Roman coins. —*Brick structures* - 2

(Contd.)

CHART II *(Contd.)*

NAME	LOCALE	EARLY SEQUENCE CENTURIES B.C.	SĀTAVĀHANA CENTURIES A.D.
			Majestic apsidal structure — one a Buddhist Chaitya? Both show no evidence of foundation. —Beads, bangles of shell and glass in considerable number *Terracottas* — a female figure and torso made of double mould. These are typical of Sātavāhana workmanship elsewhere.
Vadagaon Madhavpur[6]	Belgaum District. A suburb of the city of Belgaum	Reported stone *yupa* inscription in Brahmi assigned palaeographically to 1st century B.C.	A township of the early historic period well laid out town —Pottery — a profusion of red ware, black and red ware in early phase. Russet-coated painted ware. -- *Coins* of the Sātavāhanas and their feudatories found in the cultural phase coeval to structures. On the floor of the 2-roomed house some (2) *punch-marked coins* —*Brick structures* — with several rooms which are probably residential buildings. Also one being an apsidal structure. Roads with hardrammed surface. —A large number of *terracotta* figurines, both human and animal of Sātavāhana type.

1. R.E.M. Wheeler, 'Brahmagiri and Chandravalli — 1947', *Ancient India,* No. 4, 1948.
2. M.H. Krishna, *Excavations at Chandravalli,* Bangalore, 1931, pp.180-310. Wheeler, op.cit, 1948.
3. B.K. Thaper, 'Maski', *Ancient India,* No.13, 1957, pp. 4-143.
4. F.R. Allchin, 'Piklihal Excavations', *Andhra Pradesh Archaeological Series,* No.1, Hyderabad 1961.
5. M.Seshadri, 'Excavations of a Brick Apsidal Temple at Banavasi', *Purātattva,* No.4, *Indian Archaeology, A Review,* 1970-71, pp. 28-29. A.V. Narasimha Murthy, 'Early Brick, Arcitecture in Karnataka', *Archaeological Studies*, vol. IV.
6. A.Sundara, 'Two Thousand Year Old Town and it's Architecture in Vadgaon-Madhavpur (Belgaum) in Karnataka in *Madhu,* 1981, pp. 87-98.

CHART - III A

EARLY HABITATIONAL EVIDENCE -- CENTRAL DECCAN *

	PHASE I
1500-1000 B.C. STONE Neolithic	Stone age known in the region as a whole. Middle and Late *Stone age* sites are well attested. Neolithic present at a few places. Best exemplified at Polakonda. Some evidence at Kadambapur, Kolakonda, Budigapalli and Peddabankur.
ABSENCE OF A CLEAR-CUT NEOLITHIC-CHALCOLITHIC TRADITION AS IN THE SOUTHERN DECCAN	
	PHASE II
1000-500 B.C. IRON Megalith	*Iron age* known from Megaliths at many sites. Several burials at Maulali, Hashmatpet, Kolakonda, Kokapeta, Singapur, Palamakula, Chinna Torruru, Valigonda, Pochampadu. Habitation evidence from Kadambapur, Budigapalli and Peddabankur.
	PHASE III
500-100 B.C. PRE- SĀTAVĀHANA Early Historic	Mainly based on Numismatic data. Typical example of pre-Sātavāhana coins from Kotalingala. Excavations reveal pre-Sātavāhana levels of habitation from Kotalingala, Polakonda and Vadluru. Early phase of *stupa* at Dhulikatta. Kondapur and Peddabankur have several punch-marked coins. Continuity of Neolithic tools in early historical levels at Ped dabankur.

* V. V. Krishnasastry, 'Archaeolgical Discoveries in AP', in (ed.) B. K. Gururaja Rao, *A Decade of Archaeological Studies in South India*, Dharwar, 1978.
V. V. Krishnasastry, *The Proto and Early Historical Cultures of Andhra Pradesh*, Archaeological Series 58, The Government of Andhra Pradesh, Hyderabad, 1983.

CHART - III B
SEQUENCE OF MATERIAL EVIDENCE -- CENTRAL DECCAN*

SITE NAME/LOCALE	CULTURAL PHASES
BUDIGAPALLI Karimnagar Dist.	Neolithic settlement - stone axes, few sherds of handmade grey ware, neolithic celts and microliths. Megalithic phase.
CHINNABANKUR Karimnagar Dist.	Early Historical site of five hectares. BRW Pottery.
DHULIKATTA Karimnagar Dist. (10 km from Peddabankur)	Few microliths, cores, flakes, blades just below a sterile layer of Sātavāhana deposits. Early phase of Stupa. Rich early historical site - mud fort, BRW, Braḥmi label inscription and coins.
HASHMATPET Ranga Reddy Dist. (8 km from Hyderabad)	Megalith site --- BRW, Urn burials, Iron sickle and stirrup.

KADAMBAPUR Karimnagar Dist.	Neolithic settlement. Megalithic burial and habitation site --- iron objects (dagger with copper hilt), BRW, irrigation tanks.
KAPPARAOPET Karimnagar Dist.	Early historic sturcture --- Brahmi label inscription.
KARNAMAMIDI Adilabad Dist.	Early historic site --- 20 hectares. Sātavāhana material. Habitation upto to medieval times in its eastern part.
KOKAPET Ranga Reddy Dist. (10 km N. W. of Hyderabad)	Neolithic-Chalcolithic unburnished grey ware, polished stone axes. Megalithic pit circles. Painting of proto-historic period 1 km from burials.
KOLAKONDA Karimnagar Dist.	Neolithic stone axes. Small Megalithic deposit of habitation --- BRW and neolithic celts. Sātavāhana remains --- postholes but no structures.
KONDAPUR Medak Dist. (70 km from Hyderabad)	Middle and Late Stone Age --- factory site for stone blades and flakes. Introduction of iron. Rich early historical site --- Buddhist structures, Sātavāhana material like coins, iron objects, bricks, beads.
KOTALINGALA Karimnagar Dist.	Largest excavated mound - 50 hectares. Six layers of habitation with some pre-Sātavāhana ones. Rich historical material of Sātavāhana times --- Mud fort, Brahmi inscriptions, Coins.

(Contd.)

CHART - III B *(Contd.)*

SITE NAME/LOCALE	CULTURAL PHASES
MAULALI Ranga Reddy Dist. (8 km from Secundrabad)	Megaliths --- Cairn circles, dolmenoid cists, iron objects, copper/bronze bell.
PEDDABANKUR Karimnagar Dist.	Important Neolithic site --- stone tools, microliths axes. Megalith burials and habitation area with brick structures. Iron tools, weapons and implements. PM Coins. Early historic remains of Sātavāhana times --- several stuctures, wells, cisterns coins.
POLAKONDA Warangal Dist.	Early Neolithic Stage, Late Neolithic stage. Megalith burials and habitation area — irrigation tanks. Early historical site situated to the north of the village --- 3 levels of Pre-Sātavāhana, Sātavāhana and Medieval habitation.
POCHAMPADU Nizamabad Dist.	Microliths. Rich Megalith Burial site. Iron objects, BRW, skeletal remains of horse, iron implements.

* V. V. Krishnasastry, *The Proto and Early Historical Cultures of Andhra Pradesh*, Archaeological Series 58, The Government of Andhra Pradesh, Hyderabad, 1983.
G. Margabandhu, *Archaeology of Sātavāhana-Kshatrapa Times*, Delhi, 1985.
K. P. Rao, *Deccan Megaliths*, Delhi, 1988.

CHART - IV

EVIDENCE OF CIVILIZATION -- HISTORICAL PERIOD -- CENTRAL DECCAN*

SITE NAME	EARLY SEQUENCE CENTURIES B.C.	SĀTAVĀHANA CENTURIES A.D.
DHULTKATTA	Stupa dated to last quater of 3rd century B.C. Mud brick fortifications of pre-Sātavāhana times.	Buddhist *stupa,* Mud-fort with ramparts, Granaries, fragmentary Brahmi inscriptions, Sātavāhana and Roman coins, BRW, iron objects, beads, terracottas.
KONDAPUR	Middle and Late stone age site -- flakes, blades geometric microliths	Early Buddhist structures, Building with underground chambers, cisterns, Brahmi script on storage jar, PM coins, Sātavāhana and Roman coins and coin moulds, Rouletted ware, iron plough-share (?), beads, terracottas.

(Contd.)

CHART - IV *(Contd.)*

SITE NAME	EARLY SEQUENCE CENTURIES B.C.	SĀTAVĀHANA CENTURIES A.D.
KOTALINGALA	Pre-Sātavāhana levels of habitation and coins of the Gopa and Gobhadra kings -- 2nd century B.C.	Mud-Fort, gateways, early Sātavāhana coins, Brahmi label inscriptions, pottery beads, iron slags and ore.
PEDDABANKUR	Neolithic and Megalithic site, Neolithc tools continue in early historical period. Brick structures of pre-Sātavāhana times.	Brick structures called Enclosures, wells, cisterns, Brahmi script on seals, PM coins, Sātavāhana and Roman coins BRW, iron objects-ploughshare (?), archaic terracottas, beads, copper and gold objects.

* V.V. Krishnasastry, 'Archaeological Discoveries in AP', in (ed.) B.K. Gururaja Rao, *A Decade of Archaeological Studies in South India,* Dharwar, 1978. V.V. Krishnasastry, *The Proto and Early Historical Cultures of Andhra Pradesh,* Archaeological Series 58, The Government of Andhra Pradesh, Hyderabad, 1983.

3

SOCIAL AND ECONOMIC TRANSITION
4TH - 7TH CENTURY A.D.[1]

J. KRISHNA PRASAD BABU

In recent years there has been the realization of underlining the importance of socio-economic history as this is understood as providing a base which enables us to discern the changes that have taken place at a broader level of historical change. If the main aim of socio-economic history is to project the totality of the past, the integration of this socio-economic history with political history is imperative.

The period under study can be considered a period of transition from ancient to medieval when several new elements of change were taking place *viz.*, the importance of land grants as a mode of exchange between the state and religious institutions, the growth of landed intermediaries, and the consequent subjection of peasantry and, importantly, the spread of new kinds of settlements. Transition is also discernible in the form of economic and social organization and we intend to take up details of some of these aspects during the course of this paper.

The sources for the period and the region under study are largely in the form of Copper Plate inscriptions. Some archaeological material is also available of which coins form an important segment. No extant literary works are exclusively available for this period and region of study. The total number of inscriptions for this study are sixteen comprising of nine belonging to the main family of the Viṣṇukuṇḍins beginning with the Tummalagudem plates and ending with the Polamuru I plates (Chart V 'A') [Two chronological phases are denoted by the letters 'A' and 'B']. Seven of the inscriptions under study are said to belong to their so called 'feudatories' and successors beginning with the Godavari I plates and ending with

Polamuru II set of plates (Chart V 'B').[2] The reason why one has taken into account the set of charters listed in Chart V 'B' is because they indicate continuing trends of economic and social change which is the primary area of inquiry in the present study. Therefore, we would like to underline that change in political power did not result in a break in the social and economic conditions that prevailed during this period.

The archaeological data for our period of study varies in material remains from small artifactual items to structural remains that have been identified with Viṣṇukuṇḍin layers of habitation. The data relating to Viṣṇukuṇḍin coins is particularly important in this regard. For our study we have taken into account six excavated sites [MAP IV] *viz.*, Keesaragutta[3] (Ranga Reddy district); Yelleswaram[4] (Nalgonda district); Gollathagudi and Gummadam (Mahabubnagar district);[5] Vaddamanu (Guntur district);[6] Nelakondapally (Khammam districtsct);[7] and sites such as Tellakunta (Karimnagar district); Tummalagudem (Nalgonda district)[8] that have come to light from explorations done by the State Department of Archaeology and Museums, Hyderabad. Keesaragutta and Yelleswaram give rich archaeological material in contrast to sites such as Vaddamanu and Nelakondapally which give relatively less material relating to the Viṣṇukuṇḍin layers of habitation. All the above sites, except Vaddamanu, have been excavated by the State Department of Archaeology and Museums of Hyderabad. Vaddamanu has been excavated by the Birla Archaeological and Cultural Research Institute located in Hyderabad. The total number of the Viṣṇukuṇḍin coins so far collected is roughly 2,000. All of them are copper coins. The State Department of Archaeology and Museums has 1,200 copper coins and Birla Archaeological and Cultural Research Institute in Hyderabad has 800 copper coins.[9]

Central and Eastern Deccan, [shaded areas in Map IV] chosen as the main area of study, would coincide with a major part of the State Andhra Pradesh. In terms of geographical boundaries Central Deccan, in the present context, can be said to extend from the confluence of Godavari and Mañjira rivers in the north to the Krishna-Tungabhadra rivers in the South. Eastern Deccan can be said to be the region of the Lower Godavari and Krishna basin. Broadly thus, the area under study in terms of the modern districts of Andhra Pradesh would include those of Srikakulam, Visakhapatnam, East and West Godavari, Krishna, Guntur, Khammam, Nalgonda,

Karimnagar and Mahaboobnagar. Though our study is concerned with socio-economic history of the Central and Eastern Deccan between the fourth and seventh centuries A.D., it nonetheless, becomes imperative to understand the geo-political background of this as a whole region after the end of the Sātavāhana rule in these parts from about A.D. 220 onwards.

The centuries that followed the decline of the Sātavāhanas in the third century A.D., and preceded the rise of the Chalukyas in the sixth century A.D., witnessed the rise and fall of many dynasties in the Deccan. Among them the Viṣṇukuṇḍins occupy a unique position. From the point of view of power and influence exerted on the contemporary politics of the Deccan during the fourth to the seventh centuries A.D., the Viṣṇukuṇḍins, with their nucleus in Central and Eastern Deccan, came next only to the Vākatakas who had their empire in Central India and Northern Deccan.

The Sriparvatiya region which has been identified as the Rishika country of the ancient texts by H.C. Raychauduri[10] has been considered by many scholars to be the Southern part of Telangana, around the middle valley of the river Krishna in the present day districts of Mahabubnagar and Nalgonda.[11] Traditional historiography gives considerable importance to the transfer of this country from one empire to another. Thus, after the fall of the Mauryas, this region is said to have become part of the Sātavāhana empire. Around the 2nd or 1st century B.C. King Khāravela of Kalinga in his Hāthigumpha inscription[12] claims to have threatened the Sātavāhana power here in his second regnal year. Later, the Chutus are said to have continued to rule in this area. Lastly, the Viṣṇukuṇḍins are said to have taken control over this area. In this way the Rishika country was associated with various dynasties. In the Eastern Deccan and the Krishna-Godavari delta region in particular, we find that the political configurations are not easy to fathom during this period. However, it is clear that to the east of the Sriparvata region, prior to the rule of the Viṣṇukuṇḍin, the activity of ruling dynasties such as Bṛhatpālayanas and the Śālaṅkāyanas was confined to the northern part of the river Krishna whereas, those of the Ikṣavākus and the Ānandagotras was confined to Southern part of the river Krishna.

Among the above-mentioned dynasties, from a chronological point of view, the Ikṣavākus were the first to grow powerful in the Krishna-Godavari region after the decline of the Sātavāhana power.[13]

The dominions of the Ikṣavākus extended into the present day Guntur-Nellore districts and Vijayapuri was said to have been their capital.[14] Their contemporaries, the Bṛhatpālayanas ruled over an area which extended up to Kollēru lake in the north and covered the northern half of the present day Guntur district and in the South, Kudura or modern Gudur, was said to have been their capital. Both the dynasties appear to have been subdued by the Pallavas of Kāñchi.[15] With the rise of the Śālaṅkāyanas of Vengi some of the territories of the Bṛhatpālayanas seem to have passed on to them.[16] The Ānandas ruled over the northern part of the Guntur district, *i.e.*, from Kandārapura. Their rule is stated to be between 375 A.D. - A.D. 550. The contemporaries of the Ānandagotras to the north of the Krishna river were the Śālaṅkāyanas. These people ruled over the country lying betwen the two great rivers Godavari in the north and Krishna in the South (A.D. 300 - A.D. 475). Apart from these dynasties the Pallavas ruled the Southern part of the Krishna river from their main centre of power namely, Kāñchi. Whenever, they found the rulers in the Krishna-Godavari delta weak, they overpowered the ruling dynasties and occupied the area. They continued to make attempts to conquer this region during the rule of the Viṣṇukuṇḍins also.

Against the above background, in analyzing the main theme of the present paper, we begin our inquiry by discussing the various theories on the original home of the Viṣṇukuṇḍins their genealogy and their chronology. As early as 1910 Keilhorn had suggested that Vinukonda might have been the capital of the dynasty.[17] H. Krishna Sastri taking into consideration the matrimonial relations of Madhavavarman II of the Viṣṇukuṇḍin family with the Vākatakas, and the find spot of Indrabhattarkavarman's charter near Visakhapatnam has tried to locate Sriparvata in the Visakhapatnam district.[18] Some scholars, like D.C. Sircar, have gone a step further to conclude that the dynasty had its early home in the land South of the river Krishna with their capital at Amaravati. In the light of the fact that such varied views are expressed about the original home of the Viṣṇukuṇḍins it would be best to put forward the most probable view in this regard. Sankarnarayanan's study has tried to do this on the basis of a study of their inscriptions in a chronological order and by emphasizing on a link between the Viṣṇukuṇḍin and the Chutus he has concluded that the earlier Viṣṇukuṇḍin activities were confined to the Sriparvatiya region, *i.e.*, the present day Nalgonda and

Mahabubnagar districts.

Apart from the above indications, the location of some of their early inscriptions *viz.*, the Tummalagudem charters and the distribution of the villages donated by them mentioned in these early inscriptions are all located in present day Nalgonda district of the State. Further, Krishna Sastry's hypothesis that the Viṣṇukuṇḍin capital must be located in this region for which he has suggested Keesaragutta near Hyderabad as the possible place on the basis of archaeological sources,[19] also tends to support the above as the region of their origin and early control. Therefore, on the basis of the present knowledge and the evidence that is available the early hypothesis that the earlier Viṣṇukuṇḍins belonged to the Sriparvatiya region can be accepted.

Regarding their chronology and genealogy also there is no agreement among scholars. In this regard six theories have been put forward which can be divided into two groups: (A) H. Krishna Sastri (1920); K.V. Laxman Rao (1924); D.C. Sircar (1933); K.S. Panchamukhi and K.A.N. Sastry (1936) belong to one group and (B) Sankarnarayanan (1977); Ajay Mitra Sastri(1987) belong to the other group. In our opinion Sankarnarayanan's argument having taken the view of all his predecessors gives the most convincing conclusions on this matter. The first group of scholars had depended upon limited source material whereas Sankarnarayanan has used ten charters and has arranged them in a chronological order (Chart VI) on the basis of their paleography and content. Further, his arguments seem free from unnecessary assumptions. He argues that though the dynasty became an important power under Govindavarman I (A.D. 420), it had a previous history of at least two generations from A.D. 375 and, as mentioned earlier, during this phase they had been confined to the region of Sriparvata.[20]

Govindavarman I started his reign sometime in the twenties of the fifth century A.D. He used his skill, might and energy and carved out a sizable kingdom of his own and continued to follow a policy of expansion by conducting aggressive wars into the territories of the neighbouring chiefs.[21] It is likely that Govindavarman I made matrimonial alliances with the chiefs. He was not only a conqueror but is also described as a righteous ruler and a great builder. According to his inscription he is characterized as *paramadhārmika.*[22] Some scholars depict him as a Buddhist because the charter issued by him belongs to a Buddhist monastery. The next ruler

Madhavavarman II who came to power in the early sixties of the fifth century A.D. took full advantage of the situation in the Central Deccan and declared his aim to extend his kingdom as far as the banks of the Godavari in the north. The Śālaṅkāyana power in the east was on the wane around A.D. 475. Madhavavarman II must have enhanced his prestige by overthrowing the last Śālaṅkāyana ruler and occupied Vengi which was under the latter's control. Thus, the Bay of Bengal came to be the eastern boundary of the Viṣṇukuṇḍin kingdom.

Madhavavarman II's rule ended in 502 A.D. His son Vikramendravarman II who succeeded him issued no charter. Madhavavarman II's grandson Indrabhattarakavarman ruled from 526-27 A.D. In the meanwhile Madhavavarman III who was put as the governor of the Guntur region joined in the expedition of Vākatakas against the Trikutakas and Malayas.[23] The most interesting period in the rule of the Viṣṇukuṇḍins begins with the period identified with the rise of Indrabhattarakavarman, as his records and those of his successors, unanimously credit him with repeated victories in innumerable battles. It seems from these records that by the power and strength of his army he had put down the rebels which comprised of a confederacy of the Gaṅgās, the Prithivimulas (Durjayas) and the Rāmakaśyapas.

The Tummalagudem set II plates recount the details of the reign of Vikramendravarman II. The record notes that the king after crippling the power of the Pallavas returned to Śakrapura and issued the above charter to a Buddhist monastery. His successor Madhavavarman IV was the last ruler of this family. The reasons for, and the period of the end of the Viṣṇukuṇḍin family, still hangs in a mystery. Their rule roughly ended around A.D. 612 when the eastern Chalukyas came to power. In outlining the above political background one can conclude that the Viṣṇukuṇḍins gradually expanded their territorial control from their earlier home in the Sriparvata region to the Vengi country in the east.

Questions pertaining to the political history of the Viṣṇukuṇḍins and their polity are of crucial importance in the discussions to follow. Most of the scholars who have done work on the Viṣṇukuṇḍins have defined the territorial base of their rule as an 'empire' and have thus concluded that theirs was a centralized polity with an administration which was divided into *rāṣtra, deśa* and *viśaya* for convenience.[24] On the other hand, a recent study on the history of Andhradeśa in

MAP-IV

SETTLEMENTS OF THE VISHNUKUNDINS

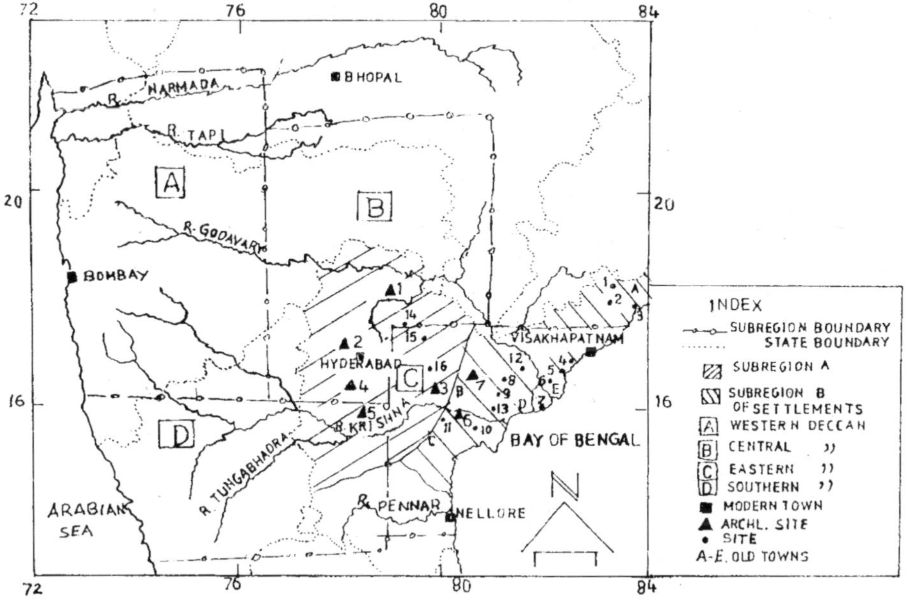

LIST OF SITES IN MAP IV
[SETTLEMENTS OF THE VIṢṆUKUṆḌINS]

EASTERN DECCAN = ZONE 2 on Map

1. PERUVĀTAKA
2. TEKKALI
3. KUDRĀVALI
4. VILĒṀBALI
5. TUNI
6. PULOMBŪRU
7. CHŪYIPĀKA
8. KATTUCHERUVULU
9. TANUKU
10. RĀVIRĒVA
11. VĒLPŪRU
12. MURODYAKALIKI
13. MĀRUTŪRA

PURAS

A. PURĀNISANGAMA
B. DENDULURU
C. CHĀMUPURA
D. PIṢṬAPURA

CENTRAL DECCAN = ZONE 1 on Map

14. PRĒNKARPAṚU
15. ĒRMADĀLA
16. IRUNDOṚO

ARCHAEOLOGICAL SITES

▲ 1. TELLAKUNTA
▲ 2. KEESARAGUTTA
▲ 3. YELLESWARAM
▲ 4. GOLLATHAGUDI
▲ 5. GUMMADAM
▲ 6. VADDAMANU
▲ 7. NELAKONDAPALLI

general by K. Satyanarayana has described the period of Viṣṇukuṇḍin rule as part of a feudal polity.[25] The characterization of the post-Sātavāhana polity stems very much from the varied methodological perspectives adopted by historians as also, how they have viewed the Sātavāhana polity. Many historians have also visualized the Sātavāhana rulers as 'empire-builders' with a centralized polity.[26] However, recent scholarship in the writings of R.S. Sharma has viewed the Sātavāhana period as the beginning of a feudal polity.[27]

A recent article by B.D. Chattopadhyaya points out that the role that the various social groups played in integrating the Sātavāhana polity should be looked at from a different angle. This can only be done if we accept that pre-state formations, before the rise of the Sātavahāna power, were rooted in strong local traditions.[28] These 'localities', as he calls them, were integrated into the pan-Deccan empire of the Sātavāhanas.[29] However, what is significant in his analysis is the point that he visualizes that these local traditions reasserted themselves in the post-Sātavāhana period. The emergence of the Ikṣavākus and the Kādambas in the post-Sātavāhana period may be considered as a 'local' manifestation and continuance of the same process.[30] In other words, Chattopadhyaya's suggestion is that the character of 'localities' which had begun to assert themselves from the second century B.C. itself, continued to be embedded in the Sātavāhana period, and they re-emerged in the post-Sātavāhana period. In a period like the one under study where there was a simultaneous existence of dynasties vying with each other for power, and about each of whom when there is often confused information, the 'empire' concept cannot be legitimately used to characterize the polity of the period. This segmented political picture perhaps can best be understood if we view political change along with the larger process of social and economic change. Among the various dynasties of the period we have chosen to focus on the Viṣṇukuṇḍins who, though they achieved political stability only for a short while, saw a period which set in the forces of economic and ideological change within the larger framework of the processes of historical change. Their political stability may have been only transient but the activities and endeavours through which they attempted to attain an economic stability need to be further studied.

On the basis of the above conclusion it can be suggested that the Viṣṇukuṇḍins, in terms of their territorial expansion, moved from their original home, *i.e.*, modern Mahaboobnagar-Nalgonda region in the west to the Vengi region in the east. In support of this we would like to further suggest on the basis of a study of the archaeological and inscriptional sources that this expansion can be established firmly in terms of the settlement patterns that emerged during this period. Before attempting a study of these settlement patterns it is pertinent to describe the geographical specificities of the two zones described as Central and Eastern Deccan [shaded areas in Map IV] for a better understanding of their spatial distribution. In terms of the geographical boundaries we have broadly divided the region under study into two zones (1) one which is delineated in the north by the confluence of rivers Godavari and Mañjira, in the south by the confluence of the rivers the Krishna and Tungabhadra and which has been called the Central Deccan (2) the other is defined as the Lower Godavari Krishna basin and the coastal belt from Srikakulam in the north to Nellore in the South and which has been called the Eastern Deccan. [MAP IV].

Though these two zones are contiguous to each other, they have distinctive features even in geographical terms which then has an impact on understanding these two units of socio-political and economic study.[31] We shall try and specify below how the historical changes occurred in these two zones during the period of our study, particularly in terms of the shift in settlements as a result of the economic activity based on the granting of lands to religious beneficiaries by the kings.

Central Deccan is largely characterized as a rocky and hilly area and the land here is not considered very fertile. This region can be placed between latitudes of 18.00° and 19.45° and longitudes 77.32° and 80.30°.[32] Though the region is drained by the rivers Godavari and Krishna in their upper reaches and tributaries such as Mañjira, Musi and Dindi, particularly during the dry season, it does not get much water from the flow of these rivers since the entire area slants from west to east. In addition to this, the soils of this area are generally and mainly red earth comprising sandy loams, sandy clay loams, and only in some patches, are the black cotton soils available.[33] The average rainfall of this sub-region today is 711.3 mm. On an average there are 46 to 50 days of rain in a year. The highest temperature is 40°C and minimum 16°C in a year.[34] Such climatic features as less rainfall, high tempratures and edaphic and topographic features as outcrops of granite and the composition of the soil leading to circumstances which are not suitable for the production of paddy cultivation and other wet crops, mark the Central Deccan. However, production of such crops as maize and jowar is possible in these parts. According to archaeologists this zone was the habitation area of largely Palaeolithic[35] and Early Neolithic communities. Even at the Sātavāhana levels of habitation there is no widespread distribution of sites in this region as a whole. There is, however, a large scale concentration of sites in such areas as the present day Karimnagar and Warangal districts where some of them like Peddabankur, Dhulikatta, Kotilingala show important settlements.[36] These are largely due to the pockets of black cotton soils available here and also because these were iron-ore yielding areas.[37] Central Deccan is generally considered very rich in mineral resources. Apart from iron it can be seen that copper is available in Nalgonda district[38]

In contrast to the above, Eastern Deccan is known for its very fertile land from ancient times.[39] The topography of the eastern region is generally characterized by plains. The length of coastal belt is 600 miles. This region is drained largely by Godavari and Krishna deltas. To the northeast it is drained by such rivers as the Suvarnamukhi and the Nagavali.[40] The soils of this area are generally fertile constituted of the black cotton, deltaic alluvial and coastal sandy ones.[41] The soils are the most fertile in this region having been periodically renewed. The average rainfall in these parts is 1.1376 mm. With the maximum temperature being 37.3°C and minimum being 27.7°[42] it enjoys a typical tropical climate with oppressive summer, good rainfall and high humidity. For the above reasons it has been called by Subba Rao as a 'nuclear area of attraction'.[43]

Against this geographical background we now turn to a description of the distribution of sites in these two zones during the period between the fourth to seventh centuries A.D. All the sites where archaeological data for this period has been found namely, Tellakunta, Keesaragutta, Tummalagudem, Nelakondapally, Yelleswaram, Gollathagudi, Gummadam, except Vaddamanu and the Undavalli and Mogalragapuram caves, are located amidst the plateau rocky areas of the Central Deccan. Though this area as a whole does not have good fertile soil two localities *viz.*, the Ramannapeta and the Devarkonda taluks, have been identified with patches of the black cotton soil. [4] In other words, one can suggest that the Yelleswaram settlement which is situated in these taluks has a fertile surrounding. The remaining settlements of the Central Deccan are situated in a topographic and climatic environment which is generally not favourable for agriculture. These factors have inhibited the development of the region in terms of large-scale settlements during the historical period under discussion.

In explaining the existence of the settlements described above, we have to turn to other plausible reasons that made this possible. It has been suggested that during the early historical period the nature of these settlements was determined by the trading and manufacturing activity and the location of these centres on important trade routes.[45] In the period between fourth to seventh centuries the settlements attributed to the Viṣṇukuṇḍins were either political or religious centres as is evident on the basis of palace-like buildings or religious structures found at sites like, Keesaragutta, Yelleswaram *etc.* Only the site of Tellakunta, which was an iron-ore area, can perhaps be designated as a manufacturing centre. The connection between the peculiar nature of the settlements and the particular environment suggests that one has to apply caution in defining the above settlements as full-fledged urban centres as for doing so, the contextual situation[46] must be taken into account. In an overview of Central Deccan one can conclude that it was not a totally barren landscape and that people in these parts had been able to develop a style of life which cannot of course, be identified in terms of monumental remains found in abundance. It displays, as Subba Rao has suggested for most regions of 'relative isolation', a curious pattern of survival and progress. The reason why Subbarao has coined some of these areas a 'areas of relative isolation'[47] is because they were zones between totally isolated areas and the nuclear fertile areas and therefore, generated communication, migration and habitation which was never absolutely permanent or uniform but reflected the exigencies of the historical situation of the period under study. Except for two inscriptions which are found in Central Deccan almost all the others under consideration have been found in Eastern Deccan during this period.

In Eastern Deccan we intend to describe the settlement pattern based on a study of inscriptional sources only, as here, hardly any archaeological data from sites attributed to the period under consideration has been found. The distribution of the villages *(Grāma)* which have been mentioned in these inscriptions are confined to the present day districts of Srikakulam (3), East Godavari

(6), West Godavari (3), Krishna and Guntur one each [MAP IV]. Two of them, namely, *Ermadāla, Preṇkapaṛu* and *Irundoṛo* are those which can be located in the Central Deccan [MAP IV]. This clearly shows that the land grants mention villages donated largely in the fertile tracts of the coastal belt which has been called by Subba Rao as a 'nuclear area of attraction'. This also probably indicates that a search for new cultivable lands motivated the activities of the Viṣṇukuṇḍin rulers to grant villages in the Eastern Deccan and thereby, control the economic surplus of these lands. It is also interesting to note that the two villages donated in Central Deccan were found in the earliest inscriptions and this was a grant made to a Buddhist monastery (Chart VIII 'A'). On the other hand, all the other subsequent inscriptions indicate that lands were granted to *Brāhmaṇas* (Chart VIII 'A' + 'B') and these have been located in the fertile zones of the Eastern Deccan.

The villages viz., *Peruvātaka, Jijjika, Kudrāvali, Vilēmbali, Murodyakaliki, Tuṇḍi, Pulombūru, Chūyipāka, Kattucheruvulu, Tāndivāda, Mārutūra, Regōnṛam, Rāvirēva, Vēlpūru, Prēnkapaṛu, Ērmadāla* [MAP IV] mentioned in the inscriptions indicate that these were settlements of the Viṣṇukuṇḍin period. Apart from these *grāmas* some other places and locality names such as *purās, viṣayas* and *nagaras* are also noted in the inscriptions (Details in Chart VII). This differentiation indicates that apart from village settlements some towns and military camps were also known to be located in the Eastern Deccan. These were further placed in larger territorial units called *viṣayas* and *deśas* in the inscriptions.

An analysis of the inscriptional data reveals that in the Eastern Deccan the various types of settlements during the fourth to seventh century A.D. tend to reflect a contemporary concern to contrast villages with towns as two ends of the spectrum of a settlement. These settlements can be deduced on the basis of the various terms used to describe them as:-

Village grāma is mentioned in all the inscriptions under study.

Military Camp is mentioned *five* times. It is significant to note that these camps were either in the *purā* areas or in the *nagara* areas Chart VII, nos. 5, 6, 13) and sometimes in the *vāda* areas (Chart VII, nos. 3, 9).

Vāda/Vātika is mentioned *three* times (Chart VII, nos. 3, 9, 14) and denotes an enclosure of a village consisting of boundaries of trees. It can be taken to mean a village.[48]

Purā is mentioned *nine* times (Chart VII, nos. 4, 5, 6, 7, 8, 10, 11, 12, 14). It commonly denotes a town. These types of settlements can be seen in Vākataka inscriptions as well.[49]

Nagara is mentioned only *twice* (Chart VII, nos. 3, 13), to mean a city.

Viṣaya is mentioned *seven* times (Chart VII, nos. 3, 6, 8, 9, 12, 13).

An analysis of these settlements can be done against the background of the current controversy about the nature of towns during the early medieval period. Almost all the scholars agree with Sharma's hypothesis that there was a decline of the early historical urbanization (which is said to have reached a climax around 300 A.D.),[50] but, that there was no total disappearance of towns. However, scholars argue that in the post sixth century A.D. period the town or urban settlement re-emerged under a different economic situation.[51] In the light of the above discussion on the nature of urban centres we can use some of the evidence from archaeological sites located in the Central Deccan to draw conclusions in the present study.

These sites yield either religious structures or palace-like buildings. For instance, the Yelleswaram excavation defines the religious structures and the Keeseragutta excavation defines both religious structures and buildings that have been identified as palace-like structures. This temple building activity seems to indicate that there was a transition from the earlier emphasis on Buddhist structures in many parts of Andhra to the emergence of Brahmanical temples. Buddhist settlements do not totally disappear. However, there is a clear tilt towards the Brahmanical religion during this period. Other structures like votive tanks, shrines, remnants of drainage system can also be seen in the Keesaragutta excavations. [Summarized from the two reports cited in notes 3 and 4]. V.K. Thakur points out that the temple building activity was aided by the emergence of certain religious beliefs and this, in a way, tended to provide the very ideological sustenance to the feudal system itself.[52] In describing the social background of terracotta art between 300-600 A.D. Devanagana Desai also gives suggestions as to how this art seems to have been prepared under feudal patronage.[53] In other words, one could suggest that it was the transformation in the societal power structure which led to a significant alteration in the constitution of the patron class of art under feudalism. Thus, it can be suggested that the joint efforts of the artisans like potters and carpenters in making the temple decorations with large figures and plaques functioned under feudal patronage. Similarly, in the iron manufacturing areas metal smiths probably catered to the military and political set-up of the times. An iron manufacturing area has been identified by P.V.P. Sastry in the Guntur region. He points out that this region between fourth to seventh centuries A.D. was an area for manufacturing armours and these were most probably sold on a commercial basis to other regions.[54]

While drawing upon the inscriptional sources in discussing the settlements of the Eastern Deccan we need to point out, on the basis of B.D. Chattopadhyaya's[55] suggestions, that in methodological terms settlements can be identified on the basis of their suffixes and classified into various categories. Adopting this method we find 24 villages, 9 towns, 2 cities in this region and 3 villages and one town in the Central Deccan. The largest concentration of villages mentioned in the inscriptions under study are found located in the East Godavari district (see Chart VII). In this district nearly 10 villages surrounded by *purās* like Chāmupura, Dantapura can be identified (Chart VII) [MAP IV]. Next, in Srikakulam district we have three villages surrounded by *purās* like Piṣṭapura, Purānisangama, Mangalapura and Kudūrapura (Chart VII) which are situated at some distance from the above mentioned villages. Chāmupura (Chart VII, no. 11) has been identified by Sankarnarayanan as 'fortress with a division of the army'. He gives an explanation for this in breaking it up into *chāmu* which in the Sanskrit language means 'an army' and *pura* which is understood in the sense of a 'city'.[56] Thus, most of the above settlements as 'towns' or 'cities' in both zones can be noted as either weapon manufacturing areas or what is generally understood as 'military camps'.

The existence of trade in the period under study can be suggested on the basis of coins found at Keesaragutta, Yelleswaram, Nelakondapally in Central Deccan and Dharanikota, Sattenapalli, Sankaram[57] in Eastern Deccan. This indicates some sort of trade but when one identifies it with the nature of material remains found, one can suggest that it was mainly due to supply of luxury and military goods to the royalty and feudal elite.

In an overview of this description we can say that in the region under study settlement patterns need to be understood in their contextual sense. We may postulate that a minimal amount of trade is evident from the availability of the Viṣṇukuṇḍin coinage. It is interesting to note that at about the same time the Vākatakas who ruled northern Deccan did not strike any coins of their own.[58] The settlement patterns in Central Deccan were thus probably nurtured by some volume of trade being located as they were in an area of communications. The settlements in the Eastern Deccan, on the other hand, have to be understood in the context of the nature of the agrarian economy that had emerged during this period which we turn to examine next.

In order to assert their control in the new localities namely, the fertile zones of coastal regions, the Viṣṇukuṇḍin rulers made effective use of the traditionally sanctioned mode of granting lands which thus enabled them to strengthen their economic base in the new regions, particularly of the fertile coastal belt, of the Eastern Deccan. As noted above their original homeland can most probably be identified in the Central Deccan. R.S. Sharma has pointed out for India as a whole, that the main motive behind giving land grants was economic and, therefore, an analysis of these can help us understand the problems relating to the ownership of land, agrarian relations of production, the tax system, the position of peasantry *etc.*, in early India.[59]

A significant point that has emerged in the present study is that the majority of the donations that were made comprised of villages and not pieces of land (Chart VIII 'A' & 'B' column 5). The transaction of all these grants was mainly between the kings and *brāhmaṇas*(Chart VIII 'A', column 4, nos. 2, 3, 4, 5, 8, 9 . . .) and in a few cases, between the king and the Buddhist monasteries (Chart VIII 'A', column 4, nos. 1, 7, VIII 'B', no. 11) or temples (Chart VIII 'A', column 4, no. 6). In this way both the *brāhmaṇas* and the religious institutions emerged as powerful landed intermediaries between the king and the people. However, it must be stated that their interests coincided with those of the kings and during this early period, it is difficult to suggest that they were able to establish independent local spheres of power totally free from the king's control.

The economic privileges in the Viṣṇukuṇḍin inscriptions, in the majority of the cases, mention general phrases like *Sarvva bādha parihāreṇa, Sarvva parihāreṇa, Sarvva kara parihāreṇa, Sarvva kara bhara vimukta* and do not specify the exemptions granted to the donees as is done in inscriptions of other contemporaries like the Vākatakas and Pallavas (Chart VIII 'A' & 'B', column no. 6). To elucidate the wider ramifications of the land grant system and its operation we shall take up each of these and exemptions specified in one or two donations made by them (Chart VIII 'A', no. 1). The grant made by king Govindavarman I to a Buddhist monastery mentions the term *kara*. In this situation one can suggest that the use of such a general term definitely implies that the donee could collect a variety of taxes from the peasantry. On the whole, the grants do not specify to the kind of taxes that were required to be paid, the amount of taxes that was to be levied and so on. Therefore, this indicates the possibility that the donee had the freedom to extract as much as he wished to and how he wished to do so. This was naturally in the donee's favour as when the production increased the demands on the peasantry could be freely exercised.

There is also the use of the terms *bhāga* and *bhoga* in the same inscription to indicate the transfer of fiscal rights to the donee (Chart VIII 'A', no. 1). In the inscription of Govindavarman I both these terms are mentioned as a mode of payment. The transfer of the right to collect *bhāga* and *bhoga* had serious implications. Having accepted that *bhāga* generally denotes 'royal share of the produce',[60] it becomes clear that in the grants of this period the king transferred this right to the donee. It can be presumed that the ordinary peasants of the granted villages, in this case, *Ērmadāla*, *Preṇkāpaṛu* were responsible for the payment of *bhāga* and *bhoga*. R.S. Sharma has pertinently pointed out that in the case of such payments the beneficiaries may have insisted on having certain types of produce for their own particular consumption and with all the 'seigniorial' rights that they possessed they could compel the peasants to produce those cereals which they most needed.[61] Moreover, the people of the two villages had to supply the daily needs which were required by the monks. In other words, the transfer of the rights on *bhāga* and *bhoga* to the beneficiaries adversely affected peasants' rights on producing the crops which they really needed.

It has been noted in studies on ancient and early medieval India that an important item of the kings' income was the right to forced labour.[62] This became a well accepted means of controlling the peasantry. Forced labour was unpaid labour service with an element of compulsion and was probably common in monasteries which needed extensive labour services for getting lands cultivated. In addition to this, the inscription informs us that king Govindavarman I gave away thousands of girls, male and female servants for the repairs of tanks, buildings of the monastery.[63] In this context, R.S. Sharma has drawn our attention to Fahsien's comments that monasteries built for the monks around the seventh century A.D. were furnished with houses, gardens and fields and supplied with husbandmen and were also given cattle to cultivate them.[64] This suggests that *Viṣṭi* was used for activities such as repairs of tanks and buildings. Once this right was transferred to the beneficiary through a land grant, it marked the beginning of an important feudal practice. Though this is not mentioned many times in the inscriptions under study, in ultimate analysis, it can be said that the execution of forced labour undoubtedly made the monastery a powerful force in the rural setting at the cost of both the dominant and ordinary peasant in these granted villages who, on the other hand, gradually become both economically and socially deprived.

Early Indian sources often refer to mines as an important item of royal income. This income was also transferred by the kings to the donees in the early medieval period. The Tummalagudem plates of Govindavarman I authorized the beneficiary to enjoy all that is hidden under the earth. For this the grant refers to the term *sanidhi-s-opanidhi* (Chart VIII 'A', column, 6 no.1). Sharma is of the opinion that there was no sense in specifying these resources of the villages in the inscriptions unless the idea was to place them at the disposal of the donees. In the above mentioned inscription hidden treasures of the donated villages *Ērmadāla*, *Preṇkāpaṛu* have been referred to. These villages have been identified to be located in the present day district of Nalgonda which according to the archaeologists of the BACRI was an iron minting area.[65] Once this exclusive control over the iron and other types of mines passed into the hands of the beneficiaries they could also control the supply of agricultural implements to the peasants.[66] Other transferred villages *viz.*, *Retturaka*, *Rāvirēva*, *Polamuru*, (Chart VIII 'A', Nos. 3, 6, 9) with their natural resources most certainly helped the beneficiaries to increase their superior rights in land. Such provisions connected agrarian produce directly to the beneficiaries and more importantly, transferred almost all communal agrarian resources to him. In this context, Sharma points out that if a peasant did not have free access to various agrarian resources his autonomy in production was substantially crippled. Only a free exercise of the agrarian rights mentioned above could make his unit effective in production.[67]

An important administrative power which was given to the

beneficiaries was the right to punish the people i.e., *sadaṇḍa* (Chart IX, no.1 column 5) which effectively resulted in exercising their general control over the means of production. Sharma, however, explains that the grants of the fifth century A.D. show that the ruler generally retained the right to punish the thieves.[68] In our study on the other hand, the first inscription of Govindavarman I (Chart VIII 'A') dated to around 375 A.D. explicitly authorizes the monastery, which is the beneficiary in this case, to punish the people. In this situation one can suppose that this right must have been used effectively for demanding the payment of taxes from the peasants in the villages granted. It further also implies general control over the labour of the peasants which was undoubtedly an essential element in the means of production.

The Ramatirtham plates (Chart IX, no. 5) is the one inscription which mentions clearly that the people of the village were to carry out the orders of the beneficiary.[69] Rai interprets this carrying out the orders of the beneficiary as an indication of obeying the commands of the donees.[70] The economic and administrative privileges became further sanctified and acceptable because all the grants (Chart IX) contained certain religious clauses. The common stanza in all the inscriptions is :

"Yasya yasya yadā bhūmis-tasya tadā phalaṁ
sva dattām paradattam vā yo hareta vasundharam
Shaṣṭhim vārshe sahasrāṇi narake pachyate-dhruvam"

In fact, these can be considered a kind of protection for the perpetration of both the economic and administrative privileges to the donees. Therefore, all the grants with their religious sanctions we^re trying to control the people of their respective villages through emphasizing the religious ideology.

In analyzing some of the above explicitly stated privileges and disabilities of the different social groups certain implicit implications emerge which can be said to directly the result of the former. With an increase and spread of the land grant system the powers of the king began to be eroded in both political, judicial and economic terms. This erosion of the king's individual control over the segments of land or villages did not mean that the state powers disappeared. They were now exerted through a class of people that had emerged as landed intermediaries.[71]

In the inscriptions that have survived, as specified in Chart VIII 'A' & 'B', twelve *brāhmaṇas* emerged as landed intermediaries. Among the *brāhmaṇa* intermediaries some had migrated from other areas to receive land grants as is indicated by the Tundi land grant (Chart VII, no. 8). In this case the donee Śiva Śarman was a resident of the locality of Aki which has been identified as Akividu[72] of Bhimavaram Taluk in West Godavari district and he was given the village of Tundi of Tuni taluk located in East Godavari district.[73] This in turn, had an important implicit impact on the existing ownership rights of peasants in the village community as a whole. It led to the disturbance of particularly the dominant traditional rights over the land in the donated areas. A considerable amount of historiographical literature[74] has emerged on the subject of ownership rights in land and it is now largely concluded that it is not absolute ownership that has to be identified in the ancient records, but rather, multiple land rights co-existing on the same piece of land. Therefore, one should not be confused and consider that the royal ownership was opposed to the individual rights. In fact, the former should be considered to have certain kinds of superior rights which enabled him to grant the land in the first place. In the same way, the landed intermediaries also did not enjoy absolute ownership of land but enjoyed superior rights at the cost of the individual owner. It was the individual peasant family that was worst affected by the creation of the new rights in land which had resulted by the transfer of king's rights to the intermediaries. For example, the Tummalagudem inscription of Govindavarman I refers to the Buddhist monastery with economic, political and judicial rights over the two villages viz., *Ērmadāla* and *Preṇkāpaṛu*. In this way there emerged a heterogeneous strata of dependent peasantry.

Provisions such as *sadaṇḍa* and *viṣṭi* were said to carry out the orders of the beneficiary indicating that the people of the concerned villages, namely *Ērmadāla*, *Preṇkāpaṛu*, *Peruvātaka* (Charts VIII & IX, nos 1 & 5) were made totally subject to the beneficiary. In other villages, not specifically mentioned to be effected by the above, people began to get gradually over-burdened with taxes because it was now in the hands of the beneficiaries to decide the quantum of taxes to be levied. The concomitant increase in the rights and privileges of the donees was further intensified because of the religious sanctions which affected the subservience of the peasantry in whom the ideology was so internalized that it made any protest ineffective. (Chart IX).

From the political point of view these land grants were important in that their settlement in the form of the new *agrahāra* villages was created in some cases to be located in the border areas of the kingdom. These *agrahāras* were bestowed with instructions that did not permit the entry of outsiders and so in a way, they acted as a protection for the kingdom. In addition to this in the *agrahāra* villages it was the primary duty of the *brāhmaṇas* to spread Vedic teachings through which control over the people could be exerted. Thus, political expansion in new zones of the coastal areas was strengthened effectively by the grant of lands which enhanced the religious and economic privileges of some sections of society, who then became the effective social base of the newly emerging political elites.

In an overview of this study we can conclude that a spatial shift of Viṣṇukuṇḍin power may be suggested from the upland regions of the Central Deccan to the Eastern Deccan. If one accepts the suggestion of V.V. Krishna Sastry that Keesaragutta can be identified as the capital city of the Viṣṇukuṇḍins and that their original nucleus of power lay in Telangana part of the present day Andhra Pradesh, then the concern of these rulers to grant villages in the more fertile areas of the Krishna-Godavari basin can be well appreciated. Apart from this, we can also see that there was an ideological shift in the patronage given by the Viṣṇukuṇḍin rulers. As has been discussed by us above in the areas of their original home land, on the basis of two of their earlier inscriptions, and structural evidences,[75] their patronage of Buddhist monasteries can be deduced. Later, when they expanded their kingdom towards eastern side, *i.e.* the Vengi region, there was an increasing support to the Brahmanical religion.[76] It was mainly to strengthen their economic base and to establish an effective control over the agricultural surplus of these new regions that the land grant system was carried forward by these rulers so effectively. This practice had begun in the Deccan with the Sātavāhanas. However, a major line of departure and conscious concern that had emerged in this period was that it now began to be effectively used, not simply for religious patronage, but also as a means of achieving political, economic and social control of new regions and people.

NOTES

1. This article is based on my M.Phil thesis (unpublished) approved for degree by the University of Hyderabad in 1989. I am grateful to Dr. Aloka Parasher who helped me to give final shape to this article.
2. All the texts and translations of these inscriptions are available from such journals as *Epigraphica Indica; Epigraphica Andhrica; Bharati* (Telugu) *Andhra Pradesh Government Archaeological Series; Journal of Andhra Historical Research Society* and the *Journal of Bombay Branch of the Royal Asiatic Society.*
3. V.V. Krishna Sastry, 'Excavation at Keesaragutta', *Annual Report of the Department of Archaeology and Museums*, Hyderabad 1981-82, pp. 12-27.
4. Abdul Waheed Khan, *A Monograph on Yelleswaram Excavations*, Archaeological Series no. 14, Hyderabad, 1963, pp. 16-48.
5. K. Rama Mohan Rao, *Early Dynasties of Āndhradeśa from the fall of Sātavāhanas to the Rise of Eastern Chalukyas*, unpublished Ph.D. thesis, Karnatak University, 1981.
6. 'Excavation at Vaddamanu, Guntur District', *IAR*, 1981-82; 82-83; 84-85 pp.4; p.4; p.3.
7. N.R.V. Prasad, 'Nelakondapalle Excavation', *ARDAM*, Hyderabad, 1977-78.
8. K. Rama Mohan Rao, op. cit., 1981.
9. Personal information from State Department of Archaeology --1,200 coins and BACRI -- 800 coin collection which makes a total of 2,000 coins.
10. H.C. Raychauduri, *Political History of Ancient India* (7th edition), Calcutta, 1970, p. 602 (First edition 1923).
11. D.C. Sircar, *Studies in the Geography of Ancient and Medieval India*, Delhi, 1971, p. 31.
12. R.C. Majumdar (ed.), *The Classical Age*, vol. III, Bombay, 1954, p. 93.
13. D.C. Sircar, *Successors of the Sātavāhanas in the Lower Deccan*, Calcutta, 1939, p. 14.
14. Ibid., p. 14.
15. G. Sambasiva Rao, 'Pallava rule over the Guntur District', *JAHRS*, vol. 29, 1963-64, p. 73.
16. M. Rama Rao, 'Successors of the Sātavāhanas', *JIH*, vol.XL, pt. iii, Dec. 1962, p. 560.
17. *EI*, vol. IV, p. 195.
18. As mentioned in Sankarnarayanan, *Viṣṇukuṇḍins and Their Times*, Delhi, 1977, p. 18.
19. V.V. Krishna Sastry, 'Keesaragutta – A capital of Visnukundins', *JAAP*, vol. I, no.1, 1979, p. 103.
20. S. Sankarnarayanan, op. cit., 1977, p. 5.
21. *EA*, vol. II, p. 9, LL. 4-6.
22. *EI*, vol. XVII, p. 334, LL. 2-3.
23. S. Sankarnarayanan, op. cit., 1977, p. 63.
24. Ibid., pp. 130-136.
25. K. Satyanarayana, *Andhrula Samskriti – Charitra*, vol.1, (Telugu) Hyderabad, 1981, p. 156.

26. K.A.N. Sastri, *A History of South India*, (4th edition) Madras, 1987, p. 92 (First edition, 1955).
27. R.S. Sharma, *Indian Feudalism (c. 300-1200 A.D.)* (2nd edition) Delhi, 1980, p. 22 (First published 1965).
28. B.D. Chattopadhyaya, 'Transition of the Deccan in Early Historical Phase' in B.M. Pande & B.D. Chattopadhyaya (ed.), *Archaeology and History*, Delhi, 1987, p. 730; D. Nagamani, *Material Culture and Social Formation in Early Deccan*, Unpublished M.Phil Dissertation, University of Hyderabad, 1990, Chapter III.
29. Ibid., p. 728.
30. Ibid., p. 730.
31. B. Subba Rao, *The Personality of India Pre and Pro-historic Foundation of India and Pakistan*, Baroda, 1958, p. 21.
32. V.V. Krishna Sastry, *The Proto and Early Historical Cultures of Andhra Pradesh*, Hyderabad, 1983, p. 1.
33. Ibid., p. 3.
34. Ibid., p. 4.
35. Bridget and Raymond Allchin, *The Rise of Civilisation in India & Pakistan*, Delhi, 1983, p. 22. The Deccan plateau is predominant in its physical features of hills which favoured the Palaeolithic settlements and whenever the hills contained suitable caves or rock shelters these were used for habitation and often enlarged by the construction of a levelled stone terrace in front of them.
36. V.V. Krishna Sastry, op. cit., 1983, pp. 123-126. Their details discussed in Aloka Parasher, 'Social Structure and Economy of Settlements in the Central Deccan (200 B.C. - 200 A.D.)' in Indu Banga (ed.), *The City in Indian History*, Delhi, 1991, pp. 19-46.
37. *The Andhra Pradesh District Gazetteer*, Nalgonda, 1974, p. 9.
38. Ibid., p. 11.
39. Amita Ray, *Life and Art of Early Andhradeśa*, Delhi, 1983, pp. 15-16.
40. *The Andhra Pradesh District Gazetteer*, Srikakulam, 1979, p. 3.
41. *The Andhra Pradesh District Gazetteer*, East Godavari, West Godavari, Krishna, Guntur, 1973, 1974, pp. 69, 75, 15.
42. Ibid., p. 15, 24, 30.
43. B. Subba Rao, op. cit., 1958, p. 28.
44. *The Andhra Pradesh District Gazetteer*, Nalgonda, 1974, p. 23.
45. H.P. Ray, *Monastery and Guild (Commerce under the Sātavāhanas)* Delhi, 1986, pp. 144-151. Ray finds that the sites like Kondapur, Dhulikatta *etc.*, participated in the trade activity during the Sātavāhana period.
46. Om Prakash Prasad, 'Trade in the Growth of Towns: A Case Study of Karnataka' (600-1200 A.D.), *PIHC*, 41st Session, Bombay, 1980, p. 154. He has described several towns in Karnataka during the period from the fifth to tenth century A.D. which appeared to have been either administrative or religious centres.
47. B. Subba Rao, op. cit., 1958, p. 126.
48. K.M. Shirmali, *Agrarian Structure in Central India and the Northern Deccan. A Study of Vākataka Inscriptions*, Delhi 1987, p. 12.
49. Ibid., p. 11.

50. R.S. Sharma, *Urban Decay in India* (300-1200 A.D.), Delhi, 1987, pp. 88-101. Here Sharma has made an attempt to add the empirical base to his hypothesis where he takes examples from Andhra Pradesh also.
51. B.D. Chattopadhyaya, 'Trade and Urban Centres in Early Medieval North India', *IHR*, vol. I, no.2, 1974, pp. 215-277.
52. V.K. Thakur, 'Feudal Content of Pālā Art: A Framework for Enquiry', *PIHC*, 48th Session, Goa, 1987, p. 104.
53. Devangana Desai, 'Social Background of Ancient Indian Terracottas (600 B.C. - 600 A.D.)' in Debiprasad Chattopadhyaya (ed.), *History and Society* (Essays in honour of Niharanjan Ray), Calcutta, 1978, p. 161.
54. P.V.P. Sastry, 'Some Urban Centres in Early Medieval India', *JTS*, Vol.1. no.1, April, 1988, Hyderabad, pp. 18-19.
55. B.D. Chattopadhyaya, 'Urban Centres in Early Medieval India: An Overview' in S. Bhattacharya & Romila Thapar (ed.), *Situating Indian History*, Delhi, 1987, pp. 9-33.
56. S. Sankarnarayanan, op. cit., 1977, p. 135.
57. B.D. Chattopadhyaya, *Coins and Currency System in South India*, Delhi, 1978, p. 135
58. K.M. Shirmali, op. cit., 1987, p. 4.
59. R.S. Sharma, *Perspectives in Social and Economic Hisstory of Early India*, (reprint), Delhi, 1983, p. 226.
60. D.C. Sircar, *Indian Epigraphical Glossary*, Delhi, 1966, p. 47.
61. R.S. Sharma, 'How Feudal was Indian Feudalism', *JPS*, vol.12, no. 23 Jan-April, 1985, p. 23.
62. D.N. Jha, *Revenue System in Post-Maurya and Gupta Times*, Calcutta, 1966, p. 66.
63. *IA*, vol. II, 9, LL. 7-8.
64. R.S. Sharma, op. cit., 1980, p. 36.
65. V. Pandit Rao & Gayatri, 'A Study of Visnukundin Coins', *Bulletin of Material Sciences*, Vol. 9, June, 1987, p. 145.
66. R.S. Sharma, op. cit., 1985, p. 24.
67. Ibid., p. 23.
68. R.S. Sharma, op. cit., 1980, p. 3.
69. See Chart IX inscription no. 5.
70. G.K. Rai, *Involuntary Labour in Ancient India*, Allahabad, 1981, p. 183.
71. Raghavendra Vajapayi, 'Brahaspati's Brāhmaṇa Landlords : Their Rights and Privileges', *PIHC*, 37th Session, Calicut, 1976, p. 92.
72. S. Sankarnarayanan, op. cit., 1977, p. 81.
73. Ibid., p. 82.
74. a)V.A. Smith, *Early History of India*, (4th edition), Oxford, 1924, p. 1241, (First Edition 1919). He states that land was a crown property.

    b)K.P. Jayaswal, *Hindu Polity*, (5th Edition), Bangalore, 1978, p. 330 (First published in 1924). He has viewed that land was an individual property.

    c)L. Gopal, *Aspects of History of Agriculture in Ancient India*, Varanasi, 1980, pp. 87-89. He sees land was a common property of both the king and the peasants.

    d)Dharma Kumar, 'Private Property in Asia? The Case of Medieval South India', *CSSH*, vol. 27, no. 2, April, 1985, p. 348. She states that the problem lies in the translation of the English word 'ownership' itself.

e)R.S. Sharma, *op. cit.*, 1980, p. 123. He explains that there existed multiplicity of rights in land; *i.e. svatva* of the king, *svatva* of the intermediary and *svatva* of the tenant (*svatva* means 'rights').

75. See Chart V & VIII – Inscription nos. 1 & 8 in Chart V found in Nalgonda district *i.e.* the Telangana area; nos. 1 & 7 in Chart VIII belong to a Buddhist monastery.

76. From the second ruler of the Viṣṇukuṇḍin family Mādhavavarman II onwards the kings used to do *Aśvamedhas, Agnisthomas* and *Kratus: eg. E.I*, vol. XVII, p. 338, LL. 1-2 says Mādhavavarman III performed the *agnisthoma* and *kratu*.

CHART - V A
THE DISTRIBUTION OF VIṢṆUKUṆḌIN INSCRIPTIONS

Sl. No.	NAME OF THE INSCRIPTION AND DATE	FIND SPOT PLACE	TALUK/ DISTRICT	NO. OF PLATES	SEAL	REFERENCE	REMARKS
1.	TUMMALAGUDEM PLATES I OF GOVINDAVARMAN I 459 A.D.	Tummala-gudem	Ramanapeta (Nalgonda District)	5	a ring with a circular seal bearing the figure of lion	*E.A.*, II pp. 9-13	It is doubted as a forged one. It mentions mainly economic privileges.
2.	VELPURU PILLAR INSCRIPTION OF MADHAVAVARMAN II 495 A.D.	Velpuru	Sattannapalle (Guntur District)	--	--	*E.I.*, XXXVII pp. 128-29	Completely damaged.
3.	IPURU PLATES I OF MADHAVAVARMAN II 499 A.D.	Ipuru	Tenali (Guntur District)	3	a ring with a circular seal	*E.I.*, XVII p. 334	This has Prakrit and local pronunciation.
4.	KHANAPUR PLATES OF MADHAVAVARMAN II 499-502 A.D.	Khanapur	Satara District (MAHA-RASHTRA)	3	The ring and seal are lost	*E.I.*, XXVII pp. 316-17	It is doubted as a forged one. First plate is missing, second plate broken to some extent. It does not mention any privileges.

5.	IPURU PLATES II OF MADHAVAVARMAN III 510 A.D.	Ipuru	Tenali (Guntur District)	3	--	*E.I.*, XVII p. 338	Writing on the second plate, second side is destroyed.
6.	RAMATIRTHAM PLATES OF INDRAVARMAN 544 A.D.	Ramatir-tham	(Visakha-patnam District)	3	The ring with an oval seal bearing the lion figure	*E.I.*, XII p. 134	--
7.	CHIKKULA PLATES OF VIKRAMENDRAVARMAN II 565 A.D.	Chikkula	Tuni (East Goda-vari District)	5	The ring with a circular seal bearing the lion figure	*E.I.*, IV pp. 196-97	It does not mention economic privileges.
8.	TUMMALAGUDEM PLATES II OF VIKRAMENDRAVARMAN II 566 A.D.	Tummala-gudem	Ramanapeta (Nalgonda District)	5	Not available	*E.A.*, II pp.15-17	This has Prakrit and local pronunciation.
9.	TUNDI PLATES OF VIKRAMENDRAVARMAN II 569 A.D.	Kandula-palem	Tundi (East Godavari District)	5	The ring with a seal bearing the emblem of a standing humped bull	*E.I.*, XXXVI pp.10-12	--
10.	POLAMURU PLATES I OF VIKRAMENDRAVARMAN IV 612 A.D.	Polamuru	Ramachand-rapuram (East Goda-vari District)	4	Seal is missing	*JAHRS*, VI pp.19-21	It is doubted as a forged one.

CHART - V B
INSCRIPTIONS OF VISNUKUNDIN FEUDATORIES AND SUCCESSORS

Sl. No.	NAME OF THE INSCRIPTION AND DATE	FIND SPOT PLACE	TALUK/ DISTRICT	NO.OF PLATES	SEAL	REFERENCE	REMARKS
11.	GODAVARI PLATES I OF PRITHIVIMULA 535 A.D.	--	(Godavari District)	5	A copper ring with a seal that contains on its surface some figures now totally indistinct	*JBBRAS*,XVI pp. 116-117	--
12.	GODAVARI PLATES II OF PRITHIVIMULA	--	(Godavari District)	5	-do-	*APGAS*, No. 6 pp. 241-242	--
13.	JIRJINGI PLATES OF GANGA INDRAVARMAN I 535-37 A.D.	Jirjingi	Tekkali (Srikakulam District)	3	A copper ring. The seal is missing	*E.I.*, XXV p. 286	--
14.	TANDIVADA GRANT OF PRITHIVIMAHARAJA 613 A.D.	--	--	4	Not available	*E.I.*, XXIII pp. 96-97	--

15. GOLLAVALLI GRANT OF PRITHIVIMAHARAJA 616 A.D.	--	--	3	Not available	*E.I.*, XXXV pp. 222-23	--
16. MARUTURA GRANT OF PULAKESI II 616 A.D.	--	--	5	Not available	*APGAS*, No. 6 pp. 36-38	--
17. POLAMURU PLATES II OF THE EASTERN CHALUKYA JAYASIMHA I 634 A.D.	Polamuru	Ramachandra-puram (East Godavari District)	3	A copper ring with an oval shape with a circular seal but emblem is not distinct.	*JAHRS*, IV pp. 74-75	--

CHART - VI
THE GENEALOGY AND CHRONOLOGY OF VISṆUKUṆḌINS

INDRAVARMAN [c.375-400 A.D.]

MADHAVAVARMAN I [c.400-422 A.D.]

GOVINDAVARMAN II [c.422-462 A.D.]

MADHAVARAMAN II [c.462-502 A.D.]

DEVAVARMAN	VIKRAMENDRAVARMAN I [c. 502 - 527 A.D.]	MANCHYANNA BHATTARAKA
MADHAVARAMAN III		

INDRABHATTARAKAVARMAN [c. 527-555 A.D.]	GOVINDAVARMAN II
VIKRAMENDRAVARMAN II [c. 555-572 A.D.]	
	MADHAVAVARMAN IV [c. 564-612 A.D.]

NOTE: This chart is borrowed from S. Sankarnarayanan's book, *The Vishṇukuṇḍis and their Times.*, Delhi 1977.

CHART - VII
TYPES OF SETTLEMENTS BETWEEN
4TH TO 7TH CENTURIES A.D.

Sl. No.	NAME OF THE INSCRIPTION AND DATE	GRĀMA (Village)	VĀDA/ VĀTIKA	PURA (Town)	NAGARA (City)	VIṢAYA (Province)	DĒŚA/ Others	REFERENCE
1.	TUMMALAGUDEM I 459 A.D.	*ĒRMADĀLA PRENKAPAṚU* (Nalgonda District)		--	--	--	--	*E.A.*, II, p.11, L - 23.
2.	VELPURU PILLAR INSCRIPTION 495 A.D.	--	--	--	--	--	*VĒLPŪRU* (Guntur District)	*E.I.*, XXXVII p.128, L - 4.
3.	IPURU I PLATES 499 A.D.	*VILĒMBALI* Velampalem** (Ramchandrapuram Tq) (East Godavari District)	*KUDAVĀDA* Gudivada** (Peddapuram Tq.) (East Godavari District)	--	*TRIVAR NAGARA* Tiruvuru** (Krishna District)	*GUDDĀDI* (East Godavari District)	--	*E.I.*, XVII, p. 334. L - 4; L - 8; L - 9

(Contd.)

CHART - VII *(Contd.)*

Sl. No.	NAME OF THE INSCRIPTION AND DATE	GRĀMA (Village)	VĀDA/ VĀTIKA	PURA (Town)	NAGARA (City)	VIṢAYA (Province)	DĒŚA/ Others	REFERENCE
4.	IPURU II PLATES 510 A.D.	*MURODYA-KAḶIKI*	--	*KUDŪRA-PURA°* Guduru** (Masuli-patnam)	--	--	--	*E.I.*,,XVII, p. 338. L - 1; L - 7.
5.	RAMATIRTHAM PLATES 544 A.D.	*PERUVĀTA-KA* Perumali** (Srikakulam (District)	--	*PURĀNI-SANGAMA* (Palakonda Tq.) Srikakulam District)	--	--	--	*E.I.*,,XII,p.134. L - 1; L - 7.
6.	CHIKKULA PLATES 565 A.D.	*REGONṚAM* Ravirela** *RAVIRELA* (Krishna District)	--	*DENDULŪRU* Denduluru** (West Godavari District)	--	*VATAPTI* (Krishna District)	--	*E.I.*,IV, pp 196-97,L-1; L-19;LL-20-21.
7.	TUMMALAGUDEM II 566 A.D.	*IRUNDORO**	--	*INDRAPURAM*	--	--	--	*E.A.*,II, pp.16-17, L-29; L - 33.

8. TUNDI PLATES 569 A.D.	*TUNDI* Tuni** (East Godavari District) *AKIVĪDU* (West Godavari District)	--	*CHĀMUPURA* (East Godavari District)	--	--	--	*APGAS*, No.8, L - 25; L - 28
9. POLAMURU PLATES I 612 A.D.	*PULOMBŪRU* Polamuru** (East Godavari District)	--	*KUNUPŪRA* Konduru** Sattana- palli Tq. (Guntur District)	--	*KUDDAVĀDI* Guddavadi (East Godavari District)	*KARMMA-* *RASHTRA* (Guntur District)	*JAHRS*, VI, p.19, L-19; L-20;L-24.
10. GODAVARI PLATES I 535 A.D.	*CHŪYI-* *PĀKA** *VILENDI** *RENGUTA** *KARMPAR** *ANUKURANAM**	*KANDĀLI* Tatipaka (East Godavari District)	--	--	*TAḶUPĀKA* Tatipaka** (East Godavari District)	--	*JBBRAS*, XVI, pp.116-117 L-10;LL-22-24.
11. GODAVARI PLATES II	*KATTUCHERU-* *VULU*(East Godavari District) *KONARALA* *GANRU* *PARIYAPAṚU* *TRULPAṚU*	--	*GUNAPĀ-* *ŚAPURA*°	--	*TĀLUPĀKA* Tatipaka** (East Godavari District)	--	*APGAS*, No. 6 p. 242 L - 15; LL - 19-20.

(Contd.)

CHART - VII (*Contd.*)

Sl. No.	NAME OF THE INSCRIPTION AND DATE	GRĀMA (Village)	VĀDA/ VĀTIKA	PURA (Town)	NAGARA (City)	VIṢAYA (Province)	DĒŚA/ Others	REFERENCE
12.	JIRJINGI PLATES 535-37 A.D.	*JIJJIKA*** Jirjingi Tekkali (Srikakulam District)	--	*DANTAPURA*° (East Godavari District)		--	*VONKARA-BHOGA* (Srikakulam District)	*E.I.*, XXV, p.286 L - 1; L - 11.
13.	TANDIVADA PLATES 613 A.D.	*TANDIVADA* Tanuku (East Godavari District) *KONDAMANCHI**	--	*PISHTAPURA*° Pithapuram** (Srikakulam District)	--	*PĀGUNARA* Tanuku (East Godavari District)	--	*E.I.*, XXIII, pp. 96-97 L - 1; L - 8; L - 17.
14.	GOLLAVALLI PLATES 616 A.D.	*GOLLĀVALLI* Gollavalli** Bobbili Tq. (Srikakulam District)	--	--	*VIRAJO-NAGARA* (Orissa)	*RANADU* (Srikakulam District)	--	*E.I.*, XXXV pp. 222-23 L - 1; L - 7.
15.	MARUTURA GRANT 616 A.D.	*MĀRUTŪRU* Tanuku (East Godavari District)	*NATAVĀDA**	*MANGALAPURA* *KUDURAPURA* (Guntur District)	--	--	--	*APGAS*, No.6 p.36 L - 14; L - 31.

Note: *denotes places not identified, **denotes modern identifications, °denotes place of issue. Translation of place names based on *Sabda Ratnakaramu*, A Dictionary of the Telugu Language.

CHART - VIII A
THE ECONOMIC PRIVILEGES IN VIṢṆUKUṆḌIN INSCRIPTIONS

Sl.	NAME OF THE INSCRIPTION AND DATE	ADDRESSED TO	DONEE	VILLAGES GRANTED	ECONOMIC PRIVILIGES GRANTED	REFERENCE
1.	TUMMALAGUDEM PLATES I OF GOVINDAVARMAN I 459 A.D.	--	*ārya-sangham* (Buddhist Monastery)	*Ērmadāla* & *Prēṇkaparu*	a)Collection of Taxes(*kara*) b)Payment of *bhāga* & *bhōga* (*svōchchishṭa bhāga-bhōga*) c)Forced Labour (*Visṭi*) d)Hidden Treasures (*sa-nidhi-sōpa-nidhi*) e)Exemption from all troubles (*sakala parihārau*)	*E.A.*, II. pp.11-13 LL- 23-25.
2.	IPURU PLATES I OF MADHAVAVARMAN II 499 A.D.	*jñān-sarvvān ēvamājñā-payati* (people of the village)	Agni-śarmmaṇē (*Brāhmaṇa*)	*Vilēmbali*	a)Exemptions from taxes and obligations (*sarvva-parihārēṇa*)	*E.I.*, XVII p. 334, L - 10.
3.	KHANAPUR PLATES OF MADHAVAVARMAN II 499-502 A.D.	--	Bālā-svāminē &Kēśava-svāminē (*Brāhmaṇas*)	*Rēṭṭūrakaṁ*	--	*E.I.*, XXVII pp. 316-17

(*Contd.*)

CHART - VIII A *(Contd.)*

Sl.	NAME OF THE INSCRIPTION AND DATE	ADDRESSED TO	DONEE	VILLAGES GRANTED	ECONOMIC PRIVILIGES GRANTED	REFERENCE
4.	IPURU PLATE II OF MADHAVAVARMAN III 510 A.D.	*jñān-evam ājñāpayati* (people of the village)	Agni-śarm-Ēndra śarmma-bhvā *(Brāhmaṇas)*	*Murōdya-kaḷiki*	--	*E.I.,* XVII, p. 338
5*.	RAMATIRTHAM PLATES OF INDRAVARMAN 544 A.D.	*grāma-sama) vētan-kutum binas-samājñā-payati*(house holders of the village	Nagna-śarmmaṇē *(Brāhmaṇa)*	*Peruvātaka*	a) It was made an *agrahāra (agrahārakṛtya)* b)Exemptions from all taxes and burdens *(sarvva kara bhara vipramuktō)* c)People must give customary produce *(yadatra-phalaṁ-uchitaṁ tad-dātavyam)*	*E.I.,* XII p.134 LL 8-10.
6.	CHIKKULLA PLATES OF VIKRAMENDRAVARMAN II 565 A.D.	*evam-ājñā payati* (people of the village)	*Sōmagirē-śvarānāthāya* (Temple)	*Rēgōnran*	—	*E.I.,* IV, pp.196-97

7.	TUMMALAGUDEM PLATES II OF VIKRAMENDRAVARMAN II 566 A.D.	—	*arya-vara-bhikshu samgha* (Buddhist Monastery)	*Irundōro*	a)With all constituents of the gift(*sarva-dāna-sahita*) b)Free from all burdens (*sarva bādha parihārēṇa*)	*E.A.*, II pp.15-17 LL 32-33
8.	TUNDI GRANT OF *VIKRAMENDRAVARMAN* II 569 A.D.	*evam-ājñā payati* (people of the village)	Svāmi-śarm-manē (*Brāhmaṇa*)	*Tūṇḍi*	a)Free from all burdens (*sarva bādhā parihārēna*)	E.I.,*XXXVI* pp.11-12 & *APGAS*, No. 8 L-29.
9*.	POLAMURU PLATES I OF GOVINDAVARMAN IV 612 A.D.	*mahāttarān-adhikārapuru-shām cha imam artham ājñā payati* (officials and Mahāttarān of the village)	Śiva-śarmmanē (*Brāhmaṇa*)	*Pulōṁbūru & Chatur nivartanān nene kshētraṁ* (4 nivartanas of land)	a)Exemption from all taxes (*sarvva - kara - parihārēna*) b)It was made as an *agrahāra* (*agrahārakṛtya*)	*JAHRS*, VI pp.19-21 L - 27

CHART - VIII B
THE ECONOMIC PRIVILEGES IN VISNUKUNDIN FEUDATORIES AND SUCCESSORS INSCRIPTIONS

Sl. No.	NAME OF THE INSCRIPTION AND DATE	ADDRESSED TO	DONEE	VILLAGES GRANTED	ECONOMIC PRIVILIGES GRANTED	REFERENCE
10*.	GODAVARI PLATES I OF PRITHIVIMULA 535 A.D.	*sarvvān-eva rāshṭrakūta pramukhānē-vam ājñāpayati* (rāshṭrakūta officials of the village)	*tri-chatvārim śad-Ātharv-vanika kulibhyō* (43 *brāhmaṇas* of Atharvakula)	*Chūyipākō*	a)It was made an *agrahāra* (*agrahārikṛtya*)	*JBBRAS*, XVI pp.116-117 L-26.
11.	GODAVARI PLATES II OF PRITHIVIMULA	*rāshṭrakūta-grāma vṛddha-pramukha viṣaya nivāsinaḥ sarvvān-itham-ājñāpayati* (elders and rāshṭrakūta officials of the village)	*ārya-vara-bhikshu-*sangha (Buddhist Monastery)	*Kaṭṭucheruvula*	a)Exemptions from taxes and obligations (*sarva-parihārēna*)	*APGAS* No. 6 pp.241-42 L.24.
12*.	JIRJINGI PLATES OF THE GANGA INDRAVARMAN I 535-37 A.D.	*grāma sarvva-samāvētan-kutumbinah-samājñā-payatyasa* (householders of the village)	Agnisvāminē Rudrasvāminē Saṁvibhajya (two equal shares) (*brāhmaṇas*)	*Jijjika*	a)It was made an *agrahāra* (*agrahārikṛtya*) b)Exemption from all taxes (*sarva kara parihārēna*)	*E.I.*, XXV, p. 286 L - 15; L - 17

13*. TANDIVADA GRANT OF PRITHIVIMAHARAHA 613 A.D.	*sarva samāvētan kutuṁbinas-samājñāpayati* (householders of the village)	Bhavaśarmmanē (*Brāhmaṇa*)	Tāndivāda	a) Free from all taxes (*sarva kara parihārēṇa*) b) It was made an *agrahāra* (*agrahārikṛtya*)	*E.I.*, XXIII pp. 96-97 L-20
14*. GOLLAVALLI GRANT OF PRITHIVIMULA 616 A.D.	*sarvva samā-vētan kutuṁ-binaḥ samājñā payati* (householders of the village)	*Padma-śarmmanē* (*brāhmaṇa*)	*Gollāvalli*	a) Free from all taxes (*sarvva kara parihārēṇa*) b) It was made an *agrahāra* (*agrahārikṛtya*)	*E.I.*, XXXV pp.222-23 L-13
15* MARUTURA GRANT OF PULAKESI II 616 A.D.	---	Twelve *brāhmaṇas* and one other caste person *varṇa-traya nivrittaya*	*Mārutūru*	a) An *agrahāra* village (*agrahāra bhōga*)	*APGAS* No. 6 pp.36-38 L - 31.
16* POLAMURU PLATES II OF THE EASTERN CHALUKYA JAYASIMHA I 634 A.D.	*mahāttaram-adhikāra puru-sham-cha ārtham ājñāpayati* (Officials and *mahāttaran* of the village)	Rudra-śarmmanē (*Brāhmaṇa*)	*Pulombūra*	a) An old *agrahāra* renewed (*Purvvagrahārika . . .agrahārh-kṛtya*) b) Free from all taxes (*sarvva kara parihārēna*)	*JAHRS*, IV, pp. 74-75 LL - 19-20.

Note: *denotes an *agrahāra* village.

CHART - IX
THE POLITICO - JUDICIAL AND RELIGIOUS IMPRECATIONS IN VIṢṆUKUṆḌIN INSCRIPTIONS

Sl. No.	NAME OF THE INSCRIPTION AND DATE	AIM	SCRIBE	POLITICO-JUDICIAL PRIVILEGES	RELIGIOUS IMPRECATIONS	REFERENCE
1.	TUMMALAGUDEM PLATES OF GOVINDAVARMAN I 459 A.D.	*māta-pitrōh sarvva-satvanān cha nikhila dāridye dukhō-paśana hētoḥ* (alleviating all miseries of poverty of all beings and his parents the continuity of the roots of merit L - 21	--	a)Right to Punish *(Saḍaṇḍa)* b)Immunity from the entry of royal troops and officials *(chara-bhata-dūta-vallabha-rājapuru-shair-apraveśyau)* LL - 24-25	Merit of giving land accrues to him who possess it, either it was made by him or by others should not be disturbed and one who disturbs it he will go to *naraka* for 60,000 years and one who obeys he will go to *svarga* for 60,000 years. *(Bahubhir-vvasudha datta bahubhis chānupālita Yasya Yasya Yadā bhūmis - tasya tasya tadā phalaṁ Sva-dattām para-dattām vā yō hāreta vasundharam Shashtim varsha sahasrāani svargge vasati bhūmidāḥ achchhetta chānumanta cha tānyeva narake vaset* LL - 29-32	*E.A.*, II pp.11-13
2.	IPURU PLATES I OF MADHAVAVARMAN II 497 A.D.	*asmad-vaṁśa-vibhūtyārttham* (for the sake of the prosperity of his own family) L-10	Manchyanna-bhattarakaḥ L-11	a)Immunity from the entry of royal troops and officials *(sarvva-rājapurushair parihārttavyaḥ pālayitavyas cha LL-10-11*	(Imprecations same as above) LL -12-13	*E.I.*,XVII p.334.

3.	KHANAPUR PLATES OF MADHAVAVARMAN II 497-502 A.D.	---	kayāsthena sripālena L - 31	---	-do- LL - 23-30	*E.I.*,XXVII pp.316-17
4.	IPUR PLATES II OF MADHAVAVARMAN III 510 A.D.	---	Guna-bhartta L - 13	---	-do- LL - 14-16	*E.I.*,XVII p.338
5.	RAMATIRTHAM PLATES OF INDRAVARMAN I 544 A.D.	*sva-puṇy-ābhiphala vriddhaye* (for the increase of the rewards of his own good deeds) L - 7	---	a)People must carry out the orders *(vachana-preshan adikam cha kāryyam sarvvam sadā karttavyām* L - 10	-do- LL - 13-15	*E.I.*,XII p.134
6.	CHIKKULLA PLATES OF VIKRAMENDRAVARMAN II 565 A.D.	---	---	---	- do -(+) Disturbing the grant is equal to *killing a cow, brāhmaṇa (Gavo bhūmi tatha bhāryyas kramya hara ma naya Sravayanti rājānām brahmahatyā cha lipyate* LL - 27-32	*E.I.*,IV
7.	TUMMALAGUDEM PLATES II OF VIKRAMENDRAVARMAN II 566 A.D.	-- Mularajaḥ	Sri- L-45	LL - 38-41	(Imprecations same as above) pp.15-17	*E.A.*, II

(Contd.)

CHART - IX *(Contd.)*

Sl. No.	NAME OF THE INSCRIPTION AND DATE	AIM	SCRIBE	POLITICO-JUDICIAL PRIVILEGES	RELIGIOUS IMPRECATIONS	REFERENCE
8.	TUNDI PLATES OF VIKRAMENDRAVARMAN II 569 A.D.	---	---	---	- do - LL - 33-34	*E.I.*, XXXVI pp. 11-12
9.	POLAMURU PLATES II OF MADHAVAVARMAN IV 612 A.D.	---	---	---	(Imprecations same as Sl.No.1.) LL - 35-40	*JAHRS*,VI pp. 19-21 LL - 35-40
10.	GODAVARI PLATES I OF PRITHIVIMULA 535 A.D.	---	---	---	- do - LL - 27-33	*JBBRAS*,XVI pp.116-117
11.	GODAVARI PLATES II OF PRITHIVIMULA	---	---	---	- do -(+) Disturbing the grant is equal to killing a cow, *brāhmaṇa*, child, sage *(Viggnnatām bhartri-gō-vipra-bāla-youshit-tapasvinaḥ* *Ya gatis sa bhaved-vrittim harataḥ śāsanānkitam* LL - 26-33	*APGAS* No. 6 pp. 241-42
12.	JIRJINGI PLATES OF GANGA INDRAVARMAN I 535-37 A.D.	*sva-puṇyā yuryyaso bala-varddhanartha māta-pitrōscha puṇya-vāpta*	Deva-singha *(sandhi vigrahika)* L-26	---	(Imprecations same as Sl.No.1.) LL - 24-25	*E.I.*, XXV p. 286

	(For the increase of their own family religious merit, king's life, fame strength) L-16				
13. TANDIVADA GRANT OF PRITHIVIMAHARAJA 613 A.D.	*māta-pitri-pādānud-dhyātaḥ* (For the merit of his parents) L - 7	---	---	- do - LL - 24-28	*E.I.*, XXIII pp. 96-97
14. GOLLAVALLI GRANT OF PRITHIVIMAHARAJA 616 A.D.	*māta-pitri-pādānud-dhyātaḥ* (for the merit of his parents) L - 6		---	- do - LL - 19-20	*E.I.*XXXV pp.222-23
15. MARUTURA GRANT OF PULAKESI II 616 A.D.	---	---	---	- do - LL - 34-37	*APGAS* No. 6 pp.36-38
16. POLAMURU PLATES OF THE EASTERN CHALUKYA JAYASIMHA I 634 A.D.	*māta-pitri-Pādānud-dhyātaḥ* (for the merit of his parents) L - 12	---	---	- do - LL - 23-24	*JAHRS*,IV pp. 74-75

4

SOCIAL GROUPS AND ECONOMIC CHANGE 7TH - 13TH CENTURY A.D.[1]

TEJASWINI YARLAGADDA

The early medieval period (a term coined only in recent historiography), in the context of Indian history has been identified as an important phase of socio-economic transition. Fundamental changes occurred in the social, economic, political and ideological spheres during this period. This period in Indian history has generated a potential for research and, in recent times there has been a great spurt of historical writing focusing on the nature of the socio-economic structure of early medieval India.[2] In order to comprehend the complexities of the social formation of this period greater significance is now being attached to analyses which integrate the study of social and economic history with the political and the ideological and also, those that focus on the need to understand the regional specificities of social formations. We have in this regard a few serious attempts by such eminent scholars as R.N. Nandi, M.G.S. Narayanan, Burton Stein, K.M. Shrimali, R. Champakalakshmi, Hermann Kulke, Noboru Karashima, who have enhanced the importance of micro-level studies. All these studies have significant bearing on our understanding of the regional specificities of the complex social relationships in early India which defy any rigid universalization at an all India level and further, go to remind us for the need to penetrate the hitherto historically unresearched regions and bring to light specific structural formations of these regions.

MAP- V

POLITICAL BOUNDARIES OF MAJOR DYNASTIES OF DECCAN 6th 12th CENTURY A.D.

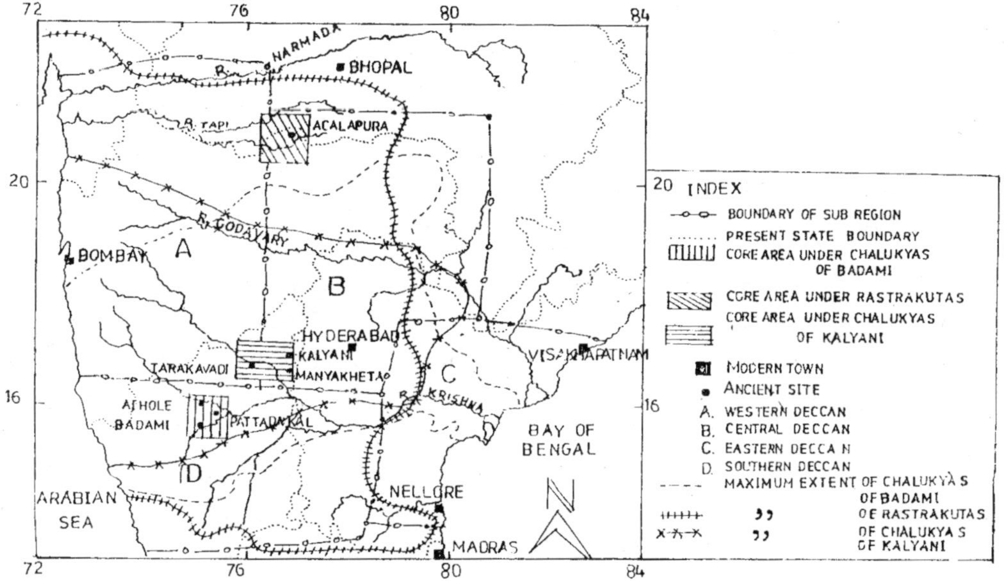

The Western part of the Deccan region, [MAP V] which does not fall under the category of what B. Subba Rao had defined as 'nuclear zones',[3] has not been able to attract enough attention from historians and we still find rather descriptive and compartmentalized versions of the historical formations of the region.[4] As much remains to be done on identifying periods, elements and nature of change in this region, we have made a small attempt at the analysis of the social structure of this region within the overall framework of economic change in the hope that this would initiate further historical research in greater depth at a later stage.

To initiate our understanding of the nature of the socio-economic structure of the early medieval Western Deccan, we have taken up an analysis of the social groups of the region. As the social groups and their relationships are the ultimate expression of the interplay of the existing structural phenomena, their study therefore enjoins an integrative analysis of the economic, political, ideological and the social forces under operation, thus providing us with an effective perspective to comprehend the totality of the historical past. To understand the nature of the social groups under consideration, we have relied upon the inscriptional sources pertaining to the period between 6th century A.D. and 13th century A.D. These inscriptions belong to such dynasties as the Chalukyas of Badami, Rashtrakutas of Malkhed, Chalukyas of Kalyani and their subordinate rulers who ruled over different parts of the Western Deccan during various periods [MAP V]. Inscriptions of the early medieval period are nothing but legal documents recording the dominant economic activity of the time, namely land transactions, and we get to know about the social groups under study through the functions they performed, terms used to describe them, their designations, titles and their *varṇa, gotra*, status wherever available in the context of these land transactions. It would be pertinent to state that we have attempted the study of various social groups of the region not merely in terms of the official capacities in which they are described but also as groups involved in production on a large scale. In this context, we see the emergence of a hierarchically organized structure of the social groups (see Charts X 'A', 'B', & 'C', appended to the essay). The levels of hierarchy are determined chiefly by the hold that these groups had over landed property. We observe at this juncture that those groups that had an access to landed property possessed the privilege of acquiring both the political and ideological control over the numerically large section of those social groups who did not have any control over the means of production and were deprived of any access to landed property. Far from being a homogeneous society, these can be perceivable as two broad categories of social groups with a highly stratified element giving rise to complex social relations of economic interdependence between them, as also within them.

The nature of stratification among various social groups undergoes significant transformation throughout the period of our study. To comprehend not only the dynamic nature of what constitutes social groups over a certain period of time, but also the underlying economic basis for such a change, we have divided our study into three broad phases chiefly on the basis of the changes in the nature and the number of social groups mentioned in the inscriptional sources of the period. The first phase (Three phases denoted by the letters 'A', 'B' and 'C' in the Charts) of our study (Middle of the 6th century A.D. - Middle of the 8th century A.D.) has been considered as a background phase and we have mention of very few social groups operating in the land transactions. This phase, however, becomes crucial for our study as it sets the stages for changes that occur later (Chart - X 'A'). The second phase of our study (Middle of the 8th century A.D. - the latter half of the 10th century A.D.), has been taken up as one of transition in which the mention of social groups relatively speaking, begins to increase in number (Chart - X 'B'). It is chiefly in the third phase (latter half of 10th century A.D. - 13th century A.D.) of our study, that we find numerous social groups picturing in the land transactions of the period, either as directly participating in the dealings or emerging as holders of various shares of the temple property (Chart - X 'C'). Increase of the social base at every subsequent phase of our study is indicative of the changing economic structure of the period. This was, in turn, a direct result of the changing agrarian economy and the growth of temple-centered activities in the context of the proliferation of the land grant economy.

Economic structure of the period under consideration has been postulated to have been dominated by the features of decline in the urban economy of towns, leading to a subsistence economy of agriculture, based largely on rural settlements.[5] In such a situation, a lot of significance began to be attached to landed property as can be attested by the growth in the grants of lands of various measurements found mentioned in the inscriptional sources of the period in the

Western Deccan (Charts XII 'A' 'B' 'C' on economic transactions). These land transactions indicate to us the mechanisms of surplus appropriation and distribution adopted by the privileged sections of the society of the period, and thus form the prime factors in defining the socio-economic set-up of the period. It was in fact the interaction of these material forces with the political and the ideological ones which determined the status of various social groups in the hierarchical social structure of early medieval Western Deccan.

Transfer of lands of various sizes was effective only within a minority section in society which, nonetheless, led to a significant change in the landholding pattern when compared to earlier times and became a crucial factor in determining the hierarchical levels of social organization. The fact that certain sections of society had the ability to grant lands raises the pertinent question of the nature of rights in land that these groups traditionally held. The question of landed rights becomes pertinently significant for our study because it were these rights which were most frequently transferred at the time when the transactions were made and it very rarely involved actual transfer of land itself. The relative nature of these rights held over land determined the status of an individual in the hierarchical social structure of the period.

There has been considerable controversy between the Western scholars writing during the late 19th and the early 20th century on the one hand, and the nationalist historians of India on the other, over the nature of rights in land in pre-British India. Writings of the former, represented by such scholars as Karl Marx and later Vincent Smith, negated the existence of privately owned land in early India as in those times, according to these scholars, all land was owned by the despotic ruler.[6] On the other hand, nationalist scholars such as U.N. Ghoshal, K.P. Jayaswal *etc.* have argued for the existence of a clear notion of the concept of private ownership of land in early India.[7] Attitude of the nationalist writers on the nature of rights held in early India can, however, be best exemplified in the work of A.S. Altekar. As the author of the *History of Village Communities in Western India*, he completely rules out the possibility of any communal holding of land in early India and even goes to the extent of characterizing the early Indian land tenures as those of individual peasant proprietorship with the principles of Ryotwari system present in them.[8] It is from the middle of the 20th century that the writings on early India begin to be written from a diferent perspective by such scholars as D.D. Kosambi[9] and R.S. Sharma.[10] These scholars, adopting the tool of historical materialism, have studied the material basis of the property relations of various periods of early India. Their studies have brought out the fact that not only is there evidence to prove the existence of private property in land, but also, that there were changes in the nature of property relations over the centuries. Thus for instance, they point out that the rights held in land in the early medieval period were not the same as they were earlier in the Vedic and the post-Vedic ages.[11] This was because, the nature of rights held in the landed property began to take shape according to the imperatives imposed by the prevalent economic structure of the time. D.D. Kosambi and R.S. Sharma have dealt largely with the economic structure of Northern and Central India.

In recent times, we have significant contributions being made in terms of understanding the specific nature of the economic patterns of various Southern regions of India. Among these, we have works of such eminent scholars as R.N. Nandi, N. Karashima and Dharma Kumar, who have brought out valuable information regarding the nature of rights held in land in the early medieval period, particularly in the Peninsular region of India. While Dharma Kumar[12] and Karashima[13] have focused chiefly on the extreme South , the work of Nandi focuses chiefly on the Karnataka region.[14] All these scholars attest to the growth of private property in land in the early medieval period at the cost of the previously held communal holdings. Through their respective areas of studies, R.S. Sharma[15] and Dharma Kumar,[16] have brought out the possibility of the existence of a multiplicity[17] of rights in a single landholding in the early medieval period. The specific nature of these rights, however, varied in its content and terminology from region to region. It was chiefly the nature of the multiplicity of rights held over a single plot of land, that actually led to the definition of 'superior' and 'inferior' rights in landed property and formed the basis for the hierarchical relations between various sections of the society.

To comprehend the nature of the rights held in landed property in the context of our study, one has to analyze the nature of the land transactions in the area under consideration. It has been shown for other regions of South India that during this period there were two principal categories of landholdings, namely the beneficial and the non-beneficial holdings. While the former were held by the *brāhmaṇas (brahmadeyas)* and the temples *(devadāna)*, the latter were held by rich peasant communities.[18] While the former category of land rights have been considered private in nature, it has been suggested that the latter or the non-beneficial landholdings paid full taxes and had communal rights over them.[19] Communal rights in the latter case were mostly those of the peasant families as large kin groups located in particular areas. It is chiefly the nature of rights transferred to the donee that goes to determine the exact nature of landholding.

In the first phase of our study, we find that numerous villages were granted predominantly by the chiefs of the main ruling family, termed here as *rāja* (Chart X 'A', ii, 2)[20], *mahi-patir* (Chart X 'A', ii, 4), *mahārāja* (Chart X 'A', ii, 5), and *mahārājadhirāja* (Chart X 'A', ii, 8). In this phase we have the emergence of the social groups belonging to the *brāhmaṇa varṇa* as the chief beneficiaries of the grants. (Chart X 'A', iii). In the second phase, we have alongside the grants made by the chiefs of the main ruling family, a considerable number of lesser chiefs of the State also making such grants (Chart X 'B'). The lesser chiefs are indicated to us through the use of such terms as the *mahāsāmantadhipati* (Chart X 'B', ii, 6), *perggaḍe* (Chart X 'B', ii, 16), *gāvuṇda* (Chart X 'B', ii, 16), *perggāvuṇda* (Chart X 'B', ii, 14) and *rāja* (Chart X 'B', ii, 20) and governors of various provinces whose exact titles have not been specified here. However, they have been noted as ruling over a specific area (Chart X 'B', ii, 11). These groups of donors, however, indulged in making grants of small measurements of lands, goods and tax concessions to the temples and to the *mahājanas* (a locally powerful section of society, usually comprising of *brāhmaṇas*). In the third and final phase of our study, we have a greater number of lesser chiefs (Chart X 'C') emerging as donors and these are indicated to us as the *urodeya* (Chart X 'C', ii, 3), *mahāpraċhṇdadaṇḍanāyakaṁ* (Chart X, 'C', ii, 3), *mahāsāmantanāḷgāvuṇda* (Chart X, 'C', ii, 7), *mahāpradhānaṁ* (Chart X 'C', ii, 7), *pasāyite* (Chart X 'C', ii, 8), *mahāmaṇḍaleśvara* (Chart X 'C', ii, 9), *mahāsandhivigrahādhikāri* (Chart X 'C', ii, 10), *mahāmātya*, (Chart X 'C', ii, 11), *mahāmātya vaḍḍa rāvuḷda perggaḍe* (X 'C', ii, 12), *mahāsāmanta* (Chart X 'C', ii, 14), *mahārāja* (Chart X 'C', ii, 13), *mahāpradhānaṁ piriya perggaḍe daṇḍanāyakaṁ* (Chart X 'C', ii, 15), *mahāpradhānaṁ perggaḍe* (Chart X 'C', ii, 14) *daṇḍanāyaka* (Chart X 'C', ii, 20), who donated chiefly to the brahmanical temples.

In all the three phases of our study we find that while the granting of villages and large measurement of lands remained the privilege of the chiefs of the main ruling family, the lesser chiefs made grants of small measurements of lands. The very fact that the main ruling family chiefs had the capacity to grant large number of villages, goes to indicate the extensive rights that these groups enjoyed in their territory. It has been held by earlier scholars such as U.N. Ghoshal that what was usually granted by the king was his own fiscal and semi-fiscal claims over the villages granted. It has further been stated that the land of the grants was often waste land which thus helped in the extension of cultivation.[21] In other words, the idea of the ownership of land by the main ruling family chiefs, which would have armed them with the exclusive right of granting lands and villages, has been negated in the early historical works on India. In the legal texts of early India we, however, find that on the one hand, there is staunch support for the royal ownership of land and on the other, there are texts which also encourage the growth in the private ownership of landed peroprty.[22] This apparent contradiction in the attitude of the legal writers of the early medieval period, it has been argued, only helped in the growth of private property in land of both the king and the dominant landholding peasants. The theory supporting the royal ownership of land only tended to legalize the grants made by the main ruling family chiefs to the brahmanical ideologues, thus leading to the growth of the private ownership over land held by the *brāhmaṇas*.[23] In the context of our study too, we find that it was chiefly in the grants made to the *brāhmaṇas* and the brahmanical temples that extensive economic and juridical immunities were attached (Chart XII 'A', 'B', 'C'). These immunities indicate the transfer of various rights that the donor had over the grant to the donee and, further, they were not necessarily in the form of usufructary rights but rather, they tended to confer different kinds of proprietary rights to the donees on the grants made.

In all the three phases of our study, we find that beneficial tenures were created by different levels of State power, irrespective of whether they were by the chiefs of the main ruling family or the lesser chiefs, in the form of grants to the *brāhmaṇas* and the brahmanical temples. Evidence of economic privileges attached to these grants begin in the context of our study, around the beginning of 7th century A.D. We have in this context, the use of various terms to indicate the specific nature of the economic privileges granted. Thus we have terms such as *bhoga* (Chart XII 'A', iv), *bhogābhyantarasiddhi* (Chart XII 'B', iv), *tribhogābhyantarasiddhi* (Chart XII 'C', iv), *uparikara* (Chart XII 'A', 'B', iv), *udraṅga* (Chart XII 'A', 'B', iv), *sādhānyahiraṇyadeyaḥ* (Chart XII 'A', 'B', iv), *namasya* (Chart XII 'B', 'C', iv), *śulka-kara-vādha-parihāraḥ* (Chart XII 'C', iv), *nidhi-nidhānasametaḥ* (Chart XII 'C', iv), *bhūtopattapratyāya* (Chart XII 'B', iv) used to describe the various economic rights transferred to the donee for the usage of different kinds of rights specified in the grant. Towards the end of 7th century A.D. and thereafter, we have instances of economic rights enjoined with such phrases as, 'to be preserved as long as the sun, moon, earth and the ocean last' (*āchāndrākarṇavakṣiti-sarit-parvata-samakalīnaḥ*) (Chart XII 'A', v, 5), 'to be free from conflicting claims' (*sarvabādhāparihāraṁ*) (Chart XII 'A', v, 10) and so on. Further, particularly in the second phase of our study (Chart XII 'B', v), frequent use of such phrases as 'the right to either cultivate the land or get it cultivated' (*kriṣatoḥ-karṣayataḥ)*[24] and 'enjoy the grant or cause it to be enjoyed' (*bhumjato-bhojayataḥ*) occur.[25] Further, it was also to be enjoyed by the future generations of the donee (*putra-pautrānva-yakram-ōpabhōgyaḥ*).[26] We also have the 'principle of the rent-free enjoyment of land by one who brings it under cultivation for the first time' (*bhūmichhidraṇyāya*)[27] attached to the grant. These rights conferred upon the donees indicate the hereditary, permanent and the proprietary nature of the grants made. The economic and the juridical immunities thus attached to the grants get proliferated by the middle of the 8th century A.D. and undergo a significant change by the middle of the 10th century A.D., wherein we find relatively less number of immunities being granted. This was so mainly because of the change in the nature of the donors making grants, whose status as the lesser chiefs of the State restricted their capacity to make large grants with extensive immunities attached to them, as had been done by the chiefs of the main ruling family in the earlier phase.

With regard to some of the lesser grants made in the second and the third phases of our study (Chart XII 'B', 'C'), we do not have any specific immunities attached to them. We get to know about the existence of these land tenures, termed broadly as the 'non-beneficial' tenures, chiefly through the grants that the lesser chiefs made to various donees, such as the *brāhmaṇas* and the brahmanical temples as has been explained below. According to Y. Subbarayalu the ordinary villages, which constituted the non-

brahmadeya tenures, 'enjoyed just customary rights and privileges and were subject to normal governmental revenue assessment'.[28] The author has made these conclusions chiefly on the basis of the non-*brahmadeya* tenures under the Chola rulers. One may argue that the assumption that the non-*brahmadeya* holdings were subject to normal governmental assessment is equally relevant to the tenures of the Western Deccan. We find in the context of our study that the grants made by the lesser chiefs were made revenue-free when transferred to religious persons and institutions (Chart XII 'B', 'C'). This would further entail the assumption that these tenures before their donation were subject to the payment of revenue. Landholdings in the non-*brahmadeya* villages were considered communal in nature. Lands in these cases were held by the cultivators themselves who collectively owned the landed property leaving no room for the private ownership of land.[29] Karashima, in his study of the non-*brahmadeya* village of Allur, has further argued that by the end of the 9th century A.D. and the beginning of the 10th century A.D., the earlier held communal rights were being impinged upon by the landlords who owned large areas of land covering several villages. This in its turn led to the growth in the rights held by the individual peasant families at the cost of the collective rights of the peasant communities.[30] In the context of our study, we may discern a similar growth in the individual rights over the landed property by various landowning families (Chart XII 'A', 'B', 'C'). This phenomenon can be studied through an analysis of the inscriptional sources available to us, which attest to the growth and the proliferation of the grants made, particularly in the second and third phases of our study. In the first phase of our study, it is difficult for us to come to any conclusion over the nature of the non-*brahmadeya* land tenures chiefly because we have very negligible evidence of the grants being made by the lesser chiefs (Chart X 'A'). At this juncture, we may simply presume that communal land-holding in the non-*brahmadeya* villages, must have been firmly entrenched which must have made it difficult for the dominant peasant families to make any gifts or grants.

Evidence of the grants of lands made by the lesser chiefs begin in the context of our study around the latter half of the 9th century A.D. (Chart X 'B') and their number goes on increasing hereafter in the second and the third phases (Chart X 'C'). In fact in the third phase (Chart X 'C'), we find that the grants made by the lesser chiefs predominate those made by the chiefs of the main ruling family. As a result of the proliferation of the grants of lands made by the lesser chiefs we find a significant change in the nature of grants made. As opposed to the predominance of grants of villages made in the first phase (Chart XII 'A'), and to a certain extent in the second phase (Chart XII 'B') of our study, we find that a majority of the grants made in the third phase are those of small measurements of lands and sites of houses (Chart XII 'C'). The fact that the lesser chiefs were in a position to make revenue-free grants to various religious beneficiaries goes to prove that they possessed ownership or proprietary rights in land, which alone made it possible for them to part with a portion of their rights in land. Rights of sale, gift and enjoyment are generally included in the rights of private ownership of land. In the context of our study, one may argue that these rights were fully exercised by the donors of small measurements of land. For example, evidence for the gifts of land by the lesser chiefs go on increasing right from the 9th century A.D. In the latter half of the 11th century A.D. we also have an inscription of the reign of Chalukya Someśvara I, in which there is mention of the purchase of land by the queen from a local potentate which was then granted to a Jaina monastery.[31]

Growth in the private property in land which had also gained legal sanction during this period placed the landowners in a 'dominant' position. This enabled them to command advantages of productive processes such as having control over labour as well as the means and fruits of production. It is in the context of the dominance exercised by the privileged sections of the society, that one can explain the servile position of several other social groups who had no access to the economic, political and ideological privileges that the former groups enjoyed and, therefore, remained subject to the regulations imposed by the former. It is in this context that we have categorized the former as the 'dominant' social groups and the latter as the 'subject' groups. Here, when we use the term 'dominant' to characterize the privileged sections of the society that we have discussed above at some length, we use it in terms of the economic status of these groups which in its turn helped them to attain a significant status in the political power structure thus enabling them to use legal and ideological sanction for their dominance over the numerically larger sections of the subject population. In the latter category one may include various groups of the subject peasantry and professional artisan groups who catered to the needs of the rural population and were listed as servants of the brahmanical temple establishment. 'Peasant' has been defined as a person who undertakes agriculture on his own, working with his own implements and using labour of his family.[32] However, when we talk of the subject peasantry, we have in our mind stratified and heterogeneous peasant groups such as sharecroppers, landless labourers, permanent and temporary tenants and so on whose livelihood was directly related to their dependence on agricultural activities.[33] They were the actual tillers of land irrespective of their ownership of the tools which they used for purposes of production.

Professional artisan groups on the other hand, included primarily those who were involved in various artisanal and craft activities. These groups were involved in ancestral occupations and formed a 'subject' group in the sense that owing to the economic conditions of the period (marked by relative decline in the commercial activity during the early medieval period), they were dependent upon the dominant sections of the society for their livelihood and were thus tied to either, temple centered agrarian settlements or *brahmadeya* villages. At this juncture, one would like to state that these groups too cannot be considered in terms of a homogenous entity. Distinct levels of stratification can be traced within these groups, which largely depended upon the nature of the professional activity they were involved in. We have a couple of instances in the third phase(Chart X 'C') of our study wherein the guilds into which these professional groups were organized have been mentioned. In this context we have mention of such guilds as the stone-cutter's guild, the brazier's guild, the carpenter's, the balcksmith's and the goldsmith's guilds (Chart X 'C', ii, 18). It has been suggested that the guilds in the context of the period under study emerged as superior groups vis-a-vis the individual artisans and craftsmen.[34] Therefore, some of the guilds have been mentioned as donors of various commodities (Chart X 'C', ii, 18). We have several references to various artisan guilds in the work of G.R. Kuppuswamy pertaining to the early medieval period of the Karnataka region. We have references to such guilds as that of *telligas* (oil mongers), artisans, carpenters, goldsmiths, tailors, weavers and so on.[35] Among these we find that the oil mongers emerge as the most powerful group, 'who lived in their own streets and had their own tanks and temples'.[36] Since a hierarchy was established even among various guild organizations depending upon the nature of economic activity they were involved in, we have to identify their particular nature of subjection vis-a-vis other guilds of the temple to which they were attached. Also, when we refer to professional groups as subject groups, it does not necessarily imply that they were all formed into guilds, but rather, to those individual artisans and craftsmen, who functioned outside the guild organization and were dependant on the landlords or the dominant religious institutions, namely the temples.

We do not have direct explicit mention of the peasant and the individual artisans in the inscriptional sources as these groups had no say in the politico-economic transactions of the time and therefore could not articulate their actions. However, one can get a rough indication of the existence and the status of the subject peasantry with the help of the study of various immunities granted to the donees by the donor when either, a village or, land was granted (Chart XII 'A', 'B', 'C') In these cases, the mention of the names of various taxes, nature of the rights conferred upon the donee, owner of the granted area *etc.*, indicate to us the existence of a tax paying population on the one hand, and also, the extent to which the existing rights were impinged upon by the donee and so on. One of the striking features of the immunities granted, alluding strongly to the existence of a servile population is the right to impose *viṣṭi (sotpadyamānaviṣṭikaṁ)* or forced labour. Our evidence of the imposition of *viṣṭi* begins towards the beginning of the 9th century A.D. in a grant of a village made by the Rashtrakuta ruler Govinda III (Chart XII 'B', V, 3). While mention of *viṣṭi* is made more often in the second phase of our study, between the period 9th - 10th century A.D. (Chart XII 'B'), we however, do not find any mention of the term in the third phase of our study. The decline in the mention of the term *viṣṭi* in the context of the third phase of our study, should not lead us to infer, that it has been given up completely by this time. According to G.K. Rai, a firmly entrenched social practice which had been in existence for more than a thousand years, affecting all segments of society in all parts of India, could not have disappeared suddenly in a few decades.[37] The possible reasons suggested for the disappearance of the term *viṣṭi* are, commutation of forced labour into money payment and peasant rebellions.[38] While for our area of study, we have no evidence of peasant rebellions, the growth of the commercial economy in this phase as a result of the spread of land grants, postulated by R.N. Nandi[39] for the early medieval Karnataka, could have probably enabled the commutation of the forced labour into money payment. This would mean that the servile status of the peasantry was in any case not on the decline. The evidence available to us about the prevalence of *viṣṭi* is, nevertheless, suggestive of the existence of the notion of servile labour during the period under study.

Further, mention of taxes such as *udraṅga* and *uparikara*, which have been interpreted to mean 'principal tax' or tax on permanent tenants[40] and 'minor taxes' or tax on temporary tenants[41] respectively, become an important source for us to define a section of the subject peasantry, namely the temporary and the permanent tenants. Further, the above immunities have been mentioned in the grants exclusively made to the *brāhmaṇas* by the chiefs of the main ruling family (Chart XII 'A', 'B'). We have, however, no such immunities attached to the grants made by the lesser chiefs, and therefore, one may presume that a different kind of subjection existed in the non-*brahmadeya* villages. Thus for instance, in an inscription of the beginning of the 10th century A.D. of the time of the Rashtrakuta king Amoghavarsha, we have the mention of the term *okkaltnam* or the rights of cultivation of a certain group over the area donated.[42] In this instance we get an idea of a particular kind of peasant group who had the rights to cultivate, irrespective of the change in the ownership of land itself. Thus we get an idea of the stratified nature of the peasant groups which was effectively exploited by the dominant groups during this time for their own benefit. The stratified nature of the peasant groups can be viewed in the context of three categories of peasantry as suggested by Irfan Habib. These are the peasant proprietor, who emerges as a landlord in the context of our study either, in the capacity of a donee or, a donor. On the other hand, there are those peasants, who had claims to permanent or long term occupancy rights,[43] who can, in the context of our study, be equated to those who payed *udraṅga*. B.N.S. Yadava has characterized for us the nature of stratification as it existed in the early medieval context in general. He underlines the fact that a number of those free peasants to whom landed property descended by right of inheritance, may have been reduced to mere tenants due to the growing claims of greater rights over land as a result of land grants.[44] This phenomenon can be clearly discerned in the second phase of our study, wherein the donees were conferred upon permanent rights over lands and villages and were given the special privilege of either, cultivating the lands granted to them or, getting them cultivated.[45] These rights bestowed the donee with the right to evict the existing cultivators which by implication would mean conversion of permanent tenants into tenants-at-will leading to the growth of several layers of subject peasantry.

The extensive economic privileges thus granted to the donees, were further reinforced by various administrative immunities, attached to the grants, such as the protection of the grant from the entry of soldiers *(chāta-bhaṭa-dūta-rajāpuruṣāṇām apraveśanīyaṁ)* (Chart XII 'A', v, 5), right to punish the people for ten kinds of offences *(daṇḍa-doṣa-dasaparādhaḥ)* (Chart XII, A, v, 22), and so on. These must have armed the donees with effective political and economic authority to impose their domination over the stratified subject peasantry. Further, the ideological imprecations attached to almost all the grants making threats of punishments of going to hell in case of violation of the grant and rewarding heaven for preserving the grant, must have left no room for the peasant groups to raise their voice against their exploitation.[46] Therefore, some categories of peasants during this period, probably possessed land, but were compelled to pay rent in cash, kind or labour to the landlords and function in response to the needs of the landlord.[47]

By the middle of the 9th century A.D., we also have the emergence of the brahmanical temple as the landlord resulting in the growth of a category of subject social groups different from those we have discussed above. These were involved in the professional/craft activities centering around the temples. We encounter a few examples of these groups in the inscriptional sources of our study. From the last quarter of the 10th century A.D. onwards, we have mention of such groups as drummers *(parey-oy)* (Chart XI 'B', iii, 1), temple girls *(sūḷeya)* (Chart XI 'B', iii, i), horn blowers *(kāleyatamge)* (Chart XI 'B', iii, 1), stone-mason *(kalkutiga)* (Chart XI 'C', iii, 3), flute players *(vamsigarggaṁ)* (Chart XI 'C', iii, 5), and producers and sellers of betel leaves *(tambuliga sāsirvvar)* (Chart XI 'C', iii, 5). These groups received a few *mattars* of land for their subsistence, as a part of the temple establishment. While referring to all these groups in his study, Appadorai considers them as the employees in the service of the temple, and the variety of interests represented by these groups take the position of the temple as an employer predominant.[48] The stratified nature of these groups is indicated to us by the differential measurements of lands granted to each of these groups. In the Hebbel inscription of the last quarter of the 10th century A.D., pertaining to the second phase of our study, we have, out of the cultivable land allotted to God, distribution of various shares to the servants of the temple.[49] Thus the drummer was given 14 *mattars* of land, five dancing girls were given 20 *mattars*, the horn blower received 2 *mattars* and the builder of the temple received 12 *mattars* of it. This exemplifies clearly the nature of hierarchical relations as they existed among the professional groups centered around the temple institutions. According to C.J. Fuller, who has conducted a sociological study of the present day Minakshi temple in Tamil Nadu, the priests, more than any other group in the temple, by virtue of their being closest to God, occupy the highest place in the hierarchy, after the deities themselves.[50]

This aspect of hierarchy can be seen in the context of our study as well, wherein in the second and the third phases (Chart XII 'B', 'C') of our study, we have instances of a major part of the grants made to the temple, being allotted to the priests, which enabled these groups to emerge as a dominant group as controllers of the temple. In laying emphasis on the ideological control the *brāhmaṇas* had on society, Fuller goes on to state that the hierarchical ranking within the temple was primarily defined by the relationships that different groups had with the deities. The priests, as they performed the most vital services for the deities formed the principal servants of the temple and were superior to other servants of the temple, such as the chanters, musicians, dancing girls and so on, whose roles are said to pertain to subsidiary parts of worship.[51] While almost all these groups emerge as the recipients of the land grants (Chart XI 'B', 'C'), we cannot attribute to them the status of dominant groups. This is mainly because these grants were in most cases shares in a larger grant that was made to the temple in which these groups served. In the inscription of Chalukya Someśvara I, in the latter half of the 11th century A.D., a grant was made to the temple establishment for plastering the temple, for an officiating priest, for the God's scents, incense, lamps, oblations, for drummers, a dancing woman and flute players.[52] Since specific shares for each of these groups in this case, are not mentioned, it implies their dependence on the will and fancy of the temple authorities. This provides an interesting evidence to exemplify the lack of identity for temple-centered professional groups independent of the temple institution. Further, the very nature of appointment of the temple servants goes to indicate their servile status. According to Ismail, if a majority of the temple servants coming from the above-mentioned source were not adequate, then the temple had to recruit necessary servants and maintain them on its own.[53] Further, service in the temple was considered hereditary,[54] which then meant that continuation of the servile status of these groups for the future generations as well, was ensured. Thus, the professional groups working in the temple were dependant on the dominant social groups who were patrons of the temple establishments which employed these groups. One may summarize at this juncture that these social groups were in a way servile to the dominant social groups, and served them in an indirect way, through the means of temple services.

Growth in the individual rights of dominant peasant families, the brahmanical ideologues and the brahmanical temples, had several implications for the larger socio-economic structure. It is noteworthy that this phenomenon led to the accentuation of the social stratification within the village community. On the other hand, in some cases, it led to new agricultural settlements, and the growth in the private property. The latter led to the concentration of surplus in the hands of a few rich people, thus leading to the growth of a superior landowning group. All these features had further implications for the socio-economic organization of society engendering several changes in the nature of the economy as a whole. At this juncture, we find that the growth of temples as the landlords in the latter half of our study, had a significant bearing on the changing economy of the time. The temples had several clusters of villages surrounding them and with the political patronage and ideological significance attached to them, they were in a position to command and manage the productive activities of the period. As a result of the concentration of surplus by the dominant peasant families, *brāhmaṇas* and brahmanical temples, we find significant growth in the productive activities of the period. We have several instances in the context of our study, of tank irrigation being paid a lot of attention in the inscriptions of the period belonging to the third phase of our study. In a Western Chalukya grant of A.D. 1052-3, we find a *mahāmaṇḍaleśvara* granting house-tax to the Great Tank of the *agrahāra* of Nirili.[55] Similarly , in another inscription of the same period we have a *mahamatya*, granting twenty *mattars* of cultivatable land for the upkeep of the tank of Kelawadi.[56] Through these examples, we get an idea of the care being shown by the local chiefs of the period towards a betterment of agrarian activity. According to

R.N. Nandi, the beginnings of bonded labour in the 8th century A.D., coincides meaningfully with the expansion of private farms, improved techniques of agriculture and increase in crop-production.[57] The fact that there has been an increase in the crop-production of the period is attested by several scholars writing on the region of Karnataka.[58]

Surplus production led to a spurt in the commercial activities and we find that by the latter half of the second and the beginning of the third phases of our study, an urban-like economic activity begins to emerge. This can be attested by the following examples. It has been suggested that the epigraphic evidence for the coins in the Deccan region, for the period which roughly starts with the consolidation of the Western Chalukya power in the Deccan and ends again with the restoration of the Chalukyan power by the rulers of Kalyana, is not as profuse as they are from the later Chalukyan period onwards.[59] A monetized economy has been considered as a significant characteristic of an urban economy. In the third phase of our study, we have several instances of wages in gold being mentioned. Thus in an early 11th century A.D. grant of Jayasimha II, we have the grant being made in terms of 50 *gadyanas* of gold.[60] We have another instance of an early 12th century A.D. grant in which ten *gadyanas* of gold is granted out of an impost.[61] Further, we have mention of several instances of cash taxes, such as *śulka, vaḍḍa-rāvulda, perjuṁka* and so on, mentioned along with various categories of tax officials associated with the collection of dues in an urban-like setting (Chart X 'C', ii, 6, 12, 14, 16). We also have mention of a few guilds of both artisans and merchants in the latter half of the second and the beginning of the third phase of our study. These are the *śresṭhi* (Chart X 'B', ii, 13), *nakhara* (Chart X 'C', ii, 7), *nānādesi* (Chart X 'C', ii, 17), which have all been explained as merchant guilds and such other artisanal guilds as 120 *kottali, kalkutiga gottali, kamchagarara gottali* (Chart X 'C', ii, 18), have also been mentioned in the third phase of our study. Thus the data in hand is indicative of growth of a relatively urbanized economy from an earlier chiefly rural setting. We find that most of the urban activity begins to be centered around the brahmanical temples which emerged as the focal points of marketing and trading activities and the commercial groups now begin to seek validation by participating in gift giving and temple management functions. Their status was hardly different from that of the agricultural groups, for they were agriculturists now taking to trade.[62] Thus we find that the change in the land tenurial structures significantly brought into being new operational factors in the economy which in their turn, brought about change in the nature of dominant social groups and the groups dependent upon them. Gradually the former began to interest themselves in the changed economic activity of the time, namely, the commercial activities. The agrarian nexus of the commercial groups was, however, never lost as it remained the chief source of surplus appropriation.

The socio-economic change discussed above, would not have been possible without the political and ideological patronage it enjoyed through various means. In the context of our study an analysis of the political power set-up along with its ideological base would help us immensely in comprehending the socio-economic change in its totality. The social groups involved in the administration of the period, have been either, described in terms of a part of the centralized bureaucratic structure by the conventional historians[63] or, in terms of a decentralized bureaucracy, trying to entrench themselves at the grassroot levels by the Marxist scholars.[64] We may, on the other hand, argue with the help of our study, that it were primarily the dominant social groups, located chiefly at the local and supra-local levels[65] which formed an integral part of the political power structure of the early medieval Western Deccan. The landlords at the local level, as we have seen above, were able to exercise a great control over the population of their localities, by virtue of their ownership of land and the subsequent involvement in the local power structure. In this context, we have an interesting example of the term *mahattara* (Chart X 'B', ii, 19), which has not been interpreted as functionary of the State. The very fact that this term has been interpreted as denoting an elder of a village or, a family goes to indicate that the *mahattara* with strong local kin ties must have occupied a locally powerful position by virtue of his ownership of landed property, which accorded him both political and social status. This goes to explain the reason why he was elected or selected as member of the village council. According to R.S. Sharma, the term *mahattara* was elevated at the cost of the other sections of the rural population and they provided a suitable base for the recruitment of higher functionaries and for the growth of 'feudalism' under the Rashtrakuta rulers.[66]

This can be further substantiated through the way in which the functionaries at the village level itself are described with the use of various terms as *urodeya, perggaḍe, gāvuṇda, nal-gāvuṇda, ur-gāvuṇda, grāmakutā* (Chart X 'A', 'B') and so on. Use of these different terms indicate various levels of power held by the rural groups and this in turn, shows the stratified nature of society at the local level and further, it is significant to note here that all these terms are described in the context of the grants made by the dominant groups either, as donors of the grant, or as their protectors and witnesses and also, as builders of temples (Chart X 'C', ii, 5, 14, 19). These evidences best exemplify our contention that the prominent position in the political power structure was acquired by the dominant social groups through their control of the landed property. Dominance exercised over the peasant groups, by a few peasant families during this period in the Western Deccan region can be partly related to a certain extent to the geography of the region. Owing to the nature of the region, it may be surmised that the necessity to have irrigation facilities must have arisen.[67] We have, in the context of our study, several examples of the grants of lands being made for the upkeep of tanks etc. which have been cited above.[68] This is indicative of irrigation facilities being managed and controlled by the dominant sections of the village community. It were these social groups which entrenched themselves in terms of local and supra-local elite and were integrated into the state structure of the period. Around 9th century A.D., we have an interesting evidence of a *mahāsamantādhipati* belonging to the Rashtrakuta dynasty, emerging subsequently as a *mahārājadjirāja*[69] thus establishing dynastic control over the area by overthrowing the earlier ruler.

It was essential for these newly emerging dynastic powers to have a tenacious support of the locally powerful groups in order to assist them, on the one hand, to establish their sovereignty over the area conquered and on the other, to fight wars for extending their control over neighbouring fertile tracts. Constant wars were fought by the main ruling families of the Western Deccan region in order to gain the fertile tracts of the Eastern Deccan namely, Vengi or, to get hold of the Kaveri delta in the extreme South. Thus the Chalukya rulers of Badami were involved in battles with the Pallava and the Pandya rulers of the extreme South and on the other hand, held several campaigns against the Vishnukundin rulers of the Eastern Deccan. After conquering the latter, the Chalukyas of Badami even succeeded in founding a dynastic line of their own in the Vengi region.[70] The Rashtrakuta rulers of Malkhed were in a similar way involved in the battles with the Chalukya rulers of Vengi and the Chola rulers of the extreme South, whom they succeeded in subduing several times and extended their sway over these regions.[71] Similarly, Chalukyas of Kalyani were involved in battles with the Cholas of the extreme South and the rulers of Vengi.[72] These urges of the rulers to gain vast fertile tracts can be linked up chiefly to the geographical configuration of their core areas in the Western Deccan, [MAP V] which was largely a plateau area,[73] [MAP II] devoid of vast tracts of fertile land to enable a constant flow of agrarian surplus required to maintain the ruling strata. Vengi region, on the other hand, lying between the Godavari and Krishna deltas was extremely fertile and was frequently the bone of contention between the plateau kingdoms of the Western Deccan and the coastal kingdoms of the East who had the desire to control the entire water way.[74] It would not have been possible for the ruling families to fight these wars without adequate support of the local people represented by their chiefs. The latter were integrated into the State power structure mainly through the conferment of the so-called 'feudatory' titles and ranks upon them by the main ruling family. In the second and the third phases of our study we find that several new terms emerge to describe the dominant social groups. We have emergence of such terms as the *perggaḍe*, *nāl-gāvuṇda*, *mahāmaṇḍaleśvara*, *mahāpradhānam* and similar other new groups from the 8th century A.D. onwards. This would then imply that new bases of power were brought into the picture by each branch of the main ruling family (belonging to a powerful supra-local group) by conferring titles and ranks, which was then integrated into the State structure. If these terms had indicated merely bureaucratic titles of the State, then they would not have undergone such rapid changes.

Apart from the coercive power exercised by the main ruling family, one may postulate here, that the ideological apparatus was also effectively made use of for the socio-political integration required for the early medieval state system. This could be explained in terms of land grants made extensively to the *brāhmaṇas* particularly by the chiefs of the main ruling family. Apart from helping in agrarian expansion and strengthening the State system at the local levels, these religious beneficiaries must have also helped in the process of acculturation. In the third phase of our study, we have seen the emergence of brahmanical temples as landlords on a large scale. This phenomenon went hand in hand with the spread of the *bhakti* cult during the 11th and 12th century A.D., for which the brahmanical temples became the centres of proliferation with the support of the local bases of power. This can be substantiated by the fact that in the second and third phases of our study, (Chart X 'B' & 'C') the lesser chiefs made grants mostly to temples. By providing patronage to such institutions, the State system could effectively establish its hold over the society. Thus 'the contributive potential of temple in the legitimization of a political power, based on social differentiation is clearly discernible in the active participation of the agencies of political power in the creation and promotion of a network of temple centered monastic groups.'[75]

Role of ideology became crucial at the level of economic relations as well. This is where the principle of *varṇa* system becomes important for us to comprehend the role played by ideology in governing the economic relationships of the period. We find that in the early medieval Western Deccan, all the four traditional *varṇa* divisions are not mentioned in the inscriptions. With the exception of the mention of *brāhmaṇa varṇa* (Chart X 'A', 'B') and one or two instances of the *vaiśya-jāti* (Chart X 'B'), *beḷḷaḷa-kula* (Chart X 'B') and *kamma kula* (Chart X 'B'), we hardly have any mention of the social groups in terms of their 'caste' status. It has been postulated that in the region under study, we do not have the spread of the *kṣatriya* and *vaiśya varṇas*. Instead, we have the proliferation of the *brāhmaṇa* and the *śūdra varṇa*. The members of the latter *varṇa* now began to be equated with agriculturists, which was earlier considered the profession of the *vaiśya varṇa*.[76] The menial jobs for the dominant social groups, which were earlier performed by the *śūdra varṇa* now began to be considered as the duty of the *cāṇḍāla*[77] who has been mentioned a couple of times in the third phase of our study (Chart XI 'C', iv, 2, 7). The members of the *pañcama varṇa* to which the *cāṇḍāla jāti* belongs, according to Vivekanand Jha, proliferated during the early medieval period.[78] The *cāṇḍāla* considered as an untouchable, was made to live outside the precincts of the village community and was associated with the profession of dealing in hides and armour etc., jobs which were considered abhorrent by the higher castes. We may consider the *cāṇḍāla* as the lowest in the scale among those who offered professional service in the villages. The very fact that to be born as a *cāṇḍāla* became one of the punishments to suffer in case of the violation of the grants made, goes to indicate to us the contempt with which this group was held.[79] Thus the *varṇa* system was not only an instrument for regulating social relations, but, a mechanism through which not only the surplus produce, but also the labour could be appropriated by those who were not directly engaged in production.[80]

Thus we see that, while changes in the social structure are related to the broader changes in the land relations, we cannot at the same time establish that the social change is totally independent of the dominant ideology and the political system of the time. In this context, we would like to conclude by highlighting the difficulty in the interpretation of the term *mahājana*, which exemplifies in our study, a close nexus between the political, economic and ideological dominance exercised in the maintenance of the hierarchical social relations of the period. The *mahājanas* in the context of our study emerge as donors (Chart X 'B'), recipients (Chart X 'B'), approvers (Chart X 'B', 'C'), witnesses (Chart X 'C'), and acknowledgers (Chart X 'C') of grants. We may surmise at this juncture that the *mahājanas* enjoyed both political and economic status. The fact that several of the grants were made only after washing the feet of the *mahājanas*[81] also goes to indicate the privileged position held by these groups. This was regarded as an auspicious act and goes to prove that in ritual terms, the *mahājanas* must have enjoyed the position similar to that of the *brāhmaṇas*, or, as has been suggested by scholars, were indeed *brāhmaṇas*. Thus, the *mahājanas* emerge as not only politically and economically powerful groups, but also in terms of the ideological hold they had over the society of the time. It is perhaps due to these reasons that a variety of modern historical writings on the actual status of the *mahājana* group, agree to conclude that they were powerful rural elites. Accordingly, Altekar suggests that *mahājanas* included almost all the heads of the families residing in a village that were the members of the village community.[82] According to R.S. Sharma, *mahājanas* were the leading members of the local bodies.[83] Kuppuswamy considers the *mahājanas* as part of local authority.[84] Dikshit, while discussing the *mahājanas* in the context of the *agrahāra* villages considers them as *brāhmaṇas* residing in and enjoying the *agrahāra* grants.[85]

Thus it is the relationship between the ideological and the material factors which explains the totality of societal organization and change in the pre-modern Indian context.[86] We have attempted to understand this by organically relating the social groups to the given economic, political and ideological milieu of the period. Our aim here was not to fit our analysis into any given historiographical framework, but to comprehend the relationship between the material and ideological forces that had given rise to a particular kind of social organization in a given geographical setting. We hope to have in a small way explained that though it is generally believed that society in early India was organized on normative, prescriptive lines of descriptions as given in the *Dharmaśāstras*, in the context of the case study of the early medieval Western Deccan, we would like to emphasize that it functioned within a very pragmatic and realistic environ of an economic and political order that was instrumental in bringing about change while maintaining, at the same time, certain elements of continuity that apparently give the impression that Indian society in the past was static and stagnant.

NOTES

1. Based on my M.Phil dissertation accepted by the University of Hyderabad in 1989. I am thankful to Dr. Aloka Parasher for suggestions while writing this paper.
2. For ex. D.D. Kosambi, *An Introduction to the Study of Indian History*, Bombay, (rp) 1985. First published in 1956; R.S. Sharma, *Indian Feudalism* (A.D. 300 - A.D. 1200), Delhi, (2nd ed.) 1980. First published in 1965; B.N.S. Yadava, *Society and Culture in Northern India in the 12th Century* A.D., Allahabad, 1973, and so on.
3. B. Subba Rao, *Personality of India : Pre and Proto Historic Foundation of India and Pakistan*, Baroda, 1958, pp.85-141. In this work, regions with vast tracts of fertile lands, which have direct impact on the development of civilizations, have been defined as 'nuclear' areas or areas of 'attraction'. Under this category, we have such examples as the Indo-Gangetic basin of the Northern India, Raichur Doab of the Deccan region and the Kaveri delta of the extreme South.
4. For ex. K. Sundaram, *Studies in Economic and Social Conditions of Medieval Andhra*, A.D.1000-A.D.1600, Madras, 1968; G.R. Kuppuswamy, *Economic Conditions in Karnataka*, Dharwar, 1975; Jyotsna Kamat, *Social Life in Medieval Karnataka*, Delhi, 1980 and so on.
5. B.N.S. Yadava, 'Problem of the Interaction Between Socio-Economic Classes in the Early Medieval Complex', *IHR*, vol. III, 1976-77, pp. 43-44. This view is held by the Marxist historians of India who look upon the developments in the socio-economic set-up of the early medieval Indian subcontinent within the framework of 'feudal mode of production'. We have several other scholars working outside the framework of 'feudalism' and who have brought to light evidence to indicate the existence of urban phenomenon in certain regions of India in the early medieval period. For ex. B.D. Chattopadhyaya, 'Trade and Urban Centres in Early Medieval North India', *IHR*, vol. I, 1974.

6. D.N. Jha, *Studies in Early Indian Economic History*, Delhi, 1980, pp. 2-3.
7. Ibid., p. 10.
8. A.S. Altekar, *A History of Village Communities in Western India*, Bombay, 1927, pp. 80-81.
9. D.D. Kosambi, *op. cit.,* 1985, pp. 13-14.
10. R.S. Sharma, *op. cit.,* 1980, pp. 110-126.
11. Romila Thapar, *Ancient Indian Social History*, New Delhi (rp), 1984, p. 19.
12. Dharma Kumar, 'Private Property in Asia? The Case of Medieval South India', *CSSH*, vol. 27, no. 2, April, 1985, p. 343.
13. N. Karashima, *South Indian History and Society* (Studies from inscriptions, A.D. 850 - 1800), New Delhi, 1984, p. xvii.
14. R.N. Nandi, 'Growth of Rural Economy in Early Feudal India', Presidential Address, Section I, *PIHC*, 45th Session, Annamalainagar, 1984, p. 3.
15. Sharma, *op. cit.*, 1980, pp. 10-126. Here the author has highlighted with the help of legal texts of the period the existence of superior rights held by the *brāhmaṇas* on the one hand, and also of the inferior rights held by the actual cultivators on the other.
16. Dharma Kumar, *op. cit.*, 1985, pp. 351-355. In this work, the author has highlighted the existence of multiple rights over the lands in early medieval South India in the form of both communal ownership of land and joint family ownership.
17. Ibid., p. 351.
18. Ibid., p. 345.
19. Ibid., p. 348.
20. The capital Roman numerals indicate the Chart Number and the alphabetical notation attached to it, indicates the chronological phase. The small Roman numerals are further attached to indicate the column number. Separate Arabic numerals indicate the serial numbers of the example cited in the Chart. This pattern has been followed throughout for references to the Charts.
21. Summarized from Irfan Habib, 'The Social Distribution of Landed Property in Pre-British India', in R.S. Sharma, & V. Jha (ed.), *Indian Society : Historical Probings,* New Delhi, 1974, p. 281.
22. Sharma, *op. cit.*, 1980, p. 124.
23. Ibid.
24. J.F. Fleet, CXXV, 'Sanskrit and Old Canarese Inscriptions', (A.D. 806-7), *IA*, XI, 1882, p. 166.
25. Ibid.
26. V.V. Mirashi and N.A. Gore, '35', 'Dharvar Plates of Rashtrakuta Govinda III' (A.D. 806-7), *EI*, XXVI, p. 294.
27. D.C. Sircar, *Indian Epigraphical Glossary*, Delhi, 1966, p. 339.
28. Y. Subbarayalu, 'The Place of Ur in the Economic and Social History of the Early Tamil Nadu, from A.D. 750 to A.D. 1350', in A.V. Narasimha Murthy and B.K. Gururaja Rao (Ed.), *Rangavali : Recent Researches in Indology*, Delhi, 1983, p. 172.
29. Dharma Kumar, *op. cit.*, 1985, p. 348.
30. N. Karashima, *op. cit.*, 1984, p. 23.
31. Lionel D. Barnett, 10, 'Arasabidi Inscription of the Reign of Someśvara I

(A.D. 1047), *EI*, XVII, p. 122.

32. Irfan Habib, 'The Peasant in Indian History', General President's Address, *PIHC*, 43rd session, Kurukshetra, 1982, p. 3.
33. B.N.S. Yadava, 'Immobility and Subjection of Indian Peasantry in Early Medieval Complex', *IHR*, vol. I, 1974, pp. 18-27.
34. This has been deduced on the basis of a discussion held with Dr. S. Nagaraju, Professor, Department of History, University of Hyderabad.
35. G.R. Kuppuswamy, *op. cit.*, 1975, pp. 102-103.
36. Ibid., pp. 103-105.
37. G.K. Rai, 'Forced Labour in Ancient and Early Medieval India', *IHR*, vol. 3, 1976-77, p. 34.
38. Ibid.
39. Nandi, *op. cit.*, 1984, p. 4.
40. Sircar, *op. cit*, 1966, p. 344.
41. Ibid., p. 352.
42. R.S. Panchamukhi (ed.), 'Venkatapur Inscription of Amoghavarsha (A.D. 906-7), *EI*, XXVI, p. 62.
43. Irfan Habib, *op. cit.*, 1982, p. 48.
44. B.N.S. Yadava, *op. cit.*, 1976-77, p. 48.
45. Terms used to describe this cited on page 8 (footnotes 24-27) above.
46. For ex. J.F. Fleet, 168, 'Kautheem Plates of Vikramaditya V (A.D. 1008)', *IA*, XVI, 1887, p. 24.
47. Sharma, *op. cit.*, 1980, p. 213.
48. A. Appadorai, *Economic Conditions in South India* (A.D. 1000-1500), Madras, 1936, p. 275.
49. J.F. Fleet, 50, 'Hebbal Inscription of A.D. 975', *EI*, IV, 1898, p. 358.
50. C.J. Fuller, *Servants of the Goddess : The Priests of a South Indian Temple*, London, 1984, p. 23.
51. Ibid, p. 47.
52. J.F. Fleet, II 'C', 'Of the Reign of Someśvara I (A.D.) 1066)', *EI*, XVI, 1922, p. 85.
53. K. Ismail, *Karnataka Temples : Their Role in Socio-Economic Life*', Delhi, 1984, p. 112.
54. Ibid.
55. Lionel, D. Barnett, 10 'A', 'of the Reign of Someśvara I' (A.D. 1052-3), *EI*, XVI, 1922, p. 67.
56. J.F. Fleet, 36, 'Kelawadi Inscription of the time of Someśvara I', (A.D. 1053), *EI*, IV, 1898, p. 261.
57. R.N. Nandi, *op. cit.*, 1984, p. 25.
58. Ibid, pp. 40-49 and G.R. Kuppuswamy, *op. cit.*, 1975, pp. 56-66.
59. B.D. Chattopadhyaya, *Coins and Currency Systems in South India*, A.D. 225 - 1300, New Delhi, 1977, p. 118.
60. Lionel, D. Barnett, 38 'A', 'Of the Reign of Jayasimha II (A.D. 1022)', *EI*, XIX, p. 224.
61. J.F. Fleet, XXXIII, 'Western Chalukya Grant of Jagadekamalla' (A.D. 1139-40) *IA*, VI, p. 141.
62. R. Champakalakshmi, 'Urbanization in South India : The Role of Ideology and Polity', Presidential Address, Section I, *PIHC*, 47th Session, Srinagar,

1986, p. 20.

63. For ex. A.S. Altekar, *Rashtrakutas and their Times,* Poona, 1934; K.R. Basavaraja, *Administration Under the Chalukyas of Kalyana*, Madras, 1983, and so on.

64. For ex. R.S. Sharma, *op. cit.*, 1980, pp. 1-3.

65. B.D. Chattopadhyaya, 'Political Processes and Structure of Polity in Early Medieval India : Problems of Perspective', Presidential Address, Section I, *PIHC*, 44th Session, Burdwan, 1983, p. 44.

66. Sharma, *op. cit.*, 1980, p. 85.

67. J.F. Richards, *Mughal Administration in Golconda*, Oxford, 1975, p. 4.

68. See notes 55-56 above.

69. S.K. Dikshit (ed.), '4', 'Ellora Plates of Dantidurga' (A.D. 742), *EI*, XXV, 1939, p. 29 and Fleet (ed.), CXXI, 'Sanskrit and Old Canarese Inscriptions', *IA*, XI, 1882, p. 112.

70. K.A. Nilakanta Sastri, *A History of South India*, Madras, 1976 (4th ed.), p. 163.

71. Ibid., pp. 158-160.

72. Ibid., pp. 180-192.

73. Himanshu Prabha Ray, *Monastery and Guild : Commerce Under the Sātavāhanas*, Delhi, 1986, p. 13.

74. Romila Thapar, *A History of India*, Vol. I, Harmondsworth (rp), 1984, p. 168.

75. Ashok Shettar, 'Aspects of Agricultural Expansion in Early Medieval Southern Karnataka', in K. Veerathappan (ed.), *Studies in Karnataka History and Culture* (Proceedings, Vol. II, of the Karnataka History Congress), Mysore, 1987.

76. Summarized from Suvira Jaiswal, 'Changes in the Concept of *Śūdra Varṇa* in Early Middle Ages', *PIHC*, 41st Session, Bombay, 1980, pp. 113-114.

77. Vivekananda Jha, 'Stages in the History of Untouchables', *IHR*, vol. II, no. 1, 1975, p. 28.

78. Ibid, p. 29.

79. For ex. Lionel, D. Barnett '37' Gadag Inscription of the Reign of Jayasimha II', (A.D. 1037), *EI*, XIX, 1927, p. 219.

80. R.S. Sharma, *Śūdras in Ancient India* (A Social History of the Lower Orders down to *circa* A.D. 600), Delhi, 1980, p. 320.

81. J.F. Fleet (ed.), 15 'H', 'Ron Inscription of the time of Amoghavarsha I' (A.D. 874), *EI*, XIII, 1915, p. 185.

82. A.S. Altekar, *op.cit.*, 1934, p. 199.

83. R.S. Sharma, *op. cit.*, 1980, p. 58.

84. G.R. Kuppuswamy, *op. cit.*, 1975, p. 1.

85. G.S. Dikshit, *Local Self-Government in Medieval Karnataka*, Dharwar, 1964, p. 38.

86. Frank Perlin, 'The Material and the Cultural : An Attempt to Transcend the Present Impasse', *MAS*, vol. 22, no. 2, 1988, p. 383.

CHART - X A
THE DOMINANT SOCIAL GROUPS
PHASE I (MIDDLE OF THE 6TH CEN. A.D. - MIDDLE OF THE 8TH CEN. A.D.)

i	ii	iii	iv	v
Sl. No. Name of the Inscription	Name/Title	*Varṇa/gōtra*/Status	Context	Reference
1. No. *CXX* Sanskrit and Old Canarese Inscriptions (A.D. 567-8)	A) i. Dõnagāmuṇḍa ii. Eḷagāmuṇḍa iii. Maḷḷeyas iv. Uncharādhā-savereyas	A) Not mentioned B) Village headman C) Resider at *Chaitya* D) King	A) i,ii,iii, iv. DONORS B) BUILDER of the temple C) ACQUIRER of the grant	l.l. 15-20, *IA*, XI, 1984, pp.69-70.
	B) *gāmuṇḍa*	E) Ruling over Pāndipuram	D) ACKNOWLEDGER	
	C) Prabhāchandra/*gurāva*	F) Belongs to the main Ruling Family	E,F) Mentioned in the eulogy	
	D) Mādhavatti/*arasa*			
	E) Sinda/*arasa*			
	F) Kirtivarma/*Srimat-prithuvivallabha rājadhi rāja paramēśvara*			

(Contd.)

CHART - X A *(Contd.)*

i	ii	iii	iv	v
2) *No.XL* Sanskrit and Old Canarese Inscriptions (A.D. 578-9)	A) Mangala/*rāja* B) Priyasvāmi C) Vallabha	A) King B) *Kaśyapa gōtra* C) *Mānavya gōtra*/main ruling family chief/ father of 'A'	A) DONOR B) DONEE C) Mentioned in the Eulogy	l.l.i, 11, 15-20, *IA*, VII, 1878, pp.161-162.
3. *No. XXVII* Chalukya Grant of Pulakeśin II (A.D. 613)	A) Satyāśraya/*Prithuvi vallabha Mahārāja* B) Jyeṣṭaśarma	A) Main ruling family chief. B) *Vāsiṣṭha gōtra*/Belonged *to the school of Taittiriyas*/Acquainted with the 4 *vēdas*	A) DONOR B) DONEE	l.l. 9, 14-15, *IA*, VI, 1877, p.73.
4. *No. VIII* Chiplun Copper Plate Grant of Pulakesin II (Bet. A.D. 609-A.D. 642)	A) Satyāśraya/*Mahipatir* B) Mahēśvara C) Śrivallabha Sēnānandarāja D) *Sāmantas*	A) Belongs to the main ruling family/*Mānavya gōtra* B) *Atrēya gōtra*/performer of sacrifices. C) Maternal uncle of 'A'. D) Feudatory Chiefs.	A) DONOR B) DONEE C) EXECUTER D) GUARANTORS	l.l. 1,8,11-13, *EI*, III, 1894-95, p. 51.

5. *No. 9* Lohaner Plates of Chalukya Pulakesin II (A.D. 630)	A) Satyāśraya/*Prithuvi-vallabha Mahāṛāja* B) Dāmadikshita C) i. *Rāja* ii. *Sāmantabhōgika* iii. *Viśayapati* iv. *rāśtrakūta* v. *grāmayuktaka*	A) Main Ruling Family Chief/ *Mānavya gōtra* B) *Savarṇi gōtra*/Belonged to the Maitrāyaṇika branch of the Black Yajurveda C) i,ii,iii,iv,v - Rulers of various administrative divisions.	A) DONOR B) DONEE C) ADDRESSEES	l.l. 17-18, 22-23. *E.I*, XXVII, p. 40.
6. *No. LII* Chalukya Grant of Pulakesin II (Date not recorded)	A) Satyāśraya Pulakesi Vallabha/*Mahārājaḥ* B) i. *Brāhmaṇas* ii. Rāchārya	A) Same as above. B) ii. Varcha gōtra	A) DONOR B) i,ii, DONEES	l.l. 8-10. *IA*, VIII, 1879, p. 44.
7. *No. XXVIII* Chalukya Grant of Vikramaditya I (Date not recorded)	A) Vikramaditya Satyāśraya/ *Śriprithuvivallabha Mahārājadhirāja paramēśvara*	A) Same as above. B) i, ii. *Kaśyapa gōtra* iii.*Hārita gōtra* iv,v,vi.*Bhāradvāja gōtra* vii,viii,ix.Māṇḍavya gōtra	A) DONOR B) DONEE	l.l.28, 30-39, *IA*,VI,1877. p.77.

(Contd.)

CHART - X A *(Contd.)*

i	ii	iii	iv	v
	B) i. Nandisvāmi ii. Sāntiśarma iii. Adityaśarma iv. Agundubhōyōpiddi Sarma v. Dāmaśarma vi. Lōhasvāmi vii. Bhallasvāmi viii. Bādiśarma ix. Pidiśarma x. Nijubhōyōdōṇaśarma xi. Gandabhōyō	x,xi. *Kaśyapa gōtra*		
8. *No. XXIX* Western Chalukya Grant of *Vinayaditya* (A.D. 690)	A) Vinayaditya/Śriprithuvi-vallabha Mahārājādhirāja Paramēśvarabhattāraka.	A) Main Ruling Family Chief	A) DONOR	l.l.23, 29-31, 36, *IA*, VI 1878,p.86-87.
	B) Bhimaśarma	B) Bhāradvāja gōtra	B) DONEE	
	C) Sri Rāmapuṇya vallabha/ *Mahāsandhivigrahika*	C) Minister for war and peace	C) WRITER	

9. *No. XLVIII* Of Western Chalukya King Vinayaditya (A.D. 694-695)	A) Vinayaditya/ Same as above. B) Isāna Śarma C) Rāmapuṇyavallabha/ *Mahāsandhivigrahika*	A) Same as above. B) *Vatsya gōtra* C) Same as above	A) DONOR B) DONEE C) WRITER	l.l. 23, 26, 41-42, *IA*, VI, 1878, p.302.
10. *No. 30* Poona Plates of Chalukya Vinayaditya (A.D. 690)	A) Vinayaditya/ Same as above B) Durga Śarma and Ravi Śarma C) Rāmapuṇyavallabha/ *Mahāsandhivigrahika*	A) Same as above B) *Kaśyapa gōtra* C) Same as above	A) DONOR B) DONEE C) WRITER	l.l. 21, 25-26, 35, *EI*, XXV, 1939, p. 291.
11. *No.187* Sorab Copper Plate Grant of Vinayaditya (A.D. 692)	A) Vinayaditya/ Same as above. B) Divākara Śarma C) Chitravāha/*Mahārāja* D) Rāmapuṇya Vallabha/ *Mahāsandhivigrahika*	A) Same as above. B) *Dēvarāta Kauśika gōtra* C) Son of the Āḷupa ruler Guṇasāgara. D) Same as above	A) DONOR B) DONEE C) ACKNOWLEDGER D) WRITER	l.l. 16, 17, 30 *IA*, XIX, 1890, p.150.

(Contd.)

CHART - X A (*Contd.*)

i	ii	iii	iv	v
12. *No.LVII* Of Western Chalukya King Vijayaditya (A.D.696-7)	A) Vijayaditya Satyāśraya/ Same as above. B) Eḷtugolugasaṇi.	A) Same as above. B) Priest	A) DONOR B) DONEE	l.l. 3-4. *IA*, VIII, 1879, p.285.
13. *No.3* A Grant of the Western Chalukya Vijayaditya (A.D. 731)	A) Vijayaditya/ Same as above. B) Bhavasvāmi Bhaṭṭ C) Sri Niravadya Sri Puṇya Vallabha.	A) Same as above B) *Viśvamitra gōtra*	A) DONOR B) DONEE C) WRITER	l.l. 24, 33-35, 45, *EI*, XXV, p.24.
14. *No. 39* Jamalgama Grant of Chalukya Vijayaditya (A.D. 697)	A) Vijayaditya/ Same as above, B) i. Kotti Śarman ii. Prabhakara/*grihita Sūhasra*, *Shaḍangavit* C) Rāmapuṇya Vallabha/ *Mahā Sandhivigrahika*	A) Same as above. B) i.*Kauśika gōtra* ii.*Bhāradvāja gōtra* learned in the Sāmaveda and conversant with the six Vēdangas. C) Minister for war and peace.	A) DONOR B) DONEE D) WRITER	l.l. 31, 34-35, 42, *No. EI*, XXVI, 1965, p.315.

15. *No.LXXVII* Western Chalukya Grant of Vijayaditya (A.D. 700)	A) Vijayaditya/ Same as above. B) Dēvasvāmi	A) Same as above. B) *Vatsa gōtra*	A) DONOR B) DONEE	l.l. 30, *IA*, IX, 1880, p.128.
16. *No.LXXVII* Western Chalukya Grant of Vijayaditya (A.D. 705)	A) Vijayaditya/ Same as above. B) Eight *brāhmaṇas* belonging to various *gōtras* C) *Niravādya Puṇya Vallabha/ Mahāsandhivigrahika*	A) Same as above. B) *Bhāradvāja gōtra* *Kauśika gōtra* *Kaundinya gōtra* *Maudgalya gōtra* Kaśyapa gōtra *Vatsa gōtra* C) Minister for War and Peace	A) DONOR B) DONEE C) WRITER	l.l. 29, 42, *IA*, IX, 1880, p.131.
17. *No.3* Grant of Western Chalukya Vijayaditya (A.D. 731)	A) Vijayaditya/ Same as above. B) Bhavasvāmi Bhaṭṭa C) Niravādya Puṇyavallabha/ *Mahāsandhivigrahika*	A) Same as above. B) *Viśvamitra gōtra* C) Same as above.	A) DONOR B) DONEE C) WRITER	l.l. 31-33, 45, *EI*, XXV, 1939, p.24.

(Contd.)

CHART - X A *(Contd.)*

i	ii	iii	iv	v
18. *No.23* Narwan Plate of Chalukya Vikramaditya II (A.D. 742)	A) Vikramaditya/ Same as above.	A) Same as above.	A) DONOR	l.l. 53, 58-62, 73-74, *EI*, XXVII, 1947, pp.130-131.
	B) *Brāhmaṇas* of various *gōtras*	B) *Kauśika gōtra* *Atrēya gōtra*	B) DONEE	
	C) Anivarita Puṇyavallabha/ *Mahāsandhivigrahika*	C) Same as above.	C) WRITER	
19. *No.LVIII* Of Chalukya Vikram-aditya II (A.D. 732-3)	A) Revaḍibadda	A) Not stated	A) DONOR	l.l. 4-5, *IA*, VIII,1879, p.286.
	B) Aditya batārage	B) Priest	B) DONEE	
	C) i. Vikramaditya/ *Sriprithuvi Vallabha mahārājādhirāja paramēśvara* ii. *Mahājana*	C) i. Main Ruling Family Chief. ii. Elders of the village.	C) i, ii. PRO-CLAIMERS	
20. *No.LXXVI* Western Chalukya Grant of Nāgavardhana (Date not recorded)	A) Nāgavardhana/rājaḥ	A) Belongs to the Royal family.	A) DONOR	l.l. 14-15, 17-23, *IA*, IX, 1880, p.124.
	B) *Mahāvratibhya upabhōgaya*	B) Ascetics who live at the temple of Kapilēśvara.	B) DONEES	

21. *No.1* Pattadakal Pillar Inscription of the time of Kirtivarman II (A.D. 754)	A) Kirtivarma Satyāśraya/ Same as above.	A) Main Ruling Family Chief	A) DONOR	l.l. 12-13, 15, 18. *EI*, III, pp.5-6.
	B) Brahmamūrti - Ārya Bhaṭṭa Trivikrama	B) Priest of the temple of Vijayēśvara.	B) DONEE	
	C) Subhadēva/*rūpakāra*	C) Sculptor of the stone pillar of the temple/ *Śāndilya gōtra*	C) Living in the TEMPLE	
22. *No.4* Ellora Plates of Dantidurga (A.D. 742)	A) Dantidurga/ *mahāsāmantādhipati* *Prithuvivallabha*	A) Lesser Chief	A) DONOR	l.l. 2,3,4,7,8,9-15.*EI*, XXV,1939, pp.29-30.
	B) Revaditya Bhaṭṭaya, Bhaula, Govisarebhya.	B) *Bhāradvāja gōtra*	B) DONEES	
	C) i. *rāja* ii. *Sāmanta* iii. *bhōgika* iv. *Viśayapati* v. *rāśtrakūta* vi. *mahattara*	C) Lesser Chiefs	C) ADDRESSEES	
	D) i. Karkka Rāja/ *Samādhigata Paṇchamahāśabda mahāsāmantādhipati* ii. Indra Rāja/ *mahāsāmantādhipati*	D) i. Father of Indra Rāja ii. Father of Dantidurga	D) Mentioned in the EULOGY	

(Contd.)

CHART - X A *(Contd.)*

i	ii	iii	iv	v
23. *No.CXXI* Sanskrit and Old Canarese Inscriptions (A.D. 753-4)	A) Śri Dantidurga rājadēvaḥ/ *mahārājadhirājaḥ paramēśvara paramabhaṭṭaraka*	A) Main Ruling Family Chief.	A) DONOR	l.l. 27, 28, 29, 34-35. *IA*, XI, 1882, pp.112-113.
	B) Nārayaṇa bhaṭṭa	B) *Vasiṣṭla gōtra*	B) DONEE	
	C) i. *rāśtrakutas* ii. *viśayapati* iii. *grāmakuta*	C) Lesser Chiefs	C) ADDRESSEES	

CHART - X B
THE DOMINANT SOCIAL GROUPS
PHASE II MIDDLE OF THE 8TH CEN. A.D. - LATTER HALF OF THE 10TH CEN. A.D.

i	ii	iii	iv	v
Sl. No. Name of the inscription	Name/Title	*Varṇa/gōtra*/Status	Context	Reference
1. *No.16 'C'* Lakshmeshwar Inscription of the time of Srivallabha (A.D. 793)	A) *Mūṛuṁ-kēriya pattagāṛara Seṇiṇi*	A) Headman of the guild of weavers of *mūṛuṁkēri.*	A) DONORS	l.l. 4,5,6,7, 8. *EI*, VI, 1900-01, p. 166.
2. *No.2* Anjanavati Plates of Govinda III (A.D. 800-01)	A) Govinda III/ *paramabhaṭṭaraka mahārājādhirāja paramēśvara prithuvi vallabha*	A) Main Ruling Family Chief.	A) DONOR	l.l. 29, 30. 31-36, 43-54, 55. *EI*, XXIII, 1935, pp. 15-18
	B) 13 *brāhmaṇas* belonging to various *gōtras.*	B) *Vāsiṣṭha gōtra, Kramaitta gōtra, Hāridra gōtra, Kutimasha gōtra, Mōggala gōtra, Bhāradvāja gōtra Kaśyapa gōtra Vājasanēya gōtra, Sāngali gōtra*	B) DONEES	
			C) ADDRESSEES	
			D) EXECUTOR	
			E) WRITER	

(Contd.)

CHART - X B *(Contd.)*

i	ii	iii	iv	v
	C) i. *rāśtrapati* ii. *viśayapati* iii. *grāmakūtā* iv. *yuktaka* v. *niyuktaka* vi. *mahattara*	C) Lesser Chiefs	F) Mentioned in the Eulogy	
	D) Chakkirāja/*dūtaka*	D) Messenger		
	E) Kukkaika/*mahāsandhi-vigṛahika*	E) Minister for war and peace		
	F) Gautama/*Sāmantabalādhikṛta*	F) Father of 'E'/ Commander-in-chief		
3. *No.CXXIII* Sanskrit and old Canarese Inscriptions (A.D. 803-4)	A) Govinda III/ Same as above.	A) Main Ruling Family Chief.	A) DONOR	l.l. 4, 11, 18-19, *IA*,
	B) Śivadhari/*Gorava*	B) Śaiva priest	B) DONEE	XI, 1882, pp.126-127.
	C) Śridhara/*mahāsandhi-vigrahikrita*	C) Same as above.	C) WRITER	
4. *No.35* Dharur Plates of Rashtrakuta Govinda III (A.D. 806-7)	A) Govinda III/ Same as above.	A) Same as above.	A) DONOR	l.l. 38, 39, 40, 41, 42, 71,
	B) Duggaiyya Bhaṭṭa	B) *Vatsa gōtra*	B) DONEE	*EI*, XXXVI, 1965, pp.293-
		C) Lesser Chiefs	C) ADDRESSEES	296.

	C) i. *rāśtrapati* ii. *viśayapati* iii. *grāmakūtā* iv. *yuktaka* v. *niyuktaka* vi. *ādhikārika* vii. *mahattara*	D) Same as above.	D) EXECUTOR	
	D) Devaiyaraṇaka/*dūtaka*			
5. *No. CXXV* Sanskrit and Old Canarese Inscriptions (A.D. 806-7)	A) Govinda III/ Same as above.	A) Same as above.	A) DONOR	l.l. 33-34, 35, 36, 39, 61. *IA*, XI, 1882, pp. 159-160.
	B) Chaturvedi Damodarabhaṭṭa	B) *Bhāradvāja gōtra*/ belonged to the assembly of *Chaturvedis*	B) DONEE	
	C) i. *rāśtrapati* ii. *viśyapati* iii. *grāmakūtā* iv. *ayuktāka* v. *niyuktaka* vi. *ādhikārika* vii. *mahattara*	C) Lesser Chiefs	C) ADDRESSEES	
	D) Bhuvirāna/*dūtaka*	D) Same as above.	D) EXECUTOR	
6. *No. CXXVII* Sanskrit and Old Canarese Inscriptions (A.D. 812-13)	A) Śri Karkkarājadēva/ *mahasāmantādhipati*	A) Laṭeśvara, belongs to the main ruling family.	A) DONOR	l.l. 41-43, 45, 68, 69. *IA*, XII, 1883, pp. 160-161.
			B) DONEE	

(Contd.)

CHART - X B *(Contd.)*

i	ii	iii	iv	v
	B) Bhānu	B) *Vātsyāyana gōtra*, belongs to the Society of *Chaturvedis* and is a student of *mādhyandina śākha*	C) ADDRESSEES	
	C) i. *rāśtrapati* ii. *viśayapati* iii. *grāmakūtā* iv. *ādhikārika* v. *mahattaras*.		D) WRITER E) EXECUTOR	
		C) Lesser Chiefs	F) Conquered by the Ruler	
	D) Durgabhaṭṭa/ *mahāsandhivigrahika*	D) Minister of war and peace		
	E) Śri Dantivarmmā/*dūtaka*	E) Same as above		
	F) *mahasāmantas*	F) Lesser Chiefs		
7. *No. 28 'D'* Mantrawadi Inscription of the time of Amoghavarsha I (A.D. 865)	A) i. 40 *mahājanas* ii. *Gorava Moni* iii. *Elamalliye Sāsanāmum*	A) i. Belong to Elpunse. ii. Śaiva Priest iii. Managers of Elmvalli temple of *mahadēva*.	A) i, ii, iii. DONORS	l.l. 7-17 *EI*, VII. 1901-02, p. 200.
	B) Priest		B) DONEE	
8. *No.CXXXVIII* Sanskrit and Old Canarese Inscriptions (A.D. 866)	A) Devaṇṇaya	A) Governor of Beḷvola-300	A) DONOR	l.l. 7, 18, 20, 22, 23, *IA*, II, 1883, pp. 218-219.
	B) 200 *mahājanas*	B) Belong to Srivūr	B) DONEES	

Inscription	Names/Titles	Description	Role	
	C) i. Mādhavayya ii. Nimbichara-Bammayya iii. Sirigāvunda	C) Not mentioned	C) i. WRITER ii. COMMANDED the writing iii. SET up the charter	
	D) i. *daṇḍanāyakas* ii. *Sāmantās*	D) Lesser Chiefs of various places lying outside the purview of the main ruling dynasty.	D) Defeated by the ruling family of the inscription	
	E) *mahārājadhirāja pañchamahāśabda*	E) Main Ruling Family Chief.	E) Mentioned in eulogy	
9. *No. 11* Nilgund Inscription of the time of Amoghavarsha I (A.D. 806)	A) Amoghavarsha/ *paramabhaṭṭaraka mahārājadhirāja paramēśvara prithuvi vallabha*	A) Main Ruling Family Chief.	A) DONOR	l.l. 9, 13, 20-26. *EI*, VI 1900-01, pp.103-104.
	B) 120 *mahājanas*	B) Belonged to Nirgunda	B) DONEES	
	C) Devaṇṇayya	C) Governor of Beḷvola	C) EXECUTOR	
	D) Kulappayya	D) Governor of Mulgunda-12	D) REQUESTED the Grant to be made.	
	E) i. *daṇḍanāyakas* ii. *Sāmanta* iii. *taḷavargga*	E) i.Incharge of capitals and groups of places ii, iii. Chieftains and other lords of districts	E) SUBORDINATES OF 'A'	

(Contd.)

CHART - X B *(Contd.)*

i	ii	iii	iv	v
10. *No.15,'H'* Ron Inscription of the time of Amoghavarsha I (A.D. 874)	A) Ballavarasa	A) Local Potentate	A) DONOR	l.l. 2, 6, 7. *EI*, XIII, 1915-16, p. 185.
	B) *mahājanas*	B) Belonged to Roṇa	B) DONEES	
	C) Amoghavarsha/ *paramabhaṭṭaraka mahārājadhirāja parameśvara*	C) Main Ruling Family Chief	C) Mentioned in the Eulogy	
11. *No. 15 'I'* Ron Inscription of Turagavedeṅga (A.D. 874)	A) Turagavedeṅga/ *Jagadvikhyata Kishkindapuravareśvara*	A) Lord of the world-renowned Kishkindha, a best of towns/ local personage	A) DONOR	l.l. 3-4, *EI* XIII, p. 187.
	B) *mahājanas*	B) Belonged to Roṇa	B) DONEE	
			C) Feet were washed while making the Grant.	
	C) Santayya/*mahājana*	C) Important person among the *mahājanas*		
	D) *Samaya-paṭṭagāra*	D) Community of weavers attached to the 400 *mahājanas* of Roṇa.	D) DONORS (Separate grant)	

12. *No. 28 'F'* Nidagundi Inscription of the time of Amoghavarsha I (A.D. 874-5)	A) Kundatte	A) Governor of Nidugundage-12	A) DONOR	l.l. 2, 5-12, 15, *EI*, VII, 1901-02, pp. 212-213.
	B) Kuppanna/*perggaḍe*	B) Ruling over Nidugundage - 12	B) BUILDER OF Temple of Śiva	
	C) Gāḍiyamma	C) Local Potentate	C) PROTECTOR	
	D) Samkara/*nāl-gāvuṇda*	D) Local Chief	D) Mentioned in his official capacity	
	E) Bankeya/*arasārar*	E) Ruling over whole of Banavasi - 12000, Belgali - 300, Kundarage - 70, Kundūr - 500 and Purigere - 300	E) FATHER of 'A'	
	F) Amoghavarsha/ *paramabhaṭṭaraka mahārājdhirāja paramēśvara*	F) Chief of the main Ruling Family	F) Mentioned in the eulogy	
13. *No. 15 'K'* Mulgund Inscription of the time of Krishna II (A.D. 902-3)	A) i. *Chaturbhiḥ Śresthibhiḥ* ii. Arasārya iii. *brāhmaṇas* of *beḷḷāḷakula*	A) i. Four headmen of guilds. ii. Son of 'E' (local potentate)/*vaiśya jāti* iii. Land owners	A) i, ii, iii. DONORS	l.l.3, 4, 5, 6-12, *EI*, XIII, 1915-16, pp.192-93.
	B) Kanakasēna	B) Jaina teacher or priest.	B) TRUSTEE	
	C) *mahājanas*	C) Of the city of Mulgunda	C) APPROVERS	
		D) Governor of Dhavaḷa *viśaya*.	D) Chief of a particular place	
			E) BUILDER of a JAINALAYA	

(Contd.)

CHART - X B *(Contd.)*

i	ii	iii	iv	v
	D) Vinayambudhi	E) Local potentate/*vaiśya jāti*/Father of 'A'(ii)	F) Mentioned in the Eulogy	
	E) Arasārya	F) King/belongs to the main Ruling Family.		
	F) Krishna vallabha			
14. *No.4* Venkatapur Inscription of Amoghavarsha (A.D. 906)	A) Bagega/*Perggāvuṇḍa*	A) Senior village headman of Sirivūra	A) DONOR	l.l. 6, 9-13, *EI*, XXVI, 1941. p. 62.
	B) Chandrātēja Bhaṭṭāra	B) Pupil of Mallikārjuna Bhaṭṭara	B) DONEE	
	C) Māyiramma	C) Administrator of Mulgunda - 12	C,D) Governing over various regions	
	D) Mahāsirivanta	D) Governor of Beḷvola - 300		
	E) Amōghavarsha/ *prithuvi vallabha mahārājādhirāja paramēśvara bhaṭṭārara*	E) Chief of the Main Ruling Family	E) Mentioned in the Eulogy	
15. *No. 20* Deoli Plates of Krishna III (940 AD)	A) Krishna vallabha/ *paramabhaṭṭaraka mahārājādhirāja paramēśvara*	A) Chief of the Main Ruling Family	A) DONOR	l.l. 43, 51. *EI*, V, 1898-99, pp.195-196.
	B) Rishiyappa	B) *brāhmaṇa*/student of the *Vāji-kāṇva Śaka*/ *Bhāradvāja gōtra*	B) DONEE	

16. *No. CXXXV* Sanskrit and Old Canarese Inscriptions (A.D. 951-52)	A) i. Achapayya/*Perggaḍe* ii. Kalteyamma/*gāmuṇḍa* iii. 50 *mahājanas*	A) i. Senior village headman of Sarṭavura ii. Village headman of Saraṭavura iii. Of Saraṭavura	A) i,ii,iii. DONORS	l.l. 1, 3, 6, 8-10. 13, 27. *IA*, XII, 1883, pp.257-58.
	B) Ruddapayyana/*aṁgakaram*	B) Bodyguard/governor of the city of Saraṭavura.	B) Mentioned in the capacity of an official	
	C) *Guravas*	C) Śaiva Priest	C) TRUSTEE	
	D) Pittayya/*Ūrodaya*	D) Mayor	D) Requested the *mahājanas* to protect the grant.	
	E) Guligaverenāga	E) Local potentate	E) WRITER	
	F) Krishna III/ *paramabhaṭṭaraka mahārājādhirāja parameśvara*	F) Chief of the Main Ruling Family	F) Mentioned in the Eulogy.	
17. *No. 12* Hulgūr Inscription of Khottiga (A.D. 971-2)	A) Ankabbarasi	A) Wife of Guttiya Gaṅgā.	A) DONOR	l.l. 2, 4, 7, 14,16 *EI*,XXXIV, 1961, pp. 61-62.
	B) Guttiya Gaṅga	B) Governor of Gaṅgavādi 96,000, Kisukādu-70, Purigere-300 and Beḷvola-300	B) REQUESTED the grant to be made	
	C) Mārasinghayya/ *nālgāvuṇda*		C) PROTECTORS	

(Contd.)

CHART - X B *(Contd.)*

i	ii	iii	iv	v
	D) 12 *gāvuṇḍas*	C) Village headman of Purigere-300	D) Mentioned in the Eulogy	
	E) Khottiggadeva/ *nṛpēśvara*	D) Of the village		
		E) Belonged to the Main Ruling Family/Younger brother of Krishna III.		
18. *No. CXXXIV* Sanskrit and Old Canarese Inscriptions (A.D. 971-2)	A) i. Pañchaladēva ii. Malliga-Gādayya	A) i. Governor of Sebbi-30. ii. Local potentate	A) i.ii.DONORS	l.l. 4, 11-12, 14, 17-18. *IA*, XII, 1883, p.256.
			B) TRUSTEES	
	B) 84-*mahājanas*	B) Village elders.	C) Ruling over a particular region	
	C) Marasinghadēva	C) Governor of Gaṅgavādi-96000, Purigere-300 and Beḷvala-300.		
	D) Koṭṭigadeva/ *mahārājādhirāja paramēśvara paramabhaṭṭarakami rājā-mārttaṇḍambe*	D) Chief of the Main Ruling Family	D) Mentioned in the Eulogy.	
19. *No. CXXXVI* Rāshtrakuta Grant of Kakka III (A.D. 972-3)	A) Kakkala dēva/*rāja*	A) Belongs to the main ruling family/ruling over Manyakheta.	A) DONOR	l.l. 42, 46, 49, *IA*, XII, 1883 pp.266-67.
	B) Bhaṭṭa Chaṇṇapayya		B) DONEE	

	C) *rāśtrapati* *viśayapati* *grāmakūta* *mahattara* *āyuktaka* *upāyuktaka* *ādhikārika*	B) *Bhāradvāja gōtra* C) Lesser Chiefs D) Chief of the main ruling family.	C) ADDRESSEES D) Mentioned in the Eulogy	
	D) Akalavarshadēva/ *paramabhaṭṭaraka mahārājādhirāja*			
20. *No. LXXXVII* Rāshtrakuta Grant of Kakka III (A.D. 973-4)	A) Bolayya, Rajāyya, vojayya.	A) Being in Assembly	A) DONOR B,C,D, E,F,G Grant was made while all these persons were holding specified offices.	1.1. 3-18, *IA*, XII, 1883, p.271.
	B) Kakkaladeva/ *prithuvi vallabha mahārājādhirāja paramēśvara*	B) Chief of the main Ruling Family.		
		C) Governor of Purigere-300 and the Beḷvola-300.		
	C) Permānaḍi Mārasinghadēva	D) Governor of 96.		
	D) Pañjala-dēva	E) Governor of the village of Kadekēri		
	E) Mungula voja	F) Village headman		
	F) Bolagaditale and Rājayya/*nāl-gāmuṇḍu*	G) Village chief of a different rank.		
	G) Manayya/*ūrggāmuṇḍu*			

CHART - X C
THE DOMINANT SOCIAL GROUPS
PHASE III (LATTER HALF OF THE 10TH CEN. A.D. - 13TH CEN.A.D.)

i	ii	iii	iv	v
Sl. No. Name of the inscription	Name/Title	*Varṇa/gōtra*/Status	Context	Reference
1. *No.2* Tumbagi Inscription of the Reign of Satyāśraya (A.D. 1004)	A) i. Sethi Brahmayya ii. Aychakkabbe B) i. *urodēya* ii. *mahājana* C) Akaḷanika charitam Irivabedanigaṁ/ *Śri prithuvi vallabha mahārājādhirāja paramēśvara paramabhaṭṭaraka*	A) i. Governor of the Tumbige *Agrahāra.* ii. Daughter of Guṇṇeyya of Kalkene. B) i. Mayor of the town ii. Elders of town C) Chief of the Main Ruling Family	A) i,ii.DONORS B) i,ii.PROTEC-TORS C) Mentioned in the Eulogy	1.1. 4-6, 9-11, 25-30 *EI*, XVII, 1923, pp.8-9.
2. *No.168* Kautheem Plates of Vikram-aditya V (A.D. 1008)	A) Vikramaditya V/ Śri *prithuvi vallabha mahārājādhirāja paramēśvara parambhaṭṭaraka* B) Bhaṭṭa Dēvevisottara/ *bhaṭṭa*	A) Chief of the Main Ruling Family. B) *Śakha* of *Yajurveda* C) Various official groups.	A) DONOR B) DONEE C) ADDRESSEES	1.1.58, 59 63, *IA*, XVI, 1887, p.24.

		C) *rāśtrapati* *viśayapati* *grāmakūtaka* *āyuktaka* *niyuktaka* *adhikārika* *mahattara*			
3.	*No.7* Alur Inscription of the Reign of Vikram-aditya V (A.D. 1011)	A) i. Chattivarayya/ *urōdeya* ii. 200 of Alur B) Venneyya Bhatta/ *mahāprachaṇda daṇḍanāyakam* C) Amaracharya Bhaṭṭaraka D) Maruloja/*prasāda chakravarty* E) *mahājanas* F) Vikramaditya V/ *Chakravarti* *Śri prithuvi vallabha* *mahārjādhirāja* *paramēśvara* *paramabhaṭṭarakaṁ* G) *mahāsēnadhipati*	A) i. Village headman ii. assembly B) *brāhmaṇa* of *Kamma kula* C) Of Guheya monastery/ preceptor of Venneyya Bhaṭṭa D) Emperor of Palaces/ title of a stone mason E) Elders of village F) Chief of the main ruling family G) lesser chief.	A) i,ii.DONORS B) DONEEand DONOR C) DONEE D) WRITER E) WITNESSES F,G) Mentioned in the Eulogy	l.l. 2, 15, 21-24, 30 35, 46.*EI*, XVI, 1922-23, pp.29-30.
4.	*No. 38 'A'* Of the Reign of Jayasimha II (A.D. 1022)	A) Machimayya B) *Pannirvvar, brāhmaṇar* C) Jayasimha II/ Śri *prithuvi vallabha* *mahārājādhirāja* *paramēśvara* *paramabhaṭṭaraka*	A) Leader of the sages B) Twelve *brāhmaṇas* C) Chief of the main ruling family	A) DONOR B) DONEE C) Mentioned in the Eulogy	l.l. 1,11,15, 16, *EI*, XIX, 1927. p.224.

(*Contd.*)

CHART - X C *(Contd.)*

i	ii	iii	iv	v
5. *No. 37* Gadag Inscription of the Reign of Jayasimha II (A.D. 1037)	A) Madimayya Nāyaka/ *urōdeya* B) Damodara Setti C) *brāhmaṇas* D) The 1000 E) Dhōyipayyan/*Perggaḍe* F) Jagadekamalla Jayasingha II/ *Śri prithuvi vallabha mahārājādjirāja paramēśvara paramabhaṭṭaraka*	A) Village headman B) Local potentate C) *brāhmaṇas* D) Assembly E) Senior village headman F) Main ruling family chief	A) DONOR B) DONEE as well as DONOR C) These shall consume from whatever remains from the services of God. D) PROTECTORS E) BUILDER of the temple of 12 nārāyaṇa Gods. F) Mentioned in the Eulogy	1.1.1-2,6,7, 10-11, 19, 20. *EI*, XIX, 1927-28 pp.219-220.
6. *No. 11 'B'* of the Reign of Jayasimha II (A.D. 1037)	A) *mūṛunāḍa suṁkigaruv* B) i. Māra Gāvuṇḍa of Pottiyur, Surimayya, Poleyamma, Gettimayya. ii. Būhimayya/*Perggaḍe* iii. Dasimayya/*Sēnabōva* C) The 30	A) Three controllers of taxes. B) i. High revenue officials led by Mara Gavuṇḍa village headman. ii. Senior village headman iii. Town clerk of four towns.	A) DONORS B) i,ii,iii. Arranged for the division of the tolls on betel leaves	1.1.4,8,11 19,22-24, 27-28,31-38, *EI*,XVI, 1922-23, pp.77-79.

		between various taxation departments
	C) The Assembly	C) DONORS
D) i. Akkādevi ii. Mayuravarman/ *mahāmaṇḍaleśvara pañchamahāśabda* iii. Maragāvuṇḍa iv. Simgana Chaṭṭan/ *Samadhigata pañcha-mahāśabda-mahāsandhi-vigrahādhipati mahāprachaṇḍa daṇḍanāyakaṁ* v. Chāvaṇarasar/ *Kannada Sandhi-vigrahidaṇḍanāyakam* vi. Akalimayyaṁ/ *perggaḍe* vii. Sangavayya/ *Suṁkaverggaḍe* viii. Chavuṇḍamayya/ *Suṁkavesrggaḍe* ix. Dudiyamma/ *Suṁkaverggaḍe*	D) i. Ruling over Banavasi - 1200 ii. Ruler of Banavasi-1200 and Panungal-500 iii. Holding shrievalty over Panungal-500 iv. Ruler of Beḷvola-300 and Purigere-300 v. Lesser chief vi. Senior village headman vii,viii,ix. Controller of taxes of the *Paññakeni veḍḍa-lāguḷa*(connected with traffic and trade)	D) i,ii,iii,iv,v, vi,vii,viii,ix. were holding their respective offices.
E) Jagadekamalla Jayasinghadeva/ *mahārājādhirāja parameśvara paramabhaṭṭaraka*		E) Mentioned in the Eulogy

(Contd.)

CHART - X C *(Contd.)*

i	ii	iii	iv	v
7. *No.25* Hulgur Inscription of the Reign of Jayasimha II and the Yadava Kanhara (A.D. 1038)	A) i. Nidugundara Būta Gāvuṇḍa ii. *mahāsāmanta* Jayakesira/ *nāḷgavuṇḍu* iii. Tipparasa/ *mahāpradhānaṁ* B) i. *hamnivaru gāvuṇḍu* ii. *nakhara* iii. *mummuri daṇḍas* C) *Vāvaṇarasa/ mahāprachaṇḍa daṇḍanāyaka* D) *Irivabeḍanga Marāsingadeva/ pañchamahāśabda māhāsamanta*	A) i. Village headman ii. for the Purigere-300 iii. High minister B) i. 12 officers of Hullungur ii. Merchants of Hullungur iii. A guild. C) Ruler of Belvoḷa-300 and Purigere-300	A) i. DONOR ii. Gave the land to A i. iii. DONOR B) i,ii,iii. DONEES C,D) Were Ruling their respective provinces at this time and are mentioned in the eulogy	l.l.1-3,7,9, 11-12,19,24-25 31-33.*EI* XVI,1922-23, pp.335-336.
8. *No.28* Chikkerur Inscription of Somēsvara I (A.D. 1048)	A) i. Rēvakabbarasi/ *Pasāyitē* ii. 1000 *mahājanas* B) i. 1000 *mahājanas* ii. 32 *mahājanas*	A) i. Official of Kiriya-Kerur ii. Elders of Kiriya-Kerur B) i. Elders of	A) i. DONOR - purchased land from A ii. B) i,ii,iii,iv,	l.l. 1-3, 9, 10, 11, 16-23, *EI*, XXXVI, 1965, pp.221-222.

		iii. Kālidasayya/ *Kannada-Sandhi-vigraha mahā-prachaṇḍa daṇḍanāyaka* iv. Nāraṇayya/ *Pradhānadaṇḍanāyaka* v.Bhōgavarayya/ *Pathaḷe-verggade* vi.Gundayya/*Perggade* vii.Dāvaṇagahisa/ *purohita* C) Kētimayya/*Sēnabōva* D) Trailokyamalladēva/ *prithuvi vallabha mahārājādhirāja paramēśvara paramabhaṭṭaraka*	Kiriya-Kerur, of Iśavura and of Tilivalli ii. Elders of Taṇagundur iii. Minister for war and peace and commander of forces iv. Minister and Commander v. Village headman vi. Senior village headman of Mudrāvaṇa vii. Priest C) An Accountant D) Chief of the main ruling family	v,vi,vii. WITNESSES to the above deed. C) WRITER D) Mentioned in the Eulogy	
9.	*No. 10 'A'* of the Reign of Somēśvara I (A.D. 1052-3)	A) Harikeśarideva/ *mahamaṇḍaleśvara* B) 300-*mahājanas* C) i. Trailokyamalla Ahavamalla/ *prithuvi vallabha mahārājādhirāja paramēśvara paramabhaṭṭaraka*	A) Governor B) Elders of the *agrahāra* of Nirili C) i. Chief of the main ruling family ii. Lord of Banavasi D) i. Accountant ii. Stone mason	A) DONOR B) CONVENED and HONOURED C) i,ii. Mentioned in the Eulogy D) i. WRITER ii.EXECUTOR	l.l. 1-6, 11 12 - 15, 21-22. *EI*, XVI, 1922-23, pp.67-68.

(Contd.)

CHART - X C *(Contd.)*

i	ii	iii	iv	v
	ii. Mayuravarman/ *mahāmaṇḍalesvara pañchamahāśabda* D) i. Jōgivayya/Sēnabōva ii. Chittojam/ *kalukutigaṁ*			
10. *No. 9 'A'* Mulgund Inscription of the Reign of Someśvara I (A.D. 1053)	A) Beldēva (Jain)/ *mahāsandhivigrahādikāri* B) Nayasēna Paṅḍitadeva/ *mahāpurusha* C) *mahājanas* D) i. Trailokyamalladeva/ *mahārājādhirāja paramēśvara paramabhaṭṭaraka* ii. Somēśvara II/ *Samādhigata pañchamahāśabda mahāmaṇḍaleśvara*	A) Minister for war and peace B) Noble man. C) elders of village D) i.Chief of the main ruling family ii.Son of the above.	A) DONOR B) Grant was made after washing his feet. C) ACKNOWLEDGERS D) i, ii. Mentioned in the Eulogy	l.l. 3,5, 16, 17, 23, 30, *EI*, XVI, 1922-23. pp.55-56.

11. *No.36* Kelawadi Inscription of the time of Somēśvara I (A.D. 1053)	A) Supparasa/*mahāmātya* B) i. Chaṭṭapayyana ii. Sivoja C) i. Trailokyamalladeva/ *prithuvi vallabha mahārājādhirāja paramēśvara* ii. Bhogadēvarasa/ *pañchamahāśabda mahāsāmantadhipati mahāprachaṇḍa daṇḍanāyaka*	A) Chief Minister B) Not mentioned C) i.Chief of the main ruling family. ii.Governor of Pangaragi-12/ uncle of Supparasa, the *mahāmātya*	A) DONOR B) i.WRITER ii.Commanded the chart to be written C) i,ii.Mentioned in the Eulogy l.l. 1,4-6, 15, 22-23, 31-32. *EI*, IV, 1896, pp.261-226.
12. *No. 26* Tilvalli Inscription of the Reign of Somēśvara I (A.D. 1053-4)	A) i. Sōvanāthayya/ *mahāmātya vaḍḍa-rāvulda perggaḍe*. ii. Nāgavarmayya, Śivanāgayya and Singayya/*Keṇikāra dhishṭaya* iii. Chattimayya/ *Perjumkada Perggaḍe* B) Trailokyamalladeva/ *mahārājādhirāja*, *prithuvi vallabha*, *paramabhaṭṭaraka*, *paramēśvara*	A) i.Headman for tolls and duties. ii.Presidents of the *Keṇikāras* of the *atthāṇāntaras*(primary courts)of Palūr and Pānungal. iii.High minister and senior village headman. B) Chief of the main ruling family	A) i,ii,ii. DONORS B) Mentioned in the Eulogy l.l. 3-4, 10-12, 14, 17, 19. *EI*, XVI, 1922-23, pp.338-39.

(Contd.)

CHART - X C *(Contd.)*

i	ii	iii	iv	v
13. *No. 30 'A'* Inscription of Vishnu vardhana Vijayaditya (A.D. 1064)	A) Vishnuvardhana Vijayaditya/*mahārāja* B) Trailokymalla/ *mahārājādhirāja prithuvi vallabha paramabhaṭṭaraka paramēśvara*	A) Governor of Nolambavāḍi-32,000 province. B) Chief of the main ruling family	A) DONOR B) Mentioned in the Eulogy	l.l. 1-3, 5, 10-11, *EI*, IV, 1896, p.212.
14. *No.11 'C'* Of the Reign of Somēśvara I (A.D. 1066)	A) i. Joyiyarasa/ *mahāsāmānta* ii. Toyimadēva *mahāmaṇḍalēśvara* B) i. Suṁkigaruv ii. *uguras* iii. gāvuṇḍa C) i. Trailokyamalladeva/ *mahārājādhirāja prithuvi vallabha paramabhaṭṭaraka paramēśvara* ii. Jēmarasa/ *mahāmaṇḍalēśvara*	A) i. Ruler of Pottiyur. ii. Lord of Banavasi and Panungal-500/ *Kadamba-kula* B) i. Tax Controllers ii. Trade guild iii. Village headman C) i. Chief of the main ruling family ii. Ruler of many towns.	A) i, ii.DONORS B) i,ii,iii.iv. PROTECTORS C) i,ii.Mentioned in the Eulogy	l.l. 1-3, 8, 11, 18, 37-38. *EI*, XVI, 1922-23, pp.85-86.

15. *No. 10 'B'* Of the Reign of Somēśvara II (A.D. 1075)	A) i. Vikramadityadeva/ *mahāmaṇḍaleśvara* ii. Śantivarmadeva/ *mahāmaṇḍalēśvara* iii. Iśvaramayya/ *mahāpradhānam piriyaperggaḍe daṇḍanāyakaṁ* iv. Śōbhanayyam/ *mahāpradhānam perggade* B) 300 *mahājanas* C) Bhuvanaikamalladēva/ *prithuvi vallabha mahārājādhirāja paramēśvara* D) Sūdōja/*Kalukutiga*	A) i. Governor ii. Presides over 85 cities/*Kadamba kula* iii. High minister, Commander, headman iv. High minister, headman B) Elders of the *agrahāra* of Nirili C) Chief of the main ruling family D) Stone mason	A) i,ii,iii,iv. DONORS B) DONEES C) Mentioned in the Eulogy D) EXECUTOR	l.l. 1-6, 9, 10, 11, 21, 30, 33-34, 43. *EI*, XVI, 1922-23. pp.70-71.
16. *No.24* Hulgur Inscription of the Reign of Vikram-aditya VI (A.D. 1077)	A) i. *Samasta Suṁkige* ii. Barmaṇṇa and Achimayya/ *Suṁka perggade* iii. Dāsiyaṇṇaṁ/*talabōgi* B) i. Tribhuvanamalladeva/ *prithuvi vallabha mahārājādhirāja paramabhaṭṭaraka paramēśvara*	A) i. Tax Controllers. ii. Tax collectors. iii. Lesser chief B) i. Chief of the main ruling family. ii. Ruler of Beḷvola-300 and Purirgene-300.	A) i,ii.DONORS B) i,ii.PROTEC-TORS C) Mentioned in the Eulogy	l.l. 4-6, 9-11, 25-30. *EI*, XVII, 1923, pp. 8-9.

(Contd.)

CHART - X C *(Contd.)*

i	ii	iii	iv	v
	ii. Jayakesiyarasa/ *mahāsāmanta nārgāvuṇda* iii. Jayasinghadeva			
17. *No. 37 'C'* Of the time of Vikram-aditya VI (A.D. 1105)	A) Satyaprachāra Bhaṭṭarakadeva B) *nakharamuṁnānādesi-gatrigaru hannavaṇarum* C) Vikramaditya VI/ *prithuvi vallabha mahārājadhirāja paramabhaṭṭaraka paramēśvara* D) Raviyana Bhaṭṭa/ *daṇḍanāyaka*	A) Governor of Sagara-300 B) Merchants, foreign merchants, market officials. C) Chief of the main ruling family. D) Ruling over Yēwur	A) DONOR B) To pay customs,duty in kind for the upkeep of the temple. C) Mentioned in the Eulogy D) Mentioned in the Eulogy	l.l. 3,10,21, 32.*EI*, XII. 1913-14, p.330.
18. *No. 37 'D'* Of the time of Vikram-aditya VI (A.D. 1110)	A) i. 120 *Kottali* of Yēwur ii. *Kālkutiga gottali Kaṁchagarāra gottāli* iv. *maṁbadagi-kammārar-akkasāleyaru, berattuṁbur adiy-āgiokkala*	A) i. 120 members of the guilds of Yēwur ii. Stone cutters guild. iii. Braziers guild iv. the carpenters, black-smiths, gold smiths. B) Chief of the main ruling family.	A) i,ii,iii,iv. DONORS B) Mentioned in the Eulogy.	l.l. 1, 2-3, 11-15, *EI*, XII, 1913-14, pp.332-333.

	B) Vikramaditya/ *mahārājādhirāja prithuvi vallabha paramabhaṭṭaraka paramēśvara*			
19. *No.9* Momigatti Inscription of the 49th year of Vikram-aditya VI (A.D. 1124)	A) Udayana Gāvuṇḍa B) Vamsakti Paṇḍita/*āchārya* C) *gāvuṇḍas* D) i. Jakesi Deva/ *mahāmaṇḍaleśvara* ii. Tribhuvanamalladeva/ *prithuvi vallabha mahārājādhirāja paramabhaṭṭaraka paramēśvara*	A) Son of Malla Gāvuṇḍa of Eraṇigeneyahalli B) Priest of the establish-ment of Kali-dēva svāmi C) Headman of Kundur D) i. Governor ii. Chief of the main ruling family	A) DONOR B) DONEE C) Grant was made in the presence of these persons D) i,ii.Men-tioned in the Eulogy	l.l. 2, 12, 17, 19-20, *EI*, XVII, 1923, pp.118-119.
20. *No. XXXIII* Western Chalukya Grant of Jagadekamalla (AD 1139-40)	A) Mahadeva and Pāladeva/ *daṇḍanāyaka* B) Rāmadeva/*Perggaḍe* C) i. Jagadekamalla/ *mahāsāmantādhipati* ii. *mahāsāmantādhipati mahāprachaṇḍa daṇḍanāyaka*	A) Commander of forces B) Headman C) i. Chief of the main ruling family ii. General Superintendent iii. Most fierce commander of forces.	A) DONOR B) Grant was made at the request of him. C) i,ii,iii. Mentioned in the Eulogy	l.l. 4-6, 13-14, 27-29. *IA*, VI, 1900-01, pp.140-141.

CHART - XI A AND B
XI A THE SUBJECT SOCIAL GROUPS
PHASE I(MIDDLE OF THE 6th CEN. A.D. - MIDDLE OF THE 8th CEN. A.D.)

i	ii	iii	iv	v	vi
Sl. No. Name of the Inscription	Rural Groups	Professional Groups	*Varṇa/jāti/kula*	Context	References
No.8 1. Chiplun Copper-Plate Grant of Pulakesin II (A.D. 609-642)		a) *grihitbhṛtya* b) *viṣaya-vāsina*		a)king's benevolent attitude towards these groups b)Command issued to the inhabitants.	l.l. 6, 9. *EI*, III, 1895 p. 51.

XI B THE SUBJECT SOCIAL GROUPS
PHASE II (MIDDLE OF THE 8TH CEN. A.D. - LATTER HALF OF THE 10TH CEN. A.D.)

i	ii	iii	iv	v	vi
No. 50 1. Hebbal Inscription of AD 975		A) *Parey-oy(v)ṁge* B) *ayvar-ssuḷeya* (Dancing girls) C) *kāḷeyat-aṁge*(horn-blowers).		*A,B,C,D* were allotted various measurements of land originally donated to God	l.l.34-40, *EI*, IV, 1898 p. 354.

CHART - XI C
THE SUBJECT SOCIAL GROUPS
PHASE III (LATTER HALF OF THE 10TH CEN. A.D. - 12TH CEN. A.D.)

i		ii	iii	iv	v	vi
Sl. No.	Name of the Inscription	Rural	Professional Groups	*Varṇa/jāti/kula*	Context	References
1.	*No.2* Tumbagi Inscription of the Reign of Satyāśraya (A.D. 1004)		A) *Parekara-suḷeyar* (drummers (public/dancing women)		A) A field of 30 *mattars* is granted out of 200 *mattars* donated to God.	l.l. 18-19, *E.I*, XVII, 1923 p.8.
2.	*No.37* Gadag Inscription of the Reign of Jayasimha II (A.D. 1037)		*Caṇḍāḷa*		Mentioned in the list of punishments	l.8, *EI*, *XIX*, II p. 219.
3.	*No. 10* Arasibidi Inscription of the Reign of Someśvara I (A.D. 1047)		A) *Parekara* (drummer) B) *Kalkutiga* (Stone Mason)		A,B) are given a few *mattars* out of the main grant made to the God.	1.16, *EI*, XVII, 1923, p.122

(Contd.)

CHART - XI C (*Contd.*)

i	ii	iii	iv	v	vi
No.30'A' 4. Inscription of Vishnuvaradhanā Vijayaditya (A.D. 1064)		A) *Su(sū)leya rgga* (dancing girls)		A) A part of the grant made to the God had to be set aside for their Maintenance	1.18, *EI*,IV,1898. p. 213.
No. 11 'C' 5. Of the Reign of Someśvara I (A.D. 1066)		A) *Parekāraggam* (drummers) B) *Pātrakkaṁ* (A dancing woman) C) *Vaṁsigar-ggaṁ*(*flute* players) D) *bojaṁgar* (Plantain-leaf or betel-leaf seller E) *taṁbuliga sasirwaruṁ* (betal leaf sellers)		A,B,C) Donees of a part of the grant made	ll.33-39, *EI*, XVI, 1922, p. 85.

6.	*No.11 'A'* Of the Regin of Satyāśraya (A.D. 1077-78)	A) *taṁbūliga-sasirwar* (the 1000 of the betel-leaf sellers in assembly)	*Gāvuṇḍa*	A) Donors of one *visa* in perpetuity	1.10, *EI*, XVI, 1922 p. 75.
7.	*No. 32 'B'* Of the Time of Vikramaditya VI (A.D. 1077)		*Caṇḍāla*	Mentioned in the list of punishments.	1,280, *EI*, XII, 1913-14 p. 284.

CHART - XII A
NATURE OF GRANTS MADE
PHASE I(MIDDLE OF THE 6TH CEN. A.D. - MIDDLE OF THE 8TH CEN. A.D.)

	i	ii	iii	iv	v	vi
Sl. No.	Name of the Inscription	Grants Made	Recipients	Economic Immunities	Juridical/ Administrative Immunities	Reference
1.	*CXX* Sanskrit and Old Canarese Inscriptions (A.D. 567-8)	Field Measuring 25 *nivaratanas* and 8 *mattars* of rice land.	*dānasāla* of a Jinālaya			l.l.7-9, *IA*, XI, 1882, p.69.
2.	*XL* Western Chalukya Grant of Mangala (A.D. 578-90)	Village of Kundivaṭaka.	*brāhmaṇa*			l.l.18, 20, *IA*, *VII*, 1878,p.162.
3.	*8* Chiplun Copper Plate Grant of Pulakesin II (Bet. AD 609- (A.D. 642).	Village of Amaravaṭavaka	*brāhmaṇa*		*Chāta-bhaṭa-dūta-rājāpurushāṇaṁ apravē saniyaṁ* (Free from the right of entry by the irregular and regular troops, messengers and kings' servants).	ll.11,12, 15-16, *EI*, III, 1895, p.51.

4.	*XXVII* Chalukya Grant of Pulakesin II (A.D. 613)	Village of Makarappi	*brāhmaṇa*	*sānidhiḥ, sōpanidhiḥ sāklupta, sōparikaraḥ* (With treasures and deposits and assig- ments of major taxes)		l.l. 13, 16 17, *IA* VI, 1877, pp.73-74.
5.	*9* Lohaner Plates of Chalukya Pulakesin II (A.D. 630)	Village of Goviyanaka	*brāhmaṇa*		*Chāta-bhaṭa-dūta-rājapurushāṇāṁ apraveśanīyaṁ āchandrarkavakshitisthiti samakālīna* (To be preserved till the exsitence of moon, stars and earth).	l.l.21-24, *EI*,XXVII, 1947, p.40.
6.	*LII* Chalukya Grant of Pulakesin II (Date not Recorded)	A)Villages of Kuvalalahusu B)A field of 25 *nivaratanas*	A)*brāhmaṇas* B)*brāhmaṇa*			l.11, *IA*, VIII, 1879, p.43-44.
7.	*XXVIII* Chalukya Grant of Vikramaditya I (Date not Recorded)	Village of Chintakuntha	*brāhmaṇas*			l.l.30-39 *IA*, VI, 1877, p.77.

(*Contd.*)

CHART - XII A *(Contd.)*

	i	ii	iii	iv	v	vi
8.	*30* Poona Plates of Chalukya Vinayaditya (A.D. 690)	Field of 50 *nivaratanas* in the village of Toraveh	*brāhmaṇas*		*Sarva-bādhāpariharaṁ* (Free from all Conflicting claims).	l.l.26,27 *EI*, XXV, 1939, p.291.
9.	*XXIX* Western Chalukya Grant of Vinayaditya (A.D. 690)	Of certain dues, Perquisites of taxes called *ādityunchnamaru manna* and *mārunchhamarumanna* at various villages.	*brāhmaṇa*	*sabhōgadattaḥ* (Rent-free land)	*āchandrārkavakshitasthiti samakālina* (To be preserved as long as the sun, moon, earth and the Ocean last).	l.l.28-32, *IA*, VI, 1878, p.86-87.
10.	*XLVIII* Of Western Chalukya king Vinayaditya (A.D. 694-695)	A)Village of Kirukāgāmasi B)Partly cultivated and uncultivated field	A & B) *brāhmaṇa*	*sā-bhogadattaḥ*	*sarvva-bādha-pariharōdattaḥ*	l.l.29,37, *IA*, VII, 1878, p.302

187 11. Sorab Copper Plate Grant of Vinayaditya (A.D. 692)	Village of Salivage	*brāhmaṇa*	*sā-hiraṇyaṁ-ākaraṁ* (with gold, and free from taxes)	*a-bhaṭa pravēsaṁsarvva-bādhā-parihārōdattaḥ*	1.1.29,37, *IA*, VII, 1878, p.302.
LVII 12. Of Western Chalukya king Vijayaditya (A.D. 696-7)	Of a *Sontige* of oil on one oil-mill	Priest			1.1.4-5, *IA*, VIII, 1879, p.285.
39 13. Jamalgama Grant of Chalukya Vijay-aditya (A.D. 697)	Village of Jamalgama	*brāhmaṇa*	*sā-bhōgaḥdattaḥ*	*āchandrarkavakshitisthiti samākālīna*	1.1.36-37 40-41, *EI*, XXXVI, 1965 p.361.
LXXVII 14. Western Chalukya Grant of Vijayaditya (A.D. 700)	Village of Nerur	*brāhmaṇa*	*sā-bhōgadattaḥ*	*sarvvabādhāparihārodattaḥ*	1.1.34-35, *IA*, IX, 1880, p.128.
LXXVIII 15. Western Chalukya Grant of Vijaya-ditya (A.D. 705)	Village of Hikulambha	eight *brāh-maṇas*		*āchandrarkavakshitisthiti samākālīna*	1.1.36-38, *IA*, IX, 1880, p.131-132.

(Contd.)

CHART - XII A *(Contd.)*

i	ii	iii	iv	v	vi
LXXIX 16. Western Chalukya Grant of Vijayaditya (Not Dated)	Village of Malavura	*brāhmaṇa*	*sā-bhōgodattaḥ*	*sarvvabādhāparihāraṁ*	l.l.41-42, 45, *IA*, IX, 1880, p.133.
3 17. Grant of the Western Chalukya Vijayaditya (A.D. 731)	Village of Taravadra	*brāhmaṇa*		*āchandrārkavakshiti-sthitisamakālīna*	l.l.37-38, 43-44, *EI*, XXV, 1939 p.24.
23 18. Narwan Plates of Chalukya Vikramaditya II (A.D. 742)	Village of Naravavana	*brāhmaṇas*	*abhyantara siddhi sahitaṁ* (With internal income or taxes payable to the village authorities as against those payable to the king).	*āchāta-bhaṭa pravēśya sarvabādhāparihāraṁ, āchandrarkavakshitisthiti samakālīna*	l.l.64-66. 72, *EI*, XXVII, 1947, p.131.
LXXVI 19. Western Chalukya Grant of Nāgavardhana (Date not Recorded)	Village of Balegrana	Ascetics residing at the Kapileś-vara temple	*Udraṇga* and *upārikara* (major and minor taxes).	*achaṭa, bhaṭa pravēśya āchandrārkavakshitisthiti samakālīna.*	*IA*, IX, 1880 p.124.

1 20. Pattadakal Pillar Inscrip-tion of the time of Kirti varman II (A.D. 754)	Half of a village and fields of 30 *nivaratanas*	*brāhmaṇa*			1.23, *EI*, III, 1895, p.6.
4 21. Ellora Plates of Dantidurga (A.D. 742)	Village of Pippalapala	*brāhmaṇas*	*abhyantarasiddhi*	*āchāta-bhaṭa pravēsya*	l.l.17-21, *EI*, XXV, 1939, p.29-30.
CXXI 22. Sanskrit and Old Canarese Inscriptions (A.D. 753-4)	Village of Karandivadeja -phitadēulavāda	*brāhmaṇa*	*sāvriksha mālākulaḥ* (rows and groups of trees), *hiraṇya* (gold), *yathāsamū-chita-bhāga-bhōga Kara-sarvvotpattyā-di-sahito-dattaḥ* (proceeds of proper shares and taxes)	*a chāta-bhaṭa pravesya daṇḍa-dōṣa-dasaparā dhaḥ* (proceeds of punish-ments inflicted for ten classes of offences). *asya bhuṁjataḥ bhūmjā-payata, krišataḥ karsap-ayataḥ* (enjoy it or cause it to be enjoyed, cultivate it or cause it to be culti-vated), *bhūmichhid-raṇyāya* (rent free enjoyment of land by one who brings it under cultivation for the first time).	l.l. 28-43, *IA*, XI, 1882, p.112-113.

CHART - XII B
NATURE OF GRANTS MADE
PHASE II (MIDDLE OF THE 8TH CEN. A.D. - LATTER HALF OF 9TH CEN. A.D.)

	i	ii	iii	iv	v	vi
Sl. No.	Name of the Inscription	Grants Made	Recipients	Economic Immunities	Juridical/ Administrative Immunities	Reference
	16 'C'					
1.	Lakshmeshwar Inscription of the Time of Sri-vallabha (A.D. 793)	A proportionate quantity of the goods turned out-one (length) on each forty lengths, but below 30, above 200, half a length	Temple			l.l, 6-12, *EI*, VI, 1900, pp. 166.
	2					
2.	Anjanavati Plates of Govinda III (A.D. 800-01)	Village of Anjanavati	13 *brāhmaṇas*	*Udraṇga, upārikara, hiraṇya-dhana. bhōgābhyantarasiddhi* (Right-to enjoy the entire internal revenue income or all the taxes to be paid to local authorities).	*brahmādeya*(tax free gift to brahmins) *kriśataḥ karśayataḥ bhuṁjataḥ bhuṁjayataḥ āchandrārkava-kshitisaritparvatasa-makālinaḥ, putra-pautraṇvayakramapa bhōgābhyantarasiddhya* (To be enjoyed by sons and the sons sons).	l.l.31-32, 36,39 48-49. *EI*, XXIII, 1936, pp.16-17.

	35				
3.	Dharur Plates of Rashtrakuta Govinda III, (A.D. 806-7)	Village of Anahe	*brāhmaṇa*	*udraṇga, upārikara sabhūtopattapratyā-yaḥ*(income resulting from storms, earth quakes and other natural changes). *sōtpadyamānavisti-kaḥ*(Forced labour), *sadhānyahiraṇyādeyaḥ bhūmichhidraṇyayēna*	*Sādaṇḍadaśaparādhaḥ acāṭabhaṭapravēśya achandrārkkarṇavakshi -tisaritparvvatasama-kālīnaḥ putrapautranva-yakramopabhogyaḥ, brahmadāyarahito-bhyantara siddhaya-bhumjato-bhojayataḥ kriṣatoḥ karśayataḥ*	I.1.41-53, *EI*, XXXVI, 1965, p.294.
	CXXV				
4.	Sanskrit and Old Canarese Inscriptions (A.D. 806-7)	Village of Ambakagrāma	*brāhmaṇa*	*Udraṇga, upārikaraḥ, sabhūtopattapratyāyaḥ sotpadyamānaistikaṁ sadhānyahiraṇyādeyaḥ*	*Sādaṇḍaśaparādhaḥ ā chandr-ārk-ārṇavaks-ḥiti-saritparvvata-sama kālīnaḥ, putrapautrān-vaya-kramopabhogyaḥ brahmadāyarahitodyaḥ ntara siddhya bhūmichhi-draṇyāya. bhuṁato bhojayatoḥ kṛṣataḥ karśayataḥ*	I.1.37-56, *IA*, XI, 1882, pp.159-60.
	CXXVII				
5.	Sanskrit and Old Canarese Inscri-ptions (A.D. 812-13)	Village of Vaḍapadraka	*brāhmaṇa*	*udraṇga, upārikaraḥ, bhūtapattapratyāyaḥ sotpadyamānavistikaṁ sādhānyahiraṇyādēyaḥ*	*Sādaṇḍadaśaparādhaḥ āchandra-ārkarṇavakshiti -saritparvvata-samakālī naḥ, putrapautrānvaya kramopabhogyaḥ, brahmadā-yarahitoṭbhyantarasiddhya, bhūmicchidrāṇyaya, bhuṁjato-bhojayataḥ, kriṣatoḥkarśa-yataḥ*	I.1.43-57, *IA*, XII, 1883, p.161.

(*Contd.*)

CHART - XII B *(Contd.)*

i	ii	iii	iv	v	vi
28'D' 6. Mantrawadi Inscription of the time of Amoghavarsha I (A.D. 865)	85 *mattars* of cultivable land; 6 plots of garden land	Priest of temple of *mahādeva*		*sarva-bādha-parihāraṁ*	l.l.7-17, *EI*, VII, 1901, p.201.
CXXVIII 7. Sanskrit and Old Canarese Inscriptions (A.D. 866)	Tax on clarified butter.	*mahājanas* of Sirivura.			l.l.19-20, *IA*, XII, 1883, p.219.
'11' 8. Nilgund Inscription of the Time of Amoghavarsha I (A.D. 866).	Tax on clarified butter.	*mahājanas* of Nirgunda			l.l.24-26 *EI*, VI, 1900, p.104.
15 'H' 9. Ron Inscription of the Time of Amoghavarsha I (A.D. 874)	Tax on clarified butter.	*mahājanas* of Rona.			l.l.6-8, *EI*, XIII, 1915, p.185.
28 'F' 10. Nidagundi Inscription of the time of Amoghavarsha I (A.D. 874-5)	One *mattar* of garden land and 5 *mattars* of cultivable land	God *mahādeva*		*sarvabādhaparihāraṁ*	l.l.8-19, *EI*, VII, 1901, p.213.

15 'K' 11. Mulgund Inscription of Krishna II (A.D. 902-3)	3 fields measuring 1000 betel creepers.	Jaina Temple.		*sarvabādhaparihāraṁ*	l.l.11-12, *EI*, XIII, 1915, p.193.
4 12. Venkatapur Inscription of Amoghavarsha (A.D. 906-7)	Garden with 1000 creepers	*brāhmaṇa*		*saṁya*(proprietory Rights)	l.l.15-19 *EI*, XXVI 1946, p.62.
20 13. Deoli Plates of Krishna II (A.D. 940)	Village of Tālapuruṁshaka	*brāhmaṇa*	*upārikara, udraṅgaḥ sādhaṇyahiraṇyadeyaḥ*	*sādaṇḍadaśaparādhaḥ āchandr-ārkaṇavaksh-iti sarit-parvvata-samakālīnaḥ brahmadāyarahito bhyantarasiddhya bhumjatobhojayataḥ kriṣatoḥkarśayatāḥ*	l.l.53-58 *EI*, V, 1899 p.196.
CXXXV 14. Sanskrit and Old Canarese Inscriptions (A.D. 951-52)	12 *mattars* of cultivable land and 6 *drammas* of charcoal.	God			l.l.8-10, *IA*, XII, 1883, p.257.

(Contd.)

CHART - XII B *(Contd.)*

i	ii	iii	iv	v	vi
CXXXVI 15. Rashtrakuta Grant of Kakka III (A.D. 972-3)	Village of Pangarika	*brāhmaṇa*	*namasya*(rent free tenure), *sā-vriksha mālākulaḥ, sādhānyaḥ hiraṇyadēyaḥ śulkādisamast-ōtpatti* (all taxes and tolls and income)	*sā-daṇḍa-dōṣadaśāparadhaḥ āchandr-ārkkam kriṣataḥkarśayataḥ bhuṁjatobhotaḥ*	1.1.46-58, *IA*, XII, 1883, p.266.
CXXXVII 16. Rastrakuta Grant of Kakka III, (A.D. 973-4)	7 *mattars* of black-soil, land, and one *mattar* of rice-land.	God *mahādeva*			1.1.13-19, *IA*, XII, 1883 p.271.
50 17. Hebbal Inscription of AD 975.	100 *mattars* of cultivable black-soil, 2 *mattars* of rice land and 2 flower gardens.	God and the *māta*	*sarvvaparihāraṁ* (complete exemption from Taxes).		1.1.17,40, *EI*, IV, 1898 p.353-54.

CHART - XII C
NATURE OF GRANTS MADE
PHASE III (LATTER HALF OF 10TH CEN. A.D. - 13TH CEN. A.D.)

	i	ii	iii	iv	v	vi
Sl. No.	Name of the Inscription	Grants Made	Recipients	Economic Immunities	Juridical/ Administrative Immunities	Reference
1.	*No.2* Tumbagi Inscription of the Reign of Satyāśraya (A.D. 1004)	200 *mattar* of land	Temple of *brahmēśvara*			1.1.20-29, *EI*, XVII, 1923, p.9.
2.	*168* Kautheem Plates of Vikramaditya V (A.D. 1008)	Village of Koddasi	*brāhmaṇa*	*sarvanamasya*(rent free holding, exempt from taxes) *sā-vriksha-mālā-kulaḥhiraṇya-dhāna-nidhi-nidhāne samētaḥ*		1.1.65,67-68, *IA*, XVI, 1887, p.24.
3.	*7* Ālur Inscription of the Reign of the Vikramaditya V (A.D. 1011)	Field of 100 *mattars*	For the alms-house for the maintenance 12 *brāhmaṇas* and of ascetics.	*sarva-namasya*	*sarva-bādhāparihāraṁ*	1.1.30,37, *EI*, XVI, 1921-22, p.29.

(Contd.)

CHART - XII C *(Contd.)*

	i	ii	iii	iv	v	vi
4.	*No. 38 'A'* Of the Reign of Jayasimha I 11(1022 AD)	a) A corn field of 50 *mattars* b) 2 *mattars* and a garden land of 335 *Kamma* and 3 oil mills c) 50 *gadyāṇas* of gold.	a)the God. b)for the lamps c)for the 104		*sarva-bādhāparihāraṁ*	l.l.15-17, *EI*, XIX, 1927, p.224.
5.	*37* Gadag Inscription of the Reign of Jayasimha II (A.D. 1037)	Field of 56 *mattars* of land	12 *Nārayana* Gods			l.l.78,*EI*, XIX, 1927 p.219.
6.	*II 'B'* Of the Reign of Jayasimha II (1037 AD)	6 loads of betal leaves	Keṁgere			l.l.34-42, *EI*, XVI, 1927 p.78.

7.	*25* Hulgur Inscr-ption of the Reign of Jaya-simha II and the Yadava Kanhara (A.D. 1038)	2 *mattars* of land	God *Narayaṇa*	*sarva-namasya*		l.l.24-26, EI, *XVI*, 1922, p.336.
8.	*No.28* Chikkerur Inscription of Someśvara I (A.D. 1048)	Land and a house site	*satra*	*sāhiraṇya sarva-namasya*	*āchandrā-rkavakshiti sthitisamakālīna*	l.l.10-18, *EI*, XXXVI, 1965, p.222.
9.	*10* Arasabidi Inscri-ption of the Reign of Someś-vara I (A.D. 1047)	One *mattar* of garden land, 12 *mattars* and 50 *mattars*		*sarvanamasya*		l.19-18, *EI*, XVII, 1923, p.122.
10.	*10 'A'* Of the Reign of Someśvara I (A.D. 1052-3)	a)House Tax b)Garden of 600 trees and a field of one *mattar*	a)Great Tank, b)God Kāli			l.l.13-15, *EI*, XVI, 1922, pp.67-68.

(Contd.)

CHART - XII C *(Contd.)*

i	ii	iii	iv	v	vi
9'A' 11. Mulgund Inscription of the Reign of Someśsvar I (A.D. 1053)	Field of 12 *mattars*	Temple		*sarvabādhāparihāraṁ*	l.l.28-33, *EI*, XVI, 1928, p.55.
36 12. Kelawadi Inscription of the time of Someśvara I (A.D. 1053)	20 *mattars* of cultivable land and one site of a house.	Tank of Kelawadi			l.l.21-24, *EI*, IV, 1896, p.261.
30 'A' 13. Inscription of Vishnuvardhana Vijayaditya (A.D. 1064).	50 *mattars* of land.	God Ramēsvar		*sarva-namasya*	l.l.12-20, *EI*, IV, 1896, p.214.
II 'C' 14. Of the Reign of Someśvara I (A.D. 1066)	Field of 4 *mattars*, tax of a *paṇa* and a quarter and the petty tax on the houses.	God Kēsavēśvara.		*āchandrārkavakshitisthiti samakālina.*	l.l.30-35, *EI*, XVI, 1922, p.85.

30 'B' 15. Inscription of of Jayasimha III (A.D. 1072)	Village of Bannekal	God Ramēśvara	*sarva-namasya*	l.l.9-11, *EI*, IV, 1896, p.215.
10 'B' 16. of the Reign of Someśvara II (A.D. 1075)	Land in Basalur	God Ramē-śavara	*Sarvābhyant-arasiddhi*	l.l.8-13, *EI*, *XVI*, 1922, pp.70-71.
24 17. Hulgur Inscription of the Reign of Vikramaditya VI (A.D. 1077)	2 loads of *ekkavattige* betel leaf, 2 loads of *paḷe* betel leaf, 2 loads of *kari* betel leaf.	God Koylālē-vara		l.l.14-21, *EI*, XVI, 1922, p.331.
37 'C' 18. Of the Time of Vikramaditya VI (A.D. 1105)	a) 12 *mattars* of arable land; *6 mattars of* arable land, one *mattar* oil mill. of rice-field, one house. b) one House c) one House	a)God Kēśa-vara. b)Priest		l.l.21-32, *EI*, XII, 1913-14 p.330.

(*Contd.*)

CHART - XII C *(Contd.)*

i	ii	iii	iv	v	vi
37 'D' 19. Of the time of Vikramaditya VI (A.D. 1110)	A quarter of a gold piece, lime for drawing sacred figures.	God Kamma-tēśvara.			l.l.11-16, *EI*, XII, 1913-14, pp.332-333.
9 20. Momigatti Inscription of the 49th year of Vikramaditya (A.D. 1124)	Gravel-field of one-*mattar*, paddy field of 100 *kamma*, two houses.	*āchārya* of the establishment of Kāli-dēva-svāmi	*sarva-namasya*		l.l.17-24, *EI*, XVII, 1923, p.119.
37 'E' 21. Of the Time of Vikramaditya VI (A.D. 1125)	a land at Valvariva-pura	God Svayambhu Sōmēśvara		*āchandrārkkavakshiti sthitisamakālīna*	l.l.7-12, *EI*, XII, 1913-14, p.334.
XXXIII 22. Western Chalukya Grant of Jagadekamalla (A.D. 1139-40)	Ten *gadyānas* of gold out of of the impost-called *siddhaya* or the established hereditary due.	Temple of God Yōgēśvara		*āchandrārkavakshiti-sthitisamakālīna*	l.l.24-29, *IA*, VI, 1900, p.141.

19 23. Nilgunda Plates of Vikramaditya VI (A.D. 1087 and AD 1123)	A) Village of Nirgunda and village of Krishna along with lands thereof	A) 500 *brāhma ṇas*	A) *sā-śulkakaravādha parihāraḥsamastā-dēya-sahitonidhi-nidhāna-sanētaḥ sarvanamasyaḥ-tribhogābhyaṁtara-sidhyāsāsānīkritya dattaḥ*	*sarvabādhāparihāraṁ rājakī-yānām-anaṁguli prēkshanīyō*(not to be looked at with the finger of appropriation by royal officers).	l.l.62-71, 74-77, *EI*, XII, 1913-14, pp.154-55.
	B) Hamlet of Āditya Pallika with lands thereof	B) For the worship of God Bhimeśvara; for the purpose of feed- of *brāmah-ṇās* and ascetics and for temple services.	B) *Sā-sulka-kara-vādhā-parihāraḥ samast-ādēya-sahito nidhi-nidhā-nasaṁetaḥ sarva-namasya-tribhōgā-bhyaṁtra-sidhya*	*rājakiyānāṁ-ananiguli -prēkshanīyo*.	
32 'B' 24. Of the Time of Vikramaditya VI (A.D. 1077)	412 *mattars* of arable land.	The *ācharya* of God Sva-yambhu of Yēhur	*suṁkaṁdaṇḍaṁteja-svāmyaṁ, sarva-namas-yaṁ tribhog-ābhyantara -siddhiyiṁ*	*sarvabādhāparihāraṁ*	l.l.229-251 *EI*, XII, 1913-14, pp.283-284.

5

TEMPLE GIRLS AND THE LAND GRANT ECONOMY 8TH - 13TH CENTURY A.D.[1]

ALOKA PARASHER SEN

The alien context of our understanding of the temple girls tradition and in particular, our concern with its moral condemnation,[2] has unconsciously led us to neglect many crucial aspects of its historical analysis --- one of these being the question of their economic subsistence. This is especially imperative to analyze since it has been clearly recognized that they operated outside the traditional family structure though in close proximity to it. The 'alien context' emerged first, in the direct 'confrontation' with the practice of the system of dedicating temple girls and then, with the gradual 'discovery' of how this institution operated in the social milieu of the times by the nineteenth century ethnographers and administrators. For South India, Edgar Thurston's[3] categorization of *devadāsis*, as they have come to be popularly referred to, as a caste, and his twenty five page description of their customs, laws of inheritance etc., marked a significant step in the construction of a supposed reality but, in essential terms of a western conception of the development of the Indian dance tradition in the hands of girls who could be described in the English language only as 'harlots' and 'prostitutes'. It is to the understanding of this 'tradition' of the temple girls' practices that were in a sense the creation of the colonial mind, both western and eastern, that modern historians tend to go back to.

It would be pertinent in the present context to cite three recent studies that have taken up an exhaustive analysis of the temple girl tradition in historical and sociological perspective with reference to Orissa[4] and Tamil Nadu.[5] All these studies have questioned the

MAP-VI

CONCENTRATION OF TEMPLES IN SOUTHERN DECCAN 6th-12th CENTURY A.D.

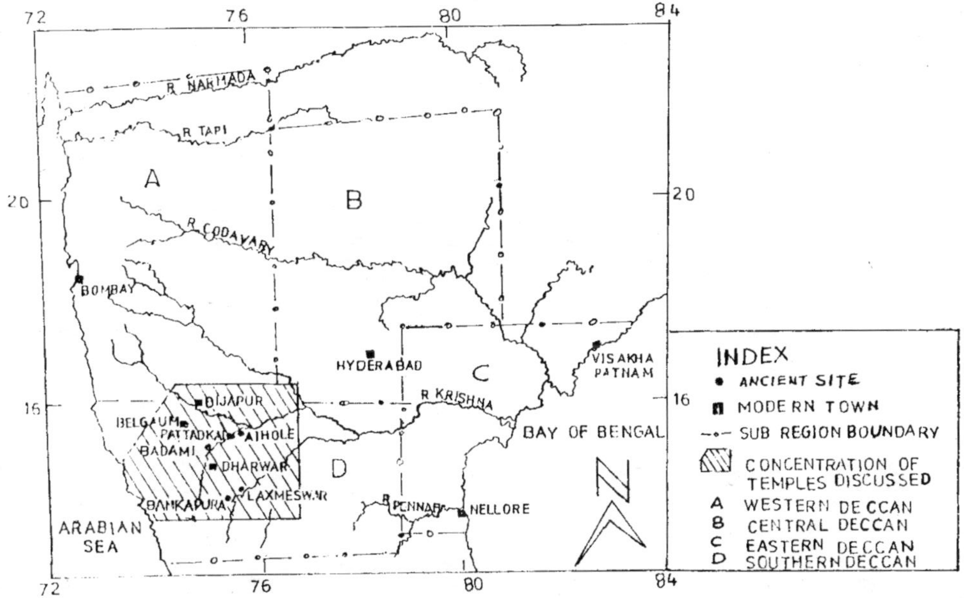

colonial perception of this tradition. Marglin has drawn our attention to the close link between the Indian motivation for social reform and the Western observations and descriptions of the system; the latter being ambivalent in their fascination for it but forceful in its condemnation, while the former, initially at least, only concerned about its obnoxious elements and thus its eradication.[6] Srinivasan has significantly related the reform movement, and later the revival movement, to the political milieu of Tamil Nadu where the struggle was most vociferous and has thereby shown that, both these adversely affected the *devadāsi* and her dance.[7] Kersenboom-Story too points out that the early studies were 'faulty, culture-bound evaluations' but, at the same time, in not claiming to give a 'truly objective' description of <u>what</u> the *devadāsi* tradition <u>was</u>,' goes on to construct an idealized picture of the same.[8] For the present we cannot deconstruct the more recent historical interpretations of the *devadāsi* tradition' nor, take up the task of reconstructing the image of the *devadāsi* and her profession in the pre-modern period, as this would require a separate paper by itself. However, it has to be pointedly stressed that the source material available for the pre-modern period which has been used by us in this study is neither concerned about describing the method of dedicating girls to temples, nor, about the moral condemnation of this system and how it operated, but rather, with information pertaining to their maintenance in the temple in terms of the grants that were made to them. One can indeed suggest that this is the only information of its kind which describes property rights of women on a large scale to a degree of certainty in the ancient and early medieval contexts.

In this paper we take a close look at this one aspect of women's access to land and its resources which is specific to their occupation and placement in society, to a geographical region [MAP VI] and to a given span in time. The specificity we try to unravel is that which pertains to temple girls who are interestingly not called by the term *devadāsi* in the inscriptions of Karnataka[9], but who are mentioned as beneficiaries in these land grant inscriptions, dated roughly between the eighth and thirteenth centuries A.D. We have presented the nature of the data available in the four charts appended to this paper which is addressed within a particular pre-industrial social formation called in certain quarters of historiographical analysis as the 'feudal'.[10] Essentially, this is a stratified society, with a complex hierarchy of graded rights in land. These rights it is well recognized, emerge over a period of time and rest primarily with either secular or religious authorities.[11] They also rest with such individuals who have certain types of power derived from special responsibilities vested in them by society.[12] The temple girls stand out as one such group of individuals. However, both the forms of authority and power were enmeshed firmly with historical changes in production relations that affected the structure of economic and cultural significance attached to the girls in the society of the times. Further, though the temple girls distinctly stand outside the patriarchal family structure, they were very much within the preview of the patriarchal values of the time which in the first place created the picture of the temple girl to be idolized in the religious context as a sort of 'courtesan of god'.[13]

A study of the history and evolution of legal ideas and institutions pertaining to property rights has hitherto always been an entry point to understanding the issue of women and their access to property. But in this connection it must be stated that the patriarchal joint family whose laws of property are normally described in the legal texts existed for only a small section of our society.[14] The rules of property, inheritance etc., described in the *Dharmaśāstras* particularly after the third century A.D. or so, mainly refer to women who were widows and their increasing access to such rights.[15] It has been pointed out that within the wider historical context during the early centuries A.D., there emerged a general tendency in the growth of individual rights in land as the development of agrarian productive forces was getting more and more closed.[16] Further, the main concern in the joint family system was closely linked with the maintenance of ownership rights in land within the family,[17] and thus women's access to property, but not their ability to dispose of it, gradually began to increase. In fact, both men and women had only limited ownership rights as the family property could not be partitioned and sold, and it has been pointed out that there are hardly any references of sale of land for the secular purposes in the records of the time.[18]

In contrast to the above explanation, a considerable amount of effort has gone into analyzing and describing the complexity of women's, particularly the widow's access to property in the Hindu legal tradition mainly because, according to some scholars, this was seen as one of the redeeming features of the Brahmanical attitude to women in an otherwise disparaging situation. Thus, Altekar, whose monograph on women is representative of this strain of thought opines: 'It is true that the doctrine of perpetual tutelage of women became popular at this time and it should normally have proved fatal to the recognition and development of their proprietary rights. But men do not always seriously believe in the solemn theories they haughtily enunciate. . . . Jurists felt no self-contradiction in declaring that women were unfit for independnce, and yet investing them with new proprietary rights.'[19] The harm that this type of historical interpretations has done is that in certain quarters it has led historians to categorically state that 'the idea of perpetual tutelage is a myth' because it is argued that the wife not only enjoyed freedom in the management of the household but also had rights of separate property.[20] This is particularly shocking because the above is a statement made in the context of a review of Manu's attitude towards women who is further credited by this scholar to have secured them a number of privileges and concessions,[21] when in fact, this law giver is generally understood to have been rather conservative on this issue.[22]

The above historiographical trends in the writing of women's history in general have on the one hand, failed to recognize that the dominant patriarchal values of the time[23] in fact vitiated against the effective control women could exert over their property and its disposal and on the other, have completely ignored the history of those women about whom information was not available from literary texts and about whom even if information was available, it was not much discussed because it went against the much cherished values of upper class morality as in the case with information on courtesans and temple girls.[24]

With reference to women's access to landed property in particualr, the case of the temple girls described in inscriptional data presents, in many ways, an interesting contrast to that which women directly under patriarchal authority had. Neither can one suggest that their case was similar to that of the widows under Hindu law who had access to inherited property only for their maintenance as the data in hand, in some cases, was particular to individual temple girls who had relatively far greater freedom than the widows. Thus, one would like to suggest that their case is one where they did not live directly under the patriarchal family but lived under its shadow. In the examples we have cited in the charts (XIII - XV) appended, it is clear that they were recipients of land grants in terms that were set by the norms of the already propertied sections and this hardly changed even if in some instances, these donors were women, either widows or wives of kings. The land grant system in fact was part of a larger economic pattern meant for the appropriation and distribution of agrarian surplus. Therefore, in the early medieval context the 'control' that the temple girls asserted over this wealth, its disposal and the power/prestige they partook in as a result of being partial/full 'Owners' of it, depended very much on the temples they were working in, where it was located and who granted them the land and wealth. Further, within the profession there was a great variety of tasks they performed and because of this diversity there was no single distinct pattern of how property was acquired, distributed and transmitted. Thus, in defining the nature of property these girls had and more so, the distinctions of status which necessarily accompanied ownership among them, we are confronted with inherently perplexing and complex issues of discussion.

We have divided the data collected into four charts. The main purpose of the inscriptions which mention temple girls was to record land grants either to them individually, or to the temple in which they were prominent beneficiaries. In the process all other information on them, their names, designations, numbers, their work etc. is incidental. On the basis of certain criteria and on an analysis we get different types of information that fall into four stages of development that has been categorized as follows:

I. In Chart XIII are listed those instances where the temple girls themselves made endowments to the temple implying their access to property which they could dispose of in the manner that pleased them.

II. In Chart XIV 'A' are listed those instances which record independent grants made to temple girls wherein sometimes they are mentioned by their names. In these cases their individuality is emphasized and implicitly a hierarchy of temple girls serving the temples emerges.

III. In Chart XIV 'B' we have listed those land grants which were made to the temple but in which it is specified that temple girls are significant beneficiaries. Here, the girls are not mentioned by their individual names but are often part of a dancing and singing group serving in the temple who are also recipients of a portion of the same or additional land grant.

IV. Finally, in Chart XV indicating the maximum number, are those instances wherein the existence of temple girls is only implied as the grant is made for a specific function/ritual in the temple which is commonly understood to have been performed by temple girls.

In taking a closer look at each of these categories further, interesting results follow. The Chart XIII examples are all early ones namely, the first two of the eighth century A.D., and the third of the first half of the eleventh century A.D. The earliest two are from the Bijapur district where the first temple building activity under the Chalukyas of Badami took place.[25] All these girls are referred to by their proper names. The designations of *sūḷe, deguḷade sūḷe* and *pāḍuvapātrā* used to define their probable status and function in the temple are all of a general nature which suggests that during this early stage they were in no way subservient to either the temple steward or the village headman as some of the later instances show. The nature of the endowments they make to the temple is however, not only in land, but also in objects and property which are transferable. But clearly, the value of these few instances is the ability of the temple girls to donate and spend wealth voluntarily without constraints and restrictions. Nonetheless, it cannot go unnoticed that in all the three instances the donations are made to the temple itself by them. It is further interesting that whereas Siriyave in the third instance, is described as *tottu* connoting either 'slave' 'concubine' or 'strumpet',[26] the name Badipoddi in the second instance, itself is said to mean 'prostitute' or 'strumpet',[27] thereby implying and emphasizing upon the sexuality of these girls.

The instances of independent grants to temple girls in Chart XIV 'A' all fall in the period between the tenth and eleventh centuries A.D. and of all the seven, six (except the sixth), are located in the Dharwar district. This is supposed to be the most fertile district in Northern Karnataka.[28] Further, except the last one which is dated to the twelfth century A.D., all the others are grants attributed in some way to the royal family of the Chalukyas of Kalyani. In terms of the girls and the lands granted to them there is a clear specificity. In all cases except the last one, the amount of land to be given to the girls is mentioned and in some cases, as in examples two and three, (Chart XIV 'A') how it was to be divided among them is also specified. These two cases are also those where the proper names of the girls are mentioned so that the land is given to them individually and not collectively to the group. It is also noticed that their number goes on successively increasing from five in the first example to sixteen in the fifth example. In all these instances they are designated both by the terms *sūḷe* and *pātrā* though the former ending is more common and in all the examples a varied terminology emerges implying the specific duties entrusted to them (Example : *chāmarada sūḷe* or girl waving chowries, *kambada sūḷe* or girl standing at the pillar of the temple etc.). In example five (Chart XIV 'A') on the basis of the land divided among the various girls, one gets an impression that there was a hierarchy in the tasks and associations of the temple girls wherein two of them -- *perggadevāḷa sūḷe* and *devarabhogakkenadeva piriyaravāḷa sūḷe* -- got a preference over the others and probably were the two who got 20 *mattars* of land each. This is deduced on the basis of the fact that the former was attached to the village headmen and the latter to the keeper of temple girls, both being powerful functionaries of the locality. That there existed a hierarchy amongst temple girls is indicated in examples two and three as well where again, in the former case, those attached to the *perggade* were perhaps privileged. In the latter case, and this is the only one of its kind, the property granted to the girls is on the basis of their division into the Right and Left hand castes.

In all the cases in Chart XIV 'A' separate grants of land were made to the accompanists like drummers, horn blowers, musicians and other individuals partaking in temple management or ritual activity. In examples three and six it is specified that a total of 500 and 250 *mattars* of land was made to the temple out of which the temple girls got certain specified amounts. This is significant because during the later period they are clubbed together as the singing and dancing group of the temple to whom the grant was made. Thus within the given structure of the land grant economy, these specific, though limited number of examples, point to the fact that there was a great variance in lands donated to temple girls, varying from a minimum of 3 *mattars* per girl in example two, to 20 *mattars* per girl in example five. Three of the donors listed in this Chart were women (XIV 'A' nos. 1, 3 and 4). Though considerable amount of evidence of this sort indicating women making land grants can be marshalled out,[29] it is difficult in the present context to analyze whether they had any independent access to this property or, that they were joint owners as example four tends to indicate. Further, all these women donors were either doing so in their capacity as administrators (Chart XIV 'A' nos. 3, 4) or, for the attainment of religious merit as they were builders of temples as well (Chart XIV 'A' nos. 1, 3). It would seem comfortable to postulate that they functioned in this capacity largely within the parameters of the joint family system (Akkadevi's importance in example 3 is because she is the sister of the Chalukya King Someśwara I) and during the later period (examples 6 and 7 in Chart XV) we have a few more instances of women making grants along with their husbands or sons. In contrast to the sisters, wives and widows in the above examples who got land either through inheritance or gifts, temple girls distinctly received land grants for their skill in the religious functions and duties they performed in the temple. It was therefore a form of payment to them not only for their subsistence but for their entire existence as they did not have families to support them during their old age.

In Chart XIV 'B' are listed those examples where temple girls were not independent recipients of land grants. This is indeed an interesting departure from the earlier period wherein the temple set up had at least clearly specified grants to them which meant that they had a certain status in the hierarchy of temple functionaries. All the examples in this Chart are of the eleventh and twelfth century A.D. -- some co-existing with the examples presented in Chart XIV 'A'. These are distributed over all the three districts of Bellary, Dharwar and Bijapur -- the maximum being in Bellary which is not considered as fertile a district as Dharwar where the maximum number of temples were said to have been concentrated between A.D. 800-1200 A.D.[30] A closer look at the status of donors in this Chart shows that except for two (Chart XIV 'B', nos. 4 and 9), which indicate them as members of the royal family, all others are local functionaries, petty feudatories or wealthy individuals. This tends to indicate that a process of sub-infeudation had taken place wherein wealth began to be concentrated at the local level. In example, seven we find a General under the Chalukyan King, who is not only the builder of the temple, but he makes a substantial grant of as much as 500 *mattars* of land. This is also the only case where the number of girls in the temple are mentioned and each of them is said to have been given a house each.

However, more pertinently these examples are significant in that in all these cases the temple as such was given the grant for various purposes which is said to maintain the temple girls as well. In three of the cases (Chart XIV 'B', nos. 3, 6, 7) the amount of land given to the temple is specified and in three other instance, (Chart XIV 'B', nos. 4, 5, 9) the girls are maintained out of the revenues of a part of the village granted to the temple. Only in one case *(e.g.* 8), they are maintained out of gold given to the temple. In all these cases there is absolutely no clarity on the access temple girls had on this wealth. This is also true for the other beneficiaries like musicians, teachers and stewards of the temple. That they all had a share in the amount donated, primarily to carry on temple activity, is the only thing that is distinctly specified in the inscriptions. It is also significant to point out that in contrast to the earlier period, now almost all the girls are subsumed under the designation *pātrā* or *pāḍuva pātrā* or *pātrā pāvuḷa* which generally means dancing and singing girls. Thus, the earlier specificity of task to be performed by them besides singing and dancing, is less noticeable. *Sūḷe* continues as a designation with its various suffixes. However, the seniority amongst the girls is indicated in the use of the term *paḷekāla pātrā*, meaning experienced dancing girl in two instances (Chart XIV 'B', nos. 1, 5). On the other hand, the term *parigrahika*, denotes that this particular girl was a female attendant (Chart XIV 'B', no. 7). But what cannot be missed is the generality with which they come to be referred to without their names and under a simple unqualified designation. In fact, in these examples it is only three instances which indicate their numbers. The reason for this trend may be postulated in that either the dedication of girls had become so common a practice and so well entrenched that details about them did not need to be specified, or, more likely, they had now begun to loose their independent access to property from their being direct recipients of land grants to their being clubbed together with the larger temple set-up. It is also possible that since the majority of donors were lesser feudatories and the majority of temples in these instances were located in comparatively less fertile regions, the revenues available must have been limited for redistribution among the Servants of the temple.

Unfortunately evidence at our disposal listed in Chart XIV 'B' does not permit us to generalize about how these grants to the temple as a whole were divided among the various people/groups maintained by it. However, in an example (Chart XIV 'A') from an inscription dated 1055 A.D. from the Kādambeśvara temple at Bantapur, Dharwar District, we get a break-up of the payments made to the temple staff.[31] They are as follows:

S.No.	Recipients	Amount Received in Land
1.	*Keti setti* (?)	12 *mattars*
2.	Drummers	10 *mattars*
3.	Musicians	6 *mattars*
4.	10 Temple girls	4-5 *mattars* each
5.	Dance master	5 *mattars*
6.	Steward of temple girls	5 *mattars*
7.	Keeper of temple girls	5 *mattars*
8.	Manager of the estates	6 *mattars*

This indicates that the temple girls were on par with the dance master and not very badly placed in comparison with the other accompanists or members of the group except the drummer who got a substantially larger share. That temple girls paid taxes is evident from two examples of the eleventh century A.D. from this region. Nilakanta Sastri points to one from the Svayambudeva temple at Bagali, Bellary District dated to 1054 A.D. wherein four temple girls (*kaṃbada suḷevaru*) were exempted for the payment of a house tax *(mane vaṇa)* and a mirror tax (*kannaḍi vaṇa*).[32] In another instance from the Koylaleśwara temple at Hulgur, Dharwar District dated to 1077 A.D. the girls (*koylālis*) of this temple had to make a payment of five *paṇas* each as part of an endowment made to the temple.[33] Ultimately, the nature of the tenurial relationship in land granted to the temple girls depended very much on what kind of land was donated, who the donor was or, whether only revenues were granted.

This brings us to the maximum number of examples available to us which have been listed in Chart XV. Here, the existence of temple girls is only implied. In this Chart except for one (Chart XV, no.1), all the other fifteen examples can be located between the twelfth and thirteenth century A.D. All these are almost equally divided between the districts of Dharwar (7) and Belgaum (9). The later inscriptions, mainly of the thirteenth century A.D. are from the Belgaum district which again is relatively a less fertile region when compared to the Dharwar district. These later examples are largely attributed to the Ratta Chieftains (Chart XV, nos. 11, 12) whose authority centered around the Belgaum region between A.D. 875 - 1250 A.D. The Sinda Chieftains on the other hand, operated from around Dharwar (Chart XV, nos. 1, 7). The examples in this Chart therefore indicate that the donors were mainly lesser chiefs and/or local feudatories and that temple building activity had now spread substantially into other parts of northern Karnataka. However, from our point of view, the nature of information on the lands granted to the temple is very vague except for the last few cases where the amount given is specified. Since the temple girls are nowhere directly mentioned it may apparently seem futile to reflect upon the examples in this Chart. On the contrary, they are particularly significant from the larger point of view in indicating how temple girls seem to have lost their earlier independent status as recipients of individual land grants. A perusal of all the examples listed in this context shows that now temple girls are only mentioned implicitly through a ritual/rituals, namely, the *aṅgabhoga* and *raṅgabhoga* of the deity. This was mainly concerned with attending upon the deity in daily services and festivals and also dancing and singing. Obviously, since the ritual is mentioned so often, the number of girls must have increased. This is also indicated by the fact that even small feudatories like headman, wealthy residents etc. (Chart XV, nos. 4, 8, 13, 15, 17) made grants for this purpose. But the fact that the girls are neither mentioned by their names, nor, are their numbers mentioned or, the fact that they were part of a specialized group of people involved in skilled activity in the temple, indicates:

1. that their access to the property/wealth was now totally subsumed to the larger concerns of temple functions with reference to its rituals;

2. that this had the effect of, on the one hand, increasing the powers of the priestly office and simultaneously, degrading the importance of those artists/dancers/musicians etc. who actually performed in the temple, and finally,

3. that this decline in their economic access to direct grants affected their social status as the elites in society who were the main patrons of temple girls, now preferred to give grants for the performance of rituals in the temples, and not to individual temple girls.

The above descriptions reflect upon a historical process of how temple girls, located in some of the temples in northern Karnataka between A.D. 700-1200, gradually began to loose their rights in land

and its resources, however limited they may have been in the first place. This loss occurred vis-a-vis the temple, and the authority vested in this institutional base made it increasingly difficult for the girls working here to exercise any independent access, control or 'share' in the property apportioned to them in return for the services rendered by them. Thus, this micro study of temple girls, as a certain type of women in early medieval times who had at least a partial access to land and its resources, brings to the forefront two inter-related issues of discussion : (1) The limited nature of rights in land that these women had in a highly stratified society is very much linked to similar limited rights that other sections of the society partook in. A considerable factor of concern in this regard was the role religious ideology played in moulding and strengthening such disparities. (2) With particular reference to women, religious ideology furthermore re-shaped and perpetuated existing patriarchal institutions. Thus, though our source material very rarely explicitly states so, the underlying premise of why temple girls were thus patronized with property, wealth etc., was predominantly because of the sexual functions they performed for the elites of the time. Their life-styles stood outside the mores of the traditional family structure but very much within the context of the religious ideology of the times which gave sanction to the practice in the first place.

Early medieval economy and polity, however it may be characterized by modern scholars[34] was, it has been suggested, essentially one in which social dominance was defined not by the actual ownership of land but rather, by the appropriation and redistribution of social surplus by the ruling elites.[35] It has further been suggested that as the British gradually evolved their legal systems, law with regard to the nature of effective control of property in land began to be accordingly defined[36] and this in fact, was then introduced for the first time as the chief determinant of wealth and private property in the modern sense.[37] It is the use of the English term ownership, as is currently understood to mean the core rights of private ownership, that creates an ambiguous situation in understanding a variety of rights in land that existed in the medieval south Indian situation. Therefore, as has been pointed out by Dharma Kumar in a recent article, one cannot talk in terms of 'absolute ownership' rights that different individuals or, even families, had in the medieval context but rather, one has to come to terms with a multiplicity of rights that people enjoyed on a given piece of land.[38]

In contrasting the pre-modern 'Land ownership' pattern with what the British introduced, Dirks emphasizes the fact that property was embedded in a complex manner with the social and political relations in medieval times. Further, the root cause for the modern historiographical debates on landowning rights in early India have emanated because historians have hitherto assumed that there was an opposition between the king's mastery over land and the peasant's rights in it.[39] Thus, he clarifies that the two terms *paṅku* and *kāṇiyāṭci* which defined property relations in medieval south India operated within a larger hierarchical structure. Whereas the former literally meaning 'share', was characterized by shares of rights to usufruct essentially in a horizontal sense among a family, group or even an entire village, the latter literally meaning a 'hereditable right', in a vertical sense, implied the entitlement to a share usually granted by a superior agent.[40] These entitlements or *kāṇiyāṭci* were in his words: 'related both to control over land and to participate in the village/lineage assembly and also, as in the case of *paṅku* to rights to a share in the local temple. . . . Indeed, the *paṅkus* were themselves shares in this *kāṇiyāṭci* or general entitlement.'[41] However, it must be stated that these varied from region to region and also depended very much on the nature of tenurial relationships that existed at a particular point in time.

It is well-known that during this period innumerable beneficial tenures were created by Kings for *brāhmaṇas* and the temple. Land grants were also made to military chiefs, village officers, various grades of temple servants and artisans. In contrasting the beneficial and non-beneficial tenures, Dharma Kumar has rightly distinguished the different types of holdings in each of these to ultimtely show that in the latter at least, examples from Chola inscriptions show that there were interesting departures from the classic family ownership patterns. Thus, she says, 'women for instance, owned property, movable and immovable, as is clear from numerous inscriptions that record gifts to temples and other charities made by women of all conditions, from queens to dancing girls and servants.'[42] We have indicated above a few examples (Chart XIII) wherein temple girls made grants to the temple but in a majority of cases (Chart XIV & XV) they were only recipients of a 'share' in larger grants that were made to the temple as a whole. Simultaneously, one cannot totally ignore that in some cases (Chart XIV 'A') these girls also received independent land grants. Nonetheless, we underline that whatever 'shares' or rights temple girls got in the land grant economy was, as was the case with various other sections of the society, inhibited by the role the various levels of State played in the appropriation of the surplus and also by the authority of the religious institutions. Fundamentally, temple girls functioned within this milieu. Dirks pertinently points out that in the early medieval situation we cannot understand landholding as an 'isolated economic fact' as rights to land were given with other types of rights.[43] In recognizing that the type of rights temple girls got in this context were mainly religious ones, their special role in these functions meant that they were some of the few people in the realm who had access to not only the inner most shrines of temples, but also, in some cases, to the King himself. Vijaya Ramaswamy has cited a thirteenth century inscription wherein a temple girl secured a land grant from the King for the temple she was working in and was thereby, honoured by the temple for this service.[44] These instances are undoubtedly few and far between but they do reflect upon a peculiar socio-economic relationship established in medieval temples where, on the one hand, economic benefits were granted to a certain type of essentially skilled women, but, on the other, they were exploited for their labour, particularly in terms of their sexuality.

Most of the scholars begin with the presumption that at a certain point in historical time the dancing and singing girls had performed purely spiritual functions and therefore, had been held in high esteem. It is, however, difficult to substantiate this and furthermore in the present study we have noted that even during the early stages when the temple girls were economically well-off and could themselves make grants to the temple, their appellation in the Karnataka inscriptions in the form of words like *sūḷe, degulada sūḷe* etc., (Chart XIII - XIV 'A' & 'B'), directly implies their being considered 'courtesans of god' in contrast to the more neutral term *devadāsi*. That this emphasizes upon their sexuality is further specified in many cases (Chart XIV 'A', nos. 3, 4, 5; Chart XIV 'B', nos. 4 *etc*) by the use of particularly the term *'bhoga'* meaning 'enjoyment'; its natural extension being understood as 'sexual enjoyment'.[45] Further, in some cases there is clear mention of their being attached to important individuals in the temple (e.g. Chart XIV 'A', nos. 2, 5). This leaves us in no doubt that the girls not only performed their professional duties, but the very nature of their work implied their being used as objects of sexual gratification. In this context then, their access to wealth and other resources unconsciously depended very much on their social accessibility to the Kings, chiefs and temple functionaries.

More significantly, these demands of the elite got sanction from the dominant ideology of the times in two ways. First, the overarching ideology focused on worship in the temple which, between the 7th and 12th centuries A.D., laid great emphasis on *bhakti* or complete devotion and surrender to god as a means of salvation. The content and spirit of this worship was Puranic which attributed *puṇya* (merit) to all those who followed the attitude of service (*dāsyabhāva*) by performing rituals in the temple. The temple girls not only performed some of the most impportant rituals like *aṅgabhoga* and *raṅgabhoga* for the deity (Chart XV) but, they were also objects of dedication to the temple. It was considered that the dedication of a dance, song or a musical instrument was far more meritorious than the dedication of flowers and food.[46] Thus, one of the ways the dancing and singing girls joined the service of the temple was through their dedication by individuals who in turn, got religious merit.[47] Secondly, apart from determining the physical presence of these girls in the temples, the Puranic ideology goes to the extent of elaborating upon their extra-religious role. In a long description in the *Matsya Purāṇa*, of the various types of services to be performed by temple girls, one of the major ones was to serve the Kings, the *brāhmaṇas* and other clients, including *śūdras*, equally. If a child was to be born of this union, both the parents were absolved of their sins. In fact, it was prescribed that the regular performance of this *vrata* was not essentially harmful to the soul's welfare and would ultimately gain them a place in *Viṣṇuloka*.[48] Though our data is limited on how these dedications were made to the temple in medieval times, it is clear that most of the grants of land/wealth to the temple girls by various sections of the population was indeed substantially also in terms of the religious merit to be gained by the latter. Ultimately, in social terms the *Bhakti* ideology became acceptable to the large majority of people and as Narayanan and Veluthat have put it : 'The ideology of bhakti served as the cementing force bringing together Kings, brahman priests and the common people in a harmonious manner. . . . This provided an illusion of equality while retaining the stubborn walls of inequality in the feudal system of production and distribution.'[49]

We would like to thus emphasize that the temple girls were integrated in a complex way into the dominant ideological framework of the society and in this sense, were automatically also, as it happens, the only women in society to have partial access to the productive resources in their own individual capacity, and not through the family structure. Though it may apparently seem that the social order accepted these girls as independent of male control, they in fact operated 'in a world in which males occupied a favored incline.'[50] Writing in the context of north India with particular reference to the access Muslim women had to property during the Mughal period, Kozlowski has pointedly stated that all women, irrespective of whether they inherited property as members of wealthy families or got it for religious purposes, as well as those who got it as dancing girls, singers and courtesans, were indeed 'indirect recipients of male controlled property'.[51] He has thus pertinently questioned if these women could, in a true sense, be regarded as independent of male authority and social control. It is well recognized that in the history of human societies with the development of patriarchy, several kin-based institutions were subverted in which women had hitherto played certain public roles. Simultaneously, with the growth of new agricultural forces of production women were relegated to the sole and essential role as wives.[52] A further consequence of this was that 'because of the privatization of property through individual inheritance the budding upper class required control of women's sexuality.'[53] In many of the earliest civilized societies rules of inheritance were often the first ones that came to be the most clearly defined. Daikonoff has drawn our attention to valuable data of the cuneiform archives (earliest -- written documents in the world) from the old Babylonian city of Ur that date to around 1800 B.C. which indicate that in the acts of the division of inheritance women were either under their father, husband or brother.[54] He, however, distinguishes the daughters, wives, sisters and widows from another category of women noted in these records, namely, the prostitutes and priestesses whom he defines as ' those not under patriarchal authority' in terms of their inheritance of property.[55] Though one cannot but recognize the value of Diakonoff's data pertaining to women for such an early period, it must nonetheless also be recognized that the image of a prostitute, her role in society and her very sustenance was also determined by the demands of men who defined her existence as such in the first place. Therefore, she, like the temple girls in the medieval times who adorned Indian temples, may not have had a direct patriarchal authority above them as they were not part of households, but their very existence outside it was the creation of patriarchal values of authority. This essentially emanated from the inherent desire of men to control female sexuality, both its normative and so-called deviant forms, so as to ultimately create the notion of an ordered society.[56]

The focus of this study on temple girls has been to highlight the significance of historically relevant data pertaining to women's access to property and wealth. We have precious little data on their caste/class affiliations for the medieval period though Ramaswamy has drawn our attention to innumerable epigraphical references to their association with the weaving community of Kaikkolas who also had a long tradition of consecrating their first born girls to the temple.[57] On joining the temple many of them ceased to have close ties with their kin and lineage based groups. This is particularly significant from the point of view of their transmission of wealth and 'shares' in the property that they had accumulated. In some cases, they stand alongside the affluent members of society in adopting conventional means of disposing of their property by making donations to religious institutions (Chart XIII). Srinivasan's study of a more recent period has shown that when grants were made for the maintenance of the girls it was usually meant for, their enjoyment 'over the generations'. Secondly the 'shares' could only be transmitted by them on a hereditary basis if their daughters were also in temple service.[58] Again, more recent accounts of the *devadāsi* system have been able to more categorically state that they were the only women under the Hindu law administered by the British courts who could inherit property and dispose of it, as well as adopt girls,[59] who could then inherit property sometimes, in preference to their brothers if they had any.[60] In fact, as the practice prevailed in the nineteenth century, the *devadāsi's* children got her father's name and not that of their father.[61] All this, Thurston argues, goes to show that 'Inheritance is in the female line, and women are the absolute owners of all property earned'.[62] Religious texts do sanction that temple girls could have children outside wedlock but medieval data does not permit us to focus upon how these girls transmitted their wealth. Srinivasan in contrasting their way of life with the conventional domestic context has highlighted that at three levels they enjoyed relative freedom vis-a-vis other women: (a) they could follow a professional activity and thereby develop their skills, (b) they were not constricted by any obligations and fidelity to their 'husbands', and (c) they had independent rights in the dispensation of their property.[63] These reflections pertain to their conditions at the turn of the present century which was also the time when it was their professional way of life itself which had ostracized them as 'fallen women'.[64] As part of the larger concerns of many of the nineteenth and early twentieth century social reformers for the 'upliftment' of women in general, the case of the *devadāsis* was also taken up by advocating marriage for them.[65] These were undoubtedly acts of middle class 'patriarchal benevolence',[66] which ironically meant that in performing 'human marriages' as opposed to their 'marriages to god,' the temple girls also gradually lost their limited access to property. Their place in society was now integrated into the fairly narrow and tightly wrapped threads of kinship and community.

NOTES

1. An earlier version of this paper was presented at the National Seminar on 'Women and Access to Land and Productive Resources, CWDS and Delhi University Centre for Women's Studies, January 10-13, 1988. In some parts it is based on work done for an M.Phil. Project in 1983 which is reported and acknowledged in Aloka Parasher and Usha S. Naik, 'Temple Girls of Medieval Karnataka', *IESHR*, vol. 23, no.1, 1986, pp. 63-91.
2. Its popular versions in Imran Qureshi, 'Yellama's Daughters of the Night,' *Indian Express*, 6 March, 1983; Chakresh Jain, '"Married" to a Goddess, Forsaken by God', *Mid-day*, 10 July, 1983.
3. Edgar Thurston and Rangachari, K. (ed.), *Castes and Tribes of Southern India*, vol. II, Delhi (rp.), 1975, pp. 125-152.
4. F.H. Marglin, *Wives of the God King*, OUP, Delhi, 1985.
5. Amrit Srinivasan, 'Reform and Revival: The Devadasi and Her Dance', *EPW*, vol. XX, no. 44, 2 November, 1985; S. C. Kersenboom-Story, *Nityasumaṅgalī*, Delhi, 1987.
6. Marglin, op. cit., 1985, pp. 3-10.
7. Srinivasan, op. cit., 1985, pp. 1873-75.
8. Kersenboom-Story, op. cit., 1987, p. xv; p. xx. See pp. 47-49 on the cultural essence of the *nityasumaṅgalīs*.
9. Aloka Parasher and Usha S. Naik, op. cit., 1986, pp. 65-68.
10. R.S. Sharma, *Indian Feudalism, A.D. 300-1200* (1st edition, 1965), Delhi, 1980. For the ensuing debate see Introduction in D.N. Jha, *Feudal Formations in Early India*, Delhi, 1987, pp. 3-25.
11. R.N. Nandi, 'Growth of Rural Economy in Early Feudal India', Presidential Address, Section I, *PIHC*, 45th Session, Annamalainagar, 1984, pp. 25-91.
12. Sister M. Liceria, 'Emergence of Brāhmaṇas as Landed Intermediaries in Karnataka — A.D. 1000-1300', *IHR*, vol I, no. 1, 1974, pp. 28-35.
13. *Matsya Purāṇa*, 70. 209-13 (SBH, vol. XVII, Allahabad, 1974).

14. A.M. Shah, *The Household Dimension of Family in India*, New Delhi, 1973, p. 12.
15. A.S. Altekar, *The Position of Women in Hindu Civilization*, Delhi (reprint), 1983, Chapters V and VI. First edition Benaras, 1938.
16. Suvira Jaiswal, 'Women in Early India : Problems and Perspectives', *PIHC*, 41st Session, Bodh Gaya, 1981, pp. 57-58. It has been pointed out by her that no attempts have been made by scholars to link developments in growth of property rights to the growth of the joint family system. See also, 'Studies in Early Indian Social History : Trends and Possibilities', *IHR*, vol. VI, nos. 1-2, 1979-1980, pp. 58-60.
17. Ibid., p. 59.
18. R.S. Sharma, *Perspectives in Social and Economic History of Early India*, New Delhi, 1983, p. 137.
19. Altekar, op. cit., 1983, p. 353.
20. R.M. Das, *Women in Manu and His Seven Commentators*, Bodh Gaya, 1962, p. 263.
21. Ibid., p. 255.
22. Sharma, op. cit., 1983, p. 48; pp. 49-61.
23. Ibid., pp. 35-48.
24. Altekar's monograph is a typical example of this. See op. cit., 1983, pp. 181-183. Only about 10 pages in a book of 300 pages is devoted to a description of temple girls, and courtesans.
25. S. Settar, 'Roots, Relations, Relevance' in Mulk Raj Anand (ed.), *Marg*, XXXII, 1.
26. *DED*, 1984, 3524, p. 309.
27. *DED*, 1984, 3869, p. 346.
28. *Bombay Gazetteer*, 1884, 2-3, pp. 7-12.
29. Jyotsna Kamat, *Social Life in Medieval Karnataka*, New Delhi, 1980, p. 106 ff.
30. R.N. Nandi, *Religious Institutions and Cults in the Deccan A.D. 600 - 1000*, Delhi, 1973, pp. 41-63; pp. 76-90.
31. *EI*, XIII, No.14, p. 175.
32. K.A.N. Sastri, 'The Chalukyas of Kalyani' in G. Yazadani (ed.), *The Early History of the Deccan*, OUP, 1960, p. 415.
33. *EI*, No. 24, p. 331.
34. Debates discussed briefly in the Introduction of N. Karashima, *South Indian History and Society*, Studies from Inscriptions A.D. 850-1800, pp. xxiv-xxxiii and D.N. Jha, op. cit., 1987, pp. 3-41.
35. Gregory, C. Kozlowski, 'Muslim Women and Control of Property in North India', *IESHR*, vol. 24, no. 2, 1987, p. 163.
36. Nicholas Dirks , 'From Little King to Landlord : Property, Law, and the Gift Under the Madras Permanent Settlement', *CSSH*, vol. 28, 1986, pp. 308-310.
37. Kozlowski, op. cit., 1987.
38. Dharma Kumar, 'Private Property in Asia? The Case of Medieval South India', *CSSH*, vol. 27, no. 2, 1985, p. 351; pp.355-357.
39. Dirks, op. cit., 1986, p. 309; p. 311.
40. Ibid., pp. 309-310.
41. Ibid., p. 310.
42. Dharma Kumar, op. cit., 1985, p. 357.
43. Dirks, op. cit., 1986, p. 311.
44. Vijaya Ramaswamy, *Textiles and Weavers in Medieval South India*, Delhi, OUP, 1985, p. 106.
45. Parasher & Naik, op. cit., 1986, p. 68.
46. Suvira Jaiswal, *The Origin and Development of Vaisanavism -- 200 B.C. - A.D.*

500, Delhi (2nd edition), 1981, p. 162.
47. Thurston, op.cit., 1975, p.125 lists six types of *devadāsis* on the basis of how they joined the temple.
48. *Matsya Purāṇa*, 70, 41-43; 208-13.
49. M.G.S. Narayanan and Kesavan Veluthat, 'Bhakti Movement in South India' in S.C. Malik (ed.), *Indian Movements : Some Aspects of Dissent Protest and Reform*, IIAS, Simla, 1978, pp. 43-44.
50. Kozlowski, op. cit., 1987, p. 180.
51. Ibid., pp. 179-180.
52. Eleanor Leacock, 'Women Power and Authority' in Leela Dube, E. Leacock and S. Ardener, (eds.), *Visibility and Power*, OUP, 1986, p. 110; p. 118; p. 125.
53. Ibid., p. 108.
54. I.M. Diakonoff, 'Women in Old Babylonia not under Patriarchal Authority', *JESHO*, vol. XXIX, no. ii, 1986, pp. 225-238.
55. Ibid., p. 228.
56. Bridget Hutler & Gillian Williams, (ed.), *Controlling Women : The Normal and the Deviant*, Croom Helm, London, 1981, pp. 12-24.
57. Ramaswamy, op. cit., 1985, pp. 55-56.
58. Srinivasan, op. cit., 1985, pp. 1871-72.
59. Thurston, op. cit., 1975, p. 151.
60. Ibid., p. 149.
61. Ibid., p. 135.
62. Ibid., p. 144.
63. Srinivasan, op. cit., 1985, pp. 1870-71.
64. Ibid., p. 1873.
65. Atlury Murali, 'Perspective on Women's Liberation: Andhra in the Nineteenth and Early Twentieth Centuries', *Studies in History*, vol. 3, no. 1, 1987, pp. 110-111.
66. Ibid., p. 120.

CHART - XIII
LAND GRANTS BY TEMPLE GIRLS
700 - 1050 A.D.

Name of Donor Name of temple Place & Date*	Status of Donor	Nature, Purpose and Amount of Endowment	Designation No.of Girls** supported	Other information	Reference
I	II	III	IV	V	VI
1. Challabbe(W) Saṅgameśwara Temple, Pattadakal, Badami Taluk, (Bijapur) 730 A.D.	Śri Vijayēśvarada *Sūḷe*[4] *i.e.*, the temple girl dedicated to this temple.	She made a votive offering of three pillars in the main hall of the *temple*	*Sūle* mentioned by her proper name Challabbe	This inscription is found on an undated pillar. Original name of the temple was Vijayēśvarada	'SOCI' *I.A.* X, No.113, p.169.
2. Badipoddi (W) Vīrupāksha Temple, Pattadakal, Badami Taluk, (Bijapur) 778 A.D.	Lokamahadeviyara *deguḷada sūḷe*[1] *i.e.* the temple girl dedicated to the Lokamahadevi temple.	She made *bhūmidānam* or 'gift of land' and *ubhyamukhi* or 'an image of a cow bringing forth a calf' to the *temple*	*deguḷada sūḷe*[1] mentioned by her proper name Badipoddi	Badipoddi is described as the daughter of Goyindapoddi	'SOCI', *I.A* XI, No. 122 pp. 126-127.

(Contd.)

CHART - XIII *(Contd.)*

I	II	III	IV	V	VI
3. Siriyāve (W) Kallēśwara Temple, Bagali, Harpanhalli Taluk, (Bellary) 1035 A.D.	A singer/dancer of the temple	Gifted *her house* to the temple on the condition that those who lived there would pay 2 *panas* per year to maintain a perpetual lamp before the god.	*Pāḍuvapātra*[8] mentioned with a proper name Siriyāve.	-	*S.I.I.* IX, 1 No. 89, p.60

CHART - XIV A
TEMPLE GIRLS AND LAND GRANTED
900 -1200 A.D.

I	II	III	IV	V	VI
1. Bujjabarasi (W) Bujjabeśwara Temple, Hebbal, Lakshmeshwar Taluk, (Dharwar) 975 A.D.	Grandmother of Ganga prince Butayya. Royal family and Builder of the temple(Feudatory)	20 *mattars*[3] of land specifically granted for *Temple girls*.	*sūḷe*[4] (*Sūḷeyar*)[4] 5 girls but their names are not mentioned	Separate grants were made to the drummer, the hornblower and others.	*E.I.*, IV, pp.350-356
2. Chāmuṇḍarāyarasa and Ketarasa Rāmeśwara Temple, Holianveri, Ranibennur Taluk, (Dharwar) 1048 A.D.	District official (Petty Feudatories)	25 *mattars* of land made specifically for *temple girls* divided as follows: 2 got 5 *mattars* land 3 got 4 *mattars* land 1 got 3 *mattars* land	*perggaḍevāḷa sūḷe*[9] *Chamaramkaṁbada sūḷe*[10] 6 girls mentioned by their names Chattabbe, Kāmatige, Kāḷabbe, Nannabbe, Ereyabbe and Devalabbe	Separate land grants were made to the flutist, musicians, the students' hostel *etc.* These officials administered Banavāsi (12,000)[+] Raṭṭapalli (70) and Iṭṭage (130)	*B.K.I*, III No.61, pp.49ff

(*Contd.*)

CHART - XIV A *(Contd.)*

I	II	III	IV	V	VI
3. Akkādevi (W) Akkeśwara Temple, Sudi, Ron Taluk, (Dharwar) 1054 A.D.	Sister of Chalukya King Someshwara I Royal family and Builder of Temple. (District Adminis-trator - Feudatory)	149 *mattars* of land made specifically for *temple girls.* Divided between 15-12 X *mattars* of land. This was done on the basis of their division into right hand and left hand castes.	*Chāmarada sūḷe*[11] *Kaṁbada sūḷe*[12] *bittiya chamarada sūḷe*[13], *pātra*[14] 13 girls mentioned by their names which are not clearly legible	Separate grants were made to the *perggaḍe*, flutists *etc.* making a total of 500 *mattars*. Admini-stered Kisukād (70)[+] Torugere (60) and Masiyavaḍi (140)	*E.I.* XV No.6e, i, pp.82-83 No.6f, p.89.
4. Harikesarideva and wife Lachchladevi (W+) Kadambeśwara Temple Bankapur, Bankapur taluk, (Dharwar) 1055 A.D.	An administrator who served under-Yuvarāja Vikram-aditya- VI (Feudal Chieftain)	44 *mattars* of land granted specifically for *temple girls* divided as follows: 6 got 4 *mattars* each 4 got 5 *mattars* each	*Kaṁbada sūḷe*[12] *balagada sūḷe*[16] 10 girls are mentioned but their names are not given	Separate grants were made to the Choultry, monas-tery, a *Kettiseṭṭi*, a drummer and musicians. He administered Banavasi 12,000[+]	*E.I.*XIII, No.14, p. 175.

5. Nāgadeva Nāgeśwara temple, Sudi, Ron taluk (Dharwar) 1060 A.D.	*Mahāsāmantādhipati*, steward of the Royal Household and General of Chalukya king Someshwara I Builder of Temple (Feudatory Minister)	203 *mattars* of land granted specifically for *temple girls* and divided as follows: 1 got 20 *mattars* 1 got 20 *mattars* 14 got 12 *mattars* each.	*Kaṁbada sūḷe*[12] *bhogada sūḷe*[17] *devarabhogakkena-deva piriyaravāla sūḷe*[18] *pātra*[14] *perggadevāla sūle*[9] *chāmarada sūḷe*[11] 16 girls are mentioned but their names are not given	A suburb was also built for the girls. Separate grants of land were made for repairs of the temple, stipends to teachers etc.	*E.I.* XV, No.6f p.89.
6. Jayasiṁha Someśwara Temple, Chinnatumbalam, Adoni Taluk(Bellary) 1068 A.D.	Brother of Chalukya King Someshwara I Royal Family (Provincial Governor - Feudatory)	12 *mattars* of land granted specifically for *temple girls*.	*Pātra*[14] (*Pātra-kke*)[14] 1 girl is mentioned but her name is not given.	He governed Nolaṁbavāḍi (32,000)+ and Sindavaḍi(1,000)+ Separate grants were made to a *Pandit*, to musicians and others. A total of 250 *mattars* was given to the temple.	*S.I.I.*IX,i No.133, p. 115.

(Contd.)

CHART - XIV A *(Contd.)*

I	II	III	IV	V	VI
7. 70 Mahājanas and some residents. Kalēśwara temple, Kaginelli, Hirekerur taluk (Dharwar) 1121 A.D.	Landlords and wealthy persons	Some land granted to the *temple girls*.	*pātra*[14] and *Svastiyama pātra pāvuḷa*[23] Number and names not specified	The inscription being *damaged* the amount of land granted in each case is not clear.	*B.K.I*,III p.141.

CHART - XIV B
TEMPLE GIRLS AND LAND GRANTED
900 - 1200 A.D.

I	II	III	IV	V	VI
1. Narasinghayya, Kallēśwara Temple, Bagali, Harpanhalli Taluk, (Bellary) 1018 A.D.	A *perggaḍe*[5] under Ganga Udayaditya (A temple official)	Land granted to the *temple* for various purposes which maintained temple dancing and singing girls also.	*Pannīrva sūḷe*[6] *paḷekāla pātra*[7] No. and name not specified	Flutists, teachers, a steward of temple girls and others were all maintained by the same grant	*S.I.I.*IX,i, p.51 ff
2. Chaṭṭiarasa, Ghaṭṭiarasa and others (Group) Uddibasavaṇṇa Temple, Morigeri, Hadagalli Taluk, (Bellary) 1045 A.D.	Wealthy merchants (?) or landlords(?)	Land granted to the *temple* for a variety of purposes which maintained dancing girls as well.	*Pāḍuva Pātra*[8] No. and name not specified	Musicians, temple servants and a mason were all maintained by this grant.	

(Contd.)

CHART - XIV B *(Contd.)*

I	II	III	IV	V	VI
3. Joyiarasa Keśaveśwara Temple Hottur, Bankapur Taluk (Dharwar) 1064 A.D.	Son of Mahāmaṇḍaleśwara Jamarasa who served as local governor (Feudatory)	4 *mattars* of land granted to the *temple* for various purposes out of which temple girls were maintained	*deguḷada sūḷe* 1 girl is mentioned without her name	He governed Poṭṭiyur. This grant was also used to maintain the priests, drummers flutists & so on. The temple was built by Kesiraja, a village Chief.	*E.I.* XVI, No.11c, p.88.
4. Viṣṇuvardhana Vijayaditya, Jatiṅga Rāmeśwara Temple, Siddapur, Malkalmuru Taluk, (Chitradurga) 1064 A.D.	Son of Chalukya King Someshvara I Royal family (Provincial governor - Feudatory)	Temple girls were maintained from the revenues of a part of a village granted to the *temple* for a variety of purposes	*Paṛukeragabhogada sūḷe*[19] No. and names not mentioned.	He governed Nolambavadi (32,000)[+] This grant was also used for the repairs of the temple, to feed ascetics and so on.	*E.I.*IV, No.30a, p.213.

5. Komaraswami - Devedibhatta and others Kallēśwara Temple, Huvina - Hadagalli, Hadagalli Taluk (Bellary) 1071 A.D.	*Mahājanas* of Pūvina Paḍaṅgile (Rich landlords? and wealthy residents?)	Temple girls were maintained from the revenues of a part of a village granted to the *temple* for a variety of purposes	*Paḷekāla pātra*[7] No. and names are not mentioned	The revenues were also used for feeding and clothing students, ascetics and other servants	*S.I.I.* IX, i, No.135, p.116
+6. Bennarasa Kadambeśwara temple, Chinnatumpalam, Adoni Taluk (Bellary) 1086 A.D.	Chief of Marāṭa (300) under *Mahāmaṇḍaleśwara* Jamarasa (Petty feudatory)	30 *mattars* of land granted to the *temple* which maintained temple girls as well.	*Pāḍuva Pātra*[8] 1 girl mentioned but without her name.	The grants was also used for the payment of musicians and their band.	*S.I.I.*, IX, i, No.155, p.138.
7. Mahādeva, Mahādeva temple Ittagi, Gadag Taluk (Dharwar) 1112 A.D.	*Mahāsāmantādhipati* general under Chalukya King Vikramaditya VI. Builder of temple. (Feudatory)	Some portion of 500 *mattars* of land given to the *temple* which also maintained temple girls.	*pātra*[14] *parigrahikka*[20] 24 girls are mentioned without their names.	A house was also given to each girl.	*E.I.*, XIII No.4, p.57.

(Contd.

CHART - XIV B *(Contd.)*

I	II	III	IV	V	VI
8. Vayijanathayya, Sevarasa and Kalamarasa. Mūlasthāna of Sindige temple, Bijapur (Bijapur) 1129 A.D.	The first one was a general The other two were local governors. (Feudatories)	Temple girls maintained from some gold gifted to the *temple*.	No. and names of girls not mentioned. *pātra pāvuḷa* [15]	This gift was also meant for the performance of ceremonies for the deity.	*B.K.I.* IV, No.100, p.126.
9. Ballaladeva Trikuteśwara temple, Gaddak, Dambal Taluk, (Dharwar) End of the 12th Century A.D.	Hoysala King builder of temple Royal Family.	Revenues of a village (Hombalalu) given to the temple.	No. and names of girls not specified. Suburbs where they lived were constructed by this King.	These revenues maintained priests, asetics & were used for performing ceremonies.	*I.A.*, II. No.2, pp.301-303.

CHART - XV
DONORS OF GRANTS TO TEMPLE GIRLS*
900 - 1250 A.D.

Sl. No.	Name of Donor Name of temple* Place & Date	Status of Donor	Nature, purpose and amount of endowment	Designation No. of Girls** supported	Other information
I		II	III	IV	V
1.	Permadideva I Kalameśwara temple, Naregal, Ron Taluk, (Dharwar) 950 - 51 A.D.	Sinda Chieftain under Chalukya Vikramaditya II. (Feudal Chief)	Some *land* out of the general grant made to the *temple*.	Existence of temple girls implied as the grant was meant for *aṅgabhoga*[2] of the deity.	Governed Kisukād (70)[+] Bagadage (70), Kelavāḍi(300), Nareyangal(12).
2.	Chenna, Galageśwara temple, Haveri Taluk (Dharwar)	A *mahāmaṇḍaleśwara* (Feudatory)	A village Pulleṇ is granted for various purposes to the *temple*.	Existence of temple girls implied in the mention of provision for *dance & music* in the temple.	Grant was to be used for worship of the god, feeding ascetics, visitors and so on.
3.	Anantamayya Someśwara temple, Lakshmeshwar (Dharwar) 1112 A.D.	*Daṇḍanāyaka* under Chalukya King Vikramaditya - VI. (Feudatory)	A *gift* of land	Existence of temple girls implied as this gift was meant for the maintenance of quarters (*Sūlekeri*)[21] for temple girls.	He constructed these quarters for the temple girls.

(Contd.)

CHART - XV *(Contd.)*

I	II	III	IV	V	VI
4.	Nidhimagamanda Jaina temple, Konur, Gokak Taluk, (Belgaum) 1112 A.D.	*Agavunda* under *mahāmaṇḍaleśwara* Raṭṭa Sena (Headmen - Feudatory)	Some land granted to the *temple*.	Existence of temple girls implied as the grant was meant for *aṅgabhoga*[2] and *raṅabhoga*[22] of the deity.	Builder of the temple. Grant also meant for repair and renovation of the temple.
5.	Vikramaditya -VI Chandaleśwara temple, Ittagi Gadag Taluka, (Dharwar) 1112 A.D.	Royal family (A Chalukyan King)	Grant of a village called Beṇṇakallu to the *temple*.	Existence of temple girls implied as this grant was meant for *aṅgabhoga*[2] and *raṅgabhoga*[22] of the deity which was performed by them.	--
6.	Jayakeśin - II and Milaladevi (W+) Mallikārjuna temple, Narendra (Dharwar) 1125 A.D.	Kādaṁba Chieftain under Chalukya King Vikramaditya -VI. (Feudal Chieftain)	Some land granted to the *temple*.	Existence of temple girls implied as part of this grant was meant for the *aṅgabhoga*[2] of the deity.	This temple was built by a *daṇḍa-nāyaka* Singarasa. The grant was also used for maintenance of temple, worship of the god and so on.

7. Demaladevi (W) and Achidevi - II Kalmeśwara temple, Naregal, Ron taluk, (Dharwar) Mid-12th Century A.D.	Wife and son of Sinda Chief Chavunda (Feudal chieftain)	300 *mattars* of land granted to the *temple*.	Existence of temple girls implied as the grant was meant for the *aṅgabhoga*[2] and *raṅgabhoga*[22] of the deity.	Chief Chavunda governed Pattada - Kisuvolal. The grant was also meant for feeding and clothing priests.
8. Merchants, Traders and Residents, of Palasige Hemmeśwara Temple, Halasi (Belgaum) Mid-12th Century A.D.	Wealthy residents of the province	Some land granted to the *temple*	Existence of temple girls implied as the grant was meant for the *aṅgabhoga*[2] of the deity.	This temple was built by a *daṇḍa-nāyaka* called Bavayya. The grant was also meant for oblations and feeding asetics.
9. Rayamurari & Sovideva Nageśwara temple, Annigeri, Navalgund Taluk (Dharwar)	A Kalachuri King Royal family.	Some land granted to the *temple*.	Existence of temple girls implied as grant was made to perform *music* and *dance*.	Grant was also to be used for oblations and offering to the deity and feeding ascetics
10. Taila, Eraha Dakshina Kedareśwara Temple Banavasi (North Kanara) 1186 A.D.	Petty Chieftains (Feudatories)	Some land granted to the *temple*.	Existence of temple girls implied as the grant was meant for *aṅagabhoga*[2] and *raṅgabhoga*[22] of the deity.	--

(Contd.)

CHART - XV *(Contd.)*

I	II	III	IV	V	VI
11.	Kartavirya - VI Sāntinātha Temple, Kalholi, Gokak Taluk, (Belgaum) End of 12th Century A.D. (Saka 1127)	A Rāṭṭa King Royal Family	A cultivable field of 2000 *Kaṁbas*[24] granted to the *temple*.	Existence of temple girls implied as this grant was meant for *aṅgabhoga*[2] and *raṅgabhoga*[22] of the deity.	He was an independent King at this time. The grant was also meant for repairs of the temple.
12.	Kartavirya -IV a)Habbeśvara b)Manikeśwara c)Siddheśwara temples Nesariage Samgaum Taluk, (Belgaum) Turn of 13th Century A.D. (Saka 1141)	A Rāṭṭa King Royal Family	1400 *Kaṁbas*[24] of land a)800 *Kaṁbas* b)400 ,, c)300 ,, granted to each temple respectively	Existence of temple girls implied as this grant was meant for the *aṅgabhoga*[2] of the deity.	The grant was also meant to supply food to asetics and repairs of the temple.
13.	12 Headmen of Sugandhavarti Mallināthadeva Temple, Samadatti Parasgod Taluk (Belgaum)	Headmen of villages (Feudatories)	600 *Kaṁbas*[24] of land to the *temple*	Existence of temple girls implied as this grant was meant for the *aṅgabhoga*[2] and *rangabhoga*[22] of the deity.	They were headmen under Rāṭṭa king Lakshamandeva. The grant was also meant for temple repairs.
14.	Purushottama Pañchalingadeva temple, Munoti Parasgod Taluk (Belgaum) 1223 - 24 A.D.	A *daṇḍanāyaka* (Feudatory)	Some land granted to the *temple*	Existence of temple girls implied as the grant was meant for the *aṅgabhoga*[2] and *raṅgabhoga*[22] of the deity.	The grant was also used for the repairs and renovations of the temple.

15. Some Individuals Pañchalingadeva temple, Munoti Parasgod Taluk (Belgaum) 1223 - 24 A.D.	Rich Residents(?)	A *Kaṇḍiga* [25] of dried fruits, grains etc. granted to the *temple*.	Existence of temple girls is implied as this grant was meant for the *raṅgabhoga* [22] of the deity.	--
16. Mallisatti Madhavadeva Temple, Chikka Bagevadi, Belgaum Taluk, Belgaum 1250 - 51 A.D.	Feudatory Minister	1000 *Kaṁbas* [24] of a field granted to the *temple*.	Existence of temple girls implied as this grant was meant for the *aṅgabhoga* [2] and *raṅgabhoga* [22] of the deity.	--
17. Some Individuals Jagadiśvara Temple, Samdatti Parasgod Taluk (Belgaum) 1252 - 53 A.D.	Rich Residents(?)	Some land granted to the *temple*	Existence of temple girls implied as this grant was partly meant for *aṅgabhoga* [2] and *raṅgabhoga* [22] of the deity.	--

NOTES: (W +) Women along with their husbands making land grants.
(W) Women making the land grants (Almost always royal ladies)
\+ Figures probably indicate the number of villages.
* The Chart is prepared in chronological order of all the inscriptions studied.
** Girls are mentioned by Name and their numbers specified only in some cases.
X The inscription is slightly damaged and the figures not clearly legible.
* Chart No. XV on Donors of Grants is based on Chapter IV, pp. 73-98 of Usha S. Naik, 'The Temple Girls in Early Northern Karnataka 700 A.D.-1200 A.D.', Unpublished M.Phil thesis, University of Hyderabad, 1983.

FOOTNOTES FOR CHART Nos. XIII-XV
[MEANINGS OF TERMS]

1. *deguḷada sūḷe*	:	a 'prostitute' of the temple.
2. *aṅgabhoga*	:	sensuous enjoyment or personal enjoyment.
3. *mattar*	:	measure of land.
4. *sūḷe* (pl. *sūḷeyar*)	:	in Kannada dictionaries of today the generally accepted meaning is 'prostitute'/'prostitutes'.
5. *preggaḍe*	:	one who has the overall controlling authority at the local level.
6. *pannīrva sūḷe*	:	'prostitute' of the scented water.
7. *paḷekāla pātra*	:	experienced girls well-versed in dance.
8. *pāḍuva pātra*	:	singing girls maintained in the temple.
9. *perggaḍevāḷa sūḷe*	:	'prostitute' attached to the steward of the temple.
10. *chāmaram kaṁbada sūḷe*	:	'prostitute' who waved chowries standing at the pillar of the temple.
11. *chāmarada sūḷe*	:	'prostitute' who waved chowries for the deity or 'prostitute' who carried silver staves during religious processions.
12. *kaṁbada sūḷe*	:	'prostitute' who stood at pillars of the temple.
13. *bittiya chāmarada sūḷe*	:	'prostitute who fanned the deity and provided free services.
14. *pātra* (pl. *pātra [kke])*	:	dancer/dancers.
15. *pātra pāvuḷa*	:	dancing/ singing girls.
16. *balagada sūḷe*	:	'prostitute' meant for the enjoyment of the public.
17. *bhogada sūḷe*	:	'prostitute' meant for the enjoyment of the public.

18. *devarabhogakkena-piriyaravāḷa sūḷe*	:	'prostitute' who was meant for the god's enjoyment and who was to be attached to the keeper of temple women.
19. *paṛukeragabhogada*	:	*paṛukeraga* probably indicates some religious duty in relation to the enjoyment of temple girls by the temple management.
20. *parigrahikka*	:	the female attendant of god.
21. *sūḷe keri*	:	quarters for temple gtirls.
22. *raṅgaboga*	:	entertainment and enjoyment for the deity.
23. *svastiyama pātra pāvuḷa*	:	one who sang and danced to the *svasti* hymn.
24. *kaṁba*	:	pillar (measure of land).
25. *kaṇḍiga*	:	three bushels.

Source : Rev. F. Kittel, *Kannaḍa-English Dictionary*, Mangalore, 1894.
M. Monier-Williams, *A Sanskrit-English Dictionary*, Oxford, 1899.

BIBLIOGRAPHY

ABRAMS, P & WRIGELY, EA, *Towns in Societies*, Cambridge, 1978.

ADHYA, GL, *Early Indian Economics*, Bombay, 1966.

AGRAWAL, DP *The Archaeology of India*, London, 1982.

AGARWAL, DP & PANDE BM, *Ecology and Archaeology of Western India*, Delhi, 1977.

AIYAR, KVS, *The Historical Sketches of Ancient Deccan*, Madras, 1917.

ALAM, SM 'The Historic Deccan - A Geographical Appraisal' in V. K. Bawa, *Aspects of Deccan History*, Hyderabad, 1975.

ALLCHIN, B & R, *The Birth of Indian Civilization,* Harmondworth, 1968.

ALLCHIN, B & R, *The Rise of Civilization in India and Pakistan,* New Delhi, 1983.

ALLCHIN, B(ed), *South Asian Archaeology* (Proceedings VIth Conf. of ASAAWE, 1981), Cambridge, 1984.

ALLCHIN, FR, *Piklihal Excavations*, APGAS, No.1 Hyderabad, 1960.

ALLCHIN, FR, *Utnur Excavations*, APGAS, No.5 Hyderabad, 1961.

ALLCHIN, FR, 'Upon the Antiquity and Methods of Gold Mining', *JESHO*, vol. 5, 1962.

ALLCHIN, FR, *Neolithic Cattle Keepers of South India*, Cambridge, 1968.

ALLCHIN, FR, 'The Relationship of Neolithic Later Settled Communities with those of Late Stone Age Hunters and Gatherers in Peninsular India', in R.S. Sharma & V. Jha (ed.), *Indian Society : Historical Probings, Essays in Honour of D.D. Kosambi*, Delhi, 1974.

ALTEKAR, AS, *History of the Village Communities in Western India*, Bombay, 1927.

ALTEKAR, AS, *The Rashtrakuta and their Times*, Poona, 1934 (2nd edition 1967).

ALTEKAR, AS, *State and Government in Ancient India*, Benares, 1949.

ALTEKAR, AS, *The Position of Women in Hindu Civilization*, Delhi, 1983 (First published Benares, 1938).

ALTEKAR, AS, *The Vākataka-Gupta Age*, Delhi, 1986 (First published 1967).

ANDREW, CF, *The True India* London, 1939.

ANSARI ZA & NAGARAJA RAO MS, *Excavations at Sanganakallu*, Bellary, 1965.

APPADORAI, A, *Worshisp and Conflict under Colonial Rule*, A South Indian Case, Orient Longman reprint, 1983.

APPADORAI, A, *Economic Conditions of South India (A.D. 1000-A.D. 1500)*, Madras, 1936.

ASAD, Talal, 'Are There Histories of Peoples Without Europe? A Review Article', *CSSH*, vol.29, no.3, July 1987.

BADEN-POWELL, *The Origin and Growth of Village Communities in India*, London 1899.

BAJPAI, KD, *The Geographical Encyclopaedia of Ancient & Medieval India*, Pt. I, Varanasi, 1967.

BALAMBAL, V, *Feudatories of South India, 800-1070-A. D.*, Allahabad, 1978.

BALARAMA MURTHY Y, *Andhrula Sanskshipta Charita* (Telugu), Vijayawada (reprint). (First published in 1953).

BALARAMA MURTHY Y, 'Sātavāhana Era: A Transition from Tribal Culture to National Culture', *JAAP*, Dr. N. Ramesan Commemoration Volume, vol. III, no.1, 1990.

BANERJEE, KD, *Middle Palaeolithic Industries of the Deccan*, DCP Dissertation, Poona, 1957.

BANERJI, NR, *Iron Age in India*, New Delhi, 1969.

BACRI, *Vaddamanu Excavations and Explorations in the Krishna Valley*, Hyderabad,1983.

BARUA, B. M., *Asoka and His Inscriptions*, 2 vols., Calcutta, 1946.

BASAVARAJA, KR, *Administration Under the Chalukyas of Kalyana*, Madras, 1983.

BAWA, VK, (ed.) *Aspects of Deccan History* Institute of Asian Studies, Hyderabad, 1975.

BEGLEY VIMLA, 'From Iron Age to the Early Historical in South Indian Archaeology' in Jerome Jacobson (ed.), *Studies in Archaeology of India and Pakistan*, AIIS, New Delhi, 1986.

BHANDARKAR, RG, *Early History of the Dekkan Down to the Mohammadan Conquest*, Delhi (reprint) 1985, (First published in 1892).

BONGARD-LEVIN, GM, *A Complex Study of Ancient India*, New Delhi, 1986.

BILGRAMI, SAA, *Landmarks of the Deccan: A Guide to Archaeological Remains in Hyderabad*, Delhi (reprint), 1984. (First published Hyderabad, 1927).

BRAUDEL, F *On History* (Tr. Sarah Mathews), University of Chicago, 1980.

BROWN, C J & DEY, AK, *India's Mineral Wealth*, London, 1955.

BRUEILLY, J,'What is Social History?' *History Today*, March 1985.

BUNBURY, EH, *History of Ancient Geography*, London, 1883.

BURGESS, JAS, *Reports on the Buddhist Cave Temples and Their Inscriptions*, London, 1883.

BURGESS, JAS, *Reports on Elura Cave Temples and Brahmanical Jaina Caves in Western India*, London, 1883.

BURGESS, JAS, *The Buddhist Stupas of Amaravati and Jaggayyapeta*, Varanasi, (reprint) 1970. First Published Madras, 1887.

CHAKRABARTI, DK, *Early Urban Centres in India* (Unpub. PhD Dissertation) Calcutta, 1972.

CHAKRABARTI, DK, 'The Beginning of Iron in India', *Antiquity*, vol. L, June 1976.

CHAKRABARATI, DK, 'The Issue of the Indian Iron Age' in S.B. Deo & K Paddayya (ed.), *Recent Researches in Indian Archaeology*, Deccan College, Pune, 1985.

CHAKRABARATI, DK, 'Ideas and Discoveries in Indian Archaeology', *IHR*, vol.V, nos.1-2, 1978-79.

CHAKRABORTI, H, *Trade and Commerce of Ancient India (200-650 A.D.)*, Calcutta, 1966.

CHANG, KC, 'Some Theoretical Issues in the Archaeological Study of Historical Reality' in R.C. Dundell & E.S. Hall (ed.) *Archaeological Essays in Honour of Irving Rouse*, The Hague, 1978.

CHAMPAKALAKSHMI, R, 'Peasant State and Society in Medieval South India: A Review Article, *IESHR*, vol.XVII, nos. 3 and 4, 1981.

CHAMPAKALAKSHMI, R, 'Urbanization in South India : The Role of Ideology and Polity', Presidential Address, Section I, *PIHC*, 47th Session, Srinagar, 1986.

CHANDRA, M, *The World of Courtesans*, Delhi, 1973.

CHATTERJEE, P, *Nationalist Thought and the Colonial World-A Derivative Discourse?*, London 1986.

CHATTERJEE, SP, *National Atlas of India Survey of India,* Hyderabad Plate 35.[MAP]

CHATTOPADHYAYA, BD, 'Trade and Urban Centres in Early Medieval North India', *IHR*, vol. I, no. 2, 1974.

CHATTOPADHYAYA, BD, *Coins and Currency Systems of South India, A.D. 225-1300*, New Delhi, 1977.

CHATTOPADHYAYA, BD, 'Political Processes and Structure of Polity in Early Medieval India : Problems of Perspective', Presidential Address, Section I, *PIHC*, 44th Session, Burdwan 1983.

CHATTOPADHYAYA, BD, *A Survey of Historical Geography of Ancient India*, New Delhi, 1984.

CHATTOPADHYAYA, BD, 'Urban Centres in Early Historical Medieval India : An Overview' in S. Bhattacharya and Romila Thapar (ed.), *Situating Indian History*, OUP, New Delhi, 1987.

CHATTOPADHYAYA, BD, 'Transition in the Deccan in the Early Historical Phase', in B.M. Pande & B.D. Chattopadhyaya (ed.), *Archaeology and History : Essays in Honour of A. Ghosh*, Delhi, 1987.

CHATTOPADHYAYA, BD, *Aspects of Rural Settlements and Rural Society in Early Medieval India*, S.G. Deuskar Lectures on Indian History, 1985, Calcutta, 1990.

CHATTOPADHYAYA, S, *Some Early Dynasties of South India*, Delhi, 1974.

CHAUDHURY, R, *Inscriptions of Ancient India* , Delhi, 1983.

CHILDE, VG, 'Civilization, Cities and Towns', *Antiquity*, vol. 31, March 1957.

CHILDE, VG, *What Happened in History*, Harmondsworth, (reprint), 1964. (First published in 1942).

CHOPRA, PN, RAVINDRAN, TK and SUBRAHMANIAN, N, (ed.) *History of South India*, vols. 3, New Delhi, 1979.

CLAESSEN JM, & SKALNIK P (Ed.), *The Early State* Theories and Hypotheses, The Hague, 1981.

CUNNINGHAM, A, *Ancient Geography of India*, London, 1871.

DAS, DR, *Economic History of the Deccan*, Delhi, 1969.

DAS, RM, *Women in Manu and His Seven Commentators*, Bodh Gaya, 1962.

DEHEJIA, V *Early Buddhist Rock Temples*, London, 1972.

DEO, SB & ANSARI, Z, *Chalcolithic Chandoli (Report on Excavations at Chandoli 1960)*, Poona, 1965.

DEO, SB *Excavations at Takalghat and Khapa 1968-69*, Nagpur, 1970.

DEO, SB & GUPTA, RS, *Excavations at Bhokardan 1973*, Nagpur, 1974.

DEO, SB, *Mahurjhari Excavations 1970-72*, Nagpur, 1973.

DEO, SB, *Problems of South Indian Megaliths*, Dharwar, 1973.

DEO, SB (ed), *Archaeological Congress and Seminar Papers*, Nagpur, 1972.

DEO, SB, *Megalithic Problems of the Deccan*, Cambridge, 1984.

DESAI, DEVANGANA, 'Social Background of Ancient Indian Terracottas (600 BC-600 AD)', in D.P. Chattopadyaya (ed.), *History and Society, Essays in Honour of Niharranjan Ray*, Calcutta, 1978.

DESAI, DINKAR, *The Mahāmaṇḍaleśvaras under the Chalukyas of Kalayani*, Bombay, 1964.

DESAI, PB (ed), *History of Karnataka*, Kannada Research Institute, Dharwar, 1970.

DEY, AK, *Geology of India*, 1968.

DEY, NL, *A Geographical Dictionary of Ancient and Medieval India*, Delhi (reprint), 1971.

DHARMA KUMAR, 'Private Property in Asia? The Case of Medieval South India', *CSSH*, vol. 27, no. 2, April 1985.

DHARMAPAL, 'A Note on the Disruption and Disorganization of Indian Society in Last Two Centuries, *Patriotic and People Orient of Science and Technology Buttetin*, November 1983, vol.3, no.2.

DHAVALIKAR, MK, 'Chalcolithic Burials: The Tekwada Evidence', *Purātattva*, no. 2, 1968-69.

DHAVALIKAR, MK, 'Daimabad – A Rediscovery', *Purātattva*., no. 3, 1969-70.

DHAVALIKAR, MK, 'Settlement Archaeology of Inamgaon', *Purātattva.*, no. 8, 1975-76.

DHAVALIKAR, MK, 'Cultural Ecology of Chalcolithic Maharashtra' in S.B. Deo & K. Paddayya (ed.), *Recent Researches in Indian Archaeology*, Deccan College, Pune, 1985.

DIKSHIT, DP, *Political History of the Chalukyas of Badami*, New Delhi, 1980.

DIKSHIT, GS, *Local Self Government in Medieval Karnataka*, Dharwar, 1964.

DIKSHIT, KN (ed.), *Archaeological Perspective of India Since Independence*, New Delhi, 1985.

DIKSHIT, MG, *Etched Beads in India, Decorative Patterns & Geographical Distribution*, Poona, 1949.

DUBOIS, AJ, *Hindu Manners, Customs and Ceremonies*, Oxford, 1897 (2nd. edition 1899),

DUBREUIL, GJ, *Ancient History of Deccan*, Delhi (reprint), 1979. (First published Pondicherry 1922).

DUMONT, Louis, (ed.), *Religion, Politics and History in India*, Paris, 1970

DUTT, KI, *Historical Geography of Andhra Pradesh*, Hyderabad, 1963.

EMMENEAU, MB & BURROW, T *Dravidian Etymological Dictionary*.

Encyclopaedia Britannica

ERDOSY, G, *Urbanization in Early Historic India*, BAR International Series, 430, 1988.

FILLOZAT, J, *Les Relations Exterieures de Pondicherry L'Inde*, 1956.

FINELY, MI, *The Ancient Economy*, London, 1973.

FORBES, RJ, *Metallurgy in Antiquity*, Leiden, 1950.

FRIED, MH, 'On the Evolution of Social Stratification and the State', in Stanley Diamond (ed.), *Culture in History: Essays in Honour of Paul Kaelin*, New York, 1960.

FRIED, MH, *The Notion of Tribe*, California, 1975.

FRIEND, JN, *Iron in Antiquity*, London, 1926.

FULLER, CJ, *Servants of the Goddess : The Priests of a South Indian Temple*, London, 1984

FUSSMAN, G, 'Central and Provincial Administration in Ancient India : The Problem of the Mauryan Empire', *IHR*, vol. XIV, no.1-2, 1987-1988.

GAIRỌLA, KC, 'The Administrative Structure of the Sātavāhana Empire', *Arts and Letters*, vol.XXIX, no. 2, 1955.

GAIROLA, KC, 'A Geographical Sketch of the Sātavāhana Empire, *Arts and Letters*, vol.XXX, no.1, 1956.

GANGULY, DC, *Eastern Chalukyas,* Benares, 1937.

GHOSH, A, *The City in Early Historical India,* Simla, 1973.

GHOSHAL,UN, *A History of Hindu Political Theories*, Calcutta, 1923.

GOPAL, BR, *Minor Dynasties of South India*, Madras, 1982.

GOPAL, L, *Aspects of History of Agriculture in Ancient India*, Varanasi, 1980.

GOPAL, S and THAPAR, R (ed.), *Problems of Historical Writing in India*, New Delhi, 1963.

GOPALACHARI, K, *Early History of the Andhra Country,* Madras, 1941.

GOTTSCHLAK, L, *Genralization in the Writing of History*, Chicago, 1980.

GREEN SALLY, 'Introduction' to the first illustrated edition of *Man Makes Himself*, by V.G. Childe, Wiltshire England, 1981.

GRIBBLE, JDB, *A History of the Deccan,* 2 vols. (vol II, 1924), London, 1896.

GUALTIERI, M, 'Fortifications and Settlement Organization : An Example from Pre-Roman Italy', *World Archaeology,* vol. 19, no. 1, 1987.

GUNAWARDANE, RALH, 'The Analysis of Pre-Colonial Social Formations in Asia in the Writing of Karl Marx', *IHR*, vol.II, no.2, 1976.

GUPTA, KM, *The Land System in South India between AD 800-1200*, Lahore, 1930.

GUPTA, PL, 'Coins from Archaeological Excavations in Deccan' in *Colloquium on South Indian Archaeology*, Hyderabad, 1990.

GUPTA, SP and RAMACHANDRAN, KS (ed.) *Readings in South Indian History,* Delhi, 1977.

GUPTA, VK, *Kautilyan Jurisprudence*, Delhi 1987.

GURUKKAL, R, 'Forms of Production and Forces of Change in Ancient Tamil Country' in *Studies in History* (New Series), vol. 5, no. 2, 1989.

GURURAJA RAO, BK, *Megalithic Culture in South India,* Mysore, 1972.

GURURAJA RAO, BK (ed), *A Decade of Archaeological Studies in South India*, Dharwar, 1978.

GURURAJA RAO, BK, 'Socio-Economic Life in Proto Historic Karnataka in B.K. Gururaja Rao & A.V. Narasimha Murthy (ed.), *Rangavalli*, Sri S.R. Rao Felicitation Volume, New Delhi, 1983.

GYAN PRAKASH,'Writing Post-Orientalist Histories of the Third World: Perspectives from Indian Historiography', *CSSH*, vol.32, no.2, April 1990.

HABIB, I, 'The Social Distribution of Landed Property in Pre-British India' in R.S. Sharma & V. Jha (ed.), *Indian Society: Historical Probings, Essays in Honour of D.D. Kosambi*, New Delhi, 1974.

HABIB, I, 'The Peasant in Indian History', General President's Address, *PIHC*, 43rd Session, 1982.

HAMMOND, N (ed.), *South Asian Archaeology* (Proceedings of Ist Conf. ASAAWE), New Jersey, 1973.

HANUMANTHA RAO, BSL, *Andhrula Charitra* (Telugu), Guntur, 1983.

HÄRTEL, H (ed.), *South Asian Archaeology* (Proceedings Vth Conf. ASAAWE, 1979), Berlin, 1981.

HILL, JN, 'The Methodological Debate in Contemporary Archaeology : A Model', in David L. Clark (ed.), *Models in Archaeology*, 1972.

ISMAIL, K, *Karnataka Temples : Their Role in Socio-Economic Life*, Delhi, 1984.

JACOBSON, J (ed), *Studies in the Archaeology of India and Pakistan*, New Delhi, 1986.

JAIN, CHAKRESH, '"Married" to a Goddess, Forsaken by God', *Mid-Day*, 10 July, 1983.

JAIN, KC, *Pre-History and Proto History of India*, New Delhi, 1979.

JAISWAL, S, 'Studies in Early Indian Social History : Trends and Possibilities', *IHR*, vol. VI, nos. 1-2, 1979-80.

JAISWAL, S, 'Changes in the Concept of the Śūdra Varṇa in Early Middle Ages', *PIHC*, 40th Session, Bombay, 1980.

JAISWAL, S, 'Women in Early India: Problems and Perspectives', *PIHC*, 41st Session, Bodh Gaya, 1981.

JAYASWAL, KP, *Hindu Polity*, 2 vols. (5th edition) Bangalore, 1978. (First published in 1920).

JHA, DN, *Revenue System in Post-Maurya and Gupta Times*, Calcutta, 1966.

JHA, DN, *Studies in Early Indian Economic History,* Delhi, 1980.

JHA, DN, 'Validity of the " Brāhmaṇa-Peasant Alliance" and the 'Segmentary State' in Early Medieval South India', *Social Science Probings*, vol. 1, no.2, June, 1984.

JHA, DN, (ed.), *Feudal Formations in Early India,* Delhi, 1986.

JHA, V, 'Stages in the History of Untouchables', *IHR*, vol. II, no. 1, 1975.

JHA, V, 'Ancient Indian Political History: Possibilities and Pitfalls', *IHR*, vol. XIV, nos.1-2, 1987-1988.

JONES, RFJ, 'A False Start? The Roman Urbanization of Western Europe', *World Archaeology,* vol. 19, no. 1, June 1987.

JOSHI, SD, *History of Metal Founding on the Indian Subcontinent,* Ranchi, 1970.

KAMAT, JK, *Social Life in Medieval Karnataka*, New Delhi, 1980.

KARASHIMA, NOBURO, *South Indian History and Society (Studies from Inscriptions AD* 850- 1800), Oxford, 1984.

KASTURI BAI, M, SASTRY TVG, VARAPRASAD RAO *Veerapuram – A Type Site for Cultural Study in the Krishna Valley,* BARCI, Hyderabad, 1984.

KENNEDY, KAR, *The Physical Anthropology of Megalith Builders of South India and Sri Lanka*, Canberra, 1975.

KENNEDY, KAR & POSSEHL, GL (ed.), *Studies in Archaeology and Palaeoanthropology of South Asia*, AIIS, 1984.

KENNEDY, RS, 'The King in Early South India as Chieftain and Emperor', *IHR*, vol. III, no.1. 1976.

KERSEN BOOM-STORY, S, *Nityasumangali Devadasi Tradition in South India*, Delhi, 1987.

KHAN, AW, *A Monograph on Yelleswaram Excavations*, APGAS No. 14, Hyderabad, 1963.

KIEPERT, Henrich, *A Maneual of Ancient Geography*, London, 1881.

KING, ANNA, 'Some Archaeological Problems Regarding Gangetic Cultures in Early Historical India' in K.A.R. Kennedy and G.L. Possehl (ed.), *Studies in Archaeology and Palaeoanthropology of South Asia,* AIIS, 1984.

KITTS, EJA, *Compendium of the Castes and Tribes Found in India, Asian Social System,* Bombay, (reprint) 1982. (First published in 1885)

KNUDSON, SJ, *Culture in Retrospect,* (Chicago, 1978).

KOSAMBI, DD, *An Introduction to the Study of Indian History*, Bombay, 1985 (First published in 1956).

KOSAMBI, DD, *The Culture and Civilization in Historical Outline*, Delhi, 1970.

KRISHNA RAO, BV, *A History of the Early Dynasties of Andhradeśa,* Madras, 1942.

KRISHNAMURTHY, K, *Nagarjunakonda, A Cultural Study,* Delhi, 1977.

KULKE, Hermann, 'Fragmentation and Segmentation Versus Integration? Reflections on Concepts of Indian Feudalism and the Segmentary State in Indian History', *Studies in History*, vol.5, no.2, 1982.

KUPPUSWAMY, GR, *Economic Conditions in Karnataka 973-1336 A.D.,* Dharwar, 1975.

LA TOUCHE, THD, *A Bibliography of Indian Geology and Geography,* 1938.

LAMBERG-KARLOVSKY, CC and SABLOFF, JAL, *Ancient Civilization and Trade,* Albuquerque, 1975.

LEACOCK, E R, (ed.) *The Origin of Family, Private Property and State*, New York, 1972.

LESHNIK, LS, *South Indian Megalithic Burials : The Pandukal Complex,* Wiesbaden, 1974.

LESHNIK, LS & SONTHEIMER, G, *Pastrolists and Nomads in South Asia,* Wiesbaden, 1975.

LEUVA, FK, *The Asur : A Study Of Primitive Iron Smelters,* New Delhi.

LICERIA, Sister M, 'Emergence of Brāhmaṇas as Landed Intermediaries in Karnataka', *IHR*, vol. I, no.1, 1974.

LOHUIZEN, JE, van (ed), *South Asian Archaeology* (Proceedings IIIrd Conf. of ASAAWE, 1975), Leiden, 1979.

MAHALINGAM, TV, *South Indian Polity*, Madras, 1955.

MAHALINGAM, TV, (ed.) *Readings in South Indian History*, Delhi, 1979.

MAJUMDAR, GG and RAJAGURU, SN, *Ashmound Excavations at Kupgal*, Poona, 1966.

MAJUMDAR, RC, (ed.), *The Classical Age*, vol. III, Bombay, 1954.

MAJUMDAR, RC, *Corporate Life In Ancient India*, Calcutta, 1920.

MAINE, H, *Village Communities in the East and West*, London, 1871.

MALONEY C, 'Archaeology in South India : Accomplishments and Prospects' in Burton Stein (Ed.), *Essays on South India,* New Delhi 1976.

MANGALAM, SJ, *Historical Geography and Toponomy of Andhra Pradesh,* New Delhi, 1986.

MARGABANDHU, C, *Archaeology of the Sātavāhana-Kshatrapa Times*, New Delhi, 1985.

MARGLIN, FH, *Wives of the God King*, OUP, Delhi, 1985.

MATSYA PURĀṆA, SBH vol. XVII, Allahabad, 1974.

MAURIZIO, T (ed), *South Asian Archaeology* (Proceedings of IVth Conf. of ASAAWE, 1977), Naples, 1979.

McINTOSH, JR, 'The Megalith Builders of South India – A Historical Survey', in H Härtel (ed.), *South Asian Archaeology,* Berlin, 1981.

MINAKSHI, C, *Administration and Social Life under the Pallavas,* Madras, 1938.

MISRA, SUDAMA, *Janapada State in Ancient India*, Varanasi, 1973.

MISHRA, VN & MATE, MS, *Indian Prehistory*, Poona, 1965.

MORGAN, L, *Ancient Societies*, New York, 1877 (Reprint) Arizona, 1985.

MOTI CHANDRA, *Trade and Trade Routes in Ancient India*, Delhi, 1977.

MUKHERJEE, R, *Chandragupta and His Times*, Madras, 1943.

MULAY, S, *Studies in the Historical and Cultural Geography of the Deccan*, Poona, 1972.

MURTHI, AV & GURURAJARAO, BK, (ed.), *Rangavalli, Recent Researches in Indology,* Delhi, 1983.

MURTY, MLK, 'Pre-Iron Age Agricultural Settlements in South India : An Ecological Perspective', *Man and Environment*, vol. XIV, no. 1, 1989.

MURTHY, RN, *Forts in Ancient and Medieval Andhra up to 1600 AD,* Tirupati, 1979.

NAGAMANI, D, *Material Cultures and Social Formation in Early Deccan*, Unpublished M.Phil Dissertation, University of Hyderabad, 1990.

NAGARAJA, RAO, MS & MALHOTRA, KC, *The Stone Age Hill Dwellers of Tekkalakota,* Poona, 1965.

NAGARAJA RAO, MS, *Protohistoric Cultures of the Tungabhadra Valley* (A Report on Hallur Excavations), New Delhi, 1977. (First published Poona, 1971).

NAGARAJA RAO, MS, 'Earliest Iron Using People in India and the Megaliths' in M.S. Nagaraja Rao (ed.), *Madhu : Recent Researches in Indian Archaeology and Art History,* Shri M.N. Deshpande Festschrift, Delhi, 1981.

NAGARAJU, SN and GURURAJA RAO, BK 'Chronology of Iron Age in South India' in D.P. Agarwal and Dilip K. Chakrabarti, (ed.), *Essays in Indian Proto-History,* vol. 5, ISPQS's History and Archaeology Series, Delhi, 1979.

NAGARAJU, SN, *Buddhist Architecture of Western India (c. 250 B.C. - c. A.D. 300)*, New Delhi, 1980.

NAGASWAMY, R (ed.), *South Indian Studies*, Madras, 1978.

NAIK, USHA S & PARASHER, ALOKA, 'Temple Girls of Medieval Karnataka', *IESHR,* vol 23, no. 1, 1986.

NANDI, RN, *Religious Institutions and Cults in the Deccan, c. A.D. 600-1000* Delhi, 1973.

NANDI, RN, 'Growth of Rural Economy in Early Feudal India', *PIHC*, 45th Session Annamalainagar, 1984.

NARAYANAN, MGS, *Aspects of Aryanization in Kerala*, Trivandrum, 1973.

NARAYANAN, MGS, *Re-Interpretations on South Indian History*, Trivandrum, 1977.

NARAYANAN, MGS, 'Trends and Prospects in Historiography', Presidential Address Section, *PIHC,* 39th Session, Hyderabad, 1978.

NARAYANAN, MGS, and VELUTHAT, K. 'Bhakti Movement in South India'. in SC Malik, (ed.) *Indian Movements : Some Aspects of Dissent Protest and Reform*, IIAS Simla, 1978.

MAJUMDAR, GG, RAJAGURU, SN *Ashmound Excavation at Kupgal*.

NEOGI, P, *Iron in Ancient India*, Calcutta, 1914.

NEOGI, P, *Copper in Ancient India*, Calcutta, 1918.

NIGAM ML, *Report on the Excavation of Two Megalithic Burials at Hashmatpet*, BACRI, Hyderabad, 1971.

PADDAYYA, K and DEO, SB, (ed.) *Recent Advances in Archaeology*, Poona, 1983.

PADDAYA, K 'The Role of Hypothesis and Traditional Archaeology' *BDCRI*, vol. 47-48, 1988-89.

PANIKKAR, KM, *India and the Indian Ocean,* London, 1945.

PANIKKAR, KM, *Geographical Factors in Indian History*, Bombay, 1955.

PARASHER, ALOKA, 'Early History of Andhra – Some Interpretations', *PAPHC*, 9th Session, Kurnool, 1985.

PARASHER, ALOKA & NAIK, US, 'Temple Girls of Medieval Karnataka' *IESHR*, vol 23, no. 1, 1986.

PARASHER, ALOKA, 'Feudal Formations', *Social Scientist*, No. 171-172, August - September, 1987.

PARASHER, ALOKA, 'Social Structure and Economy of Settlements in the Central Deccan (200 B.C. - A.D. 200) in Indu Banga (ed.), *The City in Indian History*, New Delhi, 1990.

PARPOLA, A, *Arguments of an Aryan Origin of South Indian Megaliths*, Madras, 1973.

PERLIN, FRANK, 'The Material and the Cultural : An Attempt to Transcend the Present Impasse', *MAS*, vol. 22, no. 2, 1988.

PRASAD, NRV, 'Nelakondapalle Excavation', *ARDAM*, Hyderabad, 1977-78.

PRASAD, OM PRAKASH, 'Trade in the Growth of Towns : A Case Study of Karnataka (600-1200)', *PIHC*, 40th Session, Bombay, 1980.

QURESHI, IMRAN, 'Yellamma's Daughters of the Night', *Indian Express*, 6 March 1983.

RAI, GK, *Involuntary Labour in Ancient India*, Allahabad, 1981.

RAI, GK, 'Forced Labour in Ancient and Early Medieval India', *IHR*, vol. 3, 1976-77.

RAJENDRA PRASAD, B, *Temple Sculpture of Andhra Pradesh*, Hyderabad, 1978.

RAMA RAO, M, *Andhra Through Ages,* Maruthi Books, 1957.

RAMA RAO, M, *Glimpses of Deccan History*, Orient Longmans, 1951.

RAMA RAO, M, 'Successors of the Sātavāhanas, *JIH*, vol. XL, pt. iii, December 1962.

RAMACHANDRAN, KS, *Radiocarbon Dates of Archaeological Sites in India,* APGAS 42, Hyderabad, 1975.

RAMASWAMI IYENGAR, MS, *Eminent Orientalists*, Madras, 1922.

RAMASWAMY, NS, *Amaravati : The Art & History of the Stupa & the Temple*, APGAS 4, Hyderabad, 1975.

RAMESAN, N, *Andhra Pradesh Through the Ages,* Hyderabad, 1967.

RAMI REDDY, VR, 'An Outline of the Pre and Protohistoric Cultures of South Western Andhra Pradesh', *Journal of Karnatak University,* Dharwar, vol.VIII.

RANDHAWA, MS, *A History of Agriculture in India*, vol. I, Delhi, 1980.

RAO, KP, *Megaliths of the Deccan*, New Delhi, 1988.

RAO, K RAMA MOHAN, *Early Dynasties of Andhradesa from the Fall of Sātavāhanas to the Rise of Eastern Chalukyas*, Unpublished PhD. Thesis, Karnataka University, Dharwar, 1981.

RAO V PANDIT & GAYATRI, 'A Study of Visnukundin Coins' *Bulletin of Material Sciences*, vol. 9, June 1987.

RAO, VENKATESWARA T, *Local Bodies in Pre Vijayanagar Andhra AD 1000-A.D. 1336*, Phd Thesis, Karnatak University, Dharwar, 1975.

RATNAGAR, S, *Encounters The Westerly Trade of Harappan Civilization,* New Delhi, 1981.

RAY, A, *Life and Art of Early Andhradesa,* Delhi, 1983.

RAY, A, *Villages, Towns and Secular Buildings in Ancient India*, Calcutta, 1964.

RAY, HP, *Monastery and Guild (Commerce Under Sātavāhanas),* Bombay, 1986.

RAY, HP, 'Early Historical Settlements in Deccan: An Ecological Perspective', *Man and Environment*, vol. XIV, no. i, 1989.

RAYCHAUDURI, HC, 'Geography of the Deccan' in G. Yazdani, *Early History of the Deccan*, OUP,1960.

RAYCHAUDHURI, HC, *Political History of Ancient India* (7th edition), Calcutta, 1970.

RICHARDS, JF, *Mughal Administration in Golconda*, Oxford, 1975.

ROBB, Peter (ed.) *Rural South Asia, Linkages, Change amd Development*, New Delhi, 1986.

RUSSELL & HIRALAL, *The Tribes and Castes of the Central Provinces of India*, Delhi, (reprint), 1975.

SAMBASIVA RAO, G, 'Pallava Rule over the Guntur District', *JAHRS*, vol. 29, 1963-64.

SANKALIA, HD & DEO SB, *Excavations at Nasik and Jorwe,* Poona, 1955.

SANKALIA, HD, *The Pre-History and Proto History of India and Pakistan*, Poona, 1974. (First published in 1962-63).

SARKAR, H, *Nagarjunakonda*, ASI, New Delhi, 1972.

SARKAR, H, 'Emergence of Urban Centres in Early Historical Andhradesa', in B.M. Pande & B.D. Chattopadhyaya (ed.), *Archaeology and History : Essays in Memory of A. Ghosh*, vol. II, Delhi, 1987.

SAMUEL, R,'What is Social History' *History Today*, March 1985.

SANKARANARAYANAN, S, *Vishnukundins and Their Times*, Delhi, 1977.

SARMA, IK, 'Some More Inscriptions from Amaravati Excavations and the Chronology of the Mahāstūpa', *Studies in Indian Epigraphy*, vol. I, Mysore, 1947.

SARMA, IK, 'C 14 Dates, NBPW and Early Historical Arehaeology of Peninsular India, *JIH*, vol. LII, pt.i, 1974.

SARMA, IK, *The Coinage of the Sātavāhana Empire,* New Delhi, 1980.

SARMA, IK, 'More Prakrit Inscriptions from Amaravati', *Studies is Indian Epigraphy*, Vol, VII, Mysore 1980.

SARMA, IK, 'Amaravati Stupamu - Neti Puravastu Parisodhanalu (Telugu), *Bharathi*, August, 1975.

SARMA, IK, 'Early Sculptures and Epigraphs from South East India : New Evidence from Amaravati' in F.E. Ashar and G.S. Gai (ed.), *Indian Epigraphy its Bearing on the History of Art*, New Delhi, 1985.

SARMA IK, 'Some Early Telugu Inscriptions', *Epigraphica Andhrica,* vol. IV.

SARMA, MR, *Temples of Telingana,* Hyderabad, 1972.

SARMA, MS, *History of the Reddi Kingdom*, Waltair, 1948.

SASTRI, KAN, *Historical Methods in Relation to Problems of South Indian History*, Madras, 1941.

SASTRI, KAN, A *History of South India*, 4th edition Madras, 1984. First published in 1947.

SASTRI, KAN, (ed.) *Age of Nandas and Mauryas*, Delhi,1967.

SASTRI, KRR, *South Indian Guilds,* Madras, 1925.

SASTRI, PVP, 'Simuka Satavahanudi Nanalu (Telugu), *Bharathi*, June 1978.

SASTRY, PVP, 'Coins of Simuka Sātavāhana Discovered', *JAAP*, vol, I, no. 1, 1979.

SASTRY, PVP, 'Some Urban Centres in Early Medieval India', *JTS,* vol. 1, no. 1, 1979.

SASTRY, PVP, 'Political System in Early Coastal Andhra' in Devendra Handa (ed.), *Ajaya Shri Recent Researches in Indology*, Ajay Mitra Shastri Felicitation Volume, New Delhi, 1989.

SASTRY, VVK, 'Archaeology in Andhra Pradesh' in B.K. Gururaja Rao (ed.), *DASSI*, Dharwar, 1978.

SASTRY, VVK, 'Keesaragutta - A Capital of Vishnukundins', *JAAP*, vol. I, no. 1, 1979.

SASTRY, VVK, 'Excavations at Keesaragutta', *ARDAM*, Hyderabad, 1981-82.

SASTRY, VVK, *The Proto and Early Historical Cultures of Andhra Praadesh,* APGAS No. 58, Hyderabad, 1983.

SATYANARAYANA, K, *A Study of the History and Culture of the Andhras*, vol. I, Delhi, 1975.

SATYANARAYANA, K, *Andhrula Samskriti-Charitra*, vol. I (Telugu), Hyderabad, 1981.

SENART, E, 'The Inscriptions in Caves at Nasik', *EI*, vol. VIII, 1905-06.

SENEVIRATNE, S, 'Kalinga and Andhra: The Processes of Secondary State Formation', *IHR*, vol. 7, no. 1-2, 1981.

SERIVCE, ER, *Origins of State and Civilization: The Processes of Cultural Evolution,* New York, 1975.

SETTAR, S, 'Roots, Relations, Relevance' in Mulk Raj Anand (ed.), *Marg,* vol. XXII, no.1.

SCHWARTZBERG, JE, *A Historical Atlas of South Asia,* Chicago, 1978.

SHAH, AM, *The Household Dimension of Family in India*, New Delhi, 1973.

SHARMA, RS, *Śūdras in Ancient India (Social History of Lower Orders)*, Delhi, 1958.

SHARMA, RS, *Indian Feudalism 300-1200 A.D.*, New Delhi, 1965.

SHARMA, RS, *Aspects of Political Ideas and Institutions in Ancient India,* New Delhi (reprint), 1968.

SHARMA, RS & Jha, VN (ed.), *Indian Society : Historical Probings, Essays in Honour of D.D. Kosambi,* New Delhi, 1974.

SHARMA, RS, *Material Culture and Social Formation in Ancient India,* New Delhi, 1983.

SHARMA, RS, *Perspectives in Social and Economic History of Early India,* Delhi, 1983.

SHARMA, RS, 'How Feudal was Indian Feudalism?' *JPS*, vol. 12, no. 23, January-April 1985.

SHARMA, RS (ed.) *Survey of Research in Economic and Social History*, ICSSR Publication, New Delhi, 1986.

SHARMA, RS, *Urban Decay in India (300-1200 A.D.),* Delhi, 1987.

SHASTRI, AM, *Coinage of the Sātavāhanas and Coins from Excavation,* Nagpur, 1972.

SHASTRI, AM, *Early History of the Deccan: Problems and Perspectives*, New Delhi, 1987.

SHERRING, MA, *Hindu Tribes and Castes as Represented in Benares*, London, 1872.

SHERWANI, HK, *The Bahamanis of the Deccan*, Hyderabad, 1953.

SHERWANI, HK & JOSHI, PK (ed), *History of Medieval Deccan*, 2 vols, Hyderabad, 1973-74.

SHETTAR, A, Aspects of Agricultural Expansion in Early Medieval Southern Karnataka' in K. Veerathappan (ed.), *Studies in Karnataka History and Culture* (Proceedings vol. II of the Karnataka History Congress), Mysore, 1980.

SHRIMALI, KM, *Agrarian Structure in Central India & Northern Deccan AD 300-500, A Study of Vakataka Inscriptions,* Delhi, 1987.

SIDDIQUI, A, 'A Copper Seal of Maharathi Asvaghosha', *Numismatic Digest*, vol. II, 1987.

SINGH, HN, 'Black and Red Ware - A Cultural Study in D.P. Agarwal & Dilip K Chakrabarti (ed.), *Essays in Indian Proto History*, Delhi, 1979.

SINGH, KS, *Tribal Society In India : An Anthropo-Historical Perspective,* New Delhi, 1985.

SINGH, TRR, 'Pre-Historic Sites in Karimnagar Region, Andhra Pradesh', *JAAP*, vol, I, no.2, 1979.

SINGH, TRR, 'Living Conditions of Palaeolithic Man Godavari Valley from Bastar to Bhadrachalam, Andhra Pradesh, India' *JAAP*, vol. II, no.1, 1984.

SINGH, TRR, PRASAD, K, 'Observations on the Vertebrate Fossils from Karimnagar and Adilabad Districts, Andhra Pradesh', *JAAP*, vol. II, no. 1, 1984.

SINGH, TRR, 'Some Unique Discoveries in Stone Age Archaeology in Telangana Region, Andhra Pradesh', *JAAP*, Vol. II, no.1, 1984.

SINGH, TRR, 'The Pre-Sātavāhana Andhra Kings of Central Godavari Valley. The Andhra Kings of Asmaka, Mulaka' presented at UGC Seminar on *Recent Archaeological Studies in Andhra Pradesh*, Kakatiya University, Warangal, March 1987, (cyclostyled).

SINGH, RL, *India - A Regional Geography*, Varanasi, 1971.

SIRCAR, DC, *The Successors of the Sātavāhanas in Eastern Deccan*, Calcutta, 1939.

SIRCAR, DC, *Indian Epigraphy*, Delhi, 1965.

SIRCAR, DC, *Indian Epigraphical Glossary*, Delhi 1966.

SIRCAR, DC, *Studies in the Geography of Ancient and Medieval India*, Delhi, 1971.

SITAPATI, P (ed.), *Sātavāhana Seminar*, Hyderabad, 1981.

SIVARAMA MURTI, C, *Royal Conquerors and Cultural Migration in South India and Deccan*, Calcutta, 1955.

SJOBERG, G, *The Pre-Industrial City Past and Present*, Glencoe, 1960.

SMITH, VA, *Early History of India* (4th edition), Oxford, 1924.

SPATE, OHK, *India and Pakistan A General and Regional Geography*, London, 1954.

SRINIVAS, MN, (ed.) *The Dominant Caste and Other Essays*, OUP, Delhi, 1987.

SRINIVASAN, AMRIT, 'Reform and Revival The Devadasi and Her Dance', *EPW*, vol. XX, no. 44, 2 November, 1985.

SRIVASTAVA, KM, *New Horizons in Indian Archaeology,* New Delhi, 1988.

STEIN, B, *Peasant State and Society in Medieval South India*, Delhi, 1980.

SUBBARAO, B, 'The Geographic Factors in Andhra History and Archaeology,' *BDCRI*, vol IX, pt. I, 1947-48.

SUBBARAO, B, *Personality of India : Pre and Proto-historic Foundation of India and Pakistan,* Baroda, 1958.

SUBBARAYALU, Y, *Political Geography of Chola Country*, Dept. of Archaeology, Tamil Nadu, 1973.

SUBBARAYALU, Y, 'The Place of Ur in the Economic and Social History of Early Tamil Nadu from A.D. 750 to A.D. 1350' in A.V. Narasimha Murthy and B.K. Gururaja Rao (ed.), *Rangavalli, Recent Researches in Indology,* Delhi, 1983.

SUBRAMANIA IYER, KV, *Historical Sketches of Ancient Deccan*, Madras, 1917.

SUBRAMANYAM, BR, 'Appearance and Spread of Iron in India-An Appraisal of Archaeological Data', *JOI*, vol. XIII, no. 1, Sept. 1963.

SUBRAMANYAM, KR, *Buddhist Remains in South India and History of Andhra between 225 and 610 A.D.,* Madras, 1927.(New Delhi reprint 1981.)

SUBRAMANYAM, R, *Nagarjunakonda I*, New Delhi, 1975.

SUDERSEN, V, *Geomorphology and Prehistory of South India*, Delhi, 1972.

SUNDARA, A, *The Early Chamber Tombs of South India*, A Study of the Iron Age Megalith Monuments of North Karnataka, Dharwar, 1975.

SUNDARA, A,'Cultural Ecology of the Neolithic in India' in S.B. Deo and K. Paddayya (ed.), *Recent Advances in Indian Archaeology,* Deccan College, Pune, 1985.

SUNDARA, A,'Studies in Ash Mounds' in B.M. Pande and B.D. Chattopadhyaya (ed.), *Archaeology and History Essays in Honour of A. Ghosh,* vol. I, New Delhi, 1987.

SUNDARAM, K, *Studies in Economic and Social Conditions of Medieval Andhra AD 1000-1600,* Machilipatnam, 1968.

SYED, AJ, (ed.) *D. D. Kosambi on History and Society*, Problem of Interpretation, Bombay 1985.

TAMASKAR, BG, *Contributions to Historical Geography of India,* New Delhi, 1985.

THAKUR, VK, *Urbanization in Ancient India*, New Delhi, 1981.

THAKUR, VK, 'Feudal Content of Pala Art : A Framework for Enquiry', *PIHC*, 48th Session, Goa, 1987.

THAPAR, R, *A History of India,* vol. I, Harmondsworth, (reprint) 1984.

THAPAR, R, *Aśoka and the Decline of the Mauryas*, OUP (2nd.ed.), 1963.

THAPAR, R, *Ancient Indian Social History, Some Interpretations,* Delhi, 1978.

THAPAR, R, *The Mauryas Revisited (S.G. Deuskar Lectures on Indian History 1984),* Calcutta, 1987.

THAPAR, BK, 'Maski - 1954 : Chalcolithic Site of the Southern Deccan', *AI*, vol. XIII.

THOMSON, SJ, *The Real Indian People*, London, 1914.

THURSTON, E & RANGACHARI, K, *Castes and Tribes of Southern India*, New Delhi (reprint) 1975. (First published in 1899).

TIWARY, Diwakar, *Concept of State in the Mahābhārata*, Delhi, 1990.

TRINGHAM, RUTH, 'The Concept of "Civilization" in European Archaeology' in J.A. Sabloff & C.C. Lamberg-Karlovsy (ed.), *The Rise and Fall of Civilizations*, California, 1980.

VAIDEHI, AVK, *Social and Economic Conditions of Eastern Deccan 1000-1250 A.D.*, Secundrabad, 1970.

VELUTHAT, K, *Brāhmaṇa Settlements in Kerala,* Calicut, 1978.

VELUTHAT, K, 'Monarchical Power in Early Medieval South India: The Image and Reality' paper presented at Seminar *State in South India*, JNU. New Delhi 1989 (Cyclostyled copy)

VENKATAKRISHNA RAO, B, *History of the Eastern Chalukyas of Vengi,* Hyderabad, 1973.

VENKATARAMANAYYA, N, *Eastern Chalukyas of Vengi.*

VENKATESWARA RAO T, *Local Bodies in Pre-Vijayanagara Andhra 1000-1336,* Dharwar, 1975.

VIRABHADRA RAO, *Andhracharitra* (Telugu), Madras, 1910.

WATT, G, *The Commercial Products of India*, London, 1908.

WEBER, M, *The Religion of India (The Sociology of Hinduism & Buddhism Tr.)*, New York, 1967.

WEBSTER, AM, *Third New International Dictionary*, USA, 1969.

WHEELER, REM, 'Brahmagiri and Chandravalli 1947. Megalithic and other Cultures in Mysore State', *AI*, no. 4, ASI, New Delhi, (reprint) 1984. (First published in 1947-48).

WILKS, M. and MURRAY, H, *Historical Sketches of the South Indian History*, New Delhi (rp) 1980. First Published 1817.

WITFOGEL, Karl A,' Development Aspects of Hydraulic Societies' in Irrigation Civilizations : A Comparative Study, Social Science Monographs, Washington, 1955.

YADAVA, BNS, *Society and Culture in Northern India in the Twelfth Century A.D.*, Allahabad, 1973.

YADAVA, BNS, 'Problem of the Interaction between Socio-Economic Classes in the Early Medieval Complex', *IHR*, vol. 3, 1976-77.

YADAVA, BNS, 'Immobility and Subjection of Indian Peasantry in Early Medieval Complex', *IHR*, vol. I, no.1, March 1974.

YAZDANI, G, 'The Megalithic Remains of the Deccan : A New Aspect of Them', *The Journal of Hyderabad Archaeological Society*, January 1917, No.3.

YAZDANI, G, 'Excavations at Kondapur – An Andhra Town (c. 200 B.C. - 200 A.D.)', *ABORI*, vol. XII, Pts. ii-iv, 1941.

YAZDANI, G (Ed), *The Early History of the Deccan*, Pts. I-IV, OUP, 1960.

INDEX